THE ROME STATUTE OF THE INTERNATIONAL CRIMINAL COURT

This book has been published with a financial contribution
from the Consiglio Nazionale delle Ricerche
(C.N.R.) (AI99.00449.09)
and from the Dipartimento di Scienze Giuridiche
dell'Università degli Studi di Trento.

The Rome Statute of the International Criminal Court

A Challenge to Impunity

Edited by
MAURO POLITI
GIUSEPPE NESI
Università degli Studi di Trento, Italy

Routledge
Taylor & Francis Group
LONDON AND NEW YORK

First published 2001 by Ashgate Publishing

Published 2016 by Routledge
2 Park Square, Milton Park, Abingdon, Oxon OX14 4RN
711 Third Avenue, New York, NY 10017, USA

Routledge is an imprint of the Taylor & Francis Group, an informa business

British Library Cataloguing in Publication Data
The Rome Statute of the International Criminal Court : a
challenge to impunity
1. International Criminal Court. Rome Statute of the
International Criminal Court (1998)
I. Politi, Mauro II. Nesi, Giuseppe
341.7'7

Library of Congress Control Number: 2001086761

ISBN 13: 978-0-7546-2154-6 (hbk)
ISBN 13: 978-1-138-25710-8 (pbk)

Contents

THE INTERNATIONAL CRIMINAL COURT AND THE INTERNATIONAL PROTECTION OF HUMAN RIGHTS

THE INTERNATIONAL CRIMINAL JUSTICE SYSTEM AFTER THE ROME CONFERENCE

PROSPECTS FOR THE FUNCTIONING OF THE INTERNATIONAL CRIMINAL COURT

List of Participants

Mrs. Mahnoush H. ARSANJANI, Senior Legal Officer, Codification Division, Office of Legal Affairs, United Nations, New York

Dr. Adriaan BOS, Chairman of the Preparatory Committee on the Establishment of the ICC

Professor Antonio CASSESE, former President and Judge of the International Criminal Tribunal for the Former Yugoslavia, The Hague

Professor Roger S. CLARK, Rutgers University School of Law, Camden, New Jersey

Professor Luigi CONDORELLI, University of Geneva

Professor Giorgio CONETTI, University of Insubria

Professor Giovanni CONSO, President of the Rome Conference

Ms. Patrizia DE CESARI, University of Milan and University of Trento

Mrs. Phani DASCALOPOULOU-LIVADA, Legal Service, Ministery of Foreign Affairs, Athens

Mr. Richard DICKER, Human Rights Watch, New York

Ambassador Nabil ELARABY, former Permanent Representative of Egypt to the UN – Member of the International Law Commission

Professor Luigi FERRARI BRAVO, Judge of the European Court of Human Rights, Strasbourg

Mrs. Silvia A. FERNANDEZ DE GURMENDI, Permanent Mission of Argentina to the UN, New York

Mrs. Socorro FLORES LIERA, Permanent Mission of Mexico to the UN, New York

Ambassador Francesco Paolo FULCI, Permanent Representative of Italy to the UN, New York

Professor M. Novella GALANTINI, University of Milan

Professor Gerhard HAFNER, Member of the International Law Commission

Counsellor John T. HOLMES, Permanent Mission of Canada to the UN, New York

Mr. Hans-Peter KAUL, Legal Service, Ministry of Foreign Affairs, Bonn

Ambassador Philippe KIRSCH, Chairman of the Committee of the Whole of the Rome Conference

Professor Flavia LATTANZI, University of Teramo, LUISS, Roma

Ms. Béatrice LE FRAPER du HELLEN, Legal Service, Ministry of Foreign Affairs Esteri, Parigi

Ms. Lamia MEKHEMAR, Permanent Mission of Egypt to the UN, New York

Professor Theodor MERON, New York University School of Law, New York
Professor Giuseppe NESI, University of Trento
Professor Lorenzo PICOTTI, University of Trento
Professor Fausto POCAR, University of Milan - Former President of the UN Committee for Human Rights
Professor Mauro POLITI, University of Trento
Professor W. Michael REISMAN, Yale Law School, New Haven
Professor William A. SCHABAS, Department of Legal Sciences, University of Quebec, Montreal
Ms. Cate STEAINS, Permanent Mission of Australia to the UN, New York
Professor Otto TRIFFTERER, University of Salzburg
Professor Tullio TREVES, University of Milan, Judge of the International Tribunal of the Law of the Sea, Hamburg
Ms. Francesca TROMBETTA-PANIGADI, University of Trento
Professor Gabriella VENTURINI, University of Milan
Ms. Elizabeth WILMSHURST, Legal Service, Foreign and Commonwealth Office, London

Editors' Preface

This volume brings together the papers delivered at an international meeting held at the University of Trento, Italy, in May 1999, a few months after the UN Diplomatic Conference on the Establishment of an International Criminal Court (ICC). Some of the leaders of the Rome negotiations and eminent scholars met in Trento - an environment where nobody had to worry about negotiating - to discuss the results of the Rome Conference and the future prospects of the ICC.

The idea for the Trento meeting dates back to late 1997, when the UN General Assembly decided to convene the Diplomatic Conference in Rome on 15 June to 17 July 1998. Initially no one knew whether the Rome Conference would be a success or a failure. The goal was to approve the text of a Statute that would establish a permanent, independent International Criminal Court for the purpose of trying and punishing the perpetrators of unspeakable atrocities. While such a Court had been a dream of the international community since the founding of the United Nations, a UN Conference to establish the ICC was not called until the late 1990s. Even then, the Rome Conference got off to a rocky start, confirming all the complexities and difficulties that had emerged in earlier negotiations. More than a month was dedicated to what at times seemed like an interminable series of discussions: until 17 July 1998, when on a hot Roman night the large majority of States participating in the Conference voted to approve the Statute. Those who were there that night knew that they were living an historic moment.

There is no doubt that the adoption of the Rome Statute represents a milestone in the development of international criminal law. For the first time in history, those responsible for *crimina iuris gentium* will now be aware of the fact that they could have to stand trial before an independent international Tribunal created ex *ante facto* and linked to the UN system. After the Conference had concluded, however, additional work needed to be done to integrate the Statute in view of its entry into force. To this end, a Preparatory Commission was set up to address specific issues such as the elements of crimes and the rules of procedure and evidence. Furthermore, a provision was made that amendments to the Statute could be proposed seven years after its entry into force. At the same time, the debate among politicians, diplomats and scholars over the prospects of international criminal justice could be resumed on new basis.

The University of Trento and the Autonomous Province of Trento were pleased to offer their facilities to help this debate evolve and support the organization of an international meeting on the contents of the Statute and the future of the ICC. We would like to thank those who attended the Trento meeting, those who supported it, and the students of the Faculties of Law at the University of Trento and other Universities, who followed the meeting with genuine interest and enthusiasm.

The law students of today are the lawyers of tomorrow. They will practice law in an era when the Statute has entered into force, the Court has become operational and, hopefully, the violators of international law are punished. It is for this reason that we dedicate the present volume to them.

New York, Trento

Message of the Secretary-General of the United Nations

As I had the honour to say at the Rome Campidoglio on 18 July last year, the adoption of the Rome Statute of the International Criminal Court was a gift of hope to future generations and a giant step forward in the march towards *universal* human rights and the rule of law.

By establishing the International Criminal Court, the international community proved its determination to put an end to impunity for the perpetrators of egregious violations of human rights and humanitarian law, and thus to contribute to the prevention of such crimes.

Only a permanent court with universal jurisdiction can finally lay to rest the charge that the international community is being selective or applying double standards in deciding which crimes to investigate and punish.

The work of the Preparatory Commission which started in February and recent efforts at speeding up the process of signature and ratification of the Statute are significant steps in putting the Court into operation.

In this context, events like the international meeting at the University of Trento: "The Rome Statute of the International Criminal Court, a challenge to impunity" play a significant role in maintaining the momentum achieved in July last year and in keeping the attention of States and of international public opinion focused on the need to establish the International Criminal Court as soon as possible.

I, therefore, welcome the organization of the Trento international meeting and wish its organizers and participants the best success in their endeavours.

Kofi Annan

Welcome Addresses*

MASSIMO EGIDI**

It is a great pleasure and a great honour for me to welcome the speakers and the participants to this conference on *"The Rome Statute of the International Criminal Court: a Challenge to Impunity"* on behalf of the University of Trento.

First of all, I would like to thank you for the interest you have shown in this meeting confirming the relevance of such initiative.

The importance of this conference lies, in the first place, in the topic that will be discussed here: for the first time in history, thanks to the signature of the Rome Statute, the decision of establishing an International Criminal Court competent to examine the most cruel international crimes has been taken by a large majority of countries representing the international community and not by the winners of a war or by the Security Council of the United Nations.

This is an astonishing accomplishment which only a few years ago would have seemed impossible.

The exercise of criminal jurisdiction has always been considered one of the pillars of State sovereignty, a prerogative which only the State, under exceptional circumstances, can decide to waive. The historical events we have witnessed during the last decade, however, have deeply modified the fundamental features of international relations and have influenced the very concept of State sovereignty.

Under normal circumstances States continue to be "masters", as they were, in criminal jurisdiction for all those crimes committed within their boundaries. It often happens that States, for various reasons, are not allowed to or cannot fulfil the international obligation of punishing those who have committed inhumane international crimes, such as genocide, crimes against humanity and war crimes.

---

* These welcome addresses are the transcripts of the speeches delivered on the occasion of the opening session of the international meeting on the ICC that took place in the University of Trento, Italy, on 13-15 May 1999.

** Rector of the University of Trento.

Although the emphasis is increasingly laid upon prevention and punishment of such crimes, the absence of an international criminal court would leave the individuals responsible for such international crimes unpunished.

Hence, the need to establish *ex ante* a criminal court with a permanent nature and universal competence. That is to say a court which, regardless of the place in which the crime is committed, could judge according to the law and eventually punish those who are held responsible for it even if these persons hold very important places in the State structure.

The approval of the Rome Statute has not obviously led to the immediate establishment of the international criminal court. Eighty-two countries have already signed the Statute which will come into force once the 60th ratification has been received.

Negotiations to integrate and finalize the text of the Statute began last February and are due to be completed by the middle of next year. Hence it can be stated - thanks to the attendance to this conference of many key figures of the Rome Conference actually engaged in the work of the Preparatory Commission - that this meeting represents a sort of "intersessional" step in the negotiating process.

The significance of this meeting, however, is not only related to the topic under discussion or to the future development of the negotiations.

The historical moment in which this meeting in Trento is held is one of the most dramatic and alarming since the end of World War II. In September 1998, when the promoters of this initiative began to prepare the meeting, the war in the Balkans did not seem incumbent and certainly neither were its consequences. I would like to underline that it is precisely under such circumstances that all of us realize even more how the tools of international law and diplomacy can play a key role in the prevention and peaceful solution of conflicts and in the international protection of human rights. This is one of the few certainties and one of the few indisputably positive elements that emerged lately.

In conclusion, I am confident that this conference - thanks also to the presence of eminent jurists and diplomats - will significantly contribute to re-establish the crucial role of international law in the solution of international and internal conflicts and in the international protection of human rights. In this way, the Trento meeting will constitute a very important contribution in the process leading to the affirmation of the ideals of peace and justice in international relations. These are principles to which, especially today, we cannot remain indifferent.

DIEGO QUAGLIONI*

Ladies and Gentlemen, Distinguished Colleagues and Guests,

I am pleased to welcome you all and to express my felt thanks to the participants in my personal capacity and on behalf of the Department of Legal Sciences of the University of Trento, which has promoted, supported and organized this important meeting, with the important contribution of its University, of its administrative staff and obviously in the first place of its Rector and of its Scientific Commission.

Our Department is deeply honoured in hosting this important initiative. The community of jurists in Trento is fully aware of the importance of this scientific gathering, which takes place in a very delicate moment of our history, at the end of a very dramatic century.

Let me recall as historian and not only as jurist, that in the contributions of the men of culture of our time it is felt the urgency of a reflection on the features of our time, among which there is the paradox of the constant reaffirmation of human rights and of their equally constant and ever more grave violation.

A great historian of our time, Eric Hobsbawm, introducing his beautiful book on our age: "Age of Extremes: The Short Twentieth Century", recalled the thoughts of Isaiah Berlin and William Golding, who tell us that our century is "the most terrible century in Western history", "the most violent century in human history": a century of weakening of human rights, despite the effort to reaffirm them and grant them almost in the awareness of the weakness of the great spiritual forces that had perceived human rights as not disposable and therefore untouchable.

This is the century in which the legal culture of our time spoke of a possibility of a positive law of human rights, "derecho positivo de los derechos humanos", as a famous book of Gregorio Peces-Barba Martínez says.

Professor Giovanni Conso himself also reaffirms this, when he talks of an antithesis with the hopes and of an evident proof of how international criminal law is still far from having given up at least part of its field of action to supranational criminal law. Only supranational criminal

* Head of the Department of Legal Sciences, University of Trento.

law is able to contrast, with those balanced influences of State sovereignty, the present reality and transform it into a new reality, a reality of adequate answers to the untolerable abuses which the repression of human rights, when it becomes systematic, inevitably involves: mass murder, ethnic cleansing, aggression (legitimate or not is a different problem, Professor Conso says, given that, in any case, they involve state of war, the worst enemy of human rights).

I believe that we are all here to remember that the whole international law is based and founded on a unique principle, the principle of humanity.

LORENZO DELLAI*

Rector, Illustrious Guests, Ladies and Gentlemen,

I believe that I can say that this conference highlights how often discretion and sobriety are inversely proportional to the value and importance of initiatives and meetings.

It is indeed with great discretion and with great sobriety that our University has prepared and organized this meeting, which I believe represents an occasion of extraordinary value from the civil, political and scientific point of view, in order to reflect and express trends concerning a question which is central for the future of our community.

Therefore, I wish first of all to express my sincere thanks to our University for the civil function, still more than the scientific function, which it has demonstrated itself capable of expressing and exercising in preparing and organizing today's meeting.

This consideration has been added to and made even stronger by the awareness that some of our lecturers have had a more than secondary role in the whole preliminary phase which has allowed the Conference of Rome to reach the important conclusions which we are here today to discuss.

This too is a little-known aspect of our community; but I believe that it is instead correct to emphasize it, giving the people who have had a significant role their just merits and underlining once again the civil value, even before the scientific value, of the experience which is developing within our University.

I believe that the civil and political importance of this conference has not escaped anyone. It essentially concerns discussing, considering and working around a change in the concept itself of national sovereignty, a concept which the 20th century has consigned to the next century through a process which is sometimes dramatic, sometimes full of hope and changes. Changes from the internal point of view given the drive towards a redefinition of powers subordinated to national states which is expressed in many parts of our continent, but a concept which should also and especially be redefined from the external point of view, namely as regards the

---

* President of the Autonomous Province of Trento.

construction of a new idea of a sovereignty of rights which crosses over and goes beyond state sovereignty.

I believe that the events of this period, which the Rector evoked earlier, demonstrate dramatically how the considerations which we are about to discuss are absolutely relevant and urgent, also so as not to give an answer to the question of interference in the rights within nations exclusively on conscription, which reveals, as is clear, all its limits and contradictions.

There are many good reasons for being satisfied with the initiative of our University and for associating great civil, political and institutional hopes with it. There are likewise many good reasons for associating with this initiative a particular perception of a role, a vocation which Trento and Trentino may have to express in this sphere. I believe that our city and our provincial community can genuinely put themselves forward as one of the points of reference for the great scientific and political debate on these issues. I would indeed express here the hope that our area may put itself forward as a place in which the great conflicts and the great antinomies of our times may be faced, discussed and formulated, starting just from the ethical and scientific resource which expresses itself on occasions such as this.

THE INTERNATIONAL CRIMINAL COURT: ITS MAIN FEATURES

1. Some Reflections on the Rome Conference

GIOVANNI CONSO*

Who could ever have imagined that on 13 May 1999, a day that was decided long ago for our meeting, Italy would have had a new Head of State? It is true that, recently, the schedule of the presidential election had foreseen today for the first voting, but it is also true that many electoral rounds seemed inevitable in order to have a new Head of State. On the contrary, happily, the result came very timely. If many of the States of the United Nations had worked with such speed in giving birth to the International Criminal Court, it would have been memorable!

I was proud to chair the Rome Conference. Now, however, I am less proud of it because the process of ratification is slowing down. No fault on the part of those who are here today: the very fact of meeting in Trento means that we are living intensively this event and that we want to see it realized until its end. But the others, those who really matter? Not only does it seem that some of the initial enthusiasm has come to an end, but, what is even more worrying, the adversaries of the Statute, who, on the evening of the 17 July 1998, immediately after the voting of the Assembly of the Plenipotentiaries of the United Nations, were defeated, are now raising their heads, acting as to stop the decisive path towards the ratification of the Statute. Unfortunately with undeniable success, if it is true that up to now only three States ratified the Rome Statute. A special thanks therefore to these three States. Let us name them and plaud them loudly: Senegal, Trinidad and Tobago, Republic of San Marino.

And the others, Italy first of all, where are they? "We want to be the first ones, Italy must be the first. It cannot be otherwise" has been said over and over since 18 July 1998. The same happened in France, where on last 10 December, at Palais de Chaillot, Chirac, Jospin and Badinter proclaimed solemnly: "We must be the first ones, in competition with

* President of the Rome Conference.

Italy." Something, clearly, is not working or it is working far more slowly than predicted. Let us ask ourselves why.

In the first place, there exists certainly a matter, let us say, of schedule: the first deadline for ratifying was fixed for 30 June 2000. One had the impression of having at disposal such a long period of time not to be in a hurry. In the meantime, the situation has become worrying; since 17 July has already passed by almost a year. If the signatures have become eighty-two, we only have three ratifications, which are those which really matter in the end, as just mentioned.

All this not only betrays, at least partially, the work of the plenipotentiaries, who so intensively have dedicated themselves before and during the works of the Rome Assembly, but shows also a very scarce sensibility towards all that in a tremendous way happened and continues to happen in all parts of the world after 17 July; all this demonstrates how important the need to give a concrete existence to a permanent criminal court.

From The Hague, seat of the Criminal Court for the territories of the former Yugoslavia, have come to honour this Conference Adriaan Bos, the man whose contribution in the preparatory phase was decisive for the coming into life of the Rome Statute, and Antonio Cassese, the man who was really fundamental for the start of the works of the ad hoc Tribunal. Well, nobody better than them could illustrate the growing concern for the problem of the relationship between the International Criminal Court *in itinere* and the Tribunal for the former Yugoslavia already active. Due to the growing weight upon the Prosecutor of the latter and the impossibility for the new Court, as judge established ex ante, to deal with events happened before its entry into force, it would be necessary to speed up time to avoid that The Hague Tribunal was submerged by complaints and by the necessary inquiring activities which are unfortunately continuously increasing.

Going back to the issue of ratification, the ones who followed the works on the Italian ratification know very well that, from the beginning of October 1998, the competent Ministries have drawn a law proposal for the ratification and entry into force of the Statute. The Law draft, presented to the Senate on 23 October, had a double nature. A first article contained the authorization to the President of the Republic to ratify and the executive order. A second article charged the Government with the task of introducing in the internal legal order the international provisions concerning the establishment of the new Court. The result was that of disconnecting the outcomes of the ratification from those, surely more complex, of the adjustment of the Italian legal order. But, as soon as the two competent Commissions of the Senate, Foreign Affairs and Justice, exhausted the exam of the text, the project immediately revealed the difficulties underlying the mandate: in order to reach a timely ratification on the part of Italy, it was proposed to analyse separately the two parts. The Assembly of the Senate approved the text without particular difficulties; the escamotage so reached was submitted to the other Chamber before mid-February. For a while nothing happened. Only a few days ago the Parliamentary Commission of Foreign Affairs began to work on the problem, encountering from the start a new, more frustrating type of obstacle. A few members of Parliament have asked themselves to what extent this Court will be useful when the United States have not shown their favour for the initiative; in other words - as if 120 States who voted for the Statute did not count at all - is it the case to go ahead when the United States are against? This is the question of those MPs.

Despite the inherent weakness of such argument, the Presidency ordered the informal audition of some experts on the subject. The audition took place last Wednesday, with no more than four or five MPs present. At the end of the audition, the Vice-President, Hon. Trantino, expressing satisfaction for what he heard, announced that the following day the Commission would have decided on the transmission to the Assembly. From the report of such following session we learned, however, that an MP, absent in the previous meeting, had once again suggested prudence, on the basis of the argument that the ostracism of the United States carried the risk to deliberate in a *vacuum*. From this a new *renvoi*, this time after the election of the President of the Republic. So, up to now, no prediction on the moment in which the text will be transmitted to the Assembly of the Chamber of Deputies can be made. Even more cloudy is the fate of the second part of the draft law, that stopped in the Senate after having been made object of an autonomous new draft.

And, unfortunately, the problem is present not only in Italy. In France, for instance, the need to previously modify the Constitution has emerged. But on that situation and on what is happening in other countries other speakers attending this Conference will be better able to tell us on the basis of their direct knowledge.

Nevertheless, the impression is that the euphoria of 18 July led many people to think that most of the work had already been done. Furthermore, someone thought that from that moment onwards there was plenty of time at the disposal of States for ratification, even more taking into account that in only five weeks the miracle of giving birth to the Statute had been accomplished. So, someone thought that the two following years would be enough for completing the work. On the contrary, those against the Statute sharpened their weapons and used them in different ways: the first and easiest was that of blocking or slowing down the run towards ratification; and also unexpected difficulties and unpredicted obstacles arose, of both legal and political nature, included crises of governments and economic problems.

Let me end my intervention with another nostalgia, that of 17 July, when around 8 pm, two votes in the Committee of the Whole that rejected amendments aimed at putting the project into crisis, provoked an endless applause, in an atmosphere of great happiness, repeated immediately afterwards, a few moments before midnight, in the Plenary when the result of the final vote was known. And then again on the Campidoglio, the following day, at the time of sunset, a marvellous sunset of lights and colours, when, in the gardens of the Campidoglio, a joyful toast made once again the happiness of success tangible.

We must absolutely go back to that enthusiasm, the only one able to give new impulse to a process still very difficult. We must find again that youthful spirit that precisely the University, especially if a modern one, as is the case of Trento, is able to ensure and transmit even to those who are not young anymore.

2. The Rome Statute of the ICC: Rays of Light and Some Shadows

MAURO POLITI*

1. Starting our debate on the Statute of the International Criminal Court is not an easy task. The Statute is a long and complex instrument, that reflects a number of carefully crafted compromises. The ongoing "race" to publish Articles and commentaries on the new Court has already resulted in several important studies. It will be impossible to avoid generalities, or to mention issues that have not been examined.

But for the delegates to the Rome Conference, this historic event was also a deep personal experience. Who could forget the long discussions, the moments of hope and discouragement, or the tension of the final night? These emotions themselves can greatly influence us to either celebrate what the Italian Minister for Foreign Affairs has recently described as "the most important institutional advancement of the United Nations after the Charter of San Francisco". Or to discredit the outcome of the Conference as a matter of principle. In any case, our comments can be construed as the result of the positions taken in Rome, rather than as the product of a dispassionate analysis.

However risky the attempt may be, I must try to break the ice. In doing so, I will concentrate on the main features of the Statute, and their implications for the activity of the Court. From the early preparatory process, the key points of the negotiation were clear: the list and definition of crimes; the mechanisms to activate the Court; and the relationships between the Court and national jurisdictions. The intent is to look at the relevant Articles of the Statute and to give an answer to one basic question. That is whether the Statute has devised an effective and independent Court; or instead the need for realism and mediation has prevailed to the point of creating a weak Court, unable in substance to exercise its functions. The political success of the Conference is undisputable and it was due to several

* Professor of International Law, University of Trento.

factors: the role of the "like-minded" countries (those countries most engaged in supporting the ICC project from the beginning), the unprecedented pression from the NGOs, the excellent leadership of the Conference and of its various bodies. Now we need to revisit the text, with fresh and open minds, to measure this success against the crucial legal elements of the final compromise. "Since there is a Statute" - we used to joke right after the Conference - "now we have to find out what's in it".

2. The title of my remarks is: "Rays of Light and Some Shadows." The ICC Statute contains many elements that would give the Court the powers, autonomy and procedural instruments needed to achieve its goal: in other words, to truly make a difference in preventing and punishing the most serious violations of international humanitarian law. But a price had to be paid to get the support of the vast majority of countries. There are shadows that overcarst the sky of the Statute, and some of them are pretty thick. One of the purposes of this meeting is to see to what extent these negative factors could endanger the solidity of the edifice built in Rome.

I start with a general point: the major achievement of the Conference. After 50 years of attempts, and following the trail blazed by the two ad hoc Tribunals created by the Security Council, the United Nations and the international community succeeded in establishing a permanent International Court for the repression of egregious crimes that offend the human conscience, such as genocide, war crimes and crimes against humanity. World public opinion was shocked and continues to be shocked by recent events (in the former Yugoslavia, in Rwanda and now in Kosovo) that evoke the horrors of the second world war. The Court is a concrete answer to this growing demand for justice. Despite enormous political difficulties, the Rome Conference marked a lasting defeat for the culture of impunity: a culture which nourished the atrocities of the past and is the source of those committed at present. For its part, the signature by a great number of countries (82, as of today) reaffirms the support for the Statute by a large sector of the international community, and reinforces the hope that in the years to come the Court may become a truly universal institution.

3. So, which are the brightest rays that enlighten the Statute, and which are the most troubling shadows? As I said, I will focus on the most important questions, those addressed in Part II of the Statute, entitled: "Jurisdiction, Admissibility and Applicable Law." My fellow delegates to the Conference will remember the endless talks on this Part, the rolling texts prepared by the Bureau of the Committee of the Whole, the meetings on Sundays at the Canadian Embassy, the last minute attempts to reconcile positions and avoid a vote. A vote that finally did take place on July 17th, with the result of 120 votes in favour, 7 against and 21 abstentions. While the debate on these aspects is not yet over, I wish to share with you a few thoughts.

4. There is little doubt that some of the most positive elements in the Statute relate to the definition of crimes, particularly crimes against humanity and war crimes. Together with genocide, these are the so-called "core crimes" under general international law, made subject to the Court's jurisdiction pursuant to Article 5. Aggression is also included in this list. But the Court will not be able to prosecute and punish this crime until a review conference has adopted provisions defining aggression and specifying the roles of the Security Council and the Court, respectively in determining that acts of aggression were committed by a State or by individuals. On this issue, I look forward to hearing more detailed comments from other colleagues. I may simply note that the inclusion of the crime of aggression is *per se* extremely important. Since the Nuremberg Charter aggression is considered one of the most serious crimes of concern to the international community; and the discussions in Rome, although inconclusive, showed at least that it is possible to continue the dialogue on the basis of a pragmatic and constructive approach. At the same time, the issues still outstanding remain highly controversial, and the events of Kosovo will probably not help to soften major political concerns.

Apart from aggression, the inclusion of crimes such as terrorism and drug-trafficking will also depend on future decisions by a review conference. At this stage, the ICC will thus be entrusted essentially with the gravest violations of international humanitarian law. To define these crimes was a major undertaking, once the decision had been made to include in the Statute a detailed formulation of the relevant provisions. But the overall result is more than satisfactory in having put into place an effective and "meaningful" Court.

I will not discuss genocide, since Article 6 reproduces the definition in the 1948 Genocide Convention. The desire to avoid long debates preempted any improvement in this definition, but did make it possible to reach a quick agreement already within the Preparatory Committee.

Defining crimes against humanity, on the other hand, proved more difficult than had been anticipated. The text of Article 7 still contains several positive elements, in line with the requests of the "like-minded" countries, but also of other delegations, including the United States. For the sake of brevity, I will limit my comments to the general definition.

Article 7 excludes any link between crimes against humanity and the existence of an armed conflict. It thereby confirms that these crimes may also be committed in time of peace: a principle that is essential to protecting civilian populations against the abuses of dictatorial and oppressive regimes. The chapeau also states that crimes against humanity are acts committed as part of a widespread "or" systematic attack directed against any civilian population. This was the most controversial point, since several States had demanded instead that both qualifiers, widespread and systematic, should apply in order to better distinguish crimes against humanity and ordinary crimes. In the end, these qualifiers are disjunctive, although the attack must respond to certain minimum requirements relating to both of them. Therefore, it will be sufficient for the Court to demonstrate either that the attack resulted in a large-scale action involving a substantial number of victims (and was then a "widespread attack"), or that it was conducted with a high degree of orchestration and methodical planning ("systematic attack"). Thirdly, and unlike the Statute of the "ad hoc" Tribunal for Rwanda, Article 7 does not require that all crimes against humanity (and not only acts of persecution) be committed with a discriminatory intent: namely on national, political, racial, ethnic or religious grounds. In short, the general definition of crimes against humanity captures the essence of these crimes in a clear and rather broad manner, without imposing conditions that would make it extremely cumbersome to prove their commission.

The problems in defining "war crimes" were even more substantial. The draft to be discussed in Rome was extremely long, due to the great number of options on many fundamental aspects. The major issues were the extension of the concept of "war crimes" to include internal conflicts, and the use of certain methods and means of warfare, particularly nuclear weapons and other weapons of mass destruction. Everybody agreed to include in the text the "grave breaches" of the 1949 Geneva Conventions. But the insertion of other serious violations of humanitarian law committed in international armed conflicts (namely, the grave breaches and serious violations of Protocol I) remained controversial. Some States also insisted that the Court's jurisdiction be limited to war crimes perpetrated as part of a plan or policy or on a large-scale.

On one of these issues, the provisions in Article 8 do run counter to the idea of a Court provided with wide and significant competences. I refer to the question of weapons of mass destruction, where there was a "capitulation" to the conflicting vetoes on the express reference to specific weapons. As a result, Article 8 does not place under the Court's jurisdiction either the use of nuclear weapons (the great nuclear powers were opposed, claiming that no prohibition of such utilization existed in international law);

or the use of chemical, biological, anti-personnel mines and laser weapons (crimes that many developing countries were ready to insert in the Statute, but only together with that of recourse to nuclear weapons). The provisions on methods and means of warfare thus remain very limited and quite anachronistic. Conversely, the inclusion of two sets of rules concerning "war crimes" in internal armed conflicts was a major success. I refer to serious violations of Article 3 common to the Geneva Conventions and to other serious violations of humanitarian law applicable in armed conflicts not of an international character. Here, Article 8 reaffirms recent trends in international legislation and practice, reflected especially in the jurisprudence of the Yugoslav Tribunal. The result is a significant consolidation of the principle that inhuman conduct contrary to applicable law in internal conflicts (and not only in international conflicts) deserves repression as war crime. Again, this achievement was due to the action conducted in Rome by many delegations, not only from the "like-minded" countries, who were determined to prevent the Statute from not applying to the situations in which war crimes are more frequently committed nowadays.

On the other aspects of war crimes, I will be extremely brief. The chapeau of Article 8 specifies that the Court has competence over war crimes "in particular" (and thus not exclusively) when committed as a part of a plan or policy or on a large scale. The idea of a general threshold was therefore rejected, although in the context of an appeal to the Court to act on the most serious and alarming cases of war crimes. The main violations of humanitarian law applicable to armed conflicts (including serious violations of Protocol I not defined as "grave breaches") are listed among the crimes under the Court's jurisdiction, with formulations that are often similar to the original instruments. When the Statute is different, the result is usually a clear, objective broadening of the types of acts that international law is called to repress. This is the case with crimes of sexual violence and the protection of children in armed conflicts. The Rome Conference devoted the utmost attention to these areas, also thanks to the lobbying by non-governmental organizations.

Criminalization of serious violations of humanitarian law committed in internal conflicts; inclusion of both categories of "grave breaches" of the Geneva Conventions and of Protocol I, and of other serious violations of humanitarian law; broadening of some provisions in the existing legislation, especially with regard to the protection of women and children. These are, in substance, the main achievements of the Rome Statute in defining war crimes.

5. At the same time, there is a shadow hanging over the Statute. At the last minute, a provision was added to the Bureau's proposal on war crimes. Under this "transitional" clause, contained in Article 124, a State, on becoming a party to the Statute, may declare that, for a period of seven years, it does not accept the jurisdiction of the Court over war crimes committed by its nationals or in its territory. Article 124 also states that this declaration may be withdrawn at any time, and that its provisions will be reexamined at the first review conference.

There is no doubt that this "opt-out" clause represented a substantial concession made to conservatism at the negotiating table. With respect to war crimes, Article 124 establishes precisely that system of jurisdiction "à la carte" that the "like-minded" countries had opposed during the entire preparatory process. Here, more than on any other aspect, we must look at the political constraints which led to this compromise.

In its final days, the Conference was still facing a dangerous stalemate on jurisdictional issues. Some countries (in particular, the United States) insisted in requesting that the exercise of the Court's jurisdiction be made conditional upon the acceptance by the State of nationality of the accused, both for war crimes and crimes against humanity. One of the latest American suggestions contemplated a Protocol valid for ten years and allowing a State Party to the Statute to declare that it would not accept the jurisdiction of the Court for one or the other of these two crimes (or for both of them). This declaration would have had the same effect as a new provision proposed by the U.S. on the jurisdiction of the Court towards States non-Parties: namely, the effect of requiring the acceptance of the States involved with respect to acts committed in their territory, "or committed by officials or agents of a State non-Party in the course of official duties and acknowledged by the State as such". These proposals were opposed by the "like-minded" countries, which stood firm in defending the automatic jurisdiction of the Court and rejecting the need for the consent of the State of nationality of the accused, a consent that was seen as a tool for paralysing the Court.

However, the main concern of a number of other countries related to the mechanisms for activating the Court in cases of war crimes. For example, France worried that it would face possible complaints against its political and military leaders. Many Arab countries anticipated problems with crimes committed in internal conflicts. It then became evident that an area of manoeuvering existed. To give assurances to these States by way of an "opt-out" clause limited to war crimes could guarantee a large support for the Statute, even if at the cost of a substantial exception to the principle of the Court's automatic jurisdiction. The result was the existing provision in Article 124, elaborated by the Bureau of the Committee of the Whole on the night before the final vote.

On the other hand, Article 124 is a "transitional" provision. One can predict that the first review conference will consider deleting it from the Statute. It is also possible that, upon further reflection, States who had advocated this regime in Rome will abstain from making use of the "opt-out" clause. In other words, while there is a clear, regrettable limit on the Court's jurisdiction over war crimes, only future developments will tell us the real impact this will have on the effectiveness of the Court.

6. On the other issues concerning the s.c. "trigger mechanisms", the Statute is again characterized by lights and shadows. A delicate balance was struck in the text. One major success of the "like-minded" countries is the *proprio motu* power given to the Prosecutor to start investigations on the basis of information obtained from any source. This power is subject to an authorization by the "Pre-trial" Chamber, but this authorization is an instrument of internal control, free from political interference; and should not unduly obstruct the Prosecutor's action to protect community interests. At the same time, the Statute contemplates two additional mechanisms: the complaint by a State Party, and the referral by the Security Council. This latter provision is intended to eliminate the need for the Security Council to create more "ad hoc" Tribunals. But, since the principle of complementarity remains applicable also to the cases of referral by the Security Council, it remains doubtful that this need might never arise because of the functioning of the ICC.

There are then two more aspects: the conditions for the exercise of the Court's jurisdiction, and the relationships between the Court and the Security Council with regard to those situations which are not referred to the Court by the Council. Here, in many respects the Statute is hardly consistent with the idea of an effective and independent Court. But, once again, a closer look at the relevant provisions can partially correct this negative impression.

Article 12 of the Statute provides the Court with automatic jurisdiction over the crimes within its competence. Unlike the draft prepared by the ILC, and leaving aside the special regime for war crimes, there is no need for a specific acceptance of the jurisdiction by the State, or States concerned. In cases of State complaint or Prosecutor's initiative, an additional condition must be met: either the State in which the conduct occurred (the territorial State) or the State of nationality of the accused must be Parties to the Statute or must have accepted the jurisdiction of the Court over the crime in question. Now this regime has a critical flaw. In practice, the Court will not be able to intervene where serious violations of humanitarian law are committed by the political authorities of a State non-Party to the Statute in the territory of that State, and against their own nationals. The Pol Pot's or Milosevic's scenarios would not be covered.

On the other hand, the formulation of Article 12 was probably the only way out of the impasse. In fact, many States were arguing in favour of the Court's "universal jurisdiction", while others, as I said, demanded the consent of the State of nationality of the accused. Different compromise texts (such as a Korean proposal which was close to the idea of universal jurisdiction) could not guarantee a wide support for the Statute. At the same time, the way Article 12 is formulated actually entails an important consequence, in the sense of extending the jurisdiction of the Court. In fact, the Court will be allowed to proceed even against the nationals of States non-Parties to the Statute, without the consent of these States, when the crime is committed in the territory of another State that has accepted the Statute or explicitly recognized the Court's jurisdiction. This was one of the fundamental reasons for the opposition of the United States to the Statute.

Article 16 deals with the relationships between the Court and the Security Council. The ILC draft required the Court to receive the Council's authorization before it could intervene in Chapter VII matters. Instead, the Statute gives the Council the "faculty" to request the Court not to commence or proceed with an investigation or prosecution. Such request must be made through a formal resolution and would prevent the Court from acting for a period of 12 months. It may also be renewed under the same conditions (in other words, through a resolution and each time for twelve months). This was a heavy sacrifice for the power and independence of the Court. But one may hope that the Council will use this faculty moderately. In particular, the possibility of successive renewals of the request may prove to be more theoretical than real, since a formal resolution to that effect could only be justified in exceptional circumstances. In conclusion: while Article 16 could have a negative impact on the Court, in political terms it would be extremely difficult for the Council to defend an attitude of clear and persistent obstruction of the ICC.

7. I come now to the principle of "complementarity". "Complementarity" means that, instead of replacing national jurisdictions, the Court will intervene only in those situations where national justice systems are unavailable or ineffective. Unlike the Yugoslav and Rwanda Tribunals, the ICC does not have "primacy" over national jurisdictions. Also, many countries stressed in Rome the duty of every State to exercise its repressive functions over the crimes covered by the Statute.

The main question is what criteria should determine the application of complementarity. In other words, when would the Court be authorized to act instead of a national jurisdiction? In which cases should a national justice system be deemed "unable or unwilling genuinely to carry out" an investigation or prosecution, to use the formula of Article 17?

Here, I do not share the pessimism of some commentators. Under Article 17, the Court will be able to affirm its competence in many significant situations: for example after the total or partial collapse of a national judicial system, or in the presence of "sham" proceedings undertaken to shield the accused from criminal responsibility; and also where the Court's control over national proceedings is far more incisive, such as in cases of unjustified delay, or lack of impartiality or independence in the conduct of the proceedings. In other words, the Court will be able to step in not only when there are no national courts in place, or a national proceeding appears to be, from the beginning, a false and simulated one; but even whenever the way in which the proceeding is carried out, or has been carried out, shows the absence of a true legal process (for example, having regard to the composition of the judiciary organ, the conduct of investigations and prosecutions, the timing of the judicial acts etc.). In my view, we are far from the notion of a Court which would simply "notarize" that a State is exercising jurisdiction. The "quality" and standard of national proceedings may now be subject to scrutiny. This is clearly another positive aspect of the Statute.

Furthermore, it is always up to the Court to decide on issues of complementarity. This helps to reinforce the independence and the effectiveness of the Court. Even the special mechanism of preliminary rulings regarding admissibility, established by Article 18 as an additional safeguard against undue interferences with national proceedings, does not infringe on this principle. The Prosecutor must notify all States Parties about a State complaint or an investigation started on his own initiative. If requested by the State concerned, he must defer the investigation, but he may also ask the Trial Chamber to authorize him to conduct the investigation, which is equal to saying that the Court will have the final word.

8. Despite grave political constraints, the Rome Conference has produced, in my view, a Court that can respond to the demand for justice, and the refusal of impunity, for the most serious crimes of international concern. It is difficult to say, even for the negotiators of the Statute, whether the Conference achieved the best possible result. Certainly, the risk of losing the necessary support to adopt the Statute was enormous. Those who steered the Conference, in particular Professor Conso and Ambassador

Kirsch, deserve our praise for having showed the way towards carefully balanced solutions on many crucial aspects. Not only the number of signatures, but also the encouraging start of the works of the Preparatory Commission devoted to the rules of procedure of the Court and to the elements of crimes, indicate that this balance remains valuable and adequate to allow a rapid entry into operation of the Court. And once the Court is operational, it will be able to utilize all the possibilities foreseen by the Statute, to affirm and reinforce its role.

3. The Experience of the Preparatory Committee

ADRIAAN BOS*

Introduction

I will mention a few highlights in the preparatory phase leading to the adoption of the Statute for the Establishment of an International Criminal Court (ICC) at Rome. I emphasize the word "few", since it is impossible in this context to mention all events and aspects that were important in the preparatory process aimed at the establishment of the ICC. I do hope that other participants, present in this meeting, are prepared to share their knowledge and experience by supplementing this introduction.

It seems appropriate to pay some attention to the context in which the UN Ad Hoc Committee began its work in 1995. The renewed interest in the establishment of an ICC resurfaced in the late 1980s. The call for an international criminal jurisdiction at that time was no longer a response to atrocities committed in the Second World War, as was the case with the establishment of the Nuremberg Tribunal. This change in context is important since it has influenced the course of discussions on the ICC.

Nuremberg Tribunal

At the time of the Nuremberg trials, a heated debate took place whether the principles of *nullum crimen sine lege* and *nulla poena sine lege* were fully respected in the proceedings. The same discussion took place with regard to the Tokyo Tribunal. The debate focused in particular on the convictions of individuals for crimes against peace.

Admittedly there was scarcely any codification of international

---

* Chairman of the Preparatory Committee on the Establishment of the ICC.

criminal law at that time. In 1947 Hans Kelsen wrote[1] that he definitely did not want Nuremberg to set a precedent. His view, which was common currency at the time, was that the principle of individual criminal responsibility for breaking international rules of war - especially in relation to crimes against peace - was not enshrined in international law at the time of the Nuremberg trials, but was simply a rule imposed by the victors on the states they had defeated. Kelsen was especially critical of the retroactive application of these rules to individual responsibility. Generally speaking, retroactivity has no place in criminal law, at least if it prejudices the suspect's case. Before Nuremberg, the only international applicable rule was the collective responsibility of states to refrain from the use of force.

It was in particular this view that the International Law Commission (ILC) opposed when it concluded: "The conscience of the whole civilized world has been so aroused by Nazi aggression and the attendant atrocities that the public opinion of the world now sanctions the punishment as war criminals of those persons responsible for the initiation of an aggressive war. This world public opinion is regarded as the same public opinion which first sanctioned the judicial punishment of murder, and later other crimes, without a positive pre-existing legislative act."

International Law Commission Activities

The work of the Ad Hoc Committee was based upon the Draft Statute, prepared by the ILC. It is evident that the work of the ILC since the beginning of its existence has been of great importance for the discussions in the Ad Hoc Committee. When I refer to the ILC I have two stages in mind. The first ending in 1953 with the completion of its first draft and the second beginning with the resumption of its work in 1992, together with its work on the Code of Offences against Peace and Security of Mankind (Code).

On the same day when the United Nation's General Assembly (GA) confirmed the principles of international law, acknowledged in the Nuremberg Charter and in its judgments, the GA established a Committee on the Progressive Development of International Law and its Codification. The Committee was requested to treat, as a matter of primary importance, plans for the formulation - in the context of a general codification of offences against the peace and security of mankind, or of an international criminal code - of the principles recognized in the Nuremberg Charter and

[1] The International Law Quarterly, Vol. 1, no. 2, Summer 1947, pp. 153-171.

in its judgments.[2] In 1946 still existed the conception of three different codes: one concerning the Nuremberg principles, another relating to offences against the peace and security of mankind, and the third suggesting a complete international code. During these discussions the question whether the establishment of an international judicial authority should be included was still controversial.

In 1947 the GA decided to entrust the ILC with the formulation of the principles of international law recognized in the Charter of the Nuremberg Tribunal and in the Judgments of the Tribunal and to prepare a draft Code.[3]

The first result of the codification process[4] was the Convention against Genocide in 1948. Article 6 of the Convention stated that persons charged with the crime of genocide should be tried by the competent court of the state in whose territory the act had been committed or by such international criminal tribunal as has been authorized for that purpose by states that had accepted its jurisdiction. This led the GA to invite the ILC to examine the desirability of an international judicial organ to try persons accused of genocide and, at the same time, to look into the possibility of adding a criminal division to the International Court of Justice. It should be noted here that the GA held that in view of the development of the international community there would be an increasing need for an international judicial organ for the trial of certain crimes under international law.

At its first session in 1949 the ILC concluded that the establishment of an international criminal court was both desirable and possible. The GA subsequently decided to assign the preparation of a draft statute to another committee established by the GA itself.[5] When a Draft Statute was prepared, the GA postponed consideration pending the adoption of the definition of aggression. The Committee, mandated to elaborate this definition, submitted in 1974 a recommendation, which was the basis for the resolution 3314 of 14 December 1974, containing a definition of aggression adopted by consensus.

On the basis of the reports of a special rapporteur, Jean Spiropoulos, the ILC adopted at its second session in 1950 a formulation of the principles of international law recognized in the Charter of the

[2] Res 95 (I), Affirmation of the principles of international law recognized by the Charter of the Nuremberg Tribunal, adopted on 11 December 1946.

[3] Res. 177 (II), doc. A/519.

[4] The question of genocide was raised in the GA session in 1946 by the delegations of Cuba, India and Panama. A draft text was prepared by the Secretariat of the UN, with the assistance of international and criminal law experts.

[5] Report of the Committee on International Criminal Jurisdiction, GA Suppl. No. 11 (A/2136).

Nuremberg tribunal and in its judgments, and submitted these principles to the GA.[6] In 1954 a Draft Code was completed and submitted with commentaries to the GA.

Important International Events

The cold war tensions began to cease and a more effective functioning of the UN became feasible. In the request for an agenda item of the GA in 1988, initiated by Trinidad and Tobago and supported by a coalition of Latin American and Caribbean States, reference was made to the creation of an ICC with jurisdiction over international drug offences. The request noted that the 1988 UN Narcotics Convention declared drug trafficking an international criminal activity, that international drug trafficking "threatens to engulf small states and afflicts even the superpowers" and that that an international criminal jurisdiction was necessary "for prosecuting and punishing offenders who command the means to evade the jurisdiction of domestic courts". Terrorism was also mentioned as reason to establish an international criminal jurisdiction.

Draft Statute for an International Criminal Court

The GA acted on this initiative by requesting the ILC to resume its work by considering "the question of establishing an international criminal court or other trial mechanism".

This request found a more favourable reception in the ILC than it had in the past. In the ILC was broad agreement, in principle, on the desirability of establishing an ICC and consensus that the time was particularly favourable for such a development. The ILC's initial discussions were general in character and were held in the context of its efforts to elaborate a Draft Code of Crimes against the Peace and Security of Mankind.

Work of the ILC on the Code

Although the GA in 1974 introduced the definition of aggression[7] it was not until 1981 that the ILC resumed its study of a Code. In 1981 the GA

[6] Yearbook of the ILC, Vol. II, pp. 374-378, doc. A/1316.

[7] UNGA Official Records, 29th Session, doc. A/9880 (1974).

invited the ILC to resume its work with a view to elaborating the Draft Code and to examine it with the required priority in order to review it, taking duly into account the results achieved by the process of the progressive development of international law. There were two arguments for resuming the debate on the Code. On the one hand the feeling that the existence of a Code would automatically lead to the establishment of a court to apply it, and, on the other hand, the fact that the link between the Code and the Court was used to frustrate progress towards codification.

In 1982 Doudou Thiam was appointed as Special Rapporteur. The continued discussion on an ICC in the context of the Draft Code helped to keep the idea of establishing a Court alive. In the period from 1983 to 1991 nine reports were discussed in the ILC. Among the problems with the draft Code was the scope of it. Crimes against Peace and Security of Mankind, the title of the Code, did not reflect its content accurately. The crimes mentioned, such as genocide and crimes against humanity, did not necessarily fall under the umbrella peace and security. The earlier drafts, the 1991 Draft included, contained moreover a kaleidoscopic range of crimes. This was also criticized.

Any limitation of the scope of the Draft would make it necessary to adjust the wording of its provisions.

As to the scope *ratione personae* the Code still suffered from the fact that at the beginning, the Commission had planned to cover not only the responsibility of individuals but also the criminal responsibility of states. It had ultimately decided to focus solely on the responsibility of individuals, without however excluding the responsibility of States completely.

In 1991 the ILC provisionally adopted in a first reading draft Articles of the Code and they were transmitted, through the SG of the UN, to Governments for their comments and observations. At its 44th session, in 1992, the ILC had before it the Special Rapporteur's tenth report, which was entirely devoted to the question of the possible establishment of an international criminal jurisdiction. The discussions in the ILC focused in particular on the question whether the jurisdiction of the Court should be binding or optional, and whether it should be exclusive, concurrent or of a review character. Doubts were expressed about the linkage between the Code and the Court. It was stressed that the Court's Statute and the Draft Code should constitute separate instruments and that a State should be able to become a party to the Court's Statute without becoming party to the Code.

By establishing in 1992 a working group on international criminal jurisdiction all efforts were concentrated upon the Statute. By 1993 the working group submitted to the Commission a detailed report containing a

Draft Statute. The ILC, without formally adopting the text, referred it to the GA for comment.

In 1993, the GA took note of the Draft Statute and invited the ILC to continue its work with a view to finalizing its proposals, if possible in 1994. The discussions in the GA evidenced support for the Draft Statute in principle. A Court would contribute to the development of international criminal law. It would increase the likelihood that perpetrators of international crimes would be held accountable. It would provide a more effective deterrent against such crimes by creating a standing mechanism for international prosecution and punishment. It would enhance the international legal order and thus strengthen the enforcement of international law.

A working group of the ILC, under chairmanship of Professor Crawford, undertook the task of adapting and refining the 1993 proposals in light of the views articulated by governments and other interested bodies. The revised text, consisting of 60 Draft Articles, one annex, and extensive commentary, was formally adopted by the Commission and included in its report to the GA. The ILC had transferred its Draft with the recommendation to convene an international diplomatic conference to study the Draft and conclude a convention on the establishment of an ICC.

Establishment of the ICTY

At that time the situation in the Former Republic of Yugoslavia lent already a sense of urgency to the initiative. The punishment of Saddam Hussein and other high Iraqi officials for the human and environmental consequences of the Gulf War was also mentioned as a reason for establishing an ICC. In that period the Security Council (SC) established in resolution 827 (1993) an international tribunal for the sole purpose of prosecuting persons responsible for serious violations of international humanitarian law in the former Republic of Yugoslavia after January 1, 1991.

The establishment of the International Criminal Tribunal for the Former Yugoslavia (ICTY) in 1993 has been a very important element in the process of the preparatory negotiations. Crawford mentions the combination of three elements that made it possible for the SC to reach agreement. The large scale breakdown of state order in particular societies, leading to massive violations of human rights. Support for action in the SC associated with an unwillingness by any member to veto that action. Finally the intensive and detailed media coverage of the atrocities, giving rise to public demand that "something be done".

It was argued that almost all the features of the ICTY, and subsequently also of the International Tribunal for Rwanda (ICTR), concerning the election of judges, the jurisdiction of the Tribunals and the requirements of State cooperation were unlike the provisions of the proposed ICC. Opinions were clearly divided about the significance of the establishment of the ICTY. Some authors considered it as the least serious effort of the UN, others qualified it as an important milepost along the road to a standing international criminal court. The ILC itself was also divided about the precedent-character of the ICTY for its work on the ICC. Some members felt that the Statute and Rules of the ICTY should receive particular attention in addressing similar issues in relation to a permanent court. Other members cautioned against placing too much emphasis on those instruments in the light of the essential differences between the two institutions.[8] In my view one should not underestimate the importance of the establishment of the ICTY. Psychologically it proved the feasibility of a genuine international criminal court. Moreover its functioning has provided a wealth of jurisprudence which has increasingly influenced the discussions throughout the process of negotiations.

Establishment of the Ad Hoc Committee

The intention of the SC to create an ad hoc tribunal to prosecute those responsible for genocide and other serious violations of international humanitarian law committed in Rwanda was at an advanced stage of realization when the GA in 1994 discussed the establishment of an ICC. This strengthened the argument that it would be far better to have a single permanent international court instead of ad hoc Tribunals.

Many countries participated actively in the debate in the Sixth Committee. Support was expressed for a diplomatic conference to be convened in 1996. Some delegations, however, believed such a decision premature.

It was for the GA to decide what forum is to be used for consideration and adoption of a treaty elaborated and submitted by the ILC. In the end agreement was reached to establish an ad hoc Committee, open to all members of the UN, which would facilitate a further process of intensive consultation. Its task was to review the major issues arising from the ILC Draft and consider the convening of an international conference. Alternative solutions could have been discussions in the Sixth Committee during the GA sessions, or in a working group, or through informal

[8] ILC Report 1994, par. 47.

consultations. During two sessions of two weeks in 1995 the review of the ILC Draft Statute has taken place. I believe that the procedure agreed upon has been very well chosen. It was necessary to familiarize the members of the UN with the work of the ILC. It was possible to focus upon certain key issues without committing States at that early stage too far and to investigate what was needed in addition to the ILC Draft.

Jurisdiction *Ratione Materiae*

It was very important that already in the Ad Hoc Committee a clear preference was expressed to confine the jurisdiction *ratione materiae* to a limited number of core crimes.

In the 1994 Draft Statute the ILC enumerated the crimes genocide, aggression, serious violations of the laws and customs applicable in armed conflict and crimes against humanity without defining them. All these crimes can be considered as crimes under international customary law. In addition the ILC Draft referred to crimes under or pursuant to certain treaties. This category of crimes consisted of crimes of terrorism, drug trafficking, and violations of convention on the safety of United Nations and Associated Personnel. A clear trend emerged in favour of limiting the jurisdiction of the Court to the core crimes. A majority of States had consistently opposed inclusion of the treaty crimes, since they were regarded as crimes of a different character, for which already effective systems of international cooperation were available. In selecting the crimes over which the ICC should have jurisdiction, delegations were guided by different considerations. The ILC itself mentioned acceptability by States as an important factor. Others argued that crimes should be international crimes according to international customary law.

The discussions brought together the question of international criminal offences for which persons bear individual criminal responsibility under international law and the question of the adjudication of such crimes. Aspects dealt with in the Code, such as individual criminal responsibility, punishment, international cooperation, principle of universality, concurrent jurisdiction, ne bis in idem, rights of accused, defences and definition of the crimes were already actively and intensively discussed in the ad hoc Committee and in its successor, the Preparatory Committee.

The final Draft of the Code, submitted in 1996, covered the same core crimes as in the ILC Draft Statute. The addition of the crimes against UN and Associated Personnel in the Draft Code was the only difference. The Draft Code became an additional document of reference for the discussions in the Preparatory Committee.

In the Preparatory Committee a clear majority was of the opinion that the core crimes needed to be defined in the Statute. They invoked the principle of legality to justify their demand. Mistrust in the future court has also been a factor. In practice it meant that in the preparatory phase not the selection of the crimes but their definitions took all the time. Only for genocide a clear definition in a generally accepted treaty was available. For the remaining crimes this was only partly the case. It was generally understood that the Statute was not to create new substantive law. The question what could be regarded as applicable law remained to be answered. This focused the discussion on what should be considered international customary law. An answer to this question was very difficult, since the developments of the humanitarian rules were impressive. As Meron observed international humanitarian law has developed faster since the beginning of the atrocities in the Former Yugoslavia than in the four-and-a half decades since the Nuremberg Tribunal and the adoption of the Geneva Conventions.[9] This was true for the development of the substantive rules as well as for the individual criminal responsibility related to those rules. In particular the latter aspect was much in development, in the light of the Statute for the Rwanda Tribunal, in which reference was made to common Article 3 of the Geneva Conventions and also in the light of the case law of the ICTY. Two most discussed aspects in the preparatory phase were the norms applicable in international armed conflicts and the question what use could be made of Additional Protocol I and of the Hague rules with regard to international armed conflicts. The question of the rules applicable in internal armed conflicts got relatively less attention, due to the uncertainty whether such rules should be included at all.

Complementarity

A fundamental principle of the ILC Draft, as stated in the preamble, was that the ICC is intended to be complementary to national criminal systems, in cases where such trial procedures may not be available or may be ineffective. The UK submitted in the preparatory discussions a paper in which was emphasized the primary right of states to bring criminals to justice, the need for integrating the concept of complementarity in all aspects of state cooperation and an exceptional and very restricted role for the ICC. This approach would leave the decision whether to act, in a particular case, in the hands of the state. Germany and others advocated another approach. In their view the ICC should act when states failed to

---

[9] AJIL 1998 at p. 463.

carry out their duties to bring people to justice. The test whether this is the case, will be difficult in particular in states where the judicial system is acting in good faith but nevertheless is ineffective. It became clear that the relationship between the national judiciary and the ICC needed a very delicate and refined set of rules, leaving the national judiciary intact but offering at the same time an alternative in case it fails. In view of the importance of this principle it is remarkable that its formulation in the Statute was realized without many problems. In fact the text worked out in the preliminary stage was not changed substantially in Rome. The idea of the Court is inspired by the desire to prevent serious crimes from going unpunished, be it by the national judiciary or by the Court. According to this principle the use of the Court for preventing serious crimes from going unpunished lies in the hands of the State. This made it easier for States to accept the concept of the Court.

Basis for Discussion

From the outset I have tried to organize the discussions in the Ad Hoc Committee and subsequently in the Preparatory Committee, along the ILC Draft. I saw it as a method to keep the discussions as concrete as possible and hoped that thus delegations would be encouraged to present new suggestions in the form of amendments to the ILC Draft. This approach has been followed until the production of the Zutphen-text. From 19-30 January 1998 an inter-sessional meeting took place in Zutphen (The Netherlands). Chairs of different working groups, various coordinators and the secretariat participated in this meeting. Its purpose was to identify issues that needed further discussions, issues that were not discussed at all and issues that did not appear in any paper and nevertheless must be included in the Draft.

At the time of the Zutphen-meeting also suggestions circulated of having different instruments. Arguments in favour for this were:

a) better presentation of the text, elementary rules and principles in the Statute and details in the annex;
b) the possibility of different procedures for modification of the Statute and its annex;
c) the possibility, if necessary, to adopt the Statute in Rome and postpone the adoption of the annex until a later period of time.

Out of fear to delay the whole process of the diplomatic conference, this suggestion to split the text into two was not seriously discussed in Zutphen.

The acceptance of the Zutphen-text as the basis for the further discussions in the Preparatory Committee has been very important. In view of the proceedings during a diplomatic conference it is extremely important what kind of text is transmitted as the basis for the decision making. At that time we were already half way through the preparatory phase and there was no other basis text but the one of the ILC. The discussions had clearly demonstrated that the ILC text in many respects needed to be adjusted and supplemented. The Zutphen-text for the first time offered a coherent and complete alternative for the ILC text. It contained all proposals and additions elaborated and proposed during the negotiations since the establishment of the Preparatory Committee.

Role NGO's

Speaking about the preparatory events, it is impossible not to mention the contributions of the NGO's and international organizations. The preparatory negotiations were an example of what the SG of the UN recently qualified as a new diplomacy. A diplomacy where NGO's, peoples from across nations, international organizations, the Red Cross and governments come together to pursue an objective. The NGO Coalition for an ICC, coordinating the work of more than 800 NGO's, has been very effective in these negotiations. To the maximum extent politically possible, I have tried to conduct the work in open sessions. NGO's, such as Amnesty International, Human Rights Watch, Lawyers Committee for Human Rights, the Women's Caucus for Gender Justice in the ICC and many others have published papers and commentaries on the issues under discussion, making valuable contributions in assisting delegations in preparing their national positions. The representatives of the ICRC were active in the discussions on the definition of the crimes and the presence of the representatives of the ICTY and the ICTR was very useful in particular for the discussions on the substantive and procedural penal Articles of the text.

In this respect I agree wholeheartedly with the SG of the UN that the partnership of NGO's, the private sector, international organizations and governments is a powerful partnership for the future.

4. The International Criminal Court in Perspective: From the Rome Conference to the Years to Come

JOHN T. HOLMES*

The story of the Rome Conference has been told and written about extensively since the adoption of the Statute and I do not intend to retell that history. Since the end of the Conference, however, a number of myths have emerged about what happened in Rome. Many, if not all, of these are devoid of any factual basis. Yet, they persist and indeed seem to proliferate as time distances itself from the events at "La FAO". And the fact that these myths persist is both worrisome and a call to action – to refute the claims and set the historical record straight. Allow me to outline briefly some of the more troubling myths which have emerged since the Rome Conference and to demonstrate why they are just that - myths.

Myth 1: Transparency

Some have contended that the final package on the fundamental issues contained in Part II of the Statute was conceived secretly and thrust upon the Conference in a non-transparent, undemocratic fashion.

---

* John T. Holmes is Counsellor (Legal Affairs) of the Permanent Mission of Canada to the United Nations in New York. He was a member of the Canadian delegation to the Rome Diplomatic Conference on the Establishment of an International Criminal Court. During the Conference, Mr. Holmes assisted the Chairman of the Committee of the Whole, Ambassador Philippe Kirsch, and also was coordinator for complementarity issues. The views expressed in this article are personal and do not necessarily reflect the views of the Government of Canada.

Let us return to Rome briefly to recall the events of the last few weeks and, particularly, the final hours of the Conference. Up until week three of the Conference, the Bureau of the Committee of the Whole had followed the excellent workplan prepared by Adriaan Bos and Professor Giovanni Conso at the Courmayeur meeting.[1] To a large extent, especially with respect to the procedural parts of the Statute, that workplan functioned smoothly. The various working groups met, informal negotiations were arranged and the plethora of square brackets in the Draft Statute gradually disappeared.

Such was not the case with respect to Part II and certain sections of the Statute which were intricately linked to that Part. Despite debates in the Plenary, the Committee of the Whole and the tireless efforts of the various coordinators, there was very little movement among delegations. Privately, in discussions with the Committee of the Whole Chair, Ambassador Philippe Kirsch of Canada, many delegations called for serious negotiations to begin; yet publicly these same delegations repeated their oft-stated positions without signalling areas of possible compromise.

The Bureau had no choice but to act (indeed it was encouraged to do so), first through the tabling of its Discussion Paper, then the preparation of a Bureau Proposal and ultimately the submission to the Conference of the final package. As these documents evolved, it is important to recall that the Bureau took great pains to use options or proposals which were already on the table. Cognizant of the transparency question, the Bureau papers reflected the suggestions made by delegations, indeed sometimes to the point where options favoured by very few delegations were nevertheless included. The result was that on the morning of July 17th the final package contained very few surprises. The most notable of these were:

- the jurisdictional preconditions based on State of nationality of the accused and the territorial State.[2] Both of these preconditions were part of other proposals, notably the Korean proposal, but it was a Bureau innovation to include only these;

- the so-called "opt-out provision" was not included in the Bureau Discussion Paper or Proposal.[3] However, this idea was widely discussed throughout the last week or so of the Conference (for example Ambassador Yawada of Japan

---

[1] The Courmayeur meeting was held in May 1998 and was charged with preliminary planning of the Rome Conference, including the preparation of a workplan for the Plenary, Committee of the Whole, the Drafting Committee and the Working Group.

[2] See Article 12 of the Statute.

[3] See Article 124.

conducted a series of informal consultations, including with the Like-minded Group, at which this idea was mooted);

the inclusion of the crime of aggression, albeit in an inoperative fashion, was only added in the final package.[4]

It is important to note (and this is perhaps the best argument to refute this myth) that if the final package was the product of a non-transparent approach, some, perhaps many, delegations would have seized on the 24-hour rule to object to the late tabling of the document and the Rome Conference would not have ended successfully.

Myth 2: The Vote

A second myth, somewhat related to the first, is that the rushed frenzy to adopt a Statute produced a flawed instrument and resulted in adoption by vote rather than general agreement.

There is no doubt that we could have used more time at the end of the Conference, particularly in proofreading the text (no criticism of the UN Secretariat is intended; the work of its officials was exemplary under very trying circumstances). Would that extra time have been used so constructively?

My answer is, without doubt or hesitation, no. A number of delegations used every minute of the Conference as a bargaining tool to hold out for their objectives. More time at the Conference would not have been used more effectively. The reason that the negotiations went to the wire was because the Committee of the Whole wanted to afford every opportunity for delegations to develop compromises on their own. It is noteworthy that some of the delegations which have propagated this myth were the same delegations with whom Bureau members consulted to the very last minute, endeavouring to produce a solution leading to adoption of the Statute by general agreement.

The fact that the Statute was adopted by vote remains an unfortunate historical fact. Could it have been avoided? Certainly, the Committee of the Whole Bureau did everything it could to avoid that outcome. From the outset, coordinators were strongly discouraged by the Bureau from considering votes, even on very specific issues outside the scope of Part II issues, such as the death penalty. The fear, undeniably a prescient one, was that a vote on one issue would lead to requests for

---

[4] See Article 5.

separate votes on a range of issues – embargoes, nuclear weapons, landmines and the crime of aggression were some of the issues which delegations raised bilaterally with Ambassador Kirsch as potentially requiring votes to resolve. The coordinators' insistence on negotiation resulted in many of these individual issues being resolved without separate votes. The exceptions, the amendments proposed by India and the USA, were issues on which every attempt at compromise was explored and on which a solution engendering general agreement could not be found. The fact that, regrettably, a vote was called was not due to any desire to push through a particular predetermined approach but rather an inability of a small minority of delegations to accept, after lengthy attempts at compromise, a result acceptable to an overwhelming number of States.

Myth 3: Anti-Americanism

This leads to the next myth -- that the Rome Statute is the result of anti-American sentiment. I will not dwell on this point, as this is not a conference on the USA and the ICC. Suffice it to say, that the Bureau afforded the US delegation every opportunity to advance its objectives and endeavoured up until the very last minute to accommodate legitimate American concerns. The Statute bears a strong American imprint, a result of valuable contributions by members of the US delegation -- notably in areas of crimes against humanity and war crimes, complementarity, procedure, cooperation and enforcement, which an American delegate coordinated. Many of the safeguards which are the strength of the Rome Statute, were proposed or promoted by the USA. Examples include the complementarity regime, including Article 18 on preliminary rulings, the procedural checks on the Prosecutor, the protection of national security information, Article 98 on the relationship between the Court and status of forces agreements, and so forth. On the issue which the USA felt compelled to call a vote, there was of course no solution, though strenuous efforts were made to find one. The problem was not anti-Americanism – the Bureau did not take seriously the perception that too many concessions were being made to the Americans. The problem then, as it is now, was that the Bureau was unable to find a solution to US concerns that did not in turn open a huge loophole in the Statute excluding other States, including those much more likely to perpetrate Statute crimes.

Myth 4: Confusion among Delegates

A fourth myth of the Rome Conference is that many delegations, perhaps the majority, were ill-informed, confused, without instructions or overly influenced by representatives of non-governmental organizations. This is a particularly condescending myth and one which exposes a level of ignorance about the Conference which is quite surprising. The Rome Statute is the most complex international legal instrument elaborated in many years, perhaps ever. Therefore, it is not surprising that on some of the more complex issues, some delegations did not have a full understanding. However, my role in Rome required me to be in contact with a wide range of delegations, indeed virtually all of them. I passed messages from Chairman Kirsch and the Bureau to delegations and, more importantly, I gathered information from delegations on the negotiating process and the issues contained in the Statute – primarily, but by no means exclusively, on Part 2 issues. In five weeks of "intelligence gathering", I was uniformly impressed with the depth of knowledge of many delegations on the range of issues addressed in the Statute. I recall, particularly, the fall-out after the so-called "secret" meeting at the Canadian Embassy (which was not so secret) where many delegates approached me to explain in great detail their concerns with respect to Part 2.[5] Many delegations were assisted by the voluminous information materials prepared by non-governmental organizations. In addition, the German Government on its own initiative produced and distributed a "model ICC Statute" outlining how the final outcome might look. This model contributed significantly to delegates' understanding.

Several States had non-governmental representatives on their delegations and a few of them allowed these representatives to speak. Indeed, Canada had two such representatives on its delegation and occasionally these delegates spoke on behalf on my country. Does the fact that non-governmental representatives were on delegations and participated in negotiations tarnish the contributions to the Statute of those States? I would certainly hope not. It is the sovereign right of any State to choose the composition of its delegation; far be it for any of us to cast aspersions on those States if they choose to include non-governmental representatives, or indeed even academics.

---

[5] The Bureau organized a meeting on Part 2 of the Statute at the Canadian Embassy on Sunday, July 5, 1998. Due to the size of the Embassy conference facilities, the number of delegations invited was limited.

Myth 5: The Deterrent Effect of the ICC

The final myth I wish to address is the most difficult to refute and pertains to the essence of the ICC project itself. Some contend that the ICC will have no or little deterrent effect on tyrants or on situations where tribal or ethnic passions are so aroused that logic and reason are the first casualties. Advocates of this theory point to events in Kosovo, where the existence of the International Tribunal for the former Yugoslavia and the stated intent of its Prosecutor to investigate alleged crimes have failed to deter Milosevic and Serb forces from their campaign of ethnic cleansing and terror. International criminal justice or the threat of it, so the theory goes, will not deter those determined to use any means to achieve their aims. Only force or the threat of it can realistically ensure that protagonists in conflict will be forced to limit their methods of warfare and ultimately to return to the bargaining table.

Only the most idealistic person would contend that the ICC will be a deterrent to all future combatants. The events in Kosovo prove that international intervention may be imperative where armed groups and rogue States put themselves at odds with acceptable standards of behaviour. But does this mean that the ICC will have no effect? In an excellent Article in a recent *New York Review of Books*,[6] Canadian writer Michael Ignatieff contends that international tribunals can make a difference. Citing the recent book, "Between Vengeance and Forgiveness" by Martha Minow, Ignatieff writes that, despite their limitations, international tribunals are valuable because "when they punish criminals, they also affirm, condemn, purge, and purify. They also establish concrete truths, which make it more difficult for future regimes to falsify the historical record. The successful prosecutions of senior Rwandan officials for genocide at the Arusha Tribunal and the convictions of war criminals from all sides of the Bosnian conflict at The Hague did in fact break 'the cycle of impunity' at least for these particular barbarians." Ignatieff also refers to Aryeh Neier's book, "War Crimes: Brutality, Genocide, Terror, and the Struggle for Justice", arguing that if the Court "were successful in establishing its prosecutorial independence of the great powers and bringing prosecutions, it would contribute to the emergence of an international system which denies safe havens to the future Pinochets and Pol Pots of this world".

The problem with disproving the theory that the ICC will have minimal deterrent effect is that it is extremely difficult to find supporting evidence. When atrocities are committed, they are often front page news or covered graphically by CNN. However, when fewer atrocities are

---

[6] *The New York Review of Books*, May 20, 1999, pp. 58-62.

committed than might otherwise be expected or tyrants decide not to perpetrate such crimes, little is known of the decisions which resulted in these outcomes. Was the threat of international justice the reason for hesitation or reflection? Possibly, we might argue, albeit without any certainty.

My main problem with the theory is that it suggests that, from the international legal perspective, we do nothing. Since the Court's impact will be minimal, at best, better not to raise the expectations of victims, non-governmental organizations and civil society with the false hope that few, if any, perpetrators will be brought to justice. This view is a perniciously narrow and short-sighted one. If I have learned one thing in my nearly ten years of working on multilateral legal and human rights questions, it is that progress is slow, but it is progress nevertheless.

The Way Ahead

The Rome Statute is but one step, albeit an extremely important one, in a lengthy process of codifying basic, fundamental standards of behaviour and ending impunity for those who transgress. What we accomplished in Rome is truly historic but much more remains to be accomplished. Let me briefly highlight some of the important steps ahead of us.

(1) The completion of the mandate of the Preparatory Commission (PrepCom). I can safely speak for Chairman Kirsch in expressing satisfaction (if not relief) at the outcome of the first session of the PrepCom. Serious negotiations began on two key items on the PrepCom's agenda - Rules of Procedure and Evidence and the Elements of Crime - thanks in no small part to the effective leadership of the two coordinators - Silvia Fernandez of Argentina and Herman van Hebel of the Netherlands. In addition, several coordinators or facilitators were named by the Bureau to address other PrepCom agenda items. Of note are the coordinator on aggression, Tuvako Manongi of Tanzania and Christian Maqueira of Chile.

Two aspects of the February PrepCom bear particular scrutiny. First, it is evident that there is a tremendous amount of work to be done with respect to the Rules of Procedure and Evidence and the Elements of Crime, if we are to meet the deadline of June 2000 as set out in the resolutions establishing the PrepCom. To accomplish this objective, two things must be realized, in addition to the obvious necessity of the political will of delegations to complete the task.

(a) As much available time as possible during the PrepCom must be devoted to these issues. No matter how many informal consultations are organized, the issues addressed in the Rules and the Elements must be discussed and resolved formally.

(b) Given the limited time and the range of issues, we should take advantage of the availability of intersessional meetings to advance our work. The recent meeting in Paris on issues relating to victims produced important progress. I congratulate the French Government and Béatrice Le Fraper du Hellen in particular for their important initiative. Professor Cherif Bassiouni is organizing an important meeting on the Rules of Procedure and Evidence in June in Sicily, and I am sure that this meeting will also advance our work, much as similar meetings facilitated the development of the draft ICC Statute during the old PrepCom. We must recognize that the impact of these meetings will be limited because not all countries are able to attend. Nevertheless, to the extent that they clarify issues and facilitate consensus, they are to be welcomed and encouraged.

The second potentially problematic aspect of the February PrepCom was the question of aggression. It is widely accepted, certainly by Chairman Kirsch and me, that the crime of aggression is an important issue for the PrepCom. It is why Ambassador Kirsch and the Bureau appointed a coordinator to commence consultations. Nevertheless, we cannot turn a blind eye to the mandate of the PrepCom, which is clear – the Rules and the Elements must be completed by June 2000 while other items, including aggression have no deadline. The limited time available for formal consultations on aggression should not be regarded as a diminution of its importance. Rather, it is a reflection of the mandate and deadline established for the PrepCom and, perhaps as importantly, that the still very politicized question of aggression requires more careful and flexible consultations than might be possible in a formal meeting setting.

(2) A second important step ahead is the entry into force of the Rome Statute and the actual establishment of the Court. Here, I welcome and support the comments of our Chair. There have been two ratifications thus far - Senegal and Trinidad and Tobago and a third, San Marino, is expected shortly. As well, we have over 80 signatures. This is an excellent beginning, but much work needs to be done. I know that non-governmental organizations are actively planning and beginning to work with States to ensure effective ratifications, and States themselves are exchanging information on legislative requirements. All of these steps are to be encouraged. Canada is actively engaged in its own internal process of consultation with Ministers and the preparation of draft legislation. While

the final decision rests with the government and Parliament, it is hoped that Canada will be in a position to ratify within the next year.

(3) A third step is promoting universal support for the Statute. The ICC will never be a complete success until it achieves widespread adherence and all States are pledged to cooperate with it. Those States which voted against the Statute in Rome or abstained, and, here I am thinking principally of the USA, must be brought back into the fold. To eschew this objective is to abdicate our responsibility to achieve universal support for the ICC. How can we accomplish this aim, given the positions adopted at Rome? An important step was taken at the February PrepCom, when a facilitator was named to conduct consultations "to enhance the effectiveness and acceptance of the Court". These consultations will not be easy. The USA has indicated that its problems with the jurisdictional bases of the Statute are fundamental. At the same time, the possibility of a fundamental change to the Statute is remote. There is little political will to reopen the Statute to accommodate US concerns, *as expressed thus far.* Moreover, there is a genuine fear that any reopening of the Statute would lead to an unravelling of the whole instrument. The challenge is therefore great, but the majority of States are, I believe, willing to explore every avenue to secure possible US support. Realistically, with or without a "fix" for the USA, American ratification is many years away. American support, through financial voluntary contributions and assisting with enforcement, is nevertheless both desirable and achievable. The key is dialogue and that is the mandate of the facilitator – to foster a comprehensive, non-politicized discussion on how to secure the broadest possible support for the Statute.[7]

[7] The author is deeply appreciative of the efforts of the University of Trento and the Comune of Trento for their excellent organization of the Conference. He also wishes to add his personal gratitude to Professor Mauro Politi, Professor Giuseppe Nesi, Mrs. Carla Boninsegna and Ms. Elisabetta Nones for their extraordinary work in making the Trento Conference a success.

5. The International Criminal Court: The Role of the Security Council

ELIZABETH WILMSHURST*

In any assessment of the future prospects of the Court, an important factor to be taken into account will be the strength of the Court's relationship with the United Nations, including the Security Council.

The relationship of the Security Council with the future Court is an interesting one. It was not surprising that the question of the link between the two bodies arose early in the negotiations of the Court: the functions of both bodies relate in their different ways to international peace and security. The United Nations Charter gives the council a mandate for the maintenance of peace and security. And the preamble to the Statute of the Court recognizes that crimes within the Court's jurisdiction can threaten the world's peace and security. In establishing the two ad hoc Tribunals (for the former Yugoslavia and for Rwanda) the Council was acting under Chapter VII of the Charter. It has thus recognized that atrocities of the kind which are now to be dealt with by the Court are also of concern to the Council.

The major role for the Security Council envisaged in the Statute - the referral of situations to the Court - was not a matter of great controversy at the Conference. There were objections to it, but they were largely politically motivated. It was very widely recognized to be the concern of the Council that justice should be done, and that if a situation threatened international peace and security the Council should be able to ask for action by the Court. The Council does not of course have the sole power of referral; nor do its powers preclude States Parties and the Prosecutor from seizing the Court. There is no need for further comment here on this role, except to note that in practice the referral of situations by the Council may

* Legal Service, Foreign and Commonwealth Office, London.

be of crucial importance to the early success of the Court. In the early days of the Court, few of the States then parties to the Statute are likely to be those whose territories or nationals are responsible for the commission of atrocities. Because of the jurisdictional limits of the Court, many or most of the cases before it in those early days are likely to be those referred by the Council. This is because there is no requirement for consent from States Parties before the Court has jurisdiction, if the Council refers a situation to the Court.

There was more controversy during the negotiations about the second role which the Statute provides for the Council: the requirement that the Court will have to defer an investigation or prosecution if the Council requests it to do so under Chapter VII of the Charter. In the Draft Articles prepared by the International Law Commission, the Court was not given jurisdiction in respect of any matter which the Council was dealing with, unless the Council agreed. Such a provision would indeed have given the Council wide powers: some might have said veto powers. Early on in the process of negotiation it became apparent that there was not much support for this provision in the way it was then framed. Proposals were put forward for amendment. As the provision now appears in Article 16 of the Statute, it has been turned round: the Council will have to take a positive decision to ask for deferral, and that can be done only if there are nine votes in favour and if none of the Permanent Members use a veto. Strict conditions are included. The period of deferral must be time-limited, and a new decision has to be taken if the Council wishes to renew the request for deferral. The Council can act only where a situation of a kind referred to in Chapter VII exists.

Concerns expressed by some previous speakers about Article 16 were indeed the subject of discussion at the Conference. But at the end of the day there was a recognition that *not* to include such a provision in the Statute might lead in the rare case to the Court and Council, two entities working for the maintenance of peace and security, aiming their efforts in different directions; and that would be deleterious to the common goal. An example given was the case where the dictator of a country was under investigation by the Court at the same time that his presence was necessary in peace negotiations under Council auspices. In such a case should the prospect of peace be put at risk by Court investigations?

"No peace without justice": yes. But in such a case as this, justice might need to be deferred for a while in order to ensure the adoption of a peace settlement. This will be a very rare case, and I cannot envisage that the Council will often ask for a deferral under Article 16.

The other role for the Council is not mentioned in the Statute in express terms. Article 5 gives the Court jurisdiction over the crime of aggression, but only once agreement has been reached on a provision defining the crime and setting out the conditions under which the Court will exercise its jurisdiction. Article 5 ends with the sentence: "Such a provision shall be consistent with the relevant provisions of the Charter of the United Nations". This is code for a requirement that the Court will not be able to act in relation to the crime of aggression unless and until the Council has first determined that aggression has been committed by the State concerned (this was indeed the tenor of the statement made by the United Kingdom and by the United States on adoption of the Statute at the Conference). But it is important to stress that this role for the Council will relate only to aggression, in view of the unique role given to the Council by the Charter. It does not relate to any other crime. This provision is not intended to, and will not, politicize the Court. On the contrary it will avoid the need for the Court to deal with highly political matters.

A number of comments have been made at these proceedings about informal negotiations carried on during the course of the Conference. The story of the Conference is a long and multi-faceted one, and like all good stories it has developed some myths. No one was present at every meeting in every grouping of the Conference, and something must always be left to speculation. But it is time to leave behind the politics of the Conference, to look ahead to the future of the Court and to ensure its success.

6. The Role of the Security Council and the Independence of the International Criminal Court: Some Reflections

NABIL ELARABY*

The preamble to the Rome Statute, which established the International Criminal Court, confirms a determination "to establish an independent permanent ICC". The Statute provides for a prominent and wide-ranging involvement of the Security Council in the proceedings of the ICC as a powerful over-politicized organ with an established record of sidelining legal considerations. The role assigned to the Council cast shadows on the credibility of the ICC as an independent Court of Law. Thus it is proposed to examine whether it is feasible to safeguard the independence of the ICC from the political constraints that are expected to emanate from the prominent role assigned to the Council in the Rome Statute.

At the outset I wish to emphasize that any criticism implied in my comment should not be construed as belittling the great achievement which Rome witnessed on 17 July 1998.

It is proposed to pursue this examination by briefly surveying the Security Council's present mode of operation before addressing the relevant provisions of the Rome Statute.

The Security Council has unlimited power to coerce States and enforce its will. Yet it could not be regarded from a legal perspective, as a dependable central enforcement authority due to its vague and undefined voting system. The abuse of the *veto* has, for many years, frustrated all hopes to consider the Council as the custodian for the application of the rule of law. The question of whether a decision of the Security Council may

* Permanent Representative of Egypt to the United Nations 1991-1999; Member of the International Law Commission; Former Chairman of the Special Committee of the Charter of the United Nations; Partner Zaki Hashem & Partners, attorneys at law, Egypt.

override the legal rights of States, and whether the power of the Council to characterize a situation as one justifying the making of a decision entailing such grave consequences has been the subject of debate by scholars for several years.

The experience of over half a century confirms however that the Council does not act in a norm setting manner. The Council moreover, rarely addresses the legality or even the consistency of some of its decisions. It is therefore ironic to note that the ICJ, a UN organ, while the ICC is not, is not subject to the same restrictions as the Rome Statute has subjected the ICC. A brief survey of certain aspects relating to the relationship of the two courts with the Security Council seems to be in order.

1. The ICJ like the Security Council deals with States while the ICC was created as a criminal court for individuals. It would have been expected that the scope of authority on the ICC would have been minimal.

2. Nowhere in the Charter or in the Statute of the ICJ is a reference provided that the Council is empowered to block the proceedings of the ICJ. In addition, Article 94 of the Charter provides that when the Council decides to carry out the measures to implement any ICJ decision, the Council will be acting as an agent of the ICJ. The Rome Statute permits the Council to block the proceedings of the ICC. In this context, it is relevant to recall that in the course of its consideration of the Lockerbie case in 1992 Judge Shahabuddeen raised the question of the overwhelming and ever-increasing powers of the Security Council, which is now permeating all walks of international life. He said:

> The question [...] is whether a decision of the Security Council may override the legal rights of States, and, if so, whether there are any limitations of the power of the Council to characterize a situation as one justifying the making of a decision entailing such consequences. Are there any limits to the council's powers of appreciation? In the equilibrium of forces under-pinning the structure of the United Nations within the evolving international order, is there any conceivable point beyond which a legal issue may properly arise as to the competence of the Security Council to produce such overriding results?

The Council enjoys a central and unparalleled place in our contemporary international system. It is the sole organ vested with the authority to *enforce*.

3. I now turn to the Rome Statute and propose to briefly analyse the parameter of the role of the Council, which in my view smacks of undue interference and over-politicization. Suffice it to compare the referral of a situation by the Council, which is straightforward and simplified without the conditions attached to the referral by a State or by the Prosecutor. In addition:

1. Open-ended licence to meddle: The reading of Article 5 clearly indicates that the prescribed crimes have varying links and interactions with the maintenance of world peace. *Preambular para. 3 recognizes that such grave crimes threaten the peace, security and well being of the world. So one can assume that the general umbrella of the Council will always hover over the cases before the ICC.*

2. The Council is assigned *a paramount role in the trigger mechanism.* Article 13(B) stipulates that when acting under chapter VII the Council can *refer* a situation in which one or more of such crimes appears to have been committed to the Prosecutor. To act under Chapter VII the Council has to determine the existence of a threat to breach of the peace or an act of aggression. This determination required by Article 39 of the Charter can be blocked by the casting of a negative vote by a Permanent Member. *Thus the veto controls the referral functions to be exercised by the Council.*

3. The Statute allows the Council to defer the ICC's proceedings at any time. This power does not exist in the Statute of the ICJ which is a UN organ. It can be exercised in two ways.

A. The Textual Provisions Article 16 provides that no investigation or prosecution may be commenced or proceeded with if the Council requests that ICC to that effect in a resolution adopted under chapter VII. Thus these points should be highlighted:

1. The request is for twelve renewable months. The Rome Statute does not specify time limits on how many times such a request can be made. Thus one can assume it can go indefinitely. How can this provision be reconciled with the call for "No impunity" for perpetrators of grave crimes?

2. The compliance with such a resolution is not subject to the discretionary power of the ICC. The Council is the ultimate authority.

Compare with Art. 94 where the Council for all practical purposes acts as an agent of the ICJ.

3. The adoption of a resolution not to take action *does not necessarily entail that action by the Council relating to the case under consideration is underway.* So a situation of complete paralysis may ensue.

B. Practice In practice, however, it should be recognized that a serious loophole emanates from the provisions of Article (5)1(d) regarding the crime of aggression. The loophole has two facets:

1. The nature of all crimes under the jurisdiction of the ICC intertwines with aggression, on which the Council is *the sole and ultimate arbiter.* One may therefore expect some form of "chain of event" theory to emerge in the Council to advance arguments that each of the other three crimes comprise an element of aggression which the ICC is not authorized to consider unless referred by the Council.

2. The ICC, on the other hand is prohibited from exercising jurisdiction over the crime of aggression until a provision is adopted in accordance with Articles 121 and 123, a process which would be put in motion after 7 years.

It should also be pointed out that as a general rule, no conflict is envisaged to arise when the ICC deals with a situation which the Council is seized with. Two reasons support this position:

First: The ICC deals with the criminality of individuals, while the Council's primary responsibility is the maintenance of peace and security between States.

Second: An established practice has developed, through the years, for the ICJ and the Council to be seized with the same situations (Lockerbie is a good example) which involve actions by States.

Conclusions

It has to be recognized that the independence of the ICC, as a credible judicial institution, is uncertain under the provisions of the Statute. Its independence and power can only be guaranteed when its proceedings are clearly beyond the scope of the political influence of the Security Council. Regrettably the Statute *provides an open invitation* to the Council to affect and even to dominate the proceedings. Nothing of substance can be done now to alter the relationship between the two institutions in order to free the Court from the hegemony of the Council.

In this context some have raised the possibility of shielding the Court from political influence by seeking ways and means to avoid the detrimental effect of the veto on the ICC proceedings. I have serious doubts about the feasibility of such an approach because it touches a raw nerve for the Five. They are against all forms of limitations on the veto including the call for any form of norm setting and faithful application of the rules of procedure of the Council.

A window of opportunity will be open after 7 years when the Statute will be available for review in accordance with the provisions of Article 12. This should not be lost.

But what is of great importance and relevance now is that the international community has finally established an ICC, a considerable legal and political achievement. The court is a living institution capable of evolution and growth. By itself its existence constitutes a significant deterrent and a major development which would only strengthen the contemporary legal order.

7. The Rome Statute of the International Criminal Court: Exceptions to the Jurisdiction

MAHNOUSH H. ARSANJANI*

Moulding texts sufficiently ambiguous to allow for their application to unforeseen scenarios and diverse interpretations is a useful and sometimes an indispensable negotiating skill. It is particularly useful when drafting major constitutional documents or at crucial stages of negotiations where the gaps in the views of the parties with respect to specific issues threaten to become an obstacle to reaching an agreement. In addition to such *deliberate* constructive ambiguities, ambiguities in the text are sometimes inadvertent and unintentional or due to the circumstances and the context in which the text was negotiated. The Rome Statute of the International Criminal Court provides examples of both, yet their presence poses special problems. Despite the desire of criminal lawyers for a crystal clear criminal code compatible with the principle of legality, the Statute is an international and ambitiously inclusive multilateral agreement negotiated with a deliberate and conscious effort to bring a large number of States on board. Hence two incompatible strategic and normative policies conflict in this unique instrument.

The legislative history of the Statute, beginning with its first draft by the International Law Commission, reveals the ambiguity versus clarity competition. The Commission viewed the Statute as, first and foremost, a multilateral treaty. With a view to facilitating its acceptance, the Commission incorporated the bare minimum, allowing for a great deal of subsequent interpretation by judges or further clarification by other instruments or by practice. This was a frightening idea to criminal lawyers.

---

* Senior Legal Officer, Office of Legal Affairs, United Nations. The views expressed are the author's and they do not necessarily reflect those of the United Nations.

The International Law Commission's approach also displeased the States. Pleas for the principle of legality and the demand that the States must know precisely what it is they are signing onto were also animated by the wish to leave the minimum, if possible, for interpretation by the judges of the Court.

Despite that desire and the effort made by everyone involved in the negotiations, the Statute by its very size and the range of subject matter, not to mention the abbreviated period within which it was negotiated, will oblige the judges to interpret its inconsistent Articles.[1] The requirement for interpretation extends to the very heart of the Statute, the jurisdiction of the Court.

One of the most controversial provisions of the Statute, which was negotiated to the last day, is Article 12 on the precondition to jurisdiction[2]. The very fact of being one of the last Articles negotiated could have contributed to uncertainties about its relationship with certain Articles of the Statute providing special and limited exceptions to the Court's jurisdiction for States Parties to the Statute. I am referring, in particular, to paragraph 2 of Article 11 on "Jurisdiction ratione temporis"[3]; paragraph 5

---

[1] For a review of the negotiating history of the Rome Statute see, Mahnoush H. Arsanjani, *The Rome Statute of the International Criminal Court*, 93 AJIL, 22-43, 1999.

[2] Article 12 of the Statute reads:

> 1. A State which becomes a Party to this Statute thereby accepts the jurisdiction of the Court with respect to the crimes referred to in Article 5.
>
> 2. In the case of Article 13, paragraph (a) or (c), the Court may exercise its jurisdiction if one or more of the following States are Parties to this Statute or have accepted the jurisdiction of the Court in accordance with paragraph 3.
>
>   (a) The State on the territory of which the conduct in question occurred or, if the crime was committed on board a vessel or aircraft, the State of registration of that vessel or aircraft;
>   (b) The State of which the person accused of the crime is a national.
>
> 3. If the acceptance of a State which is not a Party to this Statute is required under paragraph 2, that State may, by declaration lodged with the Registrar, accept the exercise of jurisdiction by the Court with respect to the crime in question. The accepting State shall cooperate with the Court without any delay or exception in accordance with Part 9.

[3] Paragraph 2 of Article 11 reads:

> "If a State become a Party to this Statute after its entry into force, the Court may exercise its jurisdiction only with respect to crimes committed after the entry into force of this Statute for that State, unless that State has made a declaration under Article 12, paragraph 3."

of Article 121 on "Amendments"[4] and Article 124 on "Transitional Provision".[5]

Article 12 sets a broad jurisdiction for the Court in accordance with which the Court may exercise jurisdiction when it has the consent of the State of the territory where the crime is committed *or* the consent of the State of the nationality of the accused. In addition, Article 12, paragraph 3, allows non-States Parties to consent to the Court's jurisdiction by a declaration. This paragraph has practical implications only with respect to situations where neither the territorial State nor the State of nationality of the accused is a party to the Statute.

Though the Statute does not allow reservations, it has two Articles addressing the temporal effect of the Statute. First, Article 11, paragraph 2 provides that if a State becomes a Party to the Statute after its entry into force, the Court may exercise its jurisdiction only with respect to crimes committed after the entry into force of the Statute for that State, unless that State has otherwise agreed. This means that if State A becomes party to the Statute after the Statute is already in force and, prior to its joining the Statute its nationals were involved in any of the crimes subject to the Court's jurisdiction or that such crimes occurred in its territory and for some reason the Court's jurisdiction was not triggered earlier, the Court will not have jurisdiction over those crimes of the nationals of that State. However, the apparently sought effect of Article 11(2), in view of the construction of the jurisdictional scope of Article 12, is unlikely to be achieved unless the State coming under Article 11(2) is both the territorial state and the State of nationality of the accused. In cases where either the territorial State or State of nationality of the accused is party to the Statute

---

[4] Paragraph 5 of Article 121 reads:

> "Any amendment to Articles 5, 6, 7 and of this Statute shall enter into force for those States which have accepted the amendment one year after the deposit of their instruments of ratification or acceptance. In respect of a State Party which has not accepted the amendment, the Court shall not exercise its jurisdiction regarding a crime covered by the amendment when committed by that State Party's nationals or on its territory."

[5] Article 124 reads:

> "Notwithstanding Article 12, paragraphs 1 and 2, a State, on becoming a party to this Statute, may declare that, for a period of seven years after the entry into force of this Statute for the State concerned, it does not accept the jurisdiction of the Court with respect to the category of crimes referred to in Article 8 when a crime is alleged to have been committed by its nationals or on its territory. A declaration under this Article may be withdrawn at any time. The provisions of this Article shall be reviewed at the Review Conference convened in accordance with Article 123, paragraph 1."

or otherwise has consented to the Court's jurisdiction, Article 11(2) appears ineffective.

Let me give an example. The Statute comes into force. State A is not a party to the Statute. Some nationals of State A have been allegedly involved in crimes against humanity in State B, a party to the Statute. For some reason, however, the Court's jurisdiction has not been triggered by anyone in this particular situation. State A then becomes party to the Statute and the Statute comes into force for State A after two months of its ratification in accordance with Article 126(2) of the Statute. Now State B triggers the Court's jurisdiction with respect to the crimes against humanity that were committed earlier implicating some nationals of State A. The question is whether the Court has jurisdiction with respect to these particular crimes in view of Article 11(2) without further, specific consent by State A.

Similar ambiguity also infects the relation between Article 12 and the 7 years' delay, available to States Parties under Article 124 on the non application of the Statute to war crimes. Here, again, the effect of Article 124 could only be guaranteed if the State declaring a moratorium under that Article happens to be both the territorial State and the State of nationality of the accused. Similar to the previous case, where an Article 12 State triggers the Court's jurisdiction with respect to a crime involving the State declaring the 7 years' moratorium, the declaration under Article 124 appears ineffective. Furthermore, the application of the Statute upon the completion of the moratorium, with respect to the crimes that had occurred during that 7 years is unclear.

The third provision whose relationship with Article 12 should be determined is paragraph 5 of Article 121 dealing with the effects of amendments to the Statute. Paragraph 5 of Article 121 has been criticized by some as overreaching and an example of unfair treaty vis-à-vis non-States Parties. This paragraph provides that any amendment to the Statute shall enter into force only for those States Parties that have ratified the amendment. Thus it makes it possible for States Parties not to accept the Court's jurisdiction with respect, for example, to the inclusion of a new category of crimes or the expansion of an existing definition of a crime. Of course, this option is not available to non-States Parties. Here, I only address amendments dealing with the list or definition of crimes and not amendments to other substantive Articles of the Statute that may raise other questions of interpretation. The effect of this paragraph with respect to situations where the Court's jurisdiction has been triggered by a State Party or another consenting State under Article 12 with respect to a crime involving a State Party not having accepted the new amendment to the crime is unclear.

Reconciling the inconsistencies between Article 12 and the other three Articles mentioned could not be resolved linguistically without creating a situation whereby one provision of the Statute negates the effect of another provision. Hence the major purposes of the Statute and the circumstances in which the provision in question were negotiated will have to be considered in accordance with Article 32 of the Vienna Convention on the Law of Treaties.[6]

A major purpose of the Statute was to create a standing universal International Criminal Court. Such a Court requires that as many States as possible join the Statute. Some States, while willing to join the Statute, could not do so unless the Statute addressed specific policy concerns they had. Concerns, which, it was clear, were not such as to directly and irrevocably defeat the major purposes of the Statute of dealing with serious crimes of concern to the international community. Nor were these concerns such as to paralyse the jurisdiction or the operation of the Court in the long run. Since the Statute does not allow any reservations, some of these concerns that otherwise might have been formulated as reservations, were included in the Statute as Articles 11(2), 121(5) and 124 as incentives to join the Statute that would not avail non-States Parties. The rationale is that the parties to the Statute, by signing on to it, have already undertaken major obligations and should therefore benefit from some limited exceptions. In the long run, having these states on board will enhance the effectiveness of the Statute, despite the limited exceptions for some States Parties. Furthermore, the Statute creates an institution for operating in the future and addressing future crimes. The limited exceptions, dealing as they do with some portion of the past, are not fatal to the Court's effectiveness or mission in the future. So it would seem that the relationship between Article 12 on the one hand and Articles 11(2), 121(5) and 124 should be interpreted in favour of the States invoking exceptions and thus against the jurisdiction of the Court. Otherwise, the exception Articles will be rendered ineffective or given an extremely narrow and frivolous scope.

I began by observing that ambiguity is sometimes a critical skill of the negotiator and drafter, I would conclude by observing that the ultimate effectiveness of any legal instrument depends on the skill of the interpreter.

---

[6] Article 32 on "Supplementary means of interpretation" of the Vienna Convention on the Law of Treaties reads:

> "Recourse may be had to supplementary means of interpretation, including the preparatory work of the treaty and the circumstances of is conclusion, in order to confirm the meaning resulting from the application of Article 31, or to determine the meaning when the interpretation according to Article 31:
>
> (a) leaves the meaning ambiguous or obscure; or
>
> (b) leads to a result which is manifestly absurd or unreasonable."

8. The Role of the Prosecutor

SILVIA A. FERNANDEZ DE GURMENDI*

The inclusion at the Rome Conference of statutory provisions for an independent Prosecutor with faculties to target situations on his or her own motion has been hailed by many as a major step forward in the establishment of an effective, impartial and credible International Criminal Court.

When the issue was discussed at the International Law Commission, the majority of the experts considered that the prosecution of the crimes covered by the Statute should not be undertaken without a complaint by a State or a referral by the Security Council, "at least not at the present stage of development of the international legal system" (see UN Report of the ILC on the work of the 46th session, 1994).

However, the majority of States participating in the Rome Conference considered that the *proprio motu* role of the Prosecutor was an indispensable feature of an independent and effective Criminal Court and believed it was essential to grant him or her *ex officio* powers for triggering its jurisdiction, provided that those powers would be subjected to sufficient safeguards.

Both supporters and opponents of an independent Prosecutor feared the risks of politicization of the Court, which - both sides agreed - would undermine the impartiality and independence of the Court.

For the proponents of the *ex officio* powers, an expanded role for the Prosecutor would enhance not only his or her autonomy and independence but also the independence and credibility of the Court as a whole, which would be able to function on behalf of the international community rather than of a particular complainant State or the Security Council. Subordinating the Court's activity to the decisions of political

---

* Diplomat from Argentina, Vicechair of both the Ad Hoc Committee and Preparatory Committee for the Establishment of the ICC. Vicechair of the Committee of the Whole and Chairperson of the Working Group on Procedural Matters at the Rome Diplomatic Conference. Coordinator of the Working Group on Rules of Procedure and Evidence of the Preparatory Commission for the ICC.

actors, such as States or the Security Council, could lead to impunity, discrediting the Court.

Those who argued against granting *proprio motu* powers to the Prosecutor feared an overzealous or politically motivated prosecutor targeting, unfairly or in bad faith highly sensitive political situations.

In general, it was recognized that there was some real risk of abuse of power and that some measures needed to be taken to insure the Prosecutor's accountability and to regulate the exercise of that power. Taken into account the nature of the concerns, it was important to embody statutory safeguards in order to prevent arbitrary decisions by the prosecutor and, at the same time, to help insulate him or her from excessive external pressure.

At the last session of the Preparatory Committee held in April 1998, Argentina and Germany formally proposed a system of control by the Pre-Trial Chamber of the Prosecutor's decision at a very early stage, before proceeding with an investigation. According to this proposal, victims, associations on their behalf, regional or international organizations or any other reliable source could submit information to the Prosecutor relating the commission of a crime punishable under the Statute. Upon reception of this information, the Prosecutor could not start a fully fledged investigation but was limited to a preliminary examination which could include seeking additional information and receiving written or oral testimonies at the seat of the Court. If the Prosecutor concluded there was a reasonable basis to proceed with an investigation, he or she needed to submit to the Pre-Trial Chamber a request for authorization, together with any supporting material collected.

In other words, the Prosecutor could not target a situation in a solitary manner.

In the absence of political backing under the form of a State or Security Council referral, the Prosecutor would need the judicial backing of the Court. The decision to proceed would therefore be taken in a collective manner, protecting not only the international community from possible abuse of power by the Prosecutor but also shielding the Prosecutor from external pressures.

When this proposal was presented, the sponsors underlined it was essential to give the victims an opportunity of submitting their case to the Prosecutor irrespective of the existence of a State complaint or Security Council referral. Furthermore, the victims should not be only limited to the initial information to the Prosecutor. They should also be given an opportunity to make representations to the Pre-Trial Chamber even though the suggested process of decision-making involved primarily the Prosecutor and the Pre-Trial Chamber. If the Pre-Trial Chamber or the Prosecutor refused to proceed, the victims would not be able to appeal but could present further information to the Prosecutor pertaining to the same situation in the light of new facts or evidence.

At the Rome Conference, the authorization by the Pre-Trial Chamber, was considered by the majority of States to be sufficient system of checks and balances of the powers conferred to the Prosecutor. The swift acceptance of the sole proposal put forward in this regard was certainly influenced by the fact that numerous provisions already contained in the Statute represented directly or indirectly additional safeguards, control or filter mechanisms for the Prosecutor and the Court itself.

Indeed, the system related to the Prosecutor's independent role was not created in a *vacuum* and should not be evaluated in isolation of the rest of the Statute. First and foremost, it is important to recall the detailed complementarity regime designed to insure a relation and distribution of competence between the Court and national systems that would be acceptable for the majority of States. Particularly relevant in this context, are those provisions pertaining to preliminary rulings and challenges to admissibility that give to States ample and early opportunity to question the Court's jurisdiction. Secondly, it is important to take into account the norms of Part 4 of the Statute on the Composition of the Court, which provide for the selection, accountability and, if necessary, remotion of men and women who serve at the Court as Judges or Prosecutor. Finally, one should not forget the detailed provisions on criminal procedure contained in the Statute which precise the criteria and steps that must be observed by the Prosecutor and the Pre-Trial Chamber before initiating an investigation or prosecution.

9. The International Criminal Court: Jurisdiction, Trigger Mechanism and Relationship to National Jurisdictions

HANS-PETER KAUL*

I will concentrate my remarks on the compromise on jurisdiction as outlined earlier by Mauro Politi. Given this issue, some critical comments are unfortunately necessary with regard to the very restrictive approach of our American partners in Rome. But I speak on a firm factual basis as I can base myself on the authoritative report by Ambassador Scheffer in the January edition of the American Journal of International Law.[1]

At the outset, let me say that I speak as someone who continues to believe that the complementarity regime of the Statute is probably too strong and the jurisdictional regime is probably too weak. I will try to explain this view which is, of course, my personal one.

Relationship to National Jurisdiction[2]

As you are aware, the dominating principle is of course the principle of complementarity which establishes that the Court may assume jurisdiction only when national legal systems are unable or unwilling to exercise jurisdiction. *Sedes materiae* is Article 17 which establishes a reasonable balance between the ICC and national jurisdiction and national courts

* Legal Service, Ministry of Foreign Affairs, Bonn.

[1] See David J. Scheffer, *The United States and the International Criminal Court*, in: AJIL, January 1999, Vol. 93, No. 1, pp. 12-22.

[2] The paragraph "Relationship to national jurisdiction" was contained in this statement but not read out because of time constraints.

which normally have priority. This principle of complementarity was later "strengthened" by Article 18 on preliminary rulings regarding admissibility, one of the so-called "safeguard provisions" which the American delegation forcefully pushed into the Statute. "Strengthened complementarity" sounds positive - in reality it means a considerable weakening of the Court. I invite all those who are not so familiar with the Statute to study Article 18 carefully and to understand all the procedural obstacles that a concerned State can establish by using this provision - especially if this State is not acting *bona fide*.

Jurisdictional Regime of the Statute

Maybe one can sum up the jurisdiction compromise[3] of the Rome Conference also like this: What it does is to provide for some kind of a Janus-headed double court with a double sword. But there are remarkable differences between the two faces of Janus.

One court is potentially very strong and universal and has a sharp jurisdictional sword with a long outreach.

The other court is quite weak and has only a jurisdictional sword, which is cumbersome and short.

Now, what is meant by this?

1. On one hand, you have Security Council-based, Security Council-triggered jurisdiction based on Article 13b of the Statute. Thus, the Statute contains the jurisdictional regime of a permanent ad-hoc tribunal which can be activated only by the Security Council, in particular by its permanent members. The only thing you need is a referral resolution by the Security Council under chapter VII of the Charter by which it refers a situation to the ICC. In such a case no further conditions apply, no further requirements are necessary. Moreover, this jurisdictional sword is so sharp and long that it does not matter whether the State concerned by the critical situation is a Party to the Statute or not.
2. On the other hand, you have the normal ICC jurisdiction - so to speak the one for the general membership of the Statute and of the United Nations. Here the activity of the Court can be activated or triggered either by a so-called State complaint or by the Prosecutor.

---

[3] For a report on the negotiations on jurisdiction before and during the Rome Conference see Hans-Peter Kaul: *Der Internationale Strafgerichtshof: Das Ringen um seine Zuständigkeit und Reichweite, in: Humanitäres Völkerrecht*, No. 3/1998, pp. 138-144. See also Hans-Peter Kaul, *Towards a Permanent International Criminal Court: Some Observations of a Negotiator*, in: Human Rights Law Journal (HRLJ) 18 (1997) p. 169 sequitur.

But the basic difference - which makes this jurisdictional sword so cumbersome and short is that you have the quite restrictive preconditions of Article 12[4] that either the State on the territory of which the crime was committed (territorial State) or the State of which the suspect is a national (nationality State) must be a Party to the Statute.

As many of you know, Germany had put forward a proposal[5] for a much more effective regime providing universal jurisdiction. I do not regret any more its non-acceptance because we had to recognize that this proposal enjoyed in Rome only the firm support by some 25 - 30 States.

But what I continue to deplore is the hard-to-explain disappearance or sudden death of the so-called South Korean proposal[6] replaced in the last two days by the current Article 12. The Korean proposal, which according to our notes was supported by roughly 80 percent of the States participating in Rome suggested that the Court could exercise jurisdiction if *any* of four possible States was a Party to the Statute (the territorial State, the State of nationality of the accused or of the victim or the custodial State). In particular the membership of the custodial State as a sufficient precondition for the exercise of jurisdiction would have made the general jurisdiction of the Court more effective. This is because in internal wars - the most common form of conflict today - the present compromise provision of Article 12 does not allow for any jurisdiction unless the State in question is a Party to the Statute. But if, in line with the Korean proposal the jurisdiction of the ICC could be established also by membership of the custodial State, this loophole would have been avoided. Such a provision would have meant that core crimes committed during a civil war could have been prosecuted, at least if suspects had been arrested in a State Party's territory. This way, territories of State Parties would have become a very dangerous place to be for perpetrators of such crimes. Now, how did this double compromise on jurisdiction come about in Rome?

Many explanations are possible. On my side, I will in all frankness mention two elements which were in my view decisive.

1. The very determined efforts of the American delegation to make the general jurisdiction, not Security Council-based-

---

4 For a commentary see Sharon Williams, *Article 12 Preconditions to the exercise of jurisdiction*, in: Otto Triffterer (ed.) *Commentary on the Rome Statute of the International Criminal Court - Observers' Notes, Article by Article.*

5 See UN Doc. A/AC 249/1998/DP 2. (The Jurisdiction of the International Criminal Court: An Informal Discussion Paper presented by Germany).

6 UN Doc. A/CONF. 183/C. 1/L 6.

jurisdiction of the Court as weak as possible,[7] and to build in as many safeguards as possible against such a jurisdiction.

2. Ambassador Scheffer, in his interesting article in the American Journal has reported a second decisive factor: The fact that the P 5 in the critical final phase of the conference, at least for a decisive moment, closed ranks to put together a common, very restrictive proposal for the general jurisdiction of the Court.

This explains in my view to a large extent the disappearance of the Korean proposal, and explains also that the current jurisdictional regime as contained in Article 12 is relatively weak and is further weakened by the many other safeguard provisions that our American partners so successfully distributed practically all over the Statute.

A Last Remark

It is therefore an irony that the American delegation - in my view probably the most successful delegation in Rome - was not able to vote for the Statute. It is a further irony that some American representatives continue to oppose strongly the weak Article 12 provision.

In Rome a very high number of important concessions were made to the United States. Also we on the German side - a little bit against our convictions - accepted many American safeguard proposals - this just in order to accommodate the United States, our most important ally, and if possible, to get them on board.

Let me conclude with the hope that these facts are gradually better perceived, better understood and taken into account also by some in Washington.

I remain convinced: the International Criminal Court and its challenge to impunity will become reality.

[7] The concrete expression of this American approach were US amendment proposals UN Doc. A/CONF. 183/C. 1 / L. 70 and UN Doc. A/CONF. 183/C. 1 / L 90 of 14 and 16 July 1997.

THE INTERNATIONAL CRIMINAL COURT AND THE INTERNATIONAL PROTECTION OF HUMAN RIGHTS

10. Introductory Remarks

THEODOR MERON*

One of the most interesting developments of our time has been the growing influence of human rights law on international humanitarian law.

Our panel this morning discussed one aspect of this development: the influence of human rights law on international criminal law and especially the crime of genocide, the crimes against humanity and war crimes. We also discussed the influence of human rights on the Rome Statute of International Criminal Court.

These developments are epitomized by the inclusion in the Treaty of Rome of common Article 3 and of crimes against humanity. The pertinent provisions contain norms which are virtually indistinguishable from fundamental human rights.

The Treaty of Rome made an important contribution to the protection of human rights also in its impact on the thresholds of applicability of international humanitarian law. Under the Statute, the crimes against humanity are applicable to all situations, including peace and internal wars and strife. For crimes against humanity, the Statute wisely dropped any nexus to wars, whether international or internal. They thus apply even below the threshold of applicability of common Article 3 and thus make a tremendous contribution to the protection of human rights. This has always been the case with regard to the crime of genocide, of course. It is true that crimes against humanity still require a certain level of systemacity and intensity of violations. However, with regard to non-international armed conflicts, the Statute includes in the jurisdiction of the Court some, though not enough, violations of The Hague law on methods and means of conduct of hostilities.

One of the problems with the criminalization of violations of international humanitarian law has been the lack of specificity in the definitions of the pertinent crimes, facilitating, in some cases the claim that the maxim *nullum crimen sine lege* was applicable to protect the defendant.

---

* Professor, New York University School of Law, New York.

Human rights require of course that the crimes stated in the Statute be stated with clarity, precision and specificity.

Two recent developments make a great contribution to the specificity of crimes committed against international humanitarian law. One is the work done by the Preparatory Commission on the elements of crimes. There is no question that the detailed definitions developed in this context both on substantive crimes and on general principles of criminal law, such as *mens rea*, constitute a tremendous improvement in the technical quality of international humanitarian law and will make future claims of *nullum crimen* before the International Criminal Court difficult to make. The second development is the study to be published by the ICRC of customary rules of international humanitarian law. This study - I had the honour to serve on the steering committee of ICRC experts - has drawn on national practices of very many states. It will show both that the practice is much richer than we have thought so far, and that the rules are more specific than we have imagined.

The ICC Statute itself helps to clarify the customary character of the crimes which are included in it. While not all the crimes included in the Statute are customary, there is no question that the bulk is customary. The Statute establishes that norms which in the past have been regarded as involving only the "civil" responsibility of states have become norms of criminal law as well.

The Statute makes a major contribution to rights of women, both in emphasizing gender crimes throughout the Statute, but also in matters such as in the definition of the qualification of judges. In various ways, the Statute also enables individuals and NGO's to provide information to the Prosecutor. It promotes human rights of due process, especially in various aspects of general principles of criminal law and in the statement of the sources of law, which, with regard to national laws makes it clear that such law must be consistent with internationally recognized human rights.

11. The Rome Statute of the International Criminal Court and Human Rights

FAUSTO POCAR*

The recent adoption of the Rome Statute of the International Crin Court has been rightly hailed as an important event in the development of international humanitarian law and international justice. Howeve bears a much larger impact on several other areas of international including, in particular, human rights law. In this respect, the contributi brings to the definition of the scope of the domestic jurisdiction of S cannot be underestimated; nor can the role it may play in the ong debate on immunities of Heads of States be minimized. Although these other areas may also be relevant for international human rights law, paper does not aim at identifying and discussing all fields of pos interest of the Rome Statute in this context. Rather, it will briefly foci three issues which may show how the establishment of the Internat Criminal Court may be of major significance for the development of branch of international law. They relate to: a) the relationship bet human rights and humanitarian law; b) the regime of internat guarantees for the protection of human rights; and c) the possible operation between international human rights bodies and the f International Criminal Court.

I

As to the first issue, it has to be pointed out that the Rome Statute is regarded as an extremely important instrument, whose value ca appreciated even before the actual establishment of the Court anc

* Professor of International Law, University of Milan; former President of th Committee of Human Rights.

concrete exercise of its judicial functions. Indeed, in setting up an international jurisdiction, it deals at the same time with humanitarian law and human rights, instituting a clear link between two branches of international law whose development had proceeded separately, both as far as customary and treaty law are concerned. Such a link has a twofold nature: on the one hand it results from the bringing of serious breaches of humanitarian and human rights law under the same international jurisdiction, on the other hand it depends on the codification of the crimes subject to the Court's jurisdiction, which relates to both areas.

Besides the crimes of genocide and aggression, which are selected as deserving specific provisions in the Statute, crimes coming within the Court's jurisdiction are classified in two wide categories: crimes against humanity and war crimes.

War crimes include any serious violation of humanitarian law. In particular, Article 8 of the Statute refers to grave breaches of the Geneva Conventions of 12 October 1949 and other serious violations of the laws and customs applicable in international as well as in internal armed conflicts, within the established framework of international law. Crimes against humanity, on the other hand, are referred to as grave violations of fundamental human rights listed in Article 7, when committed as part of a widespread or systematic attack directed against any civilian population, with knowledge of the attack, but without a necessary connection with an armed conflict.

The Statute itself indicates that war crimes have to be seen as violations of humanitarian law while crimes against humanity consist essentially of violations of human rights law. On one hand, indeed, it underlines that provisions on war crimes apply to armed conflict also not of an international character, but do not apply "to situations of internal disturbances and tensions, such as riots, isolated and sporadic acts of violence or other acts of a similar nature" that cannot be considered as amounting to an internal armed conflict; on the other hand, it clarifies that the attack directed against any civilian population, which is an essential element of a crime against humanity, means a course of conduct involving the multiple commission of grave violations of fundamental human rights, "pursuant to or in furtherance of a State or organizational policy to commit such attack", without mentioning the existence of an armed conflict.

While the Statutes of the existing Tribunals established by the Security Council for the prosecution of persons responsible for crimes committed in the former Yugoslavia and Rwanda defines crimes against humanity only in connection with an armed conflict, the Statute of the International Criminal Court adopts a notion of crimes against humanity which fully belongs to the field of human rights law, thus trying to set a bridge between the latter and humanitarian law. The Rome Statute can therefore be regarded as the first international instrument in which the above mentioned branches of international law are dealt with together from the point of view of the exercise of jurisdiction.

However, the angle of jurisdiction is not the only one under which the ICC Statute can be seen as having aimed at filling in the existing gap between the two areas. From the substantive point of view, its contribution to the codification of human rights law is equally important. Indeed, although the Statute does not refer to violations of all recognized human rights, the description therein provided for an important set of fundamental rights may play a relevant role in the definition of those rights not only for the purposes of the exercise of the Court's jurisdiction, but also for the development of such and related rights in other contexts. The legal concepts, definitions and indicators contained in the Statute may also be relevant and referred to by other bodies in the application of international customary as well as treaty rules. If a certain behaviour is to be considered, under certain circumstances (i.e. when it occurs as part of a widespread or systematic attack directed against a civilian population), as an international crime, the definition of such behaviour provided in the Statute can not obviously be ignored by any authority that would have to apply a treaty provision concerning the same behaviour under different circumstances. The Statute and its interpretation by the Court will therefore benefit other instances in defining the scope of the rights enshrined therein as well as the consequences of their violation when the latter occurs under different circumstances and has to be regarded in the light of different provisions.

For example, the definition of "torture" as contained in Article 7.2(e) of the Statute may be of relevance in supporting the interpretation given by the Human Rights Committee established under the International Covenant on Civil and Political Rights to Article 7 of the Covenant. Indeed, the said definition appears to suggest that a violation does not necessarily require that the offender is a person performing official functions. Similarly, the notion of "enslavement" as defined in Article 7.2(c) may be taken into account in the interpretation of the provision of Article 8 of the Covenant, especially as far as women and children are concerned; it may be equally valuable in the application of the relevant provisions of the more special Conventions adopted within the framework of the United Nations, in order to deal respectively with women's and children's rights. The same applies, again by way of example, to the definition of "enforced disappearance of persons" provided by Article 7.2(i). The reference to the "intention of removing" such persons "from the protection of the law for a prolonged period of time" may be regarded as an interesting element to be taken into account for the classification of disappearances under the provisions of another Convention under which the same violation is to be considered. This element may help, e.g., to classify disappearances as violations of Article 16 of the International Covenant on Civil and Political Rights, which affirms the absolute right of everyone to be recognized as a person in any circumstance.

It is not possible here to attempt to draft an exhaustive list of examples that may be long. However, it is worth pointing out that a codification of serious violations of human rights, as contained in the Statute, will possibly have an impact also on the definition of the scope of the restrictions inherent to certain human rights, permitted under several international instruments for purposes of protecting the internal public order of States. Such restrictions could never go beyond what would constitute a crime against humanity according to the Statute of the International Criminal Court. From a different point of view, also the detailed description of war crimes, contained in Article 8 of the Statute, may contribute to defining the minimum standard of protection that human rights deserve in any situation, including armed conflict. In this perspective, it may exercise an influence on the application of provisions like Article 4 of the International Covenant on Civil and Political Rights, which permits derogations from a series of human rights in case of emergency, at least when such emergency is due to an armed conflict of an international or internal character. Furthermore, such an influence may be regarded as a contribution to establishing a link between humanitarian law and human rights law that might reconcile certain aspects of these two domains of international law.

II

By establishing an international criminal jurisdiction competent to prosecute not only violations of humanitarian law but also serious violations of human rights law, the Statute of the International Criminal Court will have an important impact on the existing regime of international guarantees for the protection of human rights. Although limited as to the number of the rights and the gravity of their violation, the availability of an international jurisdiction to punish those responsible for such violations may add a new substantial element in order to improve that regime.

The current system of international guarantees is essentially based, both at the universal and at the regional level, on procedures aimed at establishing whether States observe their obligations to promote and protect human rights, as set forth in customary rules or treaty provisions. When violations occur, the purpose of such procedures is to make a finding in this respect and to set a pressure on the State in order that it conforms to its obligations. This applies to procedures providing for a general or specific supervision, in that they may monitor the compliance of a State with an international instrument in general terms, or focus on the violation of a particular right in a given situation. It also applies to ordinary and special procedures, being ordinary the procedures aiming at supervising the human rights situation or even specific violations in normal times in a country, and special the procedures related to exceptional situations in the constitutional life of a country, representing an emergency. Moreover, the same consideration applies both when these procedures are *ex officio,* i.e. when the monitoring body itself has the power to initiate them, without consulting the parties concerned, and when they are activated on the initiative of an interested party, be it a State or the victim of a violation. In all cases, when international obligations have not been complied with, the international guarantee intervenes with a view to inducing the State responsible for the violation to conform to them.

Under the existing international human rights instruments the findings that conclude these procedures may have different form and legal value. They may be judgments with binding force for the State concerned, recommendations, or the expression of views, or even simple comments on the situation brought to the attention of an international monitoring body. Whatever their form and value, they affirm the duty of the State responsible for the violation to give reparation or compensation to the victims. The duty of the State in this respect also includes, in the case of serious violations, the duty to punish the persons who actually committed them, even when they acted in an official capacity. The discharge of the latter duty is generally described, in decisions of human rights bodies, as essential for avoiding the spread of a climate of impunity which may favour violations of a similar nature by persons in the same position as those responsible for the condemned violation. However, no direct international guarantee is provided for in this regard by existing treaties and conventions: it is only for the State concerned to put in place such procedures, as may be in accordance with its domestic law and jurisdiction, in order to try and convict the authors of the violations.

The establishment of an international criminal jurisdiction for serious violations, *inter alia*, of human rights takes care of this issue and provides for an additional guarantee for their protection by States. Indeed, should a State not comply with its obligation to punish the persons responsible for a violation, the Court would intervene to ensure that such persons are brought to justice. In other words, the task of deterring individuals from violating human rights will be taken up directly by the international judicial body, provided that violations are of such gravity as to be of particular concern to the international community.

This approach raises a number of issues, which may deserve some brief comments. Firstly, it has to be pointed out that the new international guarantee – which, unlike the existing ones of the same kind, has a general and permanent nature – will be an additional one and will by no means replace the domestic guarantees, which consist both of providing reparation and compensation for the victims and punishing the perpetrators of human rights violations. It follows that it should be complementary to internal guarantees and intervene only in the case of inactivity of the State that has the primary duty to ensure that human rights are protected within its jurisdiction. In other words, it should be activated only when the State concerned does not or can not perform its punitive tasks.

Secondly, and in a similar perspective, the new international jurisdiction will be additional to the existing international machinery established both at the universal and at the regional level in order to provide for a guarantee of the protection of human rights. By no means may it be regarded as replacing the latter. Specific problems in this regard may however arise in the case of the establishment of another international criminal jurisdiction, whose competence overlaps with the competence of the International Court. Currently, this may however be the case of the International Criminal Tribunal for the former Yugoslavia, should it still be active at the time the Rome Statute comes into force.

Thirdly, by selecting a series of rights whose violations will come within the jurisdiction of the Court, the Statute introduces a distinction between different categories of human rights that may be seen as a departure from the principle, repeatedly affirmed by the General Assembly, that human rights are indivisible and interdependent, and that no hierarchy may be made in this regard. This is certainly true, in that the selected rights will benefit under certain circumstances from the new international guarantee while other rights will not. However, it has to be borne in mind that it has never been maintained that any violation of any human right should necessarily entail criminal sanctions for the persons responsible thereof. From the point of view of the States' obligation to ensure their protection, the principle of indivisibility and interdependence of all human rights remains therefore untouched.

Lastly, in stressing the obligation both of the State and the international community to punish the persons having committed serious violations of human rights, the Rome Statute underlines the principle of individual accountability in these matters, under municipal as well as under international law. This may add new arguments to the issue of whether the individual may be regarded, at least in certain respects, as a subject of international law. The question is not a new one: it goes back to the first international procedures which saw the individual standing as one of the parties before an international body. Progressively, the debate drew arguments from the establishment of the post-war criminal tribunals, from the various treaties and conventions which provide for monitoring procedures that can be activated by alleged victims of human rights violations before international courts or other international bodies, as well as from the currently existing *ad hoc* criminal tribunals. New weight will probably be added to the debate by the establishment of the International Criminal Court. Clearly, here is not the place to go into a discussion of a general issue of this kind. It can only be pointed out that the arguments drawn from other procedures in favour and against the subjectivity of the individual under international law are likely to be played also as far as the position of the individual before the Court is concerned.

III

Turning now to the possible cooperation between existing international human rights bodies and the International Criminal Court, there is no doubt that any interrelation of this kind may also contribute to narrow the existing gap between humanitarian and human rights law. In particular, such a co-operation may prove to be relevant in the preliminary activity leading to the exercise of the jurisdiction of the Court and at the subsequent stage of establishing the existence of a violation.

From the first point of view, it has to be recalled that the Court's jurisdiction may be exercised on the initiative of a State Party to the Statute, or of the Security Council, or after an investigation carried out by the Prosecutor according to the relevant provisions of the Statute. Thus, prosecution is basically independent from political conditioning and can take place following inquires initiated independently by the Prosecutor or after notification by other bodies, including non-governmental organizations. Whenever an international human rights body has established, within its competence, the existence of a serious violation that would come within the jurisdiction of the Court, it would seem natural that the question will be brought before the Prosecutor and that the latter will benefit from the activity of that body in carrying out his investigation. The same consideration might apply to the Security Council, which may rely on the activity of the said international body to refer a situation to the Prosecutor, although its decision may be more frequently influenced by political considerations.

A more delicate aspect concerns a possible co-operation in establishing the existence of a violation. It is well known that existing human rights bodies only have limited powers of investigation, even if these may be wider when a procedure takes place before a regional court. However, their capability to establish the factual circumstances of a specific violation should not be underestimated. Thus, an investigation conducted by the Prosecutor under the Court's Statute may greatly benefit from the evidence collected by another international body. Clearly, such evidence will by no means bind the Prosecutor, who will remain fully independent in his evaluation and in the appreciation of its value for the purposes of indicting a person. As it comes from another international body, it would however be difficult for the Prosecutor not to take it into account. The above mentioned considerations may of course apply also to the use of evidence collected by the Court's Prosecutor by other human rights bodies for the purposes of the exercise of their competence.

The practice will show if this co-operation will develop and how it will improve the Court's jurisdiction as well as the activity of other human rights bodies and international courts. Should it develop adequately, it will greatly contribute to rationalizing the existing machinery aimed at providing an international guarantee of the protection of human rights.

12. Crimes Against Humanity and the Rome Statute of the International Criminal Court

ROGER S. CLARK*

These remarks on Article 7 of the Rome Statute[1] are in three parts. In the first, I sketch the development of the concept of crimes against humanity in International law. In the second, I describe the contents of Article 7 and make some comments on the recent, somewhat confused, history of the concept. In the third, I make some general observations, particularly about the relationship (and overlap) between crimes against humanity and other crimes within the jurisdiction of the International Criminal Court ("ICC"), notably genocide and war crimes. I also introduce to an unsuspecting World what I shall call the "hierarchy of evil".

---

*Adviser to Samoa in the negotiations on the International Criminal Court. Any opinions expressed in this paper should not be attributed to that Government.

[1] UN Doc. A/CONF.183/9 (1998) (hereinafter "Rome Statute"), conveniently reproduced with corrections in M. Cherif Bassiouni, *The Statute of the International Criminal Court: A Documentary History*, Ardsley, NY 1998, 39. There is some very insightful discussion of Art. 7 by Darryl Robinson, "Defining Crimes Against Humanity at the Rome Conference", 93 *Am. J. Int'l L.* 1999, 43, by Herman von Hebel & Darryl Robinson, "Crimes within the Jurisdiction of the Court", in *The International Criminal Court, The Making of the Rome Statute, Issues, Negotiations, Results* (Roy S. Lee, ed.), The Hague 1999, 79 and by Rodney Dixon, Christopher Hall and Machteld Boot, "Crimes against humanity", in *Commentary on the Rome Statute of the International Criminal Court* (Otto Triffterer, ed.), Baden-Baden 1999, 37. I have had the advantage of reading the manuscript of a very comprehensive piece which is to be published in *Human Rights Quarterly*, in May 2000, Margaret M. DeGuzman, "The Road from Rome: The Developing Law of Crimes against Humanity". There is an excellent account of the development of the Statute in A. Hays Butler, "A Selective and Annotated Bibliography of the International Criminal Court", 10 *Crim.L.F.* 1999, 121. The best relatively short account of the fundamentals of the Statute is Leila Nadya Sadat & S. Richard Carden, "The New International Criminal Court: An Uneasy Revolution", 88 *Georgetown L.J.* (forthcoming, 2000).

1) Some History

The modern usage of the words "crimes against humanity" dates from the Nuremberg Charter, Article 6(c) of which reads:

> Crimes Against Humanity: namely, murder, extermination, enslavement, deportation or other inhumane acts committed against any civilian population, whether before or during the war, or persecutions on political, racial, or religious grounds in execution of or in connection with any crime within the jurisdiction of the tribunal, whether or not in violation of the domestic law of the country where perpetrated.[2]

Curiously enough, the term "crimes against humanity", which provided a catchy title to go along with "crime against peace" and "war crimes", did not make an appearance in the drafting of the Nuremberg Charter until the very last moment. Prior talk had been of "atrocities", "persecutions" and sometimes "deportations" (it apparently being understood that these were for the purpose of slave/forced labour).[3] The Nuremberg formulation contained two types of crimes, the murder-and-other-inhumane act types, and the persecution-on-proscribed grounds types. The two categories were overlapping since "persecution" typically involved killing, forced labour and the like which could just as easily be characterized as inhumane acts. The persecution type of offences were eventually broken out to form the core of the definition of "genocide" contained in the Genocide Convention.[4]

An earlier example of the modern usage of crimes against humanity occurred in the declaration of 28 May 1915 by the Governments of France, Great Britain and Russia concerning the massacres of the Armenian

---

[2] Charter of the International Military Tribunal, Article 6(c), in 1 *Trial of the Major War Criminals Before the International Military Tribunal,* International Military Tribunal, Nuremburg 1947, 11. See generally, Roger S. Clark, "Crimes Against Humanity at Nuremberg", in *The Nuremberg Trial and International Law,* (G. Ginsburgs and V.N. Kudriavtsev, eds.), Dordrecht/Boston 1990, 193-194. In a Protocol signed on 6 October 1945, the comma before "or persecutions" replaced the semi-colon that appeared there in the original text adopted in London on 8 August 1945. On the "semi-colon Protocol", see Clark, *ibid.* 190-192. It made it clear that the phrase "in execution with or in connection with any crime within the jurisdiction of the tribunal" modified the words "murder ... inhumane acts" as well as "persecutions". See *infra* at notes 57 and 69-71, on this limitation on the Tribunal's jurisdiction. On the history and content of crimes against humanity in general, see M. Cherif Bassiouni, *Crimes Against Humanity in International Law,* Dordrecht/Boston 1992.

[3] See generally, Clark *op.cit.* note 2, 181-90. Note that under the Rome Statute it is clear that deportations are unlawful in and of themselves. No further purpose, such as enslavement, is necessary. See *infra* note 43.

[4] G.A. Res. 260A (III), UN GAOR, 3rd Sess., Res. 174, UN Doc. A/810, 1948.

population in Turkey, killings to which the term "genocide" has also since been applied. The three-power declaration described these atrocities as "crimes against humanity for which all members of the Turkish Government will be held responsible together with its agents implicated in the massacres".[5] The novelty of the complaint is clear: this is not a complaint about war crimes inflicted on an adversary; it is about what citizens of the Ottoman Empire were doing to other citizens of the Empire. That would become the gravamen of crimes against humanity at Nuremberg, as that offence was actually applied by the Tribunal as something distinct from war crimes, crimes by Germans against fellow Germans (albeit committed during the period of the Second Word War).[6]

In even earlier usage, "crime against humanity" had a narrower meaning, applying to the slave trade.[7] References to enslavement, as we shall see, are carried forward into the Rome Statute, along of course, with the broader usage now developed via Armenia, Nuremberg, and the more recent Statutes of the International Tribunals for Rwanda[8] and Former

---

[5] Quoted in Egon Schwelb, "Crimes Against Humanity", 23 *Brit.Y.B. Int'l L.* 1946, 178, 181. Neither the Turkish Government, nor its agents were ultimately "held responsible". There were provisions (Articles 226-230) in the aborted 1920 Treaty of Sèvres between the Allies and Turkey which contemplated trials both for war crimes committed against opposing forces and for internal "massacres" (the term "crimes against humanity" does not appear). The point was not pursued in the final peace treaty.

[6] Clark, *op.cit.* note 2, 195-98.

[7] There had been other sporadic uses of the term, or something close to it, before 1915. See, e.g., Robert Lansing, "Notes on World Sovereignty", 1 *Am. J. Int'l L.* 1921, 13, 25. (distinguishing between piracy, "a crime against the world" and the slave trade, "a crime against humanity") (although it was published in 1921, a note to this Article suggests that it was written in 1906). In an unusual case in which he was justifying the extradition of a slave trader to Cuba, without the benefit of an extradition treaty, President Abraham Lincoln reported to the Senate that "a nation is never bound to furnish asylum to dangerous criminals who are offenders against the human race". See discussion in I. John Bassett Moore, *On Extradition and Interstate Rendition*, 1891, 33-35. This must be an early example of a similar usage. Jordan Paust has located an example from an 1872 speech in which "crime against humanity" was used to describe the institution of slavery itself. See Jordan Paust, "Threats to Accountability after Nuremberg: Crimes against Humanity, Leader Responsibility and National Fora", 12 *N.Y.LSch.J.Hum. Rts. 1996, 545, 549,* quoting III *Orations and Addresses of George William Curtis 1894,* 208 (Charles Eliot Norton ed.); Curtis was offering a eulogy following the demise of the anti-slavery Senator, Charles Sumner. Then there was the 1890 letter from George Washington Williams to the U.S. Secretary of State, describing King Leopold's rule in the Congo as a crime against humanity. See Adam Hochschild, *King Leopold's Ghost: A Story of Greed, Terror, and Heroism in Colonial Africa,* New York 1999, 112 (paperback). William Schabas has discovered an even earlier usage in French, with Robespierre's reference to Louis XVI as a "criminal envers l'humanité". William A. Schabas, *The Abolition of the Death Penalty in International Law*, 2d.ed., Cambridge/United Kingdom/New York 1997, 5.

[8] Statute of the International Tribunal for Rwanda, Annex to S.C. Res. 955, UN SCOR, 49th year, 3453d mtg., 1994, 1.

Yugoslavia,[9] both of which include crimes against humanity, albeit differently defined,[10] within the jurisdiction of the respective Tribunals.

These examples of the term, while evidently dealing with situations to which the laws of international armed conflict do not, by their terms at least, strictly apply, nonetheless echo the principle of the Martens clause of the Fourth Hague Convention. That is to say, to the extent that certain matters are not specifically dealt with in the Convention, "the inhabitants and the belligerents shall remain under the protection of and subject to the principles of the law of nations, as established by and prevailing among civilized nations, by the laws of humanity, and the demands of the public conscience".[11]

"Crimes against humanity" are now firmly grounded in general international law. While war crimes and genocide began their lives as customary law, or general principles of law, they have long found expression in treaty formulations. The Rome Statute serves a similar purpose for crimes against humanity. To my mind, this compensates for the way in which the wider concept of crimes against humanity has been downplayed the last five decades as many commentators tended to emphasize genocide which had been extracted from the broader concept and embedded in its own convention.[12] Crimes against humanity have now come into their own.

2) The Immediate Antecedents and the Contents of Article 7

Speaking very generally, Article 7 is a close descendant of Article 6(c) of the Nuremberg Charter[13] and of Articles 5 and 3 respectively of the Statutes of the Tribunals for Former Yugoslavia[14] and Rwanda.[15] Occasionally, it adds new elements to those instruments. But, for the most part, when it departs from their wording this is because it spells out in more detail items that were implicit in them. Exceptionally, the reference to "gender" as a proscribed ground of persecution in Article 7(1)(h) is a new element when viewed against the Nuremberg document. Its inclusion, along with the more

[9] Report of the Secretary-General pursuant to Paragraph 2 of Security Council Resolution 808, 1993, including the Statute of the Tribunal, UN Doc. S/25704 and Add. 1, 1993.
[10] See *infra* notes 74-76.
[11] Convention (No. IV) respecting the Laws and Customs of War on Land, with Annex of Regulations, done at the Hague, 18 October 1907.
[12] Cf. M. Cherif Bassiouni, "'Crimes against Humanity': The Need for a Specialized Convention", *31 Colum. J. Transnat'l L.* 1994, 457.
[13] See *op.cit.* note 2.
[14] *Op.cit.* note 9.
[15] *Op.cit.* note 8.

"traditional" grounds: political, racial, ethnic, cultural and religious,[16] is, however, consistent with more recent developments in the international law of discrimination.[17] Some participants in the drafting contended that "forced pregnancy" and "any other form of sexual violence of comparable gravity" represented new developments; others thought them implicit in the earlier instruments. "Rape", "sexual slavery" and "enforced prostitution" were more obviously implicit in the earlier instruments, although prosecutions for them were uncommon and, when there were prosecutions, they tended to be under the rubric of war crimes rather than crimes against humanity.[18] Including specific references to these matters, whether regarded as articulating the implicit, or as new breakthroughs, was nonetheless of considerable significance in the drafting process.

Article 7 is, for sure, the most detailed definition to date of crimes against humanity. It represents both a "codification" and (to a small degree) a "progressive development" of international law[19] as those terms are understood in the United Nations Charter.[20] One thing that became very

---

[16] Article 7(1)(h) also contains a residual, and probably hard to reach, category of "other grounds that are universally recognized as impermissible under international law".

[17] On the controversy about the meaning of gender, see *infra* note 26.

[18] See generally, Kelly D. Askin, "Women and International Humanitarian Law", in 1 *Women and International Human Rights Law,* (Kelly D. Askin and Dorean M. Koenig, eds.), Ardsley, NY 1999, 51-54 (contrasting failure to charge German leadership with such crimes and prosecution of Japanese leadership). See also *infra* notes 81-85 on the overlap between the concepts of war crimes and crimes against humanity.

[19] Either in the guise of customary law or of general principles of law. See Statute of the International Court of Justice, Article 38(1)(b) and (c). The most convincing explanation of the legal status of crimes against humanity in 1945-46 was as general principles of law. Clark, *op.cit.* note 2, 193 n.65. Subsequent practice adds custom to the general principles. The Statute of the ICC now gives it a treaty basis.

[20] See UN Charter Article 13 (General Assembly to initiate studies and make recommendations for, inter alia, "encouraging the progressive development of international law and its codification".) The International Law Commission, charged by the Assembly with codification and progressive development, spent many years working on a Draft Code of Crimes against the Peace and Security of Mankind. Its most comprehensive collection of crimes was contained in its 1991 draft which, however, jettisoned the Nuremberg categories of crimes against peace, war crimes and crimes against humanity. What had been crimes against humanity were covered fairly comprehensively by "genocide", "apartheid" and "systematic or mass violations of human rights". See [1991] *Y.B. Int'l L. Comm'n*, Vol. II, Pt. 2, at 101-04. The Commission's final effort in 1996 re-establishes the Nuremberg categories, but empties the Code of much of its earlier content. See Draft Code, in Report of the International Law Commission on the work of its 48th session, 6 May-26 July 1996, UN GAOR, Supp. No. 10, at 9, UN Doc. A/51/10 (1996). For commentary, see Timothy L.H. McCormack and Gerry J. Simpson, "The International Law Commission's Draft Code of Crimes against the Peace and Security of Mankind: An Appraisal of the Substantive Provisions", 5 *Crim. L.F.* 1994, 1 (discussing 1991 Draft Code); Rosemary Rayfuse, "The Draft Code of Crimes against the Peace and Security of Mankind: Eating Disorders at the International Law Commission", 8 *Crim. L.F.* 1997, 43 (discussing 1996 draft).

apparent to me in the ICC negotiations is just how difficult it is to get agreement on what represents the current customary law, or general principles of law, on any particular issue. Article 7 thus represented the limit of what a highly political process, functioning with consensus in mind, would bear. Some of us thought that we had been forced to stop short of the existing general law while others thought we were on the (possibly wrong) side of developing it.

Structurally, Article 7 consists of three paragraphs. Paragraphs 2 and 3 are definitions of the terms appearing in paragraph 1, which contains the thrust of the enacting provisions. Paragraph 1 says in its chapeau that, for the purposes of the Statute, crimes against humanity means any of a list of eleven items, described as "acts", when those acts are "committed as part of a widespread or systematic attack directed against any civilian population, with knowledge of the attack". Both of these items of the chapeau merit a little exegesis, "act" and "attack".

"Acts"

The usage of the term "acts" in the chapeau is curious to a criminal lawyer. In context, the term must be referring to more than the physical "elements"[21] of the offences created. That it contains implicit mental elements as well as physical ones is plain when one looks at items on the list such as "murder" which surely contains an element of mental culpability in addition to the obvious physical act of killing someone.[22]

---

[21] Article 9 of the Rome Statute says that the Assembly of States Parties is to adopt "Elements of Crimes" which "shall assist the Court in its interpretation and application of Articles 6, 7 and 8". The Final Act of the Rome Conference includes in the tasks of the Preparatory Commission for the Court that of drafting such elements. "Elements" is not defined in the Statute but must refer to the basic building blocks, the mental and physical matters which fit together to constitute "a crime". On the structure of mental and physical elements in the General Part of the Statute, see generally, Delegation of Samoa, *Elements of The Elements: An Informal Discussion Paper* (circulated at the ICC Preparatory Commission at its second session, 26 July-13 August 1999).

[22] Note that the last phrase of the chapeau, "with knowledge of the attack" adds an additional global *mens rea* element to any particular mental element included in the very nature of a specific "act". In terms of the structure of "elements" of offences contemplated in the "general part" of the Statute, notably Article 30, the attack is a "circumstance" element. (Art. 30 seems to envisage three types of "non-mental" elements, "conduct", "consequences" and "circumstances".) The concluding phrase of the chapeau spells out what would probably be a default rule even in the absence of particular reference to the matter: unless otherwise provided, there is criminal responsibility only if "material elements" are committed with intent and knowledge. Article 30, para. 1. In the case of a "circumstance" this seems to require knowledge in the sense of "awareness that a circumstance exists". See Article 30, para. 3. For a thorough examination of the knowledge requirement, see De Guzman, *op.cit.* note 1.

This usage of "act" to include both physical and mental aspects goes back as far as the Nuremberg formulation.[23] It is carried through (in a structure much closer to the present drafting) in the Genocide[24] and Apartheid[25] Conventions.

The "acts" listed in Article 7 are these:

(a) Murder;

(b) Extermination;

(c) Enslavement;

(d) Deportation or forcible transfer of population;

(e) Imprisonment or other severe deprivation of liberty in violation of fundamental rules of international law;

(f) Torture;

(g) Rape, sexual slavery, enforced prostitution, forced pregnancy, enforced sterilization, or any other form of sexual violence of comparable gravity;

(h) Persecution against any identifiable group or collectivity on political, racial, national, ethnic, cultural, religious, gender as defined in paragraph 3,[26] or other grounds that are universally recognized as impermissible under international law, in connection with any act referred to in this paragraph or any crime within the jurisdiction of the Court;

(i) Enforced disappearance of persons;

(j) The crime of apartheid;

(k) Other inhuman acts of a similar character intentionally causing great suffering, or serious injury to body or to mental or physical health.[27]

A few comments follow on each of these.

---

[23] See text of Article 6(c), *op.cit.* note 2.

[24] *Op.cit.* note 4, Article II.

[25] G.A. Res. 3068 (XXVIII), UN GAOR, 28th Sess., Supp. No. 30, at 75, UN Doc. A/9030 (1973) (Art. II). The Statutes for Former Yugoslavia and Rwanda, drafted rather more sparsely, use the word "crimes" to much the same effect as "acts" in the other instruments.

[26] Para. 3 provides:

For the purpose of this Statute, it is understood that the term "gender" refers to the two sexes, male and female, within the context of society. The term "gender" does not indicate any meaning different from the above.

The inclusion of "gender" occasioned some passionate exchanges and this "definition". A writer in a conservative Catholic publication claims that:

"Gender", which allegedly meant male and female, seemed to be code for homosexuals and bisexuals as well, and also seemed to be designed to put them and their lifestyles on the same legal footing as married couples.

Peter Simpson, "UN Power Grab: The International Criminal Court", *Crisis,* Sept. 1999, 17, 19. For a different view, see the careful analysis by the Coordinator on the issue in Rome, Cate Steains, "Gender Issues", in Roy Lee ed., *op.cit.* note 1, 357, 371-75. See also, Kelly D. Askin, "Crimes within the Jurisdiction of the International Criminal Court", 10 *Crim. L.F.* 1999, 33, 47-48.

[27] Rome Statute, Article 7, para. 1.

"Murder" as used here probably refers to the same kind of homicide described in the War Crimes provisions in the Statute as "wilful killing"[28] or simply "killing".[29] At the very least it includes intentional or knowing killings.[30] It is an open question whether it also includes such sophisticated national variants on murder as intent to cause great bodily harm which results in death[31] or the felony murder rule.[32] A possible reading of the preparatory work of the Statute is that the drafters of the general part meant to exclude reckless or negligent killings, or killings characterized by such concepts as *dolus eventualis* that in some domestic systems would result in a manslaughter verdict.[33] Not all commentators see it this way.[34] This is not to deny that, even if from the point of view of the actual perpetrator negligent or reckless killings would not be included, there could well be some cases of military command responsibility where the commander is responsible for murders committed by those under his or her command on the basis that the commander knew or *ought to have known* that the forces were committing or about to commit the crimes and failed to take all necessary and reasonable measures within his or her power to prevent or repress their commission.[35]

---

[28] Rome Statute, Article 8, para. 2(a)(i). See also para 2(c)(i) ("murder" in context of breaches of common Article 3 of the Geneva Conventions).

[29] *Ibid.*, Article 8, para. 2(b)(vi), 2(b)(xi), 2(e)(ix).

[30] "Intent" and "knowledge" are the basic *mens rea* elements referred to (and defined) in Rome Statute Article 30.

[31] In Prosecutor v. Akayesu, ICTR-96-4-T, at para. 589, the International Criminal Tribunal for Rwanda defined the mental element for wilful killing as:

at the time of the killing the accused or a subordinate had the intention to kill or inflict grievous bodily harm on the deceased having known that such bodily harm is likely to cause the victim's death, and is reckless whether death ensues or not.

In some other (prosecutorial) formulations, the intent either to kill or to inflict grievous bodily harm (without any further intent or recklessness) is said to be sufficient. See Working Paper, International Committee of the Red Cross, February 1999, at 14-15 (mimeo distributed at Preparatory Commission). These different formulations could lead to different results and the matter will need to be clarified either in the Elements or by the Court.

[32] With your author's doubts, compare the view of the I.L.C. in the Commentary on its 1996 Draft Code of Crimes against the Peace and Security of Mankind, *op.cit.* note 20, 96:

Murder is a crime that is clearly understood and well defined in the national law of every State. This prohibited act does not require any further explanation.

[33] See generally Per Saland, "International Criminal Law Principles", in Roy Lee ed., *op.cit.* note 1, 189, 205-06.

[34] For example, the ICRC Paper, *op.cit.* note 31.

[35] Rome Statute, Article 28 (1). "Or ought to" is surely the language of objective negligence. Cf. the situation of other (presumably civilian) "superior and subordinate" relationships where the rule is the more subjective one that the superior must be shown to have "known" or "consciously disregarded" information which "clearly indicated that subordinates were committing or about to commit such crimes". Rome Statute, Article 28(2). For a different approach, see the discussion by the Tokyo Tribunal which applied negligence principles in

"Extermination", the core meaning of which must be multiple killings, is defined[36] to include "the intentional infliction of conditions of life, inter alia, the deprivation of access to food and medicine, calculated[37] to bring about the destruction of part of a population". This language is another close echo of language in the genocide Article.[38]

"Enslavement" was a term which appeared in the Nuremberg Charter in the description both of war crimes and of crimes against humanity. I had always thought that the usage there was more of a metaphor than an attempt to incorporate classic concepts of chattel slavery. Indeed, the Nuremberg Tribunal in its decision talks about forced labour governed by the laws of war rather than about chattel slavery.[39] The definition contained in Article 7,[40] however, echoes the narrower language on chattel slavery contained in the 1926 Slavery Convention.[41] "Enslavement" is defined to mean "the exercise of any or all of the powers attaching to the right of ownership over a person and includes the exercise of such power in the course of trafficking in persons, in particular women and children. A sensible approach is to de-emphasize right of ownership here and stress that it is all about exercising power, de facto or de jure.[42]

---

the case of both military and civilian leaders, *The Tokyo Judgment, International Military Tribunal for the Far East*, Vol. I, (B.V.A. Roling and C.F. Ruter ed.) 1977, 29-31 (responsibility of Cabinet members and of Army and Navy Commanders where they knew or ought to have known of ongoing atrocities).

36 Rome Statute, Article 7(2)(b).

37 There is an ambiguity in "calculated". Does it mean that the accused intended to bring such a situation about? Or is it enough that, viewed objectively, the actions were likely to bring it about? Whose "calculation" is relevant? There will be no doubt be further debate on such issues as the "Elements" are finalized.

38 Rome Statute, Article 6(c).

39 "Judgment of the International Military Tribunal at Nuremberg", 41 *Am. J. Int'l L. 1947,* 172, 239. I can find nothing in the Nuremberg Tribunal's discussion of crimes against humanity which elucidates this matter. See also, in general, Benjamin B. Ferencz, *Less Than Slaves: Jewish Forced Labor and the Quest for Compensation,* Cambridge, Mass. 1979.

40 Rome Statute, Article 7(2)(c).

41 The 1926 Convention defines slavery as "the status or condition of a person over whom any or all of the powers attaching to the right of ownership are exercised". Slavery Convention, signed at Geneva, 25 September 1926, 82 U.N.T.S. 51.

42 To my taste, the draft definition of the elements of "sexual slavery" as a war crime produced at the August 1999 session of the Preparatory Commission emphasizes the property aspect too much. The relevant definition reads:

The accused exercised a power attaching to the right of ownership over one or more persons, such as by purchasing, selling, lending or bartering such a person or persons, or by imposing on them a similar deprivation of liberty.

UN Doc. PNICC/1999/WGEC/RT.6, at 2 (1999). There is some useful discussion which introduces the concept of "sexual servitude" which avoids some of the ownership hangups in Report of the Standing Committee of Australian Attorneys-General, Model Criminal Code, Chapter 9, Offences against Humanity, Slavery (November 1998).

"Deportation or forcible transfer of population" means "forced displacement of the persons concerned by expulsion or other coercive acts from the area in which they are lawfully present, without grounds permitted under international law".[43] This is the essence of what is involved in ethnic cleansing and why a count of crimes against humanity is so appropriate in such instances. "Deportation" carries with it the connotation that people are moved outside national boundaries; "forcible transfer" could be within the boundaries of an existing state.

"Imprisonment or other severe deprivation of physical liberty in violation of fundamental rules of international law" (not further defined in paragraph 2) catches gross violations of human rights characterized by arbitrary imprisonment.[44]

"Torture" is defined as "the intentional infliction of severe pain or suffering, whether physical or mental, upon a person in the custody or under the control of the accused; except that torture shall not include pain or suffering arising only from, inherent in or incidental to, lawful sanctions".[45] This is a stripped-down version of the definition contained in the 1984 United Nations Torture Convention[46] and the stripping-down was controversial. The 1984 treaty adds the requirement that the pain or suffering in question be "inflicted by or at the instigation of or with the consent or acquiescence of a public official or other person acting in an official capacity". Leaving this out was much debated and those who did not favour a requirement that the accused be a public official won the day. Typically that will be the case, but there will nevertheless be cases where non-officials cheerfully participate as unrecruited volunteers in an attack. The Statute catches such persons in its net.

Rape is not defined for the purposes of the Statute, and its definition has caused some difficulties in the efforts to draft Elements of the war crimes Article, where the word may also be found.[47] Nor are "sexual slavery", "enforced prostitution", "enforced sterilization" and "any

---

[43] Rome Statute, Article 7(2)(d). The deportations are proscribed in themselves. If they take place for a further purpose such as enslavement there would be a further offence.

[44] See generally, Nigel S. Rodley, *The Treatment of Prisoners Under International Law* (2d ed.), Paris/New York 1998.

[45] Rome Statute, Article 7(2)(e).

[46] Convention against Torture and other Cruel, Inhuman or Degrading Treatment or Punishment, G.A. Res. 39/46, UN GAOR, 39th Sess., Supp. No. 51, at 197, UN Doc. A/39/51 (1984).

[47] See the current efforts at drafting in UN Doc. PCNICC/1999/WGEC/RT.6 (Discussion Paper proposed by the Coordinator, 10 August 1999). There seems to be agreement that the concept is gender-neutral, but the traditional penetration requirement is controversial. Steains, *supra* note 27, 358-364, has a good discussion of the significance of including this package of offences within the definitions of crimes against humanity and war crimes.

other form of sexual violence of comparable gravity" defined. So far at the Preparatory Commission, the debate has centred on the similar provisions in the war crimes Article.[48] Whatever is agreed upon there will no doubt be carried over into the crimes against humanity Elements. "Forced pregnancy", became contentious when the Holy See saw it as opening the way to legitimizing abortions for those raped, or perhaps as an even more fundamental endorsement of abortion.[49] It was finally defined as "the unlawful confinement, of a woman forcibly made pregnant, with the intent of affecting the ethnic composition of any population or carrying out other grave violations of international law". The definition adds that "This definition shall not in any way be interpreted as affecting national laws relating to pregnancy".[50]

Aside from the proscribed grounds, which have already been mentioned,[51] the noteworthy aspects of the prohibition of persecution[52] are the definition of the concept and the concluding words of the subparagraph. "Persecution" is defined as "the intentional and severe deprivation of fundamental rights contrary to international law by reason of the identity of the group or collectivity". Persecution played a fairly significant part in the prosecution's efforts at Nuremberg, but the Tribunal did not devote much effort to illuminating its scope. The Rome Statute is generally consistent with the somewhat sketchy discussion of the concept by the Nuremberg Tribunal which seems to have included (as actions that the Statute would now consider as "severe deprivation of fundamental rights") killing political opponents and Jews and placing them in concentration camps. It also appears to have included the passage of German laws aimed at excluding Jews from economic life and from the protection of the law.[53] One suspects, however, that most of the significant cases of persecution under the Rome Statute can also be packaged under one or more of the other sub-paragraphs of Article 7(1).[54] Moreover, the independent scope of

[48] *Ibid.*

[49] See Simpson, *op.cit.* note 26, 19:

"Forced pregnancy"... could also be interpreted to mean (and has in recent court cases been interpreted to mean) that all laws preventing a woman from getting an abortion were crimes, too, for such laws "force" a woman to stay pregnant until normal birth.

[50] Rome Statute, Article 7(2)(f).

[51] *Op.cit.* at note 18.

[52] Rome Statute, Article 7(1)(h) (basic proscription), and 7(2)(g) (definition of "persecution").

[53] See generally, Clark, *op.cit.* note 2, 195-197.

[54] Thus, to consider the possibilities just mentioned in the text on the basis of the Nuremberg Judgment: killing opponents would be "murder" (para. 1 (a)); concentration camps would involve "imprisonment ... in violation of fundamental rules of international law" (para. 1 (e); excluding people from economic life and the protection of the law would be "[an]other

the persecution provision is limited by the closing words of subparagraph 1(h) which require that the persecution must be "in connection with any act referred to in this paragraph or any crime within the jurisdiction of the Court". This is a completely unnecessary limitation, insisted upon by those who had already adequately narrowed the scope of the whole Article with its chapeau. It is, of course, left over from the Nuremberg jurisdictional requirement that crimes against humanity had to be "in execution of or in connection with" other crimes within the jurisdiction of the tribunal.[55] Fears that somehow "ordinary" persecutions would become criminal were quite groundless in light of the chapeau's requirement for proving an "attack". My reading of the drafting history is that the attack requirement was designed as a general threshold that would represent an alternative to that in the Nuremberg Charter. Those who insisted in reinserting something like the Nuremberg language specifically in the persecution provision were confused and thought a further limitation necessary.[56]

"Enforced disappearance of persons" is defined to mean "the arrest, detention or abduction of persons by, or with the authorization, support or acquiescence of, a State or a political organization, followed by a refusal to acknowledge that deprivation of freedom or to give information on the fate or whereabouts of those persons, with the intention of removing them from the protection of the law for a prolonged period of time".[57] While the naming of this concept and the exposition of its elements dates from the 1980s[58] there are earlier examples that might just as easily have been given

---

severe deprivation of liberty in violation of fundamental rules of international law". (Also para. 1(e)).

[55] *Op.cit.* note 2. As a practical matter, the Nuremberg Tribunal focused on the need to show a connection to a crime against peace. See Clark, *op.cit.* note 2, 195 n.71.

[56] Robinson, *op.cit.* note 1, 55, makes a valiant attempt to salvage something of the persecution crime:

> It is not necessary to demonstrate that the "connected" inhumane acts were committed on a widespread or systematic basis; it will suffice to show a connection between the persecution and any instance of murder, torture, rape or other inhuman act, which need not amount to a crime against humanity in its own right. ... In practical terms, the requirement should not prove unduly restrictive, as a quick review of historical acts of persecution shows that persecution is inevitably accompanied by such inhumane acts.

[57] Rome Statute, Article 7(2)(i). The language is based on preambular para. 3 of the 1992 UN Declaration on the Protection of All Persons from Enforced Disappearance, G.A. Res. 47/133, UN GAOR, 47th Sess., Supp. No. 49, at 207, UN Doc. A/47/49/vol. I (1992). The reference to a "political organization" does not appear in the 1992 Declaration. See also the Inter-American Convention on the Forced Disappearance of Persons, 33 *I.L.M.* 1994, 1529.

[58] Maureen R. Berman and Roger S. Clark, "State Terrorism: Disapearances", 13 *Rutgers L.J. 1982*, 531.

the name, such as Stalin's gulag or action taken pursuant to Hitler's "Night and Fog" Decree.[59]

"The crime of apartheid" is defined as "inhumane acts of a character similar to those referred to in paragraph 1, committed in the context of an institutionalized regime of systematic oppression and domination by one racial group over any other racial group or groups and committed with the intention of maintaining that regime".[60] A few years ago, I echoed the comment of the International Law Commission that the practice is now so deeply condemned by the world's conscience that it is inconceivable that a modern code of crimes against the peace and security of mankind would omit a specific reference to apartheid.[61] Yet the Law Commission's final version of its Code in 1996 did just that, at least in as many words.[62] So too did the draft Statute for the International Criminal Court until an advanced stage of the Rome Conference.[63] It was left to the South African delegation to insist on its inclusion. (It is, however, defined with sufficient generality that it would not only catch exactly what happened in South Africa.) Personally, I took great joy in watching representatives of the West European and Other Group that had washed its hands of the Apartheid Convention when it was being drafted in 1973,[64] sagely agreeing that the Statute would be sadly incomplete unless something suitable including the word apartheid were added. My hunch,

---

[59] Robinson, *op.cit.* note 1, 58 n.76, reads the Nuremberg Tribunal's discussion of the Night and Fog Decree as characterizing the disappearances taking place under it as included in the Nuremberg Charter's "other inhumane acts" as a category of crimes against humanity. In fact, the discussion to which he refers the reader is addressed primarily to war crimes in the occupied territories, coming within the Charter Article 6(b). Nevertheless, given the Nuremberg Tribunal's frequent intertwining of war crimes and crimes against humanity, the example could be apt for crimes against humanity. (To the extent that it differentiated the categories, the Nuremberg Tribunal generally spoke of war crimes in occupied territories and crimes against humanity in Germany itself, often including Austria and sometimes Czechoslovakia in the latter category.)

[60] Rome Statute, Article 7(2)(h).

[61] Roger S. Clark, "Apartheid", in I *International Criminal Law* (M. Cherif Bassiouni ed., 2d ed.), Ardsley, NY 1999, 643, 662 (written early in 1996 before the ILC completed its final draft and referring to the 1991 draft and explanation in [1991] *Y.B. Int'l L. Comm'n*, Vol. II, Pt. Two, at 102).

[62] *Op.cit.* note 20. Article 18(f) of the 1996 Draft Code did, however, include a category of "institutionalized discrimination" which the Commentary, *ibid.* 99, describes as "the crime of apartheid under a more general denomination".

[63] The closest hint that it might be included was in footnote 17 of the Draft Statute forwarded by the Preparatory Committee to Rome. Referring to the draft language on "other inhumane acts", it noted that "It was also suggested that the list of acts should include institutionalized discrimination". See Report of the Preparatory Committee on the Establishment of an International Criminal Court, in Bassiouni, *op.cit.* note 1, 128.

[64] Clark, "Apartheid", *op.cit.* note 61, 661.

however, is that the addition is more symbolic than anything else and that the proscribed actions are already caught elsewhere in paragraph 1.[65] It is an example (not inappropriate) of the use of the law as affirmation, exclamation or denunciation rather than a string in the prosecutorial bow that is likely to see a lot of action.

Finally, there are "other inhumane acts of a similar character intentionally causing great suffering, or serious injury to body or to mental or physical health". A distinguished participant/commentator, after noting the imprecision of "other inhumane acts", adds that:

> The solution was to agree to include this final heading, but to include a clarifying threshold, specifying that the acts must be of a character similar to that of the other enumerated acts and must intentionally cause great suffering or serious injury to mental or physical health.[66]

He suggests unlawful human experimentation and particularly violent assaults as two possible candidates.[67]

An "Attack"

The requirement that there be an "attack" on a civilian population was plainly intended as a jurisdictional threshold for the ICC. Not every murder, rape, etc., especially if random, is a matter of international concern or, of more immediate significance, is appropriate to be within the jurisdiction of the Court. This matter has its origin in the limitations on the kinds of offences that could be prosecuted at Nuremberg under the rubric of crimes against humanity.[68] There, it will be recalled, the drafters were nervous about the whole concept, and ultimately decreed that the offences of crimes against humanity had to be "in execution of or in connection with any crime within the jurisdiction of the tribunal".[69] I have argued elsewhere that this was a jurisdictional limitation on the Tribunal rather than a substantive limitation inherent in the concept of a crime against humanity.[70]

---

[65] The language of the Apartheid Convention was derived substantially from that of the Genocide Convention and many of the "acts" of apartheid would also be caught by Article 6 of the Rome Statute.

[66] Robinson, *op.cit.* note 1, 6.

[67] *Id.* See also the residual provision on "other inhumane acts" in the 1996 version of the Draft Code of Offences, Article 18(k), *op.cit.* note 20, which lists "mutilation and severe bodily harm" as specific examples.

[68] It is also a close relative of the limitation in the human rights area that the human rights organs such as the Commission on Human Rights may not be able to act in individual cases but have more room where the violations are "gross". See generally, Howard Tolley, Jr., *The U.N. Commission on Human Rights*, Boulder, Colo. 1987, 55-82.

[69] Nuremberg Charter, Article 6(c), *op.cit.* note 2.

[70] Clark, *op.cit.* note 2, 194-96.

Nevertheless, the appropriate threshold has been a matter of considerable confusion ever since. It is far from clear how the notion of an "attack" came to pass as an element of the crimes against humanity offences. The word was not found in the Nuremberg Charter, although the requirement in the Nuremberg definition that the "inhumane acts" be "committed against any civilian population" carried with it a notion of scale (and even organization) inconsistent with random acts. Scale and organization are notions that are firmly located in the final "attack" definition in the Rome Statute. The Nuremberg Tribunal said at one point that "The policy of terror was certainly carried out on a vast scale, and in many cases was organized and systematic".[71] Nevertheless, the word attack still did not appear in the text of the 1991 version of the International Law Commission's Draft Code of Crimes Against the Peace and Security of Mankind.[72] Nor did it appear explicitly in the Statute of the Tribunal for Former Yugoslavia. The threshold there was that the "crimes" had to be "committed in armed conflict, whether international or internal in character, and directed against any civilian population".[73] It was, however, mentioned in the debate in the Security Council when that Statute was adopted. For example, Mrs. Madeleine Albright, the Permanent Representative of the United States to the United Nations said:

> ...it is understood that Article 5 applies to all acts listed in that Article, when committed contrary to law during a period of armed conflict in the territory of former Yugoslavia, as part of a widespread or systematic attack against any civilian population on national, political, ethnic, racial, gender or religious grounds.[74]

---

[71] *Op.cit.* note 39, 249. While the Tribunal was speaking specifically of pre-1939 events, it is clear in context that it saw subsequent events in the same light.

[72] That draft even dispensed with the title "crime against humanity". Article 21 of the draft, which defined the functional equivalent of crimes against humanity under the rubric "Systematic or mass violations of human rights", contained the element that these offences had to be done "in a systematic manner or on a mass scale". [1991] *Y.B. Int'l L. Comm'n*, Vol. II, Pt. Two, at 103. The link to the Nuremberg Tribunal's language is apparent, as are the seeds of the term "attack" which had, however, yet to be born.

[73] Statute of Tribunal for Former Yugoslavia, *op.cit.* note 9, Article 5. Commenting on this threshold, the Appeals Chamber of the Tribunal for Former Yugoslavia said:

It is by now a settled rule of customary international law that crimes against humanity do not require a connection to international armed conflict. Indeed, as the Prosecutor points out, customary international law may not require a connection between crimes against humanity and any conflict at all. Thus, by requiring that crimes against humanity be committed in either internal or international armed conflict, the Security Council may have defined the crime in Article 5 more narrowly than necessary under customary international law....

Decision on Defence Motion for Interlocutory Appeal on Jurisdiction, Tadic Case, (IT-94-1-T), 2 October 1995, para. 141.

[74] UN Doc. S/PV.3217, at 15 (25 May 1993). See also Report of the Secretary-General on the Statute, UN Doc. S/25704, para. 48 (making essentially same point but without reference

On the other hand, the Statute for Rwanda provides explicitly that the crimes must be "committed as part of a widespread or systematic attack against any civilian population on national, political, ethnic, racial or religious grounds".[75] Finally, notwithstanding these developments with the ad hoc Tribunals, the International Law Commission's 1996 version of its Draft Code of Crimes against the Peace and Security of Mankind cheerfully avoids both the word "attack" and the words "civilian population". It simply says that for a crime against humanity, the relevant acts must be "committed in a systematic manner or on a large scale and instigated or directed by a Government or by any organization or group".[76]

In short, the history is singularly unedifying. Some of the players do not seem to have had the faintest idea what they were doing.[77] The negotiations in Rome were tortured.[78] Two things are now clear: the requirement of an attack, however defined and however qualified, has been slowly working its way into the fabric of the concept of crimes against humanity. It is now firmly established in the Rome Statute. On the other hand, the reference to discriminatory grounds in the Albright statement and the Rwanda Statute, have not found their way into the Rome Statute beyond the persecution type of offences.

---

to "gender"). The Albright statement (and similar statements) and the Secretary-General's Report led to the inclusion in the jurisprudence of the Tribunal for Former Yugoslavia of requirements of both an attack and discriminatory object, in spite of neither of those elements appearing in the plain language of the Statute. See generally, John R.W.D. Jones, *The Practice of the International Criminal Tribunals for the Former Yugoslavia and Rwanda*, Irvington-on-Hudson, NY 1998, 49-55. Given that Article 5 of the Yugoslavia Statute spoke of "persecutions on political, racial and religious grounds" quite distinctly from the other "crimes", it required playing fast and loose with the language and excessive reliance on the preparatory work to require a discriminatory object for *all* of the crimes. The "attack" and "grounds" elements found their way specifically into the Rwanda Statute, *infra* note 75.

[75] The Rwanda Statute has no reference at all to armed conflict. (Any "conflict" there was presumably "non-international".) On the other hand, it provides explicitly that for all the offences there must be a discriminatory intent. This was not carried forward into the Rome Statute, except for the persecution type crimes.

[76] *Op.cit.* note 20. The Commission's explanation, at 94-96, suggests that it tried to capture the spirit of the Nuremberg Charter and Judgment, though not its exact language. It also, at 96, refers with approval to the statement in the Tadic appeal, *op.cit.* note 73, that crimes against humanity do not require a connection to international armed conflict.

[77] This sorry tale reminds me of the admonitions of Richard Baxter, "The Effects of Ill-Conceived Codification and Development of International Law", in *Recueil d'Etudes de Droit International en Hommage à Paul Guggenheim* 1968, 146. It is always possible that some of the players set out intentionally and knowingly to muddy the waters!

[78] As witness the very fair discussion in Robinson, *op.cit.* note 1.

It might perhaps be noted, moreover, that the word "armed" (as in "armed attack")[79] does not appear in the definition. Typically there will be violence by force of arms but this need not be proven as an element. A great deal of attention was given at the Preparatory Committee and in Rome to whether the attack had to be both widespread *and* systematic or whether either one would suffice. "Widespread" has objective connotations of size, a kind of volume threshold rather than a statement about the subjective purposes of those in charge. The ordinary meaning of "systematic", on the other hand, seems more subjective and has connotations of a deliberate plan (a "policy"?). There was a widespread jubilation among the NGOs and the Like-Minded States in Rome on the basis that the disjunctive "or" in the final text represented a great victory. It would be easier for a prosecutor to prove than if both prongs were required. I am not altogether sure that this euphoria was warranted. The victory for the disjunctive is tempered by the definition of "attack" in paragraph 2(a):

"Attack directed against any civilian population" means a course of conduct involving the multiple commission of acts referred to in paragraph 1 against any civilian population, pursuant to or in furtherance of a State or organizational policy to commit such attack.

"Multiple" must catch most cases of "widespread" unless one can imagine numerous incidents which are nevertheless not widespread - a difficult intellectual feat to my mind unless "widespread" means, perversely, "over a wide geographical area" rather than "large-scale". "Organizational policy" is pretty close to "systematic" as far as I can tell. In short, if an incident meets the definition of paragraph 2(a), that is, it is widespread and has a policy behind it, the "additional" elements of widespread *and* systematic seem *both* to have been met anyway! Put it the other way around, if you like: something close to both widespread *and* systematic appears to be required by the very definition of "attack".

3) Some General Observations and Herein the Hierarchy of Evil

At one stage of the Rome Statute's gestation, I had this fantasy that we might create neat definitions that did not overlap with each other. This was, of course, never realistic. The pressure to keep established concepts intact and in their "well-established" language[80] proved overwhelming. Genocide and crimes against humanity always overlapped, in that genocide was born

---

[79] For this reason, learning on the self defence provision of the UN Charter, Article 51, which uses the term "armed attack", does not appear useful.

[80] The experience of drafting the "Elements" has shown that some of the "well-established" language is in fact quite opaque.

of the persecution part of the already heinous category of crimes against humanity and was established as the most heinous of the heinous.[81] Crimes against humanity, like genocide,[82] do not require an armed conflict threshold, although we do have something of the functional equivalent in the case of crimes against humanity with the attack requirement. (As a practical matter, it is hard to imagine a genocide without an "attack" as defined for crimes against humanity, but that is not something that must be proved as an element of the offence.) In the meantime, via common Article 3 of the 1949 Geneva Conventions and the Second Protocol of 1977 to those Conventions, "war crimes" have increasingly thrust themselves into domestic, non-international conflict. With genocide being possible in time of war or peace, crimes against humanity having no required link to armed conflict and war crimes expanding their reach into non-international armed conflict, all three offences appear to have been expanding since the 1940s. Some of this expansion has been onto one another's turf. A prosecutor deciding what to prosecute in a modern setting will have ample overlapping possibilities from each of the three categories in the Statute.[83]

There is, however, an emerging "hierarchy" among them. The Erdemovic appeal and the subsequent re-sentencing[84] by the Tribunal for Former Yugoslavia underscore that, for the purposes of prosecutorial discretion, especially relating to elements that must be proved and to penalty (and possibly some rough and ready plea bargaining over guilty pleas) we now have a scale.

---

[81] As I read the Statute, virtually any genocide could also be prosecuted as a crime against humanity, but with a less demanding *mens rea* requirement. The converse is not true; crimes against humanity have a wider net than genocide.

[82] The Genocide Convention, *op.cit.* note 4, Article I, makes explicit that genocide is a crime under international law "whether committed in time of peace or in time of war". The Rome Statute is quite silent on this, but the intent is obviously the same as that in the Genocide Convention. To the extent that the Nuremberg Statute created a threshold requirement of a connection between a crime against humanity and another crime within the jurisdiction of the Tribunal, this threshold essentially disappeared in the Genocide Convention, unless one takes the view that the special intent to destroy a group in whole or in part serves a similar kind of limiting role. The special intent in the genocide definition in fact looks more like a substantive element than the jurisdictional element of the connection required at Nuremberg.

[83] At the July-August 1999 meeting of the Preparatory Commission, Portugal announced that it was drafting language designed to ensure that if the same conduct could be brought within more than one definition of the categories of offences, only one penalty could be imposed. (Author's notes.)

[84] International Criminal Tribunal for the Former Yugoslavia, *Prosecutor v. Erdemovic*: Sentencing Judgment, 5 March 1998, 37 *I.L.M.* 1998, 1182. The Separate Opinion by Judge Shahabuddeen at 1199-1200 is especially helpful. See also International Criminal Tribunal for Rwanda, The *Prosecutor v. Kambanda*, Judgment and Sentence, 4 September 1998, 37 *I.L.M.* 1998, 1413.

Genocide is the worst, crimes against humanity are next and "ordinary" war crimes are the lowest on the scale.[85] This is not to justify or excuse them; it is a question of the tariff for engaging in them!

[85] It should be added that the Nuremberg Tribunal, *op.cit.* note 39, asserted that "to initiate a war of aggression ... is not only an international crime; it is the supreme international crime differing only from other war crimes in that it contains within itself the accumulated evil of the whole". (In spite of this strong rhetoric, no one was sentenced to death by the Tribunal on the basis of a crime against peace standing alone.) When the States Parties to the Rome Statute define aggression and bring the jurisdiction of the Statute over that offence into play, the Court may have to reassess the location of aggression in the hierarchy of evil.

13. War Crimes in International Armed Conflicts

GABRIELLA VENTURINI*

1) The Jurisdiction of the International Criminal Court in Respect of War Crimes

The International Criminal Court will have jurisdiction in respect of war crimes "in particular when committed as a part of a plan or as part of a large-scale commission of such crimes" (Article 8.1). This provision is a compromise between the high threshold position ("only when committed") that had been supported by some states, and the position of the "like-minded" countries, which maintained that the Court should have jurisdiction over any individual war crime, irrespective of its scale or planning. The agreed wording does not imply reference to a threshold (as regards crimes against humanity); it merely stresses that if a large-scale commission of war crimes has occurred or a plan to commit such crimes has been executed, the Court is an appropriate tribunal to try the persons responsible for such actions.

It would not have been possible to introduce this wording in the Rome Statute, if there had not also been an agreement to accept the "opt-out" clause contained in Article 124. Following this provision, States that become party to the Statute may declare that they will not accept the jurisdiction of the Court with regard to war crimes (alleged to have been committed by their nationals or on their territories) for a period of seven years after the entry into force of the Statute. Article 124 shall be reviewed at the first Review Conference (Article 123.1), which might possibly extend its duration.

The "opt-out" clause is apparently one of the gravest restraints on the Court's jurisdiction. However, the reasons that have led to its acceptance must be considered. It would have been very difficult for most

* Professor of International Law, Director of the Department of International Studies, University of Milan.

States to accept that officers and members of their armed forces might be taken away from their own jurisdiction in relation to any individual crime committed in time of war. Without the "opt-out" clause, some States would not have been able to sign the Statute, as they did in Rome. Moreover, had the "opt-out" been excluded, reservations to the Statute would have had to be admitted in some way; and the effects of a multiplicity of reservations would have been more detrimental than the option of delaying the jurisdiction of the Court for a limited period of time. Even the consequences of the "opt-out" provision should not be over-estimated. For some of the war crimes (i.e. those corresponding to the grave breaches of the 1949 Geneva Conventions and the 1977 additional Protocol I) the so-called "universal criminal jurisdiction" of the contracting parties exists,[1] hence, States do have the concrete opportunity to directly prosecute war criminals. In any case, it will be possible to fully evaluate the effects of the "opt-out" clause only after the entry into force of the Rome Statute, depending on the number of States that will avail themselves of the provision.

2) War Crimes Committed in International Armed Conflicts

War crimes committed in international armed conflicts are listed in Article 8.2 of the Rome Statute. They are grouped into two categories: (a), the grave breaches of the 1949 Geneva Conventions; and (b), other serious violations of the laws and customs applicable in international armed conflicts.

(a) Since the 1949 Geneva Conventions are commonly considered as corresponding to customary international law, there was little doubt that the grave breaches of these Conventions would appear in the first category of war crimes envisaged by Article 8.2(a). The statute of the International Criminal Tribunal for the former Yugoslavia also distinguishes between "grave breaches" (which are covered by Article 2 of the ICTY Statute) and "violations of the laws and customs of war" under customary international law (which are listed under Article 3). The crimes listed under Article 8.2(a) of the Rome Statute exactly correspond to the pertaining provisions

[1] Each State Party to the Conventions (and to the Protocol) is under the obligation to search for persons alleged to have committed a grave breach, and to bring them before its tribunals regardless of their nationality, or extradite them to another State Party (Geneva Convention I, Article 49; Geneva Convention II, Article 50; Geneva Convention III, Article 129; Geneva Convention IV, Article 146).

of the Geneva Conventions[2] and they are subject to the same limitation, i.e. they shall be qualified as crimes only when committed in an international armed conflict, against persons (or property) protected under the relevant Geneva Convention. Rape, sexual slavery, enforced prostitution, forced pregnancy[3] and enforced sterilization occurring during international armed conflict shall also be qualified as war crimes, provided that they constitute a grave breach according to the Geneva Conventions, as well. This means that they must be committed against protected persons (belonging to the enemy State) and be equivalent to inhuman treatment or unlawful confinement, or cause great suffering or serious injury to body or health.

(b) The second category of war crimes, listed at Article 8.2(b), consists of serious violations of the laws and customs applicable in international armed conflicts, "within the established framework of international law". This wording refers to both the customary law of international armed conflicts (as codified by the 1907 Hague Regulations) and international agreements having a wide participation, such as the 1977 Protocol I additional to the 1949 Geneva Conventions and other treaties applicable in international armed conflicts.

Destroying or seizing the enemy's property (unless imperatively demanded by the necessities of war), compelling the nationals of the hostile party to take part in the operations of war directed against their own country and committing outrages upon personal dignity are war crimes generally recognized as such by customary international law (as codified by the 1907 Hague Regulations and the 1977 Protocol I). Their mention in Article 8.2 (b)(xiii), (xv) and (xxi), however, duplicates in substance the war crimes/grave breaches listed under Article 8.2(a)(ii), (iv) and (v). Since the very specific consequence of the grave breaches of the Geneva Conventions (*i.e.* the universal criminal jurisdiction) is not relevant for the International Criminal Court, a merger between analogous crimes would possibly have simplified the enumeration in Article 8.2. On the other hand, the agreed version has the virtue of throwing light on the legal derivation of each crime, while listing them within a unitary approach, a feature which constitutes one of the Statute's greatest achievements.

Other war crimes generally recognized as such by existing customary law are those envisaged by Article 8.2(b)(xvi), (xii), (xvii), (xviii), (xix): pillage, declaring that no quarter will be given, employing poisoned weapons and asphyxiating gases, employing expanding bullets. Relevant prohibitions are provided for in international instruments that are

---

[2] See Geneva Convention I, Article 50; Geneva Convention II, Article 51; Geneva Convention III, Article 130; Geneva Convention IV, Article 147.

[3] These acts are defined as provided for in Article 7.2.(f) of the Statute concerning crimes against humanity.

considered as corresponding to customary international law, like the 1868 St. Petersburg's Declaration, the 1925 Geneva Protocol and (again) the 1907 Hague Regulations. These also prohibit killing a combatant who has surrendered, as well as killing or treacherously wounding enemy individuals (H.R., Art. 23.b and 23.c). It may be observed that the war crimes listed at Article 8.2(b)(vi) and (xi) employ the Hague Regulations' wording, instead of referring to the more recent concept of *enemy hors de combat*, which was adopted in Article 85.3(e) of the 1977 Protocol I.[4] Collective punishments, on the other hand, while prohibited by Article 50 of the Hague Regulations (as well as by the Geneva Convention and by the criminal law of many states[5]) are surprisingly not covered by Article 8.2 of the Rome Statute.

A further group of war crimes, listed at Article 8.2(b), correspond to the grave breaches of the 1977 Protocol I. In three cases, the relevant provisions are identical in substance: the transfer by the occupying power of parts of its civilian population into the territory it occupies (or the deportation of the population from the occupied territory); unjustified physical mutilations or medical or scientific experiments against persons who are in the power of an adverse party; and the abolition or suspension of the legal rights and actions of the nationals of the hostile party. These are considered as crimes of war under Article 8.2(b)(viii), (x), (xiv) and as grave breaches of Protocol I under the applicable rules of that treaty.[6]

Within this group of war crimes, however, there are a number of acts defined as war crimes which do not correspond completely to the grave breaches named in Protocol I. For example, Article 8.2(b)(xxiv) mentions attacks against objects and persons which are protected under a number of provisions in Protocol I, but does not cite some of the categories expressly referred to by Article 85.2 of that treaty.[7] There is also a substantial difference between the "improper use" of the protected emblems mentioned at Article 8.2(b) (vii), and the "perfidious use" qualified as a grave breach in Article 85.3(f) of Protocol I. The broader language of the Statute is to a certain extent balanced by the specification that death or serious personal

---

[4] Article 41.2 of Protocol I explains that a person is *hors de combat* if he is in the power of an adverse party, if he clearly expresses an intention to surrender or if he is incapable of defending himself because of unconsciousness, sickness or wounds.

[5] The Italian *Legge di guerra* (War Act) of 8 July 1938 prohibits collective punishments at Article 65, although allowing an exception "in the case that liability may be deemed joint and several".

[6] See Articles 85.4(a), 85.4(e) and 11 of Protocol I.

[7] Article 85.2. of Protocol I determines new categories of victims of grave breaches, including persons who were not protected by the 1949 Conventions (see Bothe-Partsch-Solf, *New Rules for victims of Armed Conflicts*, 1982, at p. 513, and the ICRC *Commentary* to Article 85 of Protocol I, para. 3468-3470).

injury result from the improper use of protected emblems. The same requirement, in Protocol I, applies to grave breaches consisting in intentional attacks against the civilian population and against non-defended localities, or in attacks that will cause excessive losses to civilians and excessive damage to civilian objects, or excessive (long-term and severe) damage to the natural environment.[8] Yet, the corresponding provisions of the Rome Statute, Article 8.2(b)(i), (v), (iv), do not require the occurrence of that material consequence. Hence, the Court will have jurisdiction not only in respect of such acts having caused death or serious personal injury, but with regard to their commission, irrespective of the real outcome of the action. Considering that individual criminal responsibility lies on those who have committed, ordered, abetted, contributed or attempted to commit a war crime within the jurisdiction of the Court and on their military commanders and other superiors,[9] the members of a State's armed forces will be rather heavily burdened with these provisions. Once again, this explains the reasons for the "opt-out" clause, as well as the US proposal in regard to the "Elements of Crimes" (which will be dealt with subsequently).

Intentionally directing attacks against buildings dedicated to religion, education, art, science or charitable purposes, historic monuments, hospitals and places where the sick and wounded are collected (Article 8.2.b.ix) also corresponds to a grave breach of Protocol I (Article 85.4.d). But the reference to the objects which are "the cultural or spiritual heritage of peoples and that enjoy a special protection under international agreements", which is contained in the provision of Protocol I, does not appear in the Statute. During the Diplomatic Conference, a reasonable proposal to include attacks against cultural property in the list of war crimes was made by Spain.[10] Most regretfully, this item was not a priority for the "like-minded" countries and could neither be approved nor extensively discussed.

Article 8.2(b)(ii), (xxiii), (xxv), (xxvi), further enumerate in the list of war crimes certain acts that correspond to violations of Protocol I, while not being qualified as grave breaches by that treaty. These are intentionally directing attacks against civilian objects, utilizing civilians or protected persons as human shields and intentionally using starvation of civilians as a method of warfare. Conscripting or enlisting children under 15 years into the national armed forces or using them to participate actively in hostilities may certainly be considered in connection with Article 77.2 of Protocol I

---

[8] Article 85.3 (chapeau) Protocol I. See, also, Articles 55, 85.3(b) and (c). Article 85.3(d) mentions demilitarized zones as well as undefended localities.

[9] Articles 25.3(a), (b), (c), (d), (f) and Article 28 ICC Statute.

[10] A/CONF.183/C.1/L.4, 17 June 1998.

and with Article 38.2 and 38.3 of the 1989 Convention on the Rights of the Child; yet the obligations provided for in these treaties are considerably less stringent, if compared to the qualification of these practices as war crimes in the Statute.[11] Such clear wording was certainly inspired by the latest developments in the international law of human rights.

Intentionally directing attacks against humanitarian or peace-keeping forces was both included as a "treaty crime" in the Draft Statute elaborated by the International Law Commission as well as in the April PrepCom's Draft. This is the sole example of a "treaty crime" having been shifted into the list under Article 8.2(b)(iii). Here, also, the developments of international law (in this case, the completion of the 1994 Convention on the protection of the UN and associated personnel) have strongly influenced the contents of the Statute.

Employing means and methods of warfare which are of a nature to cause superfluous injury or unnecessary suffering shall constitute a war crime under Article 8.2(b)(xx), provided that "they are the subject of a comprehensive prohibition and are included in a prospective annex to the Statute" (to be agreed following the amendment procedure set forth in Articles 121 and 123). This compromise, reached at the Plenipotentiary Conference, resembles the conclusion agreed to in respect of the crime of aggression and may be endorsed. Moreover, it is consistent with the principle *nullum crimen sine lege*. Although it may be argued that means and methods of warfare that are of a nature to cause superfluous injury or unnecessary suffering are already the object of a comprehensive prohibition under Article 35.2 of the 1977 Protocol I, it was impossible to establish an agreed list of prohibited weapons, and it is even more difficult to imagine an annex which could describe in detail the criminal methods of warfare.

Among the violations of the Geneva Conventions and of Protocol I, reprisals against protected persons are not qualified as grave breaches. Nor do they appear in the long list under Article 8.2(b). This means that the very decision, or the plan, to resort to prohibited reprisals (i.e, prohibited reprisals as a means of warfare) are not themselves qualified as war crimes. Consequently, this qualification will characterize only the material conduct (e.g. the wilful killing of prisoners of war, the inhuman treatment of civilians) which carries out a reprisal. On the other hand, the question of whether reprisals may be considered as admissible grounds for excluding criminal responsibility under the Statute, will be dealt with in the application and interpretation of Article 31.1.

[11] These rules only prohibit to recruit into the armed forces of a State children who have not reached the age of 15. Protocol I adds that States Parties "shall take all feasible measures" in order that such children do not take a direct part in hostilities (this could occur, for example, in the case of the so-called "lévée en masse": see Geneva Convention III, Article 4. A. 6.).

3) The Role of the "Elements of Crimes"

Article 9 of the Rome Statute lays down that the Elements of Crimes shall "assist the Court" in applying and interpreting Articles 6, 7 and 8.

In order to give clearer guidance to the Court a stronger guidance (as well as to limit its discretionary powers) the United States first took the initiative to include further definitions of the crimes referred to in the Statute. Informal documents by the US government were circulated during the PrepCom sessions among a number of delegations. Initially, the reactions to the US suggestions were rather cautious. Some observations, however, were conveyed to the US delegation, which formally introduced a proposal concerning the "Elements of Crimes" during the Diplomatic Conference.[12] The US insisted that these "Elements" should be included in the Statute, or, at least, that the Statute itself should not enter into force before agreement on them was reached. Although the proposal certainly had the virtue of throwing light on the nature and character of the individual acts constituting war crimes, its language (and its legal philosophy as well) strictly reflected the standards of English and American criminal law. In European countries, criminal law, and especially criminal procedure, are based on different criteria; continental judges would probably not feel at ease with very detailed definitions and would not recognize the need for such rigid guidance.

At the Plenipotentiary Conference, however, the "like-minded" countries showed a favourable attitude towards the US proposal, though refusing to subordinate the entire Statute to an agreement on the "Elements". Obviously, there was not enough time to negotiate a satisfactory text in Rome. Consequently, the "Elements of Crimes" will be adopted by the Assembly of States Parties (hence, after the entry into force of the Statute) and will be consistent with the Statute (i.e., subordinate to it). In any case, the "Elements" will be essential for the Court to operate, as much as the Rules of Procedures. Their drafting is now in the hands of the Preparatory Commission.

At the first meeting of the Preparatory Commission (New York, 16-26 February 1999), the United States brought out revised proposals on the elements of crimes against humanity and on war crimes.[13] Quite clearly, the US made an effort to simplify the structure of the "Elements", adapting them in order to accommodate some of the requirements of other countries.

---

[12] *Annex on definitional Elements for Part Two Crimes* (A/CONF.183/C.1/L.10, 19 June 1998).

[13] *Draft Elements of Crimes*, Proposal submitted by the United States of America (PCNICC/1999/DP.4/Add.1 of 4 February 1999).

The discussion, however, was not easy[14] and resulted only in a limited clarification of a small number of crimes. At the end of the session, the Coordinator of the Working Group on Elements of Crimes put forward a discussion paper[15] containing the elements the war crimes listed under Article 8.2(a)(i), (ii) and (iii), which possibly constitutes a suitable basis for future consensus. This text does not substantially extend the elements already stated in the ICC Statute; and, if the elements of the remaining crimes were to be drafted in a similar fashion, the results might well be widely shared by the members of the Preparatory Commission. Unfortunately, the crimes listed under Article 8.2(b) are much more numerous and contentious than those considered up to the present; therefore, it is very difficult to predict how long the process of completing the "Elements of Crimes" will last.

At the Rome Plenipotentiary Conference, the International Committee of the Red Cross pointed out that there are plenty of cases in international judicial practice where the elements of genocide, crimes against humanity, and war crimes have been considered, and it invited the Preparatory Commission to consider these precedents in drafting the "Elements" for the Court. Subsequently, at the February session, a group of countries submitted a paper prepared by the ICRC relating to the crimes listed in Article 8.2(a) of the Statute, i.e. "grave breaches of the 1949 Geneva Conventions".[16] Unlike the US proposal, the ICRC paper does not provide more detailed definitions of these crimes; instead, it offers a comprehensive survey of and commentaries on the treaty sources as well as an overview of the national and international case law available with regard to each crime, taking into particular account the practice of international human rights bodies.[17] While not necessarily being a substitute, this approach may well serve as a complement to the process of definition.

[14] Proposals on the "Elements of crimes" were also put forward by Colombia, Japan, Hungary and Switzerland.

[15] PCNICC/1999/WGEC/RT.2 of 25 February 1999.

[16] *Request from the Governments of Belgium, Costa Rica, Finland, Hungary, South Africa and Switzerland regarding the text prepared by the International Committee of the Red Cross on Article 8, paragraph 2 (a) of the Rome Statute of the International Criminal Court* (PCNICC/1999/WGEC/INF.1 of 19 February 1999).

[17] The survey includes: international humanitarian law instruments; the Leipzig Trials, the Nuremberg and Tokyo Trials and decisions by the International Criminal Tribunal for the former Yugoslavia and the International Criminal Tribunal for Rwanda; national case law (especially concerning the United States, the United Kingdom, France and Germany); and decisions by international and regional human rights bodies, all of which provide abundant discussions on certain offences such as "torture" or "inhuman treatment". The ICRC paper also discusses extensively the definition of "international armed conflict" as well as the characteristics of potential perpetrators of war crimes (members of the armed forces, members of Government, civilians etc.).

Indeed, the ICRC document, which is to be supplemented by further research on the other war crimes listed in Article 8.2(b), constitutes a most worthy study and it will be helpful for the Court itself, when it comes into operation.

4) The Mental Element and the Grounds for Excluding Responsibility

Given the extent of the material competence of the International Criminal Court, and considering the lessons from the judicial practice related to war crimes in international armed conflicts, it is likely that in many cases, the persons convened before the Court will allege ignorance, unintentional behaviour, or the existence of a circumstance precluding wrongfulness, in order to be relieved of individual criminal responsibility. Following Article 30 of the Rome Statute, "a person shall be criminally responsible and liable for punishment for a crime within the jurisdiction of the Court only if the material elements are committed with intent and knowledge". The Article specifies that "a person has intent where (a) in relation to conduct, that person means to engage in the conduct; (b) in relation to a consequence, that person means to cause that consequence or is aware that it will occur in the ordinary course of events", and that the term "knowledge" means "awareness that a circumstance exists or a consequence will occur in the ordinary course of events". The ICRC research on grave breaches of the Geneva Conventions, quoted above, suggests that the notion "wilful" should be understood as including "intent" and "recklessness", but as excluding ordinary negligence.[18]

The grounds for excluding criminal responsibility are identified by Articles 31 to 33. These mention: (a) the incapacity to appreciate the unlawfulness or nature of his or her conduct, due to a mental disease or defect; (b) the existence of a state of unintentional intoxication that destroys the capacity to appreciate the unlawfulness or nature of that conduct; (c) self-defence; (d) duress; and (e) a mistake of facts or a mistake of law, provided that these mistakes negate the mental element required by the crime. Superior orders do not relieve individual criminal responsibility, except in the case that the person who executed the orders was under a legal obligation to obey, did not know that the orders were unlawful and the orders themselves were not manifestly unlawful.

The wording of the "superior orders" clauses in the Nuremberg Charter and in the statutes of the ad hoc Tribunals, is concise: indeed, these

---

[18] Various cases emerging from post Second World War Trials as well as from decisions delivered by the ad hoc Tribunals support this interpretation: see PCNICC/1999/WGEC/INF.1, p. 14, fn. 41-43.

clauses merely lay down that a superior order shall not relieve an accused person of criminal responsibility, but may be considered as a mitigating factor.[19] Compared to these precedents, Article 33 of the Rome Statute is considerably more detailed and specific, even though it certainly does appear more limited, to the extent that, *a contrario*, it implies that superiors' orders do relieve an accused person of criminal responsibility, provided that the person was under a legal obligation to obey those orders and he or she did not know that they were unlawful and they were not manifestly unlawful (only orders to commit genocide or crimes against humanity are presumed to be manifestly unlawful). Indeed, a proposal by the United States had suggested for Article 33 exactly this kind of (positive) language.[20] The eventual compromise is broadly consistent with the precedents, while taking into account the needs of military discipline and the rights and interests of individual members of the armed forces.

Neither military necessity nor reprisals are included among the grounds for excluding criminal responsibility mentioned explicitly by Article 31 of the Rome Statute. Military necessity, however, may justify the destruction and appropriation of property, which are otherwise considered as war crimes (Article 8.2.a.iv, 8.2.b.xiii). As for reprisals, Article 31.3 lays down that, at trial, the Court may consider other grounds (than those mentioned by Article 31.1) for excluding criminal responsibility where such grounds are "derived from applicable law as set forth in Article 21". Therefore, the Court might have to consider reprisals in applying the "treaties and the principles and rules of international law, including the international law of armed conflict" as well as "general principles of law" derived from the "national laws or legal systems of the world" (as set forth in Article 21.1.b and c). There the question of reprisals should properly be settled. Unquestionably, the prohibitions of reprisals against protected persons, which are embodied in the Geneva Conventions, do correspond to customary international law and to the general principles of law "derived from national laws or legal systems of the world"; therefore, those reprisals might not exclude individual criminal responsibility under the ICC Statute. Permissible reprisals (e.g. the use, by way of reprisal, of prohibited

[19] Nuremberg Charter, Article 8; ICTY Statute, Article 7.4; ICTR Statute, Article 7.4. The 1977 Additional Protocol I does not mention superior orders. See Aubert, *La question de l'ordre supérieur et la responsabilité des commandants dans le Protocole additionnel aux Conventions de Genève du 12 août 1949 relatif à la protection des victimes des conflits armés internationaux (Protocole I) du 8 juin 1977, Revue internationale de la Croix-Rouge*, Mars-Avril 1998, p. 109 ss.; Sacerdoti, *A proposito del caso* Priebke: *la responsabilità per l'esecuzione di ordini illegittimi costituenti crimini di guerra, Rivista di diritto internazionale*, 1997, p. 130 ss.

[20] *Proposal by the United States of America for single provision covering issues currently governed by Articles 31,32,33 and 34*, A/CONF.183/C.1/WGGP/L.2, 16 June 1998.

weapons against military objectives), on the other hand, should be admitted by the Court as grounds for excluding responsibility. Problems might arise with reference to those reprisals, which are prohibited by Protocol I, though debatable under customary international law, e.g. attacks against the natural environment by way of reprisal. Would such an attack be justifiable on the ground of belligerent reprisals, according to the ICC Statute? This is but one of the sensitive questions concerning war crimes in international armed conflicts that will be settled by the Court.

14. War Crimes and Internal Conflicts in the Statute of the International Criminal Court

LUIGI CONDORELLI*

1) Introduction

I am one of the few speakers in this meeting who has not participated in any of the negotiations of the Statute, either at the Rome Conference or in the preparatory Commissions and Committees. As a consequence, I lack the experience, the knowledge and the spirit of those who "were there": the *anciens combattants*, the old campaigners. Through their speeches, they can contribute with their personal memories (including those of their own behaviour) to the drafting of this "*De bello romano*", as the book collecting the acts of the Rome Conference will certainly end up being called.

Nevertheless, the fact that I am not an old campaigner and that my chest is not covered with medals does not only bring the disadvantages I have mentioned. I have actually also some undeniable advantages, especially insofar as I can evaluate in total independence the outcome of the Rome Conference. My evaluation will inevitably be more detached and prospective since it will not be influenced by the positions and interests that everyone had to safeguard in the course of the negotiations. Moreover, it will not be influenced by the results of the fought battles or by the consequences that followed both for those who were victorious and those defeated. But the main advantage is that I am in the most suitable condition to judge the Rome Statute not merely as the result of a specific negotiating process, but rather as a temporary stage or an intermediate conclusion of a long and complex story: the one of the reactions of the International Community to major crimes.

---

* Professor of International Law, University of Geneva.

The task I have been given is to discuss the way in which the international norms contained in the Statute deal with the issue of war crimes in internal conflicts. This subject is somehow peculiar: only a few years ago, even at the beginning of the nineties, it would have been literally inconceivable to take it into consideration. A speaker called to talk about it would have exhausted the subject matter in one unique sentence, that would have reflected the state of international law and the unanimous opinion of legal literature: there are war crimes only in international armed conflicts, never in internal ones. Eventually, he would have taken a few more minutes to explain the unfortunate reasons why international law in force did not include provisions on war crimes in internal conflicts, thus making reference to the sovereign prerogatives of States and their domestic jurisdiction on crimes committed in their territory by their own citizens (or by other persons under their jurisdiction) in the framework of subversive actions against the established order.

In the past five or six years, everything has changed in a radical way. What has happened is a well-known and tragic story. I will limit myself to recall in a telegraphic way its crucial moments. In the context of an international community which has seen its previous order subverted by the collapse of the Eastern Block, international conflicts became rare (as they were not anymore stimulated by the opposing Blocks) and there was a real explosion of internal conflicts due to uncontrolled phenomena of dislocation of States. These latter conflicts resulted in unbelievable atrocities that no one has been able (nor is able) to prevent. Though not blocked anymore, the Security Council of the United Nations is in the impossibility to intervene with the use of force for the purpose of restoring peace within the logic of *jus contra bellum*, since States are not willing (or do not want anymore) to take part, with men and material to highly risky actions which could carry unbearable human and economic costs. This explains the so-called "humanitarian drift". The United Nations tend to transform themselves, firstly into a sort of humanitarian agency (which takes care of victims in humanitarian emergencies, mainly by organizing, directing and protecting the humanitarian aid) and, secondly, into an agent for the respect of *jus in bello*, i.e. a guardian of international humanitarian law. With regards to this latter transformation, the Security Council, being unable to accomplish its mission under the Charter to maintain and restore peace by preventing hostilities, tries to impose certain combat rules to those who fight. Under this aspect, the most impressive measures it has taken are the well-known establishment of ad hoc International Criminal Tribunals in response to the publics demands for the punishment of those who had perpetrated atrocities in the former Yugoslavia and Rwanda, as well as the diplomatic action which resulted in the elaboration of the Rome Statute.

In this new context, it was evident that the existing norms of international law were totally unsuitable to serve as a basis for the prosecution of those horrible crimes that were committed (and to the extent they were committed) in the framework of an internal armed conflict. It was clearly not enough to prosecute on the sole basis of genocide and crimes against humanity and it was then necessary to establish, in an improvised and chaotic way determined by the pressure of the events, an entire *corpus* of rules concerning war crimes in internal armed conflicts. The Statute of the ICTY gave a first, rather ambiguous, response to this issue; and so did also the Statute of the ICTR, in a clearer though still partial and unsatisfactory way. The ICTY itself and later the ICTR have substantially enriched the normative framework in this subject through an imaginative and very progressive interpretation of the rules of the Statutes (especially in the first important decision on the *Tadic* case on 2 October 1995). The Tribunals have thus given a decisive contribution to integrate and develop the norms in the field and their case law has had a considerable weight in the negotiations at Rome. Despite some doubts and a widespread resistance, the negotiators at the Rome Conference had to bend themselves to these new elements and record them, even if they have adopted sometimes restrictive attitudes, as we shall see.

Before going forward in the examination of the specific aspects of the Statute with regards to war crimes in internal conflicts, I should propose two preliminary observations of a general nature. Firstly, since I have recognized the ICTY's fundamental contribution in our field, it is important to honour not only the institution itself, but also the person of its first President, Antonio Cassese. Many of us know to what great extent the Tribunal's progressive role is due to his dynamism, effort and courage.

My second preliminary observation is the following. Hopefully, the Rome Statute will enter into force as a treaty in a near future (even if, to be realist, there is not much to be expected in terms of speed). However, in the meantime, it is undeniable that customary international law has deeply changed with regards to the norms applicable in internal armed conflicts: many of us have stated this in written works, starting from Professor Meron, who chairs this session. In a period of only a few years, there has emerged what I like to call a "coutume grande vitesse", "high speed custom". This phenomenon tends to demonstrate that, in international law, there are situations in which custom constitutes a dynamic and agile way to reform conventional law. In other words, as observed by Guy de Lacharrière, custom is often a much faster law-maker than international treaties. In our case, what happened is that an old conventional set of rules (notably contained in the Geneva Conventions of 1949), that it had been impossible to update through conventional means (both in 1977 and later), has been deeply modified through a customary process.

2) The New Law Concerning War Crimes in Internal Conflicts: the "Entry"

I think it is important to stress that the customary process I am talking about was possible thanks to an "entry", an "opening" that can be found in the system of international humanitarian law set up by the Geneva Conventions of 1949. At the basis of this phenomenon, there is the well-known idea stated in Common Article 1 by virtue of which States have the obligation not only to respect humanitarian norms when taking part in an armed conflict, but also the obligation to ensure their respect. In other words, States have the responsibility to adopt any possible measure to obtain that the Parties in an armed conflict behave in accordance with international humanitarian law.

The conventional norms I am referring to do not specify the measures that are concerned. They do indicate however - in Article 89 of Additional Protocol I to the Geneva Conventions - that States shall react "jointly or individually" to "serious violations" of humanitarian rules. Beware: to all kinds of "serious violations" ("violations graves" in the French version), and not only to "grave breaches" ("infractions graves" in the French version). In other words, this obligation does not only subsist in case of the commission of such war crimes as listed in the relevant provisions of the Geneva Conventions and Additional Protocol I which can be prosecuted under the principle of universal jurisdiction. States have the obligation to "act jointly or individually" when any other "serious violation" has been committed: and this action could include a mechanism of criminal prosecution (though it is true that, in these other cases, as opposed to those in which a "grave breach" has been committed, criminal prosecution is not a necessary consequence). Now, the concept of "serious violations" is a very broad one, based on an evaluation of the gravity of the violation. Thus, by virtue of the principles of contemporary humanitarian law, criminal prosecution can be organized at the international level ("... the High Contracting Parties undertake to act... jointly...") for all those individual behaviours that could be considered in severe violation of humanitarian rules, even if they are not expressly mentioned in the Articles defining the "grave breaches" (or war crimes).

The ad hoc International Criminal Tribunals have used this precise "opening". Their jurisdiction *ratione materiae* is defined with reference to the concept of "serious violations" of humanitarian principles (as we can see in Article 1 of both the ICTY and the ICTR Statutes). This constitutes a very broad sphere of jurisdiction, since it covers not only those norms of humanitarian law that define "war crimes" (and that concern only international armed conflicts) but also all the other "serious violations" that could take place even in an internal armed conflict. These latter violations are especially referred to in Article 4 of the ICTR Statute and, implicitly, in Article 3 of the ICTY Statute as interpreted by the Appeals Chamber in the decision of 2 October 1995 in the *Tadic* case.

As it is well-known, the case law in both ad hoc Tribunals with regards to war crimes committed in an internal conflict has widely used the "open" character of the notion of "serious violation". In so doing, the Judges have taken advantage from the fact that the statutory provisions mentioned above do not give an exhaustive ("closed") list of the crimes; the enumeration of the relevant acts is preceded by the words "[s]uch violations shall include, but not be limited to...". This interpretation has allowed the Tribunals (and especially, first of all, the ICTY) to identify the acts that could be qualified as war crimes if committed in an internal conflict: they are substantially the same than those that constitute war crimes if committed in international conflicts, provided that they are sufficiently serious.

3) Article 8 of the Rome Statute and War Crimes in Internal Conflicts

Article 8 of the Rome Statute, and especially the parts concerning internal conflicts (i.e. paragraph 2, letters c), d), e and f), should be placed in that specific background. As you know, this provision identifies two types of crimes: the serious violations of Common Article 3 (see Article 8, paragraph 2, letters c), d) and the serious violations of the laws and customs of war (see Article 8, paragraph 2, letters e), f). The first category recalls Article 4 of the ICTR Statute and the ICTY's jurisprudence in interpreting Article 3 of its own Statute. The second type recalls the interpretation of Article 3 of the Statute by the ICTY: in fact, the Chamber had said that this provision shall be understood as referring to violations of the laws and customs of war in case of international conflict as well as of internal conflict. There is a clear continuity in the provisions of Article 8 of the Rome Statute, the Statutes of the ad hoc tribunals and the case law of the ICTY: the Rome Statute welcomes and retains the previous experience and confirms the existence of international rules concerning war crimes in internal conflicts. This constitutes undoubtedly an important progress, though certainly not a linear one: actually, there have been two steps forward and one backwards.

There have been two steps forward because the Rome Statute is the first written normative instrument potentially of a universal character which qualifies serious violations of humanitarian law in internal conflicts as war crimes, and the first which provides for a mechanism for their prosecution at the international level. There has been one step backwards because the definition proposed is very restrictive if compared to the results of the previous practice, in the Statutes of the ad hoc International Tribunals and their case law.

The step backwards is due particularly to two concurrent factors. The first is the abolition of an opening formula at the beginning of Article 8, as the one found in the relevant provisions of the Statutes of the ad hoc Tribunals. I am referring to the phrase "[s]uch violations shall include, but not be limited to...". The elimination of these words obviously implies that the lists contained in the Rome Statute with regards to war crimes in internal conflicts are to be considered as binding, closed, exhaustive: they could not be broadened through interpretative means to include other "serious violations" of humanitarian rules that are not expressly included. The second element is represented by the fact that the number of *figurae criminis* in internal conflicts is very limited if compared to war crimes listed with regards to international conflicts: for instance (and this is the most impressive example) the use of inhumane weapons is not taken into consideration in the context of internal conflicts. The Rome Statute does not follow the direction of progressively drawing together the humanitarian norms applicable in different types of armed conflict (international and internal), as did the decisions of the ICTY and the ICTR (as well as a series of other data of the practice that demonstrates the same trend). On the contrary, Article 8 of the Rome Statute, though stating that war crimes could be committed both in international and internal armed conflicts, sharply separates and opposes the two regimes.

Even more worryingly, there is a further distinction inherent in Article 8 between two categories of non international armed conflicts which would be subjected to different legal regimes with regards to war crimes. By virtue of Article 8, paragraph 2, letters c) and d), it could be said that war crimes constituting a serious violation of Common Article 3 of the Geneva Conventions of 1949 could take place in any kind of non international armed conflict (but obviously not in case of unrest and internal tensions). On the contrary, letters e) and f) induce us to think that those war crimes that violate the so-called combat rules (i.e. "the laws and customs of war") could be committed only in those cases where the armed conflict is "protracted". It is difficult to understand why assaults to sanitary units, mass rapes, deportation or intentional mutilation would constitute war crimes only when the internal conflict is "protracted", and not when it does not last long!

In conclusion, one should add one further opposition to the one between war crimes in international conflicts and war crimes in internal conflicts: the opposition between war crimes committed in internal conflicts in general and war crimes committed in "protracted" internal conflicts. In other words, the definition of a non international armed conflict becomes even more complicated and disparate than before. In fact, we already knew that existing humanitarian law conventions distinguished between a broad notion of internal conflict (the one described in Common Article 3 of the Geneva Conventions of 1949) and a more restrictive one, characterised by its high level of violence (as provided for under Article 1 of Additional Protocol II to the Geneva Conventions in 1977). Now, the Rome Statute adds a new overlapping distinction, and it is difficult to understand how it should be coordinated (if it could be coordinated at all) with the previous ones: that of short and long internal conflicts. In long internal conflicts, both serious violations of Common Article 3 and serious violations of the laws and customs of war can be considered as war crimes. In short internal conflicts, the latter violations are not to be considered war crimes. In my opinion, it could hardly be denied that this is a patent absurdity.

4) On the Bad Use of the *Nullum Crimen* Principle

The *travaux préparatoires* of the Rome Statute clarify the reasons why the majority of the negotiators advocated for the adoption of such restrictive solutions just described. The whole negotiation was tremendously influenced by the argument according to which the Statute had to define completely and exhaustively the crimes under the Court's jurisdiction *ratione materiae* in order to respect the principle of criminal law *nullum crimen, nulla poena sine lege*, that was considered essential by all the participants at the Rome Conference. However, this argument has no solid foundations neither from a logical nor from a legal perspective; actually, it tends to hide the real motivations lying behind the restrictive approach that was finally adopted. "Open" lists of war crimes defined in a general manner (such as the ones contained in the Statutes of the ad hoc Tribunals) leave a very broad space for the interpretation by international judges with regards to the identification of their own sphere of jurisdiction *ratione materiae*, as clearly demonstrated by the experience of the ICTY and the ICTR. And States are not willing to accept such broad and undetermined restrictions to their domestic jurisdiction (including, obviously, the prosecution of crimes). At the most - it can be suggested -, they are willing to consent that those restrictions be imposed to others (such as the former Yugoslavia or Rwanda), but not accept them voluntarily!

On the contrary, the argument based on the respect of the *nullum crimen* principle has no value at all. Actually, this principle intends to protect a human right of a fundamental character based on the idea that nobody can be prosecuted and convicted for acts that were not considered criminal offences at the time they took place. This is obvious, since in that case, the author of those acts could ignore the criminal relevance of his or her behaviour for the very reason that there was no applicable legal instrument (national or international, according to Article 11, paragraph 2, of the Universal Declaration of 1948) that defined it as a criminal offence.

If this is correct - as it certainly is -, the principle of legality is by no means violated when a system of criminal prosecution is organized at the international level to punish acts having a criminal character which the author could not possibly ignore as those acts were clearly and exhaustively defined as criminal offences by the law. What I want to stress is that, for the *nullum crimen sine lege* principle to be respected, it is not necessary at all that the international norm that organizes the system of prosecution include a complete description of the *figurae criminis* and their corresponding penalties. For that purpose, it is sufficient to demonstrate that the author of the relevant acts was subject to legal norms (no matter if national or international) identifying *ante factum* the relevant criminal offences in a clear and accessible way.

In conclusion to this point, I should say that the system of international prosecution of war crimes will certainly be respectful of the principle of legality if it can be demonstrated that any person having committed one of those crimes was submitted to norms (of an internal or international character) that he knew were applicable to his or her case and that qualified his or her behaviour as a crime. And this can be demonstrated in the vast majority of the cases.

Moreover, it should be recalled that the *nullum crimen* principle impedes to attribute retroactive effects to criminal norms of a substantive character, but that it does not exclude at all the possibility for a prosecution to be conducted by a different judge from the one who had jurisdiction at the time of the relevant facts. In other words, as it is commonly said, the principle of legality does not prohibit the retroactive effect of rules of criminal procedure. If one turns now to the Rome Statute, it is clear that this instrument creates *ex novo* an international judge having jurisdiction to prosecute criminal offences that shall be qualified as such independently from the Statute (even when such offences do not fall within the jurisdiction of the Court, for example *ratione temporis*). In the same logic, it should be added that the restrictive definition of war crimes as contained in the Statute does certainly rule out from the jurisdiction *ratione materiae* of the ICC all acts that are not described in the relevant provision, but it does not exclude that some of these acts be qualified as criminal offences under international law and, as a consequence, that the States have the legal obligation to prosecute them under the principle of universal jurisdiction. In other words, the Statute includes under the jurisdiction of the Court only certain given categories of war crimes, but nothing allows to say that the offences considered by the Statute exhaust the list of war crimes under current international law. There are certainly other war crimes, outside those under the ICC's jurisdiction, that must be prosecuted by States without relying on the International Court.

5) Notes on Imperfections, Hurried Elements and Mistakes in the Rome Statute

The previous comments have allowed us to highlight a number of rather complex difficulties arising from the Statute with regards to war crimes in internal conflicts. One could wonder then whether a more articulated and relaxed negotiation would have avoided some of these problems. This question especially arises in view of the hasty manner in which the works at the Rome Conference were conducted, under the strong pressure of international public opinion, in order to reach an immediate adoption of a definitive text. The haste that characterized the negotiations is manifest in many defective formulations in the Rome Statute, fictitious conclusions that refer to other negotiations (such as those concerning the definition of the crime of aggression or the elements of crimes) or incredible discordance between the texts in the different official languages. Everyone knows, for instance, that the English version was the only one approved at the end of the Rome Conference, and that even that unique version was incomplete at the time.

However, even if we leave aside these formalistic aspects (that are certainly important, though), there is one more issue closely related to war crimes that has found an unacceptable solution at the Rome Conference. And there is legitimate suspicion that this difficulty is the result of a deficient analysis of a crucial and very delicate issue. I am referring to the Statute's Article 31, paragraph 1, letter c) which relieves the author of an offence from criminal responsibility if it is demonstrated that the person had acted to defend himself or herself or others (or, in case of war crimes, even property) against an imminent and unlawful use of force. Some attentive observers, thinking mainly about international conflicts (but the same reasoning could be held, *mutatis mutandis*, about internal conflicts), have raised strong criticisms concerning this provision which seems to introduce a ground for exoneration of individual criminal responsibility radically incompatible with the basic principles of current international humanitarian law. This provision, for instance, could justify the attack against civilians if it were demonstrated that it was a proportionate and reasonable defensive act against an imminent and unlawful attack against own civilians. One could think of many other examples, such as the use of poisonous weapons, toxic gases and, in general, crimes concerning the use of prohibited means and methods of warfare. Actually, Article 31, par. 1, let. c), appears to go backwards in the field of war crimes in comparison with the provisions of humanitarian law, from the Hague Law to the First Protocol of 1977. It expresses the intention of reintroducing the logic of *inadimplenti non est adimplendum* and of reprisals against protected persons and property that are prohibited under humanitarian law in force.

It will be interesting to follow the rich debate that will probably arise on this issue, animated in particular by a group of Belgian jurists. The discussion will allow to better understand whether Article 31, par. 1, let. c) is to be applied as a ground of exoneration from responsibility in case of genocide and crimes against humanity: from the text of the provision, it seems to be the case.

6) Conclusion

There can be no doubt that the Rome Statute represents a major step in the evolution of international humanitarian law, especially with regards to the norms applicable in case of internal armed conflict. The rules it proclaims are fundamentally innovative if compared to those contained in conventional instruments in force (such as the Geneva Conventions of 1949 and the Protocols of 1977). First of all, the Statute articulates in a written form a Hague Law of internal armed conflicts that was almost unknown in previous legal instruments. Secondly, it identifies the cases in which the violation of humanitarian principles applicable in case of internal armed conflicts are to be qualified as war crimes; in that sense, it constitutes an innovation if compared with the conventions of 1949 and 1977 which contained no provision on the subject.

This legal regime is indisputably innovative, but it must be considered as a codification or crystallisation of the results of a customary process that took place at exceptional speed in the past years. The Statute is to be read as corresponding to the state of general international law, no matter of its fate as a convention, i.e. no matter of the fact that it enters into force in a short or long period. Thus, it can easily be anticipated that these provisions of the Statute concerning war crimes, and especially those relative to internal armed conflicts, will be widely used by domestic legislators, tribunals both at a national and international level, diplomatic practice and legal literature as a central reference to determine the state of current international law in this field.

15. The Protection of Children's Rights in the Statute of the International Criminal Court

JOHN T. HOLMES

The protection of the rights of the child arose in a number of contexts during the negotiation of the Statute of the International Criminal Court. The three aspects which were of most significance were:

1. Recruitment of children into armed forces;
2. Non-culpability of children for crimes committed;
3. Protection of children as victims and witnesses.

Victims and Witnesses

One of the most innovative aspects of the Rome Statute is the protections afforded to victims and witnesses. Many of the provisions affording protections to victims and witnesses set out specific measures for the Court to take with respect to particularly vulnerable groups, such as women and children.

Recruitment

The Rome Conference was not intended to be a codification exercise. This was particularly true with respect to the inclusion of crimes in the Statute. Nevertheless, advances in setting international humanitarian standards were achieved at Rome in a number of areas.

The prohibition on conscripting or enlisting children is included in two sections of the Statute's war crimes provision (Article 8). It is included as a crime in international armed conflicts and also in the section relating to non-international armed conflicts. The provision relating to internal armed conflicts is essentially the same as for international conflicts except the former includes conscripting or enlisting children into armed groups as well as armed forces.

The provisions in Article 8 relating to the recruitment of children into the armed forces are drawn closely from the Geneva Protocols of 1977. Article 77 of Protocol I and Article 4 of Protocol II obligate States Parties to refrain from recruiting children into their armed forces. These obligations were later included in the Convention on the Rights of the Child (Article 38), which has now been ratified or acceded to by all but two States. However, the prohibitions in the Geneva Protocols and the Convention on the Rights of the Child were not defined as crimes. The provisions in the Protocols are not included in the breaches sections of those instruments. Therefore, the inclusion as war crimes of the acts of conscripting or enlisting children under fifteen years of age into armed forces in the Rome Statute represents a significant advance in international humanitarian and human rights law.

During the Rome Conference, strenuous efforts were made to improve in the Statute the protections afforded children in the Geneva Protocols and the Convention on the Rights of the Child. The two principal issues were the age of conscription or enlistment and the use of children in hostilities.

Ultimately, success was limited. On the age of recruitment, there remains (unfortunately) no international consensus yet on raising the age of recruitment. At the time of the adoption of the Convention on the Rights of the Child, many States and non-governmental organizations were dissatisfied with the compromise which was used, based on the Geneva Protocols. Efforts have been made since to reexamine this issue with a view to raising the acceptable age of recruitment. The United Nations Commission on Human Rights has established a working group which is elaborating an Optional Protocol to Convention on the Rights of the Child. The fact that this standard-setting exercise is still underway led many delegations in Rome to accept that the age of recruitment should be retained at fifteen years. Moreover, some States argued that the issue of the age of recruitment should be kept separate from the purpose of the Rome Conference, which was to elaborate and define crimes.

While retaining the age of 15 set in previous instruments, the Rome Statute made two potentially important changes. The Statute uses the term, "conscripting or enlisting", rather than the Geneva Protocols language of "recruiting". The change was made to clarify that the crime is intended to cover active efforts by members of the armed forces to draw children into their ranks. The crime does not cover the situation where children volunteer and join such forces.

The second change related to situations where children are part of the armed forces. Geneva Protocol I prohibits children from taking a "direct part" in hostilities. The Rome Statute uses the term, "participating actively". It can be argued that the ICC language is broader and therefore represents an advance in international humanitarian law. However, it remains for the Court itself to determine whether that is the case. The Statute provision on non-international armed conflict also uses "participate actively". This may be an unfortunate departure from the Geneva Protocol II, which places no qualification on the prohibition from participation in hostilities. This change was made for two reasons. First, it was believed necessary to retain some symmetry between the provisions for international and internal armed conflicts. Second, the provision in Protocol II is not a grave breach whereas the provision in the Rome Statute is a war crime, thus a clearer standard was necessary. Again, ultimately it will be for the Court to determine the degree to which the use of children constitutes a war crime.

Non-culpability

The issue of the culpability of children for the commission of offences under the Statute generated an interesting and troubling discussion at the Rome Conference. At odds were two important principles - the desire to end impunity for perpetrators of these heinous crimes and the wish to ensure the greatest protection of the rights of the child.

In the preparatory process, there was a lengthy debate on question of the age of responsibility. Many delegations argued for the standard used in their countries and these varied widely from state to state. While no agreement could thus be found on a specific age, many delegations contended that the age of responsibility could not be placed at eighteen, given the numbers of child soldiers globally and their increasing responsibility for the commission of heinous crimes. On the other hand, many delegations insisted that if children were deemed potentially culpable under the Statute, then a separate system of criminal juvenile justice would have to be included in the Statute, in conformity with International Covenant on Civil and Political Rights, the Convention on the Rights of the Child and various instruments adopted by the United Nations in the context of crime prevention and criminal justice.

In Rome, negotiations were resumed on this question with a view to finding a solution to this dilemma. The decision taken was to separate the question of the age of responsibility from the issue of the jurisdiction of the Court. Article 26 of the Statute thus provides that the Court shall have no jurisdiction over any person who was under the age of eighteen at the time of the commission of the offence. In this way, the Statute does not take a position on whether children should be held responsible for the commission of offences; rather, it provides that the Court will not assume jurisdiction for such cases.

There were two main reasons for the approach adopted. First, it would have been extremely complex to develop a separate system of criminal juvenile justice for the Court. International human rights instruments set clear standards for states concerning juvenile justice and if the Court were to assume jurisdiction it would have to establish a separate criminal juvenile justice system, including a distinct penal institution. The creation of such a system would have engendered lengthy negotiations, assuming that states would have accepted to establish such a system.

A second, more important reason, was that if children could be prosecuted under the Statute, the ICC would victimize children twice. In the view of many, the use of children in armed forces is already a violation of their rights. Punishment for being conscripted or enlisted into the armed forces would, in effect, victimize the child twice.

It should be borne in mind that under the Statute's provision on command responsibility (Article 28), commanders of child soldiers can be prosecuted for the offences committed by their forces.

Conclusion

The Rome Statute's treatment of the rights of the child represents a modest but important advance in international humanitarian and human rights law. Unfortunately, several of the provisions in the Statute reflect the sad reality that children remain pawns in situations of armed conflicts and are frequently victims of the most heinous crimes. Hopefully, the adoption of the Statute and the establishment of the International Criminal Court will play an important role in reducing and ending this tragedy.

16. The Status of the Individual in the Statute of the International Criminal Court*

LAMIA MEKHEMAR**

In the following pages I would like to discuss briefly a point already touched upon during this session concerning the topic of "The ICC and the Protection of Human Rights", namely, the status of the individual in the Statute of the Court adopted in Rome on July 17, 1998.

My hypothesis or starting point in determining the status of the individual in the Statute is that human rights - as a legal discipline - has influenced almost every branch and field of international law; not the least international humanitarian law under which the Statute falls. The confluence of human rights and the rules of criminal justice at both international and domestic levels is equally undeniable.

During and after the feudal wars the individual was given a prominent position in a variety of local military codes and in the writings of the early authorities of international law, especially Alberigo Gentili and Hugo Grotius in the 17th century. However, the status of the individual and his rights in international humanitarian law, in general, have evolved – in an institutionalized manner - through several stages since the inception of the Lieber Code in 1863 which can be considered the starting point of international humanitarian law (or rather the "laws of war" as they were originally called, whereas the term "humanitarian law" came to existence as a result of the influence of human rights) after centuries and even millennia of

* The author discusses this subject in more detail in: Mohammed Gomaa and Lamia Mekhemar, 55 *Revue Egyptienne de Droit International*, 1999, pp. 231-69.

** First Secretary of the Permanent Mission of Egypt to the United Nations in New York. The views expressed here are purely personal and do not necessarily reflect those of the Government of Egypt.

the application of *primary facts*, short of being law, which manifested themselves in times of war as *humanistic* or *humanitarian considerations*.

In the four Geneva Conventions of 12 August 1949 for the protection of the victims of war the individual was treated as a "protected person". His rights were limited to the prohibition of reprisals against prisoners of war, wounded, sick or shipwrecked personnel as well as against civilians in the hands of the enemy. In the following stage, his rights were extended by the two Protocols Additional to the Geneva Conventions of 1949, and Relating to the protection of Victims of Armed Conflicts of 1977. But, throughout those stages the individual enjoyed only the *passive* role of being "protected"; he had no way of action or initiative. The war crimes Tribunals for the former Yugoslavia and Rwanda went a step further in allowing the Prosecutor to initiate a case upon information received from any source, thus not excluding the possibility of the individual to bring to the attention of the Prosecutor a crime over which those tribunals have jurisdiction. However, those two Tribunals were never meant to have any *universal* implication on the status of the individual. In the latest and present stage - represented by the ICC which is intended to acquire universal adherence - the individual gained more grounds influenced by human rights.

The individual appears in the Statute of the ICC in six different capacities: an individual not related to the case, a victim, a suspect, an accused, a convicted person or a witness.

For the purposes of this analysis the legal status of the individual and the dynamics involved in the rights vested in him by virtue of the Statute will be considered from the perspective of the following quadruple classification taking into consideration the various stages of the procedures of the Court, as prescribed by the Statute. In each of theses stages, the individual is considered in one or more of the different capacities mentioned above. However, this classification is not hard and fast, its purpose is to serve as a basis for clustering the different rights accorded to the individual in the Statute so as to make their presence more obvious and more appreciable.

1) The Individual as a Protected Person

The legal status of the individual as a protected object remains the same in the Statute as it exists in International Humanitarian Law where he is accorded the passive role of being a recipient of the protection of his rights. His rights as a protected person in the Statute are found in the Articles defining the crimes within the jurisdiction of the Court under Part 2.

Although the legal status of the individual did not change, the categories of individuals under protection were extended to include the vulnerable groups of women and children. This is one of the most relevant advancements of the Rome Statute with respect to existing international legislation.

2) The Individual as a Positive Actor

The Statute endows the individual with an active role. This role manifests itself in two important phases in the procedures of the Court, namely, the triggering of the case and determining the admissibility thereof.

A. The Phase of Triggering the Case

In this preliminary stage of procedure, according to Article 15, paragraph 2, the Prosecutor may initiate a case *proprio motu* on the basis of information provided to him on crimes within the jurisdiction of the Court. The Statute, however, did not specify the sources of such information, thus enabling *any individual*, whether related to the violation or not, to provide the Prosecutor with information upon which he may trigger the case. The action taken by the individual here can be looked at as an *actio popularis*. This faculty brings the individual to a status close to an implicit *locus standi in judicio*.

Nonetheless, according to the Statute, if the Prosecutor concludes that there is a reasonable basis to proceed with an investigation based upon the information provided by an individual, he shall obtain the authorization of the Pre-Trial Chamber. This requirement is a safeguard against any abuse by the Prosecutor. It may be worth noting, however, that since this requirement is not based on a any external intervention from either the Security Council or States, it is not gravely prejudicial to the independence of the Prosecutor.

B. The Admissibility Phase

Under Article 19, paragraph 2, the accused may challenge the admissibility or the jurisdiction of the Court upon certain prescribed bases for inadmissibility contained in Article 17. This also should be looked at as a development in the role of the individual in international humanitarian law.

3) Rights Deriving from General Principles of Law

The Statute confirmed as well a group of rights of the individual deriving from the general principles of law such as the principle of *ne bis in idem* which was reaffirmed in Article 20 which stipulates that "no person shall be tried before the Court ... of crimes for which the person has been convicted or acquitted by the Court, or by another court". Also the principles of *nullum crimen sine lege, nulla poena sine lege* and that of non-retroactivity are principles that constitute a solid basis of rights and guarantees aiming at the protection of the suspect or the accused as the case may be.

4) Rights and Guarantees Aimed at Ensuring a Fair Trial

The Statute provides the accused with a host of rights designed for his protection and for ensuring a fair trial throughout its different stages.

A. The Pre-trial Phase

The rights of the individual provided for in Article 55 of the Statute during an investigation in the pre-trial phase include a number of important internationally recognized safeguards. Among those are the right of a person not to be compelled to incriminate himself or to confess guilt, not to be subjected to any form of coercion, duress or threat, to torture or any other form of cruel, inhuman or degrading treatment or punishment, the right to free assistance of a competent interpreter and to translation of documents, and the right not to be subjected to arbitrary arrest or detention and not to be deprived of liberty except on grounds provided for under the Statute of the ICC.

Prior to the questioning of the suspect, Article 55 stipulates that he should be informed that there are grounds to believe that he has committed a crime within the jurisdiction of the Court, and that he has the right to remain silent, without such silence being a consideration in the determination of guilt or innocence, to have legal assistance of his choosing, or if he does not have legal assistance, to have such free assistance assigned to him if he does not have sufficient means, and finally, the right to be questioned in the presence of counsel.

The Statute further obliges the Prosecutor during the investigations, under Article 54, to respect the interests and personal circumstances of victims and witnesses, including age, gender and health, taking into account the nature of the crime, in particular, where it involves sexual violence, gender violence or violence against children. The up-lift the Statute has given to witnesses in the ICC is essential when considering that the Rwanda Tribunal in particular had suffered from interference with witnesses and their poor administration.

The arrested person also enjoys the right of the appointment by the Pre-Trial Chamber of an expert to assist him, or the authorization of a counsel of his choice, according to Article 56, paragraph 2. The Pre-Trial Chamber will, under Article 57, paragraph 3, protect the privacy of victims and witnesses, and the persons arrested or appearing in response to a summons.

B. The Trial Phase

The Statute accords to the individual, whether he is an accused, witness or a victim, a number of guarantees in this phase of the proceedings.

Article 63, paragraph 1, requires the presence of the accused during the trial, thus excluding, at least in principle, trials *in absentia*. Article 64, paragraph 2, ensures a fair and expeditious trial conducted with full respect for the rights of the accused, and accords due regard for the protection of victims and witnesses. The same Article provides that proceedings of the trial be held in public, but in some circumstances they may be held *in camera*. Under Article 67 the accused should be duly informed of his charge in a language that he understands and speaks, and to have the assistance of a competent interpreter.

Article 68 requests the Court to take measures to protect the safety, dignity and privacy of victims and witnesses. Where necessary for the protection of victims and witnesses, the Court may decide that any part of the proceedings be conducted *in camera*, as an exception to the principle of public hearings referred to above. It will also hear the views of victims when their interests are affected; but in the same time it should strike a balance between these interests and the rights of the accused in order to ensure a fair trial. The Victims and Witnesses Unit is also allowed to provide counselling to the Prosecutor on protective measures and security arrangements. Under the same Article, the Prosecutor may withhold evidence the disclosure of which may endanger the security of a witness on the condition that the rights of the accused will not be affected. The Court may, in accordance with Article 69, refuse any evidence which can affect the fairness of the trial or when it is presented to the Court by any means in violation of internationally recognized human rights.

The Statute also makes room in Article 75 for the victims to claim reparation before the Court for which a Trust Fund will be established. As a development in the protection of the rights of victims, the Statute included rehabilitation as a form of reparation.

It is also notable that the granting of the individual of a status close to an implicit *locus standi in judicio*, as suggested earlier, falls quite in place with respect to his right to claim reparation. His rights may be lost if he were not able to bring a case to the attention of the Prosecutor.

The victims' rights have been accorded more attention in the Statute of the ICC than in the Tribunal for the former Yugoslavia where, for example, the Security Council in resolution 827(1993) affirmed that the "work of the International Tribunal shall be carried out without prejudice to the right of the victims to seek, through appropriate means, compensation for damages incurred", thus recognizing the insufficiency of the Statute of that Tribunal.

In the two previous phases the influence of Article 14 of the International Covenant on Civil and Political Rights of 1966 is more than evident. The rights stipulated therein have all been introduced into the Statute with the addition of the provision of legal assistance and eventually translation free of charge in the light of the financial circumstances of the individual.

C. The Sentencing Phase

The Statute empowers the Court only to pronounce imprisonment penalties in addition to fines and forfeiture while totally excluding the death penalty.

Article 76, paragraph 4, stipulates that the sentence shall be pronounced in public and, wherever possible, in the presence of the accused. According to Article 78, the Court, when determining the sentence, shall take into account the individual circumstances of the convicted person, and will deduct from its sentence the time previously spent in detention by a Court's order.

D. The Right to Appeal

The Statute establishes a right in the convicted person to appeal on grounds of procedural error, error of fact or error of law, or any other ground that affects the fairness or reliability of the proceedings or decision, thus elevating him one step beyond the rights accorded to the Prosecutor who is granted the right to appeal on the first three grounds. The status of the individual in this respect according to the Statute of the ICC is more advanced than in the Statute of the Tribunal for the former Yugoslavia both *ratione personae* and *ratione materiae*. In the latter, the accused and the Prosecutor were given the right to appeal, in accordance with Article 25, only on two grounds, namely, an error on a question of law invalidating the decision, or an error of fact which has occasioned a miscarriage of justice.

In this connection, the Statute also gives the person who has suffered an unlawful arrest or whose conviction has been reversed the right to compensation according to Article 85.

E. Revision of the Sentence

Also as a substantial advancement over the Statute of the Tribunal for the former Yugoslavia Article 84 of the Statute of the ICC extends to the convicted person, or after his death, to his spouse, children or parents, or even a person given express instructions from the convicted person, in special circumstances, the right to apply for the revision of the final judgment of conviction or sentence upon the emergence of new evidence or that the evidence was false, forged of falsified or that one or more judges who participated in convicting him committed acts justifying his removal from the bench.

F. The Enforcement of the Sentence

The Statute adopted an international-oriented approach in that the sentence shall be served in a State designated by the Court from a list of States which have indicated to the Court their willingness to accept sentenced persons, and not in the State where the crime had been committed or the State of which the convicted is a national. On the other hand, Article 106 declares that conditions of imprisonment shall be consistent with internationally recognized treaty standards governing treatment of prisoners, and not only in accordance with the applicable law of the State of enforcement as stipulated in the Statute of the Tribunal for the former Yugoslavia.

G. International Cooperation and Judicial Assistance

During the trajectory from the pre-trial phase unto the final decision of the Court, it (i.e., the Court) may, pursuant to Article 87, paragraph 4, in relation to any request for assistance, take measures with a view to protecting the safety or physical or psychological well-being of any victims, potential witnesses and their families.

Conclusions

Although human rights are not a novel idea, the protection of human rights in international penal justice has in reality acquired attention only recently, and more so in the Statute of the ICC. Principles such as due process or *nullum crimen sine lege, nulla poena sine lege* which are found in almost any national legislation, have been elevated to an international level of application.

It is less important to determine whether human rights are converted into rules of criminal justice or *vice versa*. What imports is the positive impact of these rules on the status of the individual in international law. The convergence of human rights and the rules of penal justice does not necessarily mean that they may not conflict. This point, however, is not the concern of this short note.

The ICC, and before it the Tribunals of the former Yugoslavia and Rwanda, has gone a great deal since the law of the victors was applied in the Nuremberg and Tokyo trails. The *corpus* of objective law in the Statute will undoubtedly ensure the individual a fair, consistent and predictable course of litigation. Maybe the most important achievement for the individual in the Statute is that he has come close to having a *locus standi in judicio*, although this still does not constitute a threshold for the status he maintains in human rights courts, such as the European Human Rights Court or the Inter-American Court of Human Rights, where he can trigger a case all by himself.

By adopting an approach based on individual criminal responsibility, in line with the tribunals for the former Yugoslavia and Rwanda - albeit their limited scope *ratione loci* and *ratione personae* - the Statute added to the realization of penal justice an international dimension by which the Court surmounts legal barriers imposed by international law, such as the concept of absolute sovereignty.

The ICC definitely marks an important advancement in the implementation of international norms benefiting the individual in what may be considered a restatement of international law. However, the confirmation of such an achievement will depend, to a certain extent, on the work of the Preparatory Commission in specifying the rights of the individual as spelled out in the Statute. One such endeavour would be the exercise by the Commission to define "victims" for the purposes of the Statute, and whether it will adopt a non-restrictive approach in reaching such a definition.

17. State's Crime and Individuals' Crimes: What Relationship?

GIORGIO CONETTI*

One among the major issues that are still to be explored in the field of criminal international law concerns the relationship between individuals' and States' international crimes. First of all, one could state that facts that constitute individuals' crimes could not be always qualified as State's crimes and vice-versa. Such statement is valid also when we are dealing with the same material fact as, e.g., a crime against humanity. This one constitutes, without any doubt, an individual's international crime, but is apt to assume the nature of a State's crime, at least according to Article 19 of the 1996 Draft Articles on States' responsibility, only when it gives origin to a serious breach on a widespread scale of an international obligation of essential importance for the safeguard of human beings.

However, we must consider that many infringements of international rules could constitute, at the same time, an individual's and a State's crime. The more, a number of States' crimes involve necessarily individuals' crimes as they may be committed only through acts or omissions of State's or public agents. Also in the cases when the events that constitute simultaneously an individual and a State's crime, the International Law Commission has always assumed the autonomy and distinction of the two behaviours and of the responsibility that derives from them.

In the ILC Report on the work of its XXVIII Session (ILC Yearbook, 1976, II-2, p. 119) is stated:

> Once again the Commission takes this opportunity of stressing that the attribution to the State of an international wrongful act characterized as an "international crime" is quite different from the incrimination of certain individuals-organs for action connected

* Professor of International Law, University of Insubria, Como.

with the commission of an "international crime" of the State, and that the obligation to punish such individual actions does not constitute the form of international responsibility specially applicable to a State committing an "international crime" or, in any case, the sole form of this responsibility.

In full consistency with this approach, Article 4 of the 1996 ILC Draft Code of Crimes against Peace and Security of Mankind, dealing with cases where the entanglement of the individuals' and States' behaviours is very tight, specifies: "The fact that the present Code provides for the responsibility of individuals for crimes against the peace and the security of mankind is without prejudice to any question of the responsibility of States under international law". In its Commentary to the Code (ILC Report on the work of XLVIII Session, GAOR, LI Session, Suppl. 10), the Commission recalls its previous comments to Article 19, concerning the non exhaustion of State's responsibility through the punishment of the guilty State's agents and the consequent permanence of the duty to give reparation. A similar rule, with the same purpose, is contained in Article 25, par. 4 of the Rome Statute of the International Criminal Court: "No provision in this Statute relating to individual criminal responsibility shall affect the responsibility of State under international law".

Such separation is certainly sound as different are the incriminating rules and the consequences of their breach. The distinction, *inter alia*, is apt to consider, in a case, the different relevance of circumstances precluding wrongfulness of States' acts or excluding individual criminal responsibility; e.g. a State may still be responsible, and even more responsible, for war crimes committed, in an armed conflict, by its soldiers who are not punishable as individuals owing to their age. According to Article 26 of the Rome Statute of the ICC, the Court shall not have jurisdiction over persons under the age of 18 at the time of the alleged commission of crime and the internal legal orders, at their turn, contain rules on age limits for criminal charge.

In classical international law, punishment of responsible State's officials could constitute one among other ways of satisfaction that the injured State is entitled to obtain, but it is considered autonomous and separate from reparations and other obligations of the offender State. At the present stage of international law, the punishment of the guilty officials is a duty upon the offender State, to fulfil with a national trial, extradition or, in the near future hopefully, trial before the ICC. The compliance with this duty does not exempt from State responsibility, but the fault to comply produces further causes of responsibility.

All this said, not every issue at stake is thus settled, as more than a question concerning the reciprocate interference of assessment and characterization of the same facts by international bodies competent to establish States or individuals's responsibility lays still open. We have seen the rather unsatisfactory solution given by the ICC Statute when it recognizes, in Article 16, the prevailing political powers of the Security Council, under Chapter VII of the UN Charter, by whose exercise the Council may defer investigation or prosecution of individual international crimes for a period of 12 months and renew the deferral without any limit. By this way, the Council may proceed in a situation falling under Chapter VII without worrying about the exercise of the ICC jurisdiction upon individual international crimes. However, one might wonder what relevance the Court should assign to Security Council former binding decisions adopted under Chapter VII, in the case in which the Court jurisdiction is resumed afterwards.

Moreover, problems arising from assessments and characterizations of facts made by different bodies on State and individuals' responsibility could become very serious when the concerned bodies are of conciliatory, arbitral or jurisdictional nature, as the Conciliation Commission or the Arbitral Tribunal foreseen by the ILC Draft Articles on State responsibility, or the International Court of Justice itself; as the ICC, according to Article 21 of its Statute, shall apply, when appropriate, international treaties and the principles and rules of international law, we must consider how much binding could be for the Court a treaty or a conciliation already passed among the interested States, or an arbitral or International Court award pronounced in the case, adjudicating in appliance of the relevant international law rules.

THE INTERNATIONAL CRIMINAL JUSTICE SYSTEM AFTER THE ROME CONFERENCE

18. The Preventive and the Repressive Function of the International Criminal Court*

OTTO TRIFFTERER**

A. INTRODUCTION/GENERAL REMARKS

I. Present Situation and Tendencies

The present situation in wide parts of former Yugoslavia mirrors an important aspect of the tension between the *primary* purpose of criminal law, to *prevent* crimes and its *secondary* function, to *repress and punish* in cases where prevention with regard to the crime committed has failed to fulfil its function. Crimes against humanity and war crimes, committed there, in Rwanda and in several other places all over the world, as well as many other appearances of crimes, remind us daily that criminality on the domestic and international level is a social disease, the sources of which have to be researched and abolished, if prevention should reach its highest degree of effectiveness. Therefore, the challenge to impunity, heading our Conference here in Trento, is a challenge to all of us and on every occasion.

Both functions of criminal law are expressly mentioned in Article 28 of the Rome Statute[1] in the context with the power of military commanders or other superiors "*to prevent* or *repress* ... crimes ... committed by forces under his or her effective command and control, or effective authority and control".[2] In this context, those two functions are meant as alternatives, both of which are of equal importance with regard to

---

* For a German version, partly corresponding with this presentation, see Jung u.a., *Festschrift für Heinz Müller-Dietz zum 70. Geburtstag*, 2001.

** Professor, University of Salzburg.

[1] All further Articles, mentioned without any specification, are those of the Rome Statute.

[2] Article 28(a)(ii) and (b)(iii); emphasis added.

crimes under international law and on the domestic level. But persons who, due to their position of power, for instance, as "Head of State or Government", could prevent such crimes best, may have participated in one way or another in their commission. They, therefore, may not be interested in the prosecution of such crimes on *the national or the international* level, especially, when otherwise they personally may have to face punishment.

This peculiarity of crimes under international law has already been expressed in the Report of the Carnegie Endowment for International Peace with regard to the causes and responsibilities concerning the Balkan Wars 1912-1913. The Commission concluded that one word from those in power would have stopped all belligerent struggles and the atrocities committed during these events.[3] This result raises the question, how persons, equipped with such a power, can be motivated to speak this one word? Can those addressed by Article 27 be personally persuaded or forced by armed attacks against their State, to put their foot down to prevent (further) crimes? Is it sufficient to merely threaten them with such reactions or with prosecution and punishment by the community of nations, if they keep silent, and thus support such crimes by not interfering? May the mere expectation, to be held *individually* responsible by the international community, influence their behaviour? Could such an expectation lead to unpredictable reactions to restore peace or, on the contrary, to an intensified abuse of power and thereby increase the number and gravity of crimes committed, ordered or not sufficiently suppressed? For instance, someone facing prosecution before an *international* Court may perhaps hold the opinion that he has not much to lose, but may gain a lot, perhaps, even avoiding criminal responsibility, when *continuing* a programme of ethnical cleansing. Can such a danger of increasing criminality serve as a justification to stop or even eliminate such persons *by force*? Are the rules to admit self-defence and defence of others applicable, especially those demanding that countermeasures are only allowed if they stop the illegal attack for sure?[4]

Besides, on the domestic level it is discussed, whether the traditional penalties, especially imprisonment, are at all adequate means to "fight" criminality or if there are others more effective, like those summarized by the concept of diversion? Is what may be helpful on the

[3] See Carnegie Endowment for International Peace, Division of Intercourse and Education, *Report of the International Commission to inquire into the causes and conduct of the Balkan Wars*, publication No. 4, 21 et seq. (399) (1914), reprinted 1993 with an introduction by G. F. Kennon. See also O. Triffterer in: O. Triffterer (ed.), *Commentary on the Rome Statute of the International Criminal Court*, 1999, Article 27, margin No. 1, with further references in footnote 2.

[4] A. Eser in O. Triffterer (ed.) *Commentary, supra* note 4, Article 31 margin Nos. 32 and 33. See also O. Triffterer, *Österreichisches Strafrecht, Allgemeiner Teil*, 2 ed. 1994, chapter 11 margin Nos. 66 et seq., with further references.

national level, also effective in the field of international criminal law or, are there peculiarities in the appearances of crimes *under international* law, which demand an independent solution apart from national criminal justice systems? Is it the position of power, often held by perpetrators of the so called core crimes, the classical Nuremberg crimes, aggression, crimes against humanity, including genocide, and war crimes, that makes the situation different and unpredictable? On the domestic level, security forces and the police are more or less present on the spot to prevent and, if necessary, to investigate criminality. But there are no such executive forces of the international community in places where crimes under international law are committed. On the contrary, persons who could exercise these functions, like military commanders and other superiors, as mentioned in Articles 27 and 28, may even have ordered or tolerated, and thus promoted such crimes.

Where are the limits of using force against those responsible for the commission of such crimes, in order to stop their continuation or impunity of the perpetrators? NATO bombing led to a rapidly intensified commission of such crimes in Kosovo and did not stop them even after more than 50 days of attacking. Was this not predictable? Dictators may judge upon the end of their time in power differently, especially when committing crimes of concern to the international community as a whole, in order to preserve their position of power as long as possible.

Must it be taken for granted, that persons in charge of such power will not put their foot down to stop all atrocities, if they are sure that they have to face prosecution and trial immediately after their opponents or the international community gets hold of them? Who can get close to them or dare to speak up to change their minds? Psychological warfare cannot guarantee success as long as it is not based on well founded studies on the relevant types of perpetrators, accomplices and victims of crimes under international law.

II. Prevention, Deterrence and Repression

Prevention, deterrence and repression are, all three, rather complex concepts. The Tenth UN Congress on the Prevention of Crime and the Treatment of Offenders, held in Vienna, 10-17 April 2000, therefore, has dealt, besides other issues, with "Effective Crime Prevention: Keeping Pace with new Developments".[5] The broad spectrum of ideas, research and

---

[5] In German speaking countries, similar expressions, "Prävention" and "Repression" are used to describe the two major functions of criminal law. See, for instance, H.-H. Jescheck/Th. Weigend, *Lehrbuch des Strafrechts, Allgemeiner Teil*, 5 ed. 1996, 4 et seq. See

approaches in a merging world, which has been presented there, cannot be dealt with here. This, and the subject matter of our Conference is justification for limiting my presentation to specific aspects of crimes under international law and their expression in relevant *international* legal documents.

1. The Diversity of Concepts to "Fight" Criminality

It is the aim of criminal law to serve as *ultima ratio* for the protection of legally accepted values and interests. All concepts to "fight" criminality agree that the most effective way to achieve this aim is to prevent crimes from being committed at all. Such a result may be obtained only by combined efforts, for instance, by diminishing the sources of crimes, by educating and motivating all citizens to obey the law, and by deterring potential perpetrators. Failing this, criminal law can only *ex post* contribute to the prevention of such crimes by *preventing* recidivism and *a repetition* of such crimes by other persons. To prevent, therefore, means to hinder the commission of crimes right from the beginning, but also to stop their commission at any stage before the crime has been completed and caused harm or continue to do so.

All these aspects describe *actions* to "fight" criminality. "Deterrent" means, according to Black's Law Dictionary, "anything which impedes or has the tendency to prevent; e.g. punishment is a 'deterrent' to crime".[6] While to "deter" and to "prevent" are rather neutral verbs, covering all possible influences on potential perpetrators, others imply some pressure on persons to avoid that crimes can or will be committed (again).

"Suppression" describes "to put a stop to all things actually existing", including to achieve an "end by force".[7] The word "repressing"

---

also note 9 below. In the discussion guide for this session of the 10th UN Congress on the Prevention of Crime and Treatment of Offenders, it is expressly mentioned that "[O]ver the past two decades, the international criminal justice community has increasingly focused its attention on identifying, developing and evaluating measures to prevent crime. That process, which received fresh impetus in reaction to the contention that 'nothing works', has continued and yielded results suggesting that there are some effective crime-prevention measures based on traditional concepts (such as strengthening the role of the family and encouraging formal education). Other innovative measures are based on technological developments that permit the criminal justice community to react in a timely and effective manner to new crime situations. Indeed, especially in the last decade, keeping pace with new developments in crime and its prevention has become a major priority for many Governments and a real challenge to law enforcement and other crime-prevention practitioners"; UN doc. A/CONF. 187/PM. 1, 22 September 1998 par. 33.

[6] 7th edition 1999.

[7] *ibid.*

has the same root. However, it emphasizes a process, necessarily following the act to be suppressed. In this sense the "International Convention for the Suppression of Terrorist Bombings" refers to all methods and means, available and suitable to fight all social appearances of terrorism. It refers, accordingly, in paragraph 5 of its Preamble, to "legal provisions on the prevention, repression and elimination of terrorism" and, in paragraph 9, to "effective and practical measures for the prevention of such acts of terrorism and for the prosecution and punishment of their perpetrators". Similar wording can be found in other international documents and confirm that prosecution and punishment are measures of *re*pression and, at the same time, belong to the broad scale opened by the word *sup*pression, thus including prevention.[8]

2. Interrelationship between Different Approaches

All these expressions describe means, methods and measures to avoid violations of legally protected values and interests. Because of this common goal, all Delegations at the Rome Conference 1998 agreed that there could be no peace without justice, especially given the capacity of justice to foster reconciliation and to deter the commission of future crimes and notwithstanding the regrettable tendency of criminal justice to occasionally take on the appearance of retribution and revenge.

However, all means approach this common goal from different angles. One depends on the stages of human behaviour, developing as a continuous, complex process towards the completion of the crime and appearing as a social disease upon which society has to react. Even though decisiveness and strength may be most effective, there are various criteria, to limit the admissibility and suitability of means, methods and measures for "fighting" criminality.

Whatever means are chosen, their effectiveness should be evaluated in advance, if possible by empirical research. All reactions to crimes, interfering with individual rights and liberties, ought to be measured on their suitability "to contribute to the prevention" of crimes under international law. The legal permission of self-defence shows, for this reason, a very detailed scale of prerequisites to justify even an *individual* prevention of crime by force.

In addition, all criminal means and measures have to be proportional to the threatening violations of legally protected values and

---

[8] Just in comparison, the German language shows an even more differentiated scale of words, mirrored in international documents: "abschrecken", "vorbeugen", "verhüten", "verhindern" (the latter contains already a tendency to "fight" against criminality), "unterdrücken" and finally "bestrafen"; see also *supra* note 6.

interests, they react upon and to the aim to be achieved with their help, for instance, preservation or restoration of peace and security of mankind. This is, in principal, expressed, for instance, in Article 17 paragraph 1, subparagraph (d), according to which "the Court shall determine that a case is inadmissible where: ... (it) is not of sufficient gravity to justify further action by the Court".[9]

Equally important is that all proceedings have to respect the rights and liberties of suspects, accused and sentenced persons as much as the applicable law does not (expressly) permit limitations as unavoidable.

Considering the stages through which crimes and the procedures for their investigation and prosecution develop, prevention in the broadest sense should be promoted practically at all phases.

The mere *planning* and *preparation* of crimes is, in general, not punishable, except in very rare cases,[10] and may be difficult to detect. But, taking influence at such an early stage can be one of the most effective ways to prevent crimes; because no *concrete* harm has yet been done nor are specific values *directly* endangered. The period of time in which such an influence can be taken effectively, may be short or long. Anyhow, it appears to be worthwhile to concentrate already at this stage on corresponding cases, because successful interferences then prevent for sure violations of legally protected values and interests.

The *attempt* to commit a crime is, in general, the stage at which the punishability of a behaviour starts, independent of the fact, in which way an attempt may be defined. To deter from further action at that stage means that a more or less concrete *danger* to legally protected values and interests has been stopped or otherwise avoided, before it has developed to a *violation* of such values or interests. Prevention should, therefore, concentrate also on this phase, which finally ends with the completion of the crime.

A completed crime, which could not be prevented, needs reaction of the society, in order to demonstrate the validity of the law by its application: Repression to avoid repetition. International criminal law, a

---

[9] For more details see Sh. Williams in: O. Triffterer (ed.), *Commentary*, *supra* note 4, Article 17, margin No. 25 and for a comparable discretion of the Prosecutor M. Bergsmo, *ibid*, Article 15, margin Nos. 30 and 31. See also O. Triffterer, *Legal and Political Implications of the Domestic Ratification and Implementation Process*, in: C. Kreß/F. Lattanzi, *The ICC Statute and Domestic Legal Orders. European and Southern African Views on Implementation. Volume I Constitutional Issues*, 2000, forthcoming.

[10] See, for instance, for Austria §§151, 175, 227, 239 and 244 StGB, but also 277, 278, and 278a. For the theoretical structure of definitions of crimes shifting criminal responsibility to a behaviour *before* the attempted crime see O. Triffterer, *Strafrecht*, *supra* note 5, chapter 3 margin Nos. 120 et seq. and chapter 15 margin Nos. 20 et seq. See also O. Triffterer, in O. Triffterer (ed.) *StGB-Kommentar*, System und Praxis, 1998, §§277, 278 und 278a.

rather new and rapidly extending field in the past 100 years, especially needs its permanent confirmation by enforcement, in order to develop an awareness for what should be avoided in the interest of values inherent to the international community as a whole, and thus protecting not only this community as such, but also its members, meaning States *and* individual persons. This is demonstrated, for instance, by the protected value, "security of mankind", covering the whole and all individuals constituting this protected target.

Society's reactions to such crimes are investigation, prosecution, trial and finally - if the case is not aquitted - conviction and punishment or one of the methods of diversion, substituting punishment at least in many *national* criminal justice systems for minor crimes or those of medium gravity. All these criminal proceedings serve, at each stage, the purpose to avoid repetition of criminal behaviour in the broadest sense and, thus, to prevent further crimes by restorative justice.[11]

Every single stage of a crime or a criminal proceeding needs a specific, individual approach to fight criminality. In order to be most effective, it has to be adapted to the concrete situation, the phase of the crime and, for instance, the alternatives provided for in criminal proceedings, as, for example, a non confirmation of charges by the Pre-Trial Chamber, according to Article 61, paragraph 7, subparagraphs (b) and (c).

3. Combined Efforts "to Contribute to the Prevention of such Crimes"

All the different approaches mentioned above are, in principle, equally important to successfully "fight" criminality, because only combined efforts by substantive and procedural law, inside and outside the criminal justice system, may result in a fruitful contribution to the prevention of such crimes. The Rome Statute mentions the prevention of crimes falling within the jurisdiction of the Court in paragraph 5 of its Preamble. It follows from the context that to prevent crimes under international criminal law is the main purpose and the mission of the Court, in order to guarantee "lasting respect for the enforcement of international justice", paragraph 11.

Preambular paragraph 5 comprises the whole variety and complexity of methods and means available to society and especially those

---

[11] For the concept of restorative justice see, for instance, A. Ceretti/G. Mannozzi, *Restorative Justice - Theoretical Aspects and Applied Models*, paper presented to the Ninth Joint Colloqium on Offenders and Victims: Accountability and Fairness in the Justice Process, Courmayeur, 24-26 September 1999 and to the UN Congress in Vienna, *supra* note 6. See also G. Kaiser, *Brauchen wir in Europa neue Konzepte der Kriminalpolitik*, Zeitschrift für Rechtspolitik, (ZRP) 2000, 151.

provided for the prevention of such crimes in the Rome Statute. It starts with the determination "to put an end to impunity for the perpetrators of these crimes", a formulation which has two meanings: The more obvious one of suspects, having to face investigation, prosecution and, if convicted, punishment, appears from the context with paragraph 4; accordingly, "the most serious crimes of concern to the international community as a whole must not go unpunished and ... their effective prosecution must be ensured by taking measures at the national level and by enhancing international cooperation". The wording, "must not go unpunished", seems to refer only to crimes already committed, an interpretation backed by the following demand for "their effective prosecution".

However, at a closer second sight, the attitude of preambular paragraph 5 to crimes under international law appears in a broader context. "To put an end to impunity" by establishing an international criminal jurisdiction, has not only to be interpreted as repressing (already) committed crimes, but also as giving a signal to all *potential* perpetrators: They are informed about the existence of the Court and its mission, not to let them go unpunished. By the context with the whole Statute, especially with Articles 17 and 20, paragraph 3, they will be aware that even if their *domestic* jurisdiction is under their control or for any other reason "unwilling or unable to genuinely" prosecute and punish them, their abuses of power may lead to their individual criminal responsibility before the *International* Criminal Court (ICC), independent of their official capacity, as provided for in Article 27. This expectation may deter them from committing crimes, which, at the domestic level, may not even be punishable or will *de facto* not be prosecuted and thus would lead to impunity, if the ICC would not take care of such situations.[12]

The words in paragraph 5 of the Preamble, "thus to *contribute* to the prevention of such crimes", further imply that avoiding impunity by establishing jurisdiction and especially the ICC, is *just one* of the means to prevent such crimes and not the only one.[13] The reference in preambular paragraph 6, to "the duty of every State to exercise its criminal jurisdiction over those responsible for international crimes", confirms that criminal law was right from its beginning established as *ultima ratio* for the protection of

---

[12] Sceptical with regard to such a deterrent effect with regard to the core crimes H. Jäger, *Makroverbrechen als Gegenstand des Völkerstrafrechts*, in: G. Hanke/G. Stuby (eds.) 1995, 325 (340), but, see also 347 et seq. as well as B. Broomhall in: O. Triffterer, *Commentary, supra* note 4, Article 22 margin No. 9. See also below B I and with regard to Germany S. Wirth/J.C. Harder, *Die Anpassung des deutschen Rechts an das Römische Statut des Internationalen Strafgerichtshofes aus Sicht deutscher Nichtregierungsorganisationen*, ZRP 2000, 144.

[13] Emphasis added; see also O. Triffterer, in: O. Triffterer (ed.), *Commentary, supra* note 4, Preamble margin No. 15.

the highest values and interests of society, when all other legal possibilities seemed to be not equally suitable to sufficiently guarantee them. Therefore, one of the justifications for criminal law and punishment is that without their existence and enforcement, such violations could not, with a similar degree of probability be prevented.

However, the way in which criminal law fulfils this function best, has always been disputed. Beccaria and Lombroso are, here in Italy, the best examples, because during their time, they expressed almost revolutionary ideas on how to prevent crimes. Until now the theory of *special-* and *general* prevention is disputed; the latter appears to be only justifiable when the penalty imposed is not measured by its (alleged) *deterrent* effect on *potential* perpetrators, but in correspondence with the individual guilt of the person sentenced. The "gravity of the crime and the individual circumstances of the convicted person", also have to be taken into account, Article 78 paragraph 1 as well as Article 77 paragraph 1, subparagraph (b). Thus, conviction and determination of sentences shall demonstrate that it is worthwhile to obey the law and, at the end of the day, it does not "pay", meaning to be not sufficiently profitable, to commit crimes. This so-called "positive general prevention", therefore, is aiming at confirming loyalty to law ("Rechtstreue") and, thus, developing awareness and the conscience of the public in favour of respecting legally protected values and interests by avoiding crimes.[14]

The Statute further presupposes that "commanders and other superiors", with regard to "forces under his or her effective command and control, or effective authority and control" (the latter also with regard to subordinates), have the "power to prevent and repress" the "commission or to submit the matter to the competent authorities for investigation and prosecution", Article 28(a)(ii) and (b)(iii). This is a confirmation of what the Carnegie Endowment for International Peace has concluded in its above mentioned report, namely, that "the positions" mentioned in Article 27, as well as those in Article 28, are equipped with the power to prevent crimes.[15] The basis of this assumption is the fact that crimes under international law, are, by their very nature, not always, but quite often, committed by persons who are embodied in hierarchic structures,

[14] The contribution of J.Ch. Nemitz to this subject matter, *The purpose of Sentencing - a Comparison between Nuremberg and Rome*, which has been published in summary in Working Materials to the International Symposium: *The International Criminal Tribunal for the former Yugoslavia*, Opatja, 8 and 9 May, 2000, 144 et seq., published by the Croatian Law Center (CLC) and the Croatian Association of Criminal Science and Practice (HUKPP), could not be taken into consideration any more.

[15] See for the Report *supra* note 4.

independent of whether in a superior or a subordinated position[16] and, therefore, the latter are educated and, not rarely, (ab-)used to obey.

B. POSSIBILITIES AND LIMITS OF AN INTERNATIONAL CRIMINAL JURISDICTION

However, *in principle*, crimes under international law can be committed by everybody. But, *typically*, such crimes are committed by persons holding, because of an official capacity, a position of power on the domestic level, which they abuse, or perpetrators commit their atrocities at least with the consent or the (silent) toleration of persons holding legitimately or *de facto* such a position.[17] These appearances often make the *national* criminal justice system ineffective for the purpose, "to put an end to impunity for the perpetrators of these crimes", Preamble paragraph 5, because the State thus involved may not be willing or able to genuinely investigate or prosecute. At the same time, this structure limits the possibilities of *international* criminal law, "to contribute to the *prevention* of such crimes", because the international community has no executive forces of its own and, therefore, depends to a very great extent on the cooperation with States.

I. Differentiation between Micro- and Macro-Criminality?

1. This prevailing structure of crimes under international law characterizes one of the main differences between the so called *micro*-criminality on the *national*, in comparison with the *macro*-criminality on the *international* level.[18] However, both have in common that they are committed on some State territory independent of the fact, if macro-criminality is committed in times of peace, like, quite often crimes against humanity, or during an internal or international armed conflict, like war crimes. Since, in so far, competing jurisdiction between the national and the international level exists, complementarity is one of the fundamental principles of the Rome Statute. This is expressed, mainly, in paragraph 10 of the Preamble and in Article 1. Complementarity shall guarantee, together with the principle of universality, that crimes committed by abusing an "official capacity", shall

---

[16] See below B I and III 1.
[17] For details see O. Triffterer, in: O. Triffterer (ed.), *Commentary*, *supra* note 4, Article 27 margin Nos. 13 et seq.
[18] See H. Jäger in G. Hanke/G. Stuby, *supra* note 13, and for additional relevant publications of H. Jäger see footnote 1.

not go unpunished, because such perpetrators cannot expect any more impunity in others than their own State or to receive asylum anywhere. And, finally, if States are unwilling or unable to investigate and prosecute such crimes, the ICC has jurisdiction, according to Article 17 or 20, paragraph 3.

The end of World War I and II, as well as the end of many authoritarian regimes and dictatorships, especially in Eastern Europe and South Africa, have brought this situation worldwide to the attention of public opinion. The German endeavours to cope with their past after World War II have created a broad discussion on the question, how to account Nazi crimes, committed collectively "pursuant to or in furtherance of a State or organizational policy", by and within the Nazi regime, to individual perpetrators. Besides the expressions mentioned, others like mega-criminality and mega-dimension of crimes have been created, to better understand such appearances and to distinguish these from general criminality.[19]

The discussion has been revitalized after the unification of East and West Germany.[20] It was considered, among other issues, whether these new expressions should characterize only crimes, *amounting to a dimension* so far *unimaginable*, or those, which were *committed collectively* by a larger group of persons as a part of social conflicts and processes in society. It was further argued, the dependence of individual behaviour upon events appearing outside of his or her sphere of influence on the macro-level, would be of such a predominant character that it appears necessary to differentiate such crimes from "normal criminality". Herbert Jäger, for instance, concluded that *genocide, war crimes* and *crimes against humanity* could only be committed when the political framework in a State would permit such behaviour *and never isolated by persons* and *not even by groups or organizations*, unless *the State provides a criminogene*

---

[19] For the quotation see Article 7, paragraph 2, subparagraph (a). For the new expressions see H. Schüler-Springorum, *Kriminalpolitik für Menschen*, 1991, 235 et seq. See for South Africa, for instance, G. Wehrle, *Neue Wege. Die südafrikanische Wahrheitskommission und die Aufarbeitung von schweren Menschenrechtsverletzungen* in: P. Bock/E. Wolfrum (eds), *Umkämpfte Vergangenheit*, 1999, 269 et seq.

[20] See, for instance, E.-J. Lampe, *Systemunrecht und Unrechtssysteme*, in: Zeitschrift für gesamte Strafrechtswissenschaft 106 (1994) 683 ff, G. Jacobs, *Vergangenheitsbewältigung durch Strafrechtfrage? Zur Leistungsfähigkeit des Strafrechts nach einem politischen Umbruch* in: J. Isensee (ed.), *Vergangenheitsbewältigung durch Recht*, 1992, 37 and P. Bock/E. Wolfrum (eds), *Umkämpfte Vergangenheit*, 1999. See especially H. Jäger, *supra* note 19. See also O. Triffterer, *Was kann das Völkerstrafrecht zur Bewältigung der Regierungskriminalität in der DDR beitragen?* in: E.-J. Lampe (ed.) *Die Verfolgung von Regierungskriminalität der DDR nach der Wiedervereinigung*, 1993, 131 et seq.

exceptional situation as the condition under which such crimes can develop.[21]

This may be true for many appearances of such crimes in history and in the future. But international criminal law has been established with the mission, to protect the highest values of the international community as a whole against grave violations. It, therefore, has to fight such criminality on all levels, including those, where they may first appear: in the minds and actions of individuals.[22] This is the reason why international criminal law includes, as a contribution to the prevention of such crimes, the aim, to hold every person *individually* responsible for committing or otherwise participating in one of these core crimes. Such a responsibility should not depend upon a participation of others nor be interpreted as being *necessarily*, for instance, a part of a plan or policy of a larger group of persons or dependent on exceptional criminogene situations, provided by a State. Because, also the so-called "small fish", acting on their own initiative and without the support of others, may by individual acts endanger international peace and security of mankind. This has been experienced not only by the assassination of Sarajevo 1914, but also by the fact that war crimes and criminal violence "against any civilian population", Article 7, may lead on the battlefields and, generally in society, to an escalation of armed conflicts and, for instance, atrocities against the opposite party.

It is true that such single acts, at least *in principle*, *can* be dealt with adequately by the *domestic* legal systems. But, again, history and the endeavours of some States to exclude cases of individual atrocities *in any event* from the *international* jurisdiction, at least as far as their own nationals are concerned, for instance, with the help of Article 124, should raise suspicion. It is preferable, to support the notion of international criminal law, to hold everybody *individually* responsible even if acting alone and only assign the international criminal *jurisdiction* for some crimes *in particular* to those embodied into a broader concept.

Exactly this policy has been pursued at the Rome Conference: the definition of genocide is in this regard unlimited and the definition of crimes against humanity contain such a limitation, to exclude *isolated* acts of *individuals*. However, the latter was heavily disputed in Rome. War crimes, therefore, are not limited. It is only mentioned, that the Court shall have jurisdiction "*in particular*" when such crimes are committed "as part of a plan or policy or as part of a large-scale commission of such crimes". The reason for this dispute was that in exceptional cases even single acts of

---

[21] *Supra* note 13, 327.

[22] The commission of genocide by individual perpetrators has been accepted by the German "Bundesgerichtshof" in its decision 30 April 1999, Juristenzeitung 1999, 1176 et seq., annotated by G. Wehrle, *ibid*, 1181 et seq.

an individual may raise the concern of the international community as a whole, because they may endanger international peace and security or involve such abuses of power, which may not be dealt with properly on the national level.

But, both regulations in Articles 7 and 8 do not exclude that crimes defined in these two groups, which do not fulfil these narrowing elements, may be investigated and prosecuted on the *national* level. Complementarity means that national jurisdiction, in principle, shall have priority with regard to crimes falling within the jurisdiction of the Court. But it does not mean that States are excluded to investigate and prosecute according to a broader concept crimes against humanity and war crimes, as long as their domestic legal systems provide the necessary jurisdictional basis for such proceedings.

For genocide, none of these two "solutions" is provided in the Statute. On the opposite, elements like those contained in Article 7, "as part of a widespread or systematic attack", meaning "pursuant to or in furtherance of a State or organizational policy", where *expressly* excluded, when drafting and finally adopting Article 6 by the Rome Conference. Not even the very careful emphasis in Article 8 that *the jurisdiction of the Court* for war crimes should be "*in particular* when committed as part of a plan or policy or as part of a large-scale commission of such crimes", was accepted for genocide.

A comparison of these three Articles, therefore, clearly indicates that, with regard to genocide, any comparable limitation is not to be found in Article 6. This leads to the effect that such a limitation cannot be introduced now with the help of the Elements of Crimes, because they "shall be consistent with this Statute", Article 9, paragraph 3. To narrow the notion of genocide, as already established by Article 6, is therefore not admissible.[23]

This opinion does not deny the fact that genocide is, in practice, often committed within a political framework of a State that permits such behaviour. But acts of genocide are characterized by the individual *intent*, "to destroy in whole or in part, a ... group, as such". It is this *additional* intent, directed on something to appear in the future, which makes genocide, even if committed by a single act of killing one person, so dangerous for peace and security of mankind. It *could* set fire to an idea,

---

[23] *Ibid.* For the first reading of the Elements of genocide see Preparatory Commission for the International Criminal Court, Elements of Crimes, UN-Doc. PCNICC/2000/L.1/Rev.1/ Add.2 where an element for all cases of genocide is drafted, reading as follows: "The conduct took place in the context of a manifest pattern of similar conduct directed against that group or was conduct that could itself effect such destruction", p. 6. For details to this issue see O. Triffterer, *Implications*, *supra* note 10.

which has to be suppressed, but nevertheless *potentially* exists in many minds: violent discriminations of a group, quite often a minority, protected by Article 6, committed with the expectation, to destroy this group "in whole or in part, ... as such". Therefore, such an intent and its demonstration by one of the criminal acts listed in Article 6(a)-(e), have to be prevented, wherever they appear in their first form of the smallest crime against this group: an individual act against one individual member of this group, executed with such an intent, going beyond the harm that has already been committed.

It is this preventive aspect which should not remain unconsidered when discussing, whether crimes of genocide falling within the jurisdiction of the Court, should be limited in a way, similar to those adopted at the Rome Conference for crimes against humanity and war crimes. Because those who believe that the core crimes, including genocide, could *only* be committed when the political framework in a State would permit such behaviour and never isolated from criminogene exceptional situations as a condition under which such crimes can develop, at the same time deny, or at least raise serious doubt, whether because of this different structure such crimes could be prevented at all and the perpetrators rehabilitated.[24]

However, this assertion is not convincing. Crimes are committed by *natural persons* and not by abstract entities, as has already been stated at Nuremberg and permanently thereafter. And human beings, who are held responsible, because they have demonstrated their free will by deciding *to break* the law, when committing their criminal action, as assumed by legal theory, must be conceded to be able, because of the same free will, to change their mind and to obey the law in the future and be independent of any State policy.

They have to be influenced and educated in this direction for preventive reasons. Even though it may be difficult to oppose State policy, there is no reason visible why this should not be possible at all. On the contrary, just because the particular intent demonstrated by committing genocide is especially dangerous, we have to invest all our efforts to prevent with all means such criminal actions, wherever and whenever they appear, and independent of whether committed collectively or by a single act of only one individual - which may or may not, eventually correspond with State or organizational policy. The mission in such a case is to avoid that the particular, additional intent, expressed perhaps in an individual act of one person, killing, for instance, just one victim, may inspire somebody to continue this line, perhaps by intensified criminal actions, setting the

[24] H. Jäger, *Makrokriminalität. Studien zur Kriminologie kollektiver Gewalt*, 1989; see also *idem*, *supra* note 13.

particular intent of a perpetrator into praxis. To avoid such a development is the aim of the specific structure of such definitions of crimes: to combine a rather small criminal act with a rather broad and far-reaching intent, and not to wait till this intent has been realized, but to punish before: "vorgelagerte Strafbarkeit".

This mental element is not a *specific* intent in the sense of "Absicht" as provided in the German Penal Code, §220a and in Austria, §321. Correspondingly, it is in both countries disputed, whether the expression "Absicht" with regard to genocide describes an intensified will or just expresses that the intent of the perpetrator (dolus directus ersten Grades) goes beyond the realization of the material elements. Such a type of structure for the definitions of crimes was, for a long time, called "Absichtsdelikte", to characterize that the intent of the perpetrator was going further than the material elements. This was not a demand for an intensified will. Now, those types of crimes are more often called crimes with an extensive intent (erweiterter Vorsatz) or a mental element, going beyond the material elements which have to be established ("überschießende Innentendenz").

In addition, Germany and Austria would go beyond the wording of the Genocide Convention, if they interpret the wording "Absicht" in the strict sense, as expressed in §5 paragraph 3 of the Austrian Penal Code. Such an interpretation would also contradict all later documents referring to the definition of genocide in the Genocide Convention, like the Statutes for the ICTY, the ICTR and the ICC. Intent to destroy covers all degrees of this mental element, even though in the Akayesu case the ICTR and in the Jelisic case the ICTY demand a higher degree. According to the wording in these Statutes, any kind of intent is sufficient, even if not fulfilling the German and Austrian demands, if these would be interpreted as an *intensified* expression of the will of the perpetrator to achieve his or her aim, to destroy the group as such. Decisive is (only) that the perpetrator commits his criminal act with an intent, going beyond this commission. This is the particular mental element, well known, for instance, in Austria for crimes, where quite often such an "erweiterter Vorsatz" (überschießende Innentendenz) does not demand a specific intent as an intensified expression of the will of the perpetrator. To avoid future, greater harm, this first appearance of a "guilty mind" in reality, has to be investigated and prosecuted before it has a chance to be set into reality.[25]

---

[25] L. Katz, *Bad Acts and Guilty Minds: Conundrums of the Crimnal Law*, 1987. For the notion of *specific* intent see, for instance, F. Nowakowski, in E. Foregger/F. Nowakowski (eds.), *Wiener Kommentar*, 1984, §5, margin Nos. 5-9; especially V. Liebscher, *ibid*, §321, margin No. 25, where he emphazises that "Absicht" does not correspond with "intent", mentioned in the Genocide Convention. See also O. Triffterer, *Österreichisches Strafrecht*,

The above considered scepticism against macro-criminality as being out of the range of criminal measures to prevent crimes, has been weakened since the establishment of the ICTY and the ICTR and the adoption of the Statute of the permanent International Criminal Court.[26] One small sign is the voluntary surrender of several indicted persons to the ICTY. The main concern now, therefore, is to develop detailed principles to account such crimes to individual perpetrators. It is claimed that the traditional pattern and means to establish individual criminal responsibility are not sufficiently suitable to comprise the whole scale of concepts and underlying structures of such crimes, characterized especially by abuse of power, political influence, mutual assistance, dependence, encouragement and the tendency of such perpetrators to outdo each other.[27]

We, therefore, have to concentrate further on the question of how endeavours to contribute to the prevention of such crimes can be adapted to the needs of these new criminological appearances, in order to achieve the best possible prevention of such crimes. Information and, in addition,

---

supra note 5, Chapter 9, margin Nos. 56 and 73 and for the two corresponding demands in the German and Austrian Penal Codes see O. Triffterer, *supra* note 10. The text of the German translation for the Genocide Convention seems with regard to *internal* aspects binding, but not with regard to international aspects, as V. Liebscher has already emphazised. This is not surprising, since the notion of intent covers also the specific intent. Correspondingly the American Model Penal Code demands for genocide "specific" intent. See for details to this issue A.K.A. Greenewalt, *Rethinking of Genocidal intent: The case of a Knowledge-Based Interpretation*, 99, Columbia Law Review, 2259. How much translations, even if they are official, can deviate from the official languages of the UN, can be seen by Article 30 of the Rome Statute. "Intent and knowledge" has been translated into German by "vorsätzlich and wissentlich", which is insofar incorrect, as each concept of Vorsatz includes as one of the possible form "Wisentlichkeit". For the German translation as well as the English, Spanish and French version see Ch. Rosbaud/O. Triffterer, *Rome Statute of the International Criminal Court, including the Final Act*, 2000, I 4 page 28 of the German translation.

[26] See, for a great amount of scepticism, especially H. Jäger in: G. Hanke/G. Stuby, *supra* note 11, 347.For the development towards the ICC see Ch. Bassiouni as well as Ph. Kirsch, Preface and Introduction to O. Triffterer (ed.), Commentary, *supra* note 5.

[27] For details see, for instance, K. Marxen, Beteiligung an schwerem systematischen Unrecht. Bemerkungen zu einer völkerstrafrechtlichen Straftatlehre in: K. Lüderssen (ed.) Aufgeklärte Kriminalpolitik oder Kampf gegen das Böse?, Band III, 1998, 220. See also K. Ambos in: O. Triffterer (ed.) *Commentary, supra* note 4, Article 25. As valuable as the discussion was not only for coping with the German past, its importance for the jurisdiction of the Court lies in having drawn the attention to the question, that crimes under international law need very careful considerations before they can be accounted to an individual person. The jurisprudence of the ICTY and the ICTR have taken care of these peculiarities as far as they were an issue in specific cases. But at the same time, they have demonstrated, that adaptation of concepts of crimes from the national level to the international level is possible, especially after the experiences made, for instance, with economical or environmental crimes.

psychological training, for instance, of military personnel, especially commanders and other superiors, as already established in some armies, appear to be one of the necessary measures.

2. Looking for such divergency from *traditional* structures, to establish individual criminal responsibilities under international law, we have to keep in mind that macro-criminality, in its most frequent appearances, is orientated on a sort of "collective responsibility", in the sense that each individual contribution is a constructive and often indispensable part of the whole, albeit the persons participating in such actions may be interchangeable. In addition, the whole functioning sometimes may depend on something which is difficult to assign to individuals. It can be described as "a State or organizational policy", Article 7 paragraph 1 in connection with the definition in paragraph 2, subparagraph (a), trying to achieve political goals by abuse of power, or, more neutral, merely with the help of "a plan or policy", or by acting as a "part of a widespread or systematic commission of such crimes", Article 8 paragraph 1.

This structure may make measures to prevent such crimes extremely difficult, especially as long as individual perpetrators believe they would contribute their part to the endeavours of their State to achieve *legitimate* aims and to realize legitimate interests. But the experience that persons acting as willing or compliant tools, may be almost at any time substituted by another person, whenever one or more of them may be convinced not to commit or to participate in such crimes any more, does not free us from trying to address every single one of them, in order to prevent crimes. On the opposite, the experience that persons acting in a chain of hierarchic structures or in group activities, for whatever reasons drop out of such social or military mass-psychological constraints, disproves the above-mentioned theory that such crimes could not be prevented and those perpetrators not rehabilitated. We may need more efforts and have to develop new methods to achieve such effects with perpetrators used to exercise - and to enjoy - their personal power. But, *in principle*, the situation and the task of international criminal law and its jurisdiction is not different from the mission of criminal law on the domestic level.

3. Looking at the differentiation between macro- and micro-criminality, we also have to keep in mind that *national* criminal law is aiming at the prevention of harm to those legally protected values and interests, which are inherent to the *national* legal order and which the national legislator deems necessary to be protected, as *ultima ratio*, by domestic *criminal* law. *International* criminal law has to protect the legal values inherent to the community of nations, especially, "peace, security (of mankind) and the well-being of the world".[28] Crimes under international criminal law thus endanger or violate values and interests of a macro-society, compared with the micro-value system on the *national* level. This leads to an obligation of all members of this society, to do their best to contribute to the prevention of such crimes. One of these means is to investigate and prosecute crimes falling within the jurisdiction of the Court, according to the principle of universality within the domestic legal systems, to which the jurisdiction of the Court is (only) complementary.

Furthermore, crimes under international law may also concern legally protected *individual* values and interests, especially human rights. They have been developed as rights against the State, originally laid down in and protected by the respective *national* legal systems, exclusively. But since States did not always grant these rights *de facto*, their *international* acknowledgement and enforcement appeared more and more to be unavoidable. Now, international *criminal* law is challenged to supply an additional, but *subsidiary* protection as far as States do not guarantee and protect those rights sufficiently.[29] Such international enforcement mechanisms are especially needed to protect individual rights against threats and violations by the State itself, because in such cases criminal justice on the *national* level may *de facto* not be available or not to be achieved. Preventive measures, therefore, have to be directed, especially in such cases, not only against individual perpetrators, but, *in addition*, against States respectively against their organs, as far as they engage in such crimes or do not sufficiently prosecute and punish them. This is expressed, in particular, in Article 25 paragraph 4.

II. Additional Criminological Peculiarities of Crimes under International Law

Stimulated by the discussion about the differences between micro- and macro-criminality, the consideration of a few additional peculiarities may

[28] Paragraph 3 of the Preamble. For details see O. Triffterer in: *Commentary, supra* note 4, Preamble margin Nos. 9 et seq.

[29] For details see O. Triffterer, *Von "Nürnberg" zu einem internationalen Gerichtshof zur Verfolgung der Kriegsverbrechen im ehemaligen Jugoslawien - Zum Schutz der Menschenrechte durch das Völkerstrafrecht* - in: H. Neisser (ed.) *Menschenrechte als politischer Auftrag*, 1993, 61 (77 et seq.); *idem Preliminary Remarks: The Permanent International Criminal Court - Ideal and Reality* in: O. Triffterer (ed.), *Commentary, supra* note 4, Part 1, margin Nos. 20 et seq.

be helpful for searching the most effective prevention and repression of such crimes.

1. Perpetrators Caught in Hierarchic Structures

Article 72 clearly indicates that perpetrators of crimes within the jurisdiction of the Court may have been engaged in national security interests of their States or are at least connected with such interests, when committing their acts.[30] Otherwise, such interest could not be the reason for withholding information needed to prove "the existence or non-existence of a fact", which may be "relevant and necessary for the establishment of the guilt or innocence of the accused".[31]

The concept of macro-criminality, as considered above, assumes, in addition, that individuals, quite often, are integrated into hierarchic structures of the State in a way that may make it difficult to precisely locate their *individual* responsibility for what may appear as a common action, a policy of a State or its institutions. The Statute takes this aspect into consideration. Individual criminal responsibility directly under international law is a well established principle, referred to and serving as the foundation for every *international* criminal jurisdiction and now for the jurisdiction of the Court. This notion is expressed in the heading of Article 25 and in different paragraphs, for instance, by their wordings, "jurisdiction over natural persons" and "individually responsible and liable for punishment". Article 25 refers, in addition, to crimes committed "jointly with another or through another person" or "by a group of persons acting with a common purpose", taking into consideration that such common actions are quite typical for many appearances of all groups of macro-criminality; the last aspect also forms the basis for paragraph 4, stating that "individual criminal responsibility shall not affect the responsibility of States under international law".[32]

---

[30] For details see, for instance, R. Dixon/H. Duffy, in: O. Triffterer (ed.), *Commentary, supra* note 4, Article 72; see also O. Triffterer, *Security Interests of the Community of States, Basis and Justification of an International Criminal Jurisdiction*, in: H. Roggeman/P. Šarcevic (eds), *National Security and International Criminal Justice*, 2000 (forthcoming).

[31] See, for the quotations, Article 72, Chapeau and paragraph 7, subparagraph (a) (iii).

[32] See, for the quotations, especially paragraphs 1, 2, 3, subparagraph (d) and the already mentioned paragraph 4. In addition, individual criminal responsibility is assumed by the wording in paragraph 5 of the Preamble "for the perpetrators", in paragraph 6, "jurisdction over those responsible for international crimes", Article 1, "jurisdiction over persons", Article 20, "no person shall be ...", three times "a person shall not be ..." in Article 22 as well Articles 23 and 24. See also K. Ambos in: O. Triffterer (ed.) *Commentary, supra* note 4, Article 25, margin No. 37 and O. Triffterer *Prosecution of States for the Crimes of State*, 67 Revue Internationale de Droit Pénale (1996) 341 et seq; *idem. Der ständige*

Common actions, as mentioned above, quite often presuppose that every individual perpetrator is more or less integrated into the organizational system and the policy pursued. In many cases, both can only function, if every link of the chain is a reliable part of the plan. Being aware of this responsibility for the whole course of events, the participants sometimes have the feeling to be and typically are "caught as an indispensable part in hierarchic structures". This may not only increase his or her selfconsciousness. It also makes it difficult not to cooperate in the provided or even assigned way, because any divergency might endanger the realization of the whole concept. To stop or to step out of such criminal activities may, therefore, be more difficult as in cases of micro-criminality.[33]

This interrelationship and mutual dependence is expressed, for instance, in Article 27, "[i]rrelevance of official capacity"; accordingly, "[t]his Statute shall apply equally to all persons without any distinction based on official capacity". The merely exemplary enumeration of official capacities starts with a "Head of State or Government" and ends with "a government official", thus, not excluding any other official capacity the perpetrator may have. Whatever this position may be, legally or *de facto*, it "shall in no case exempt a person from criminal responsibility under this Statute ...".[34]

The chain of hierarchic structures appears even more visible in Article 28, "[r]esponsibility of commanders and other superiors"; there the connection is established between those finally executing the crimes to the next "commanders or other superiors". But, as long as an "effective command and control, or effective authority and control" exists, the chain of responsibility is not interrupted; it goes straight through up to the highest level of command and authority; in such cases, criminal responsibility of none of those persons engaged "in between", is excluded. They are all, if they have committed no further action, at least responsible for negligent omission to interfere and to prevent such acts or to repress them, as stated in Article 28(a)(ii).

Reference to the chain of persons being "caught in hierarchic structures" is also made in Article 33, "[s]uperior orders and prescription of law". There it is stated that, whoever acts at the low end of the chain of a hierarchic structure is, in principle, (and independent of the responsibility

---

Internationale Strafgerichtshof - Anspruch und Wirklichkeit, in: K.H. Gössel/O. Triffterer (eds.) *Gedächtnisschrift für Heinz Zipf*, 1999, 493 (505 et seq.).

[33] But these difficulties do not make prevention impossible and, therefore, should not discourage any research or endeavours in this direction.

[34] For details see O. Triffterer in: O. Triffterer (ed.), *Commentary*, *supra* note 4, Article 27 margin No. 17.

of the commander or superior), responsible, even if "only" obeying the law or a superior order. The exception mentioned in this Article does not touch this principle, which can be seen especially with regard to genocide and crimes against humanity, for which orders are always *presumed* to be "manifestly unlawful".[35]

It should not be left unmentioned in this context that most of the crimes within the jurisdiction of the Court are not committed *directly* by Heads of State or Government, but by subordinated persons, acting more or less as "willing tools", as demonstrated during the holocaust. They are at the bottom of the hierarchy and often especially trained or even paid to obey. These are not the types of perpetrators the ICC has to deal with, as long as they may be properly treated by national criminal (military) jurisdiction. However, with regard to the prevention of crimes under international law, it is worthwhile to focus on this group as well. Because, if *they all* refuse to execute "a State or organizational policy" or plan, no such crimes would be committed in most of the cases. In addition, this hierarchic structure has to be kept in mind when dealing with those perpetrators in power positions, which are mainly responsible for the policy and the institutionalization of abuses of power.

2. Power Positions on All Levels

a) It is quite usual that perpetrators commit their crimes from an *individual* position of power over victims or other people's property.[36] But, those positions of power, which are typical for the commission of crimes under *international* law, are based on *institutionalized* power, for instance of the State, and thus, not even comparable with the power of criminal groups or organizations. Looking at the definitions of crimes listed in Article 6(c)-(e), "[d]eliberately inflicting on the group conditions", "[i]mposing measures intended to prevent birth within the group" and "[f]orcibly transferring children", confirms that the perpetrator must *de facto* have the possibility to enforce the conditions mentioned on at least parts of a *group*. This presupposes a stronger power position as needed, for instance, to commit genocide by murder or an ordinary robbery.

A comparable position of power is needed to commit crimes according to Article 7 paragraph 1, subparagraphs (d), "[d]eportation or

---

[35] *Idem, ibid.* Article 33 margin No. 30.

[36] For details see O. Triffterer, *Kriminologische Erscheinungsformen des Machtmissbrauchs und Möglichkeiten zu ihrer Bekämpfung*, Zeitschrift für Rechtsvergleichung (ZfRV) 1991, 184 et seq.; *idem., Acts of Violence and International Criminal Law - A New Position of Power to Fight Abuse of Power?*, Croatian Annual of Criminal Law and Practice, 1997, 811 (818 et seq., with further references).

forcible transfer of population", and (h), "[p]ersecution against any identifiable group or collectivity".[37] In addition, *all* crimes against humanity only fall within the jurisdiction of the Court, "when committed as part of a widespread or systematic attack", as defined in paragraph 2, subparagraph (a). But, this element can be fulfilled also by subordinates, who merely obey and therefore do not hold any position of power.

Some of the war crimes defined in Article 8 presuppose similar positions of power, for instance, paragraph 2, subparagraph (a)(iv), "[e]xtensive destruction and appropriation of property" or "[a]ttacking and bombarding" in the sense of subparagraph (b)(v). The jurisdiction of the Court is, in addition, limited to war crimes only, "when committed as part of a plan or policy or as part of a large-scale commission of such crimes". But here also many persons commit such crimes, for instance, as part of the plan, who do not hold any position of power at all.[38]

Perpetrators of crimes fulfilling the conditions just mentioned, raise concern of the international community as a whole, because they act out of a position of power, more or less protected by its installation into the hierarchic structure of State institutions; the domestic criminal justice system may, therefore, not be impartial. Measures, aiming at the prevention of such crimes, therefore, have to give attention to the fact that the "plan or policy" may take on a life of its own. This may survive, even if individual perpetrators abstain from any further criminal action.

b) Common to many of these crimes is also that they are directed against persons, exposed to an unfettered discretion of those, having power over them or compared to whom they are at least in a much weaker physical and psychological position, like victims of torture, rape and other "outrages upon personal dignity". Article 8, paragraph 2, subparagraph (e)(xi) is based on this difference and protects expressly "persons who are in the power of another party to the conflict".[39]

But, such a position of power does not only exist between perpetrators committing the final act and victims or other protected targets. They are typical also *between perpetrators*, participating on different levels of hierarchic structures in the commission of such crimes. This is, for

[37] An exception is clearly Article 8 paragraph 2, subparagraph (b)(vii); subparagraph (xii) may be of the same character. It may need a position of power to enforce a declaration "no quarter shall be given". But, finally, the mere declaration completes the crime, even if later on not enforced.

[38] It rather is sufficient, if she or he wants to participate in such a plan or policy. For the opinion that "[p]lan, policy and scale are not elements of war crimes" see W.J. Fenrick, in O. Triffterer (ed.), *Commentary*, *supra* note 4, Article 8, margin No. 4 and with regard to the mentioned subparagraphs margin Nos. 14 and 52.

[39] See, for instance, A. Zimmermann, *ibid*, margin Nos. 322 and 323.

instance, expressed in Article 28 with regard to all "commanders and other superiors", participating in the chain of responsibility, as long as they fulfil the prerequisites for the application of this Article, which have already been mentioned above. Crimes within the jurisdiction of the Court are *typically* committed not by one or two persons related with each other in a chain of subordination, but by taking advantage of hierarchic structures which quite often involve more than two levels. If this is the case, every single person down to the bottom is equipped with a power which has to be abused in order that the crime can be committed. This is true also with regard to genocide, even though this core crime can also be committed, especially, as defined in Article 6(a) and (b), by a single person, holding no such position of power against a single victim.[40]

Such a chain between positions of power on all levels is presupposed equally in Article 27, as also already mentioned above. Both chains demonstrate that each person in hierarchic structures may have a double position of power: Direct in relation to the next subordinated official and indirect over the victims. The closer the person gets to the final execution of the crime, the more direct and therefore stronger, is his power position with regard to victims and other protected targets.[41]

3. National and International Criminal Jurisdiction Dealing with Abuse of Power

Completed crimes quite often appear as an abuse of power of the perpetrator over the victim or the protected legal values. On the *national* level such abuses can, *in principle*, be effectively prevented, or at least repressed, by the State, especially by its executive and judiciary bodies, because both have even international organised crime, at least partly, more or less under control.[42]

Difficult to achieve is such an effect, however, in those cases, in which the crime is part of a State policy and, therefore, the perpetrators may have a position of power in the respective State, dominating, or at least strongly influencing, the domestic criminal justice system. This is self-

---

[40] See, for instance, W.A. Schabas, *ibid*, Article 6, margin No. 4 with further references.

[41] See for the victims also below 4 and footnote 47.

[42] The difficulties in fighting international organized crimes are great and sometimes new measures like screen search (Rasterfahndung) and bugging operation (großer Lauschangriff) have to be discussed to see how much such grave interferences with personal liberty and privacy are needed to effectively prevent or repress such crimes. The same is true with regard to the increasing corruption of persons in official capacity in many States. See also W. Gropp (ed.), *Besondere Ermittlungsmaßnahmen zur Bekämpfung der organisierten Kriminalität*, 1993 and W. Gropp/B. Huber (eds) *Rechtliche Initiativen gegen organisierte Kriminalität*, 2000 (forthcoming).

evident for dictators and similar legal or de-facto power positions. But, even in democratic States, abuse of power by State organs or persons holding another "official capacity" in the sense of Article 27, not rarely give reason to complain that State organs do not sufficiently contribute to the prevention of such abuses or do not react properly to repress them. Cases annually reported by Amnesty International can serve as an example of how far-reaching and unpredictable such abuses of power can be.[43] In addition, domestic criminal jurisdiction may even be partial if someone has committed a crime without any participation of that State, but in its interest. This involvement or concern of the State itself makes it easy and may be a temptation to disguise the facts and thus bar *national* criminal jurisdiction. *International* criminal jurisdiction is, in such cases, neutral, independent and, thus, more reliable to guarantee a proper investigation and prosecution.

This connection of crimes under international law with persons holding positions of power on the domestic level and with State policy interests, is the reason why the Rome Statute provides that, if State jurisdiction is not willing or able to deal with such appearances genuinely, because there is a suspicion that the State itself is involved, the international community, as a whole, has the mandate to protect the victims.[44] International criminal jurisdiction has to deal with such cases also in order to restore peace through justice and, thus, to contribute to the prevention of such crimes, as already mentioned above.

However, it has to be kept in mind that this jurisdiction is complementary to the national jurisdiction of all States. Therefore, if one of these States exercises its jurisdiction according to the principle of universality "properly", there is no need to engage the Court.

---

[43] The annual reports of Amnesty International and other human rights organizations surprisingly complain about grave violations of human rights even in States where most of the world did not expect that such abuses of power could happen at all. I have to admit in shame, that Austria has been included in the latest Amnesty Reports as well.

[44] The "participation" of the State itself may appear in very different forms, not only in those mentioned in Article 25 paragraph 3 (a)-(e). One of the broadest concepts is command responsibility as described in Article 28, including individual responsibility for negligent omission. This accountability results to a criminal offence necessary to fight abuses of power on all levels. See for details W.J. Fenrick in: O. Triffterer (ed.) *Commentary, supra* note 4, Article 28, especially margin Nos. 12 et seq.

4. Perpetrators of Crimes under International Law and the Contribution of Victims to the Prevention and the Repression of Such Crimes

Perpetrators of crimes under international law may appear, at a first glance, as no different from those on the national level. However, if we consider that experience has proven the danger that power corrupts and absolute power corrupts absolutely, we are confronted with one element common to most of the perpetrators who commit a crime, which is punishable *directly* under international law. Such a position of power makes perpetrators quite often feel outstanding and incontestable and, therefore, it may be difficult to influence or persuade them to exercise their official capacity properly or to prohibit the abuse of such positions effectively.

In addition, victims of crimes under international law are quite often even more at the disposal or mercy of their perpetrators than victims of ordinary crimes. Everybody can more or less effectively protect himself against micro-criminality, like theft, especially with the help of State authorities. But victims of abuse of institutionalized (State-) power are mainly those who have no such power to protect them against State authorities and their representatives. In addition, such abuses are often not clearly visible and may occur secretly, thus making the estimated number of unknown cases even higher than in the average of domestic criminality, for instance, unknown disappearances or cases of rape. Again, the regrettable and terrible events around the ethnical cleansing on the territory of former Yugoslavia and especially in Kosovo, are only one example of world-wide comparable violations of human rights in many other States, victims of which are the poorest and powerless people, like in Burundi.

Further, it has to be taken into consideration, that, *in principle,* each of us, and especially young subordinates, are to a great extent susceptible to and tempted to participate in the commission of such crimes. This has not only been experienced during World War II, but also in many events happening since then all over the globe. We can see a similar "infectious" result when "bystanders" to crimes of violence keep more or less inactive in a way, appearing under the circumstances as an inspiring toleration, quite often amounting to a silent participation.[45]

Prevention appears also to be more difficult, since perpetrators of crimes under international law, may, until now, because of their official capacity, and the lack of a permanent international jurisdiction, believe that

[45] See for details Schwind/Gietl/Zwenger, *Der (non-helping) bystander-Effekt*, Kriminalistik 1991, 233. See also O. Triffterer, *Die gesellschaftspolitische Verpflichtung als Herausforderung der heutigen Juristen?*, Festvortrag Österreichischer Juristentag Salzburg 9.9.1997, in: Verhandlungen des 13. Österreichischen Juristentags, 1999 Eröffnungs- und Schlusssitzung, 25-71, especially II 2 a, text between footnotes 8 and 10.

they will not be held criminally responsible for such abuses. Such a conviction may lead to an increasing escalation making the individual, acting within a State policy programme, insensible, indifferent to, or at least, not sufficiently respectful for the rights of other human beings, especially when dealing with "the enemy". The permanent training in using deadly weapons necessarily favours such a rudeness, reduces the natural inhibition threshold of individuals and, thereby, makes all endeavours to prevent such crimes more difficult, even if the exercise always is labelled as preparing merely for "emergency situations".

Individual perpetrators, acting as part of a common plan or policy, may also be inspired by a psychological mass phenomenon, which may lead to progressive brutality and the tendency to be more violent than others. Such a trend makes it difficult for the individual to withdraw his or her participation, when the group leaves the sphere of legality in order to achieve advantages over the enemy. Such a situation is further promoted by the fact that potential victims may appear (and often are) to potential perpetrators as dangerous as *vice versa*. The interest to survive or to stay unhurt increases the willingness to interfere with the rights and interests of others, especially when the expectation to eliminate the enemy appears as to reduce all danger for the perpetrator himself and only actions prohibited under humanitarian law promise to bring the desired relief.

Motivating may also be the knowledge of fulfilling political demands, especially if an ordered suppression or ethnical cleansing is carried out, because of corresponding propaganda, to be (or is pretended as allegedly to be) in the interest of the State; lower ranking persons in the hierarchy may want to fulfil their task "correctly" in order to serve these interests, because they do not see their illegality. In the long run, it is, therefore, very difficult to predict who may be endangered to become a perpetrator of a crime, when exceptional and unexpected circumstances place him or her in a position, where an abuse of power may - at a first glance - appear to be in the interest of that State and other participants do not hesitate to proceed.

Equally unpredictable is who may be victimized at what time, where and why by such crimes. This has been demonstrated already by the NATO bombing in Yugoslavia and especially by the killing of people in the Chinese embassy in Belgrade. Sometimes, even *ex post* the scope of victimization may not be reconstructed precisely. The modern technique, used in Hiroshima and Nagasaki, led to an unlimited circle of victims. But, even in Nagasaki and Hiroshima, some potential victims were just accidentally not hurt. This demonstrates that we are all almost completely helpless against such situations, which we often do not even recognize as being "criminogen". The situation is in so far comparable with those concerning economical and environmental crimes.[46] Living in situations, like in Kosovo at the beginning of 1999, makes persons aware of the risk. But even if they flee, they may not escape from victimization if they are not quick enough or hindered to cross the border to a neighbouring State, willing to accept them. This makes it difficult to take precautions against being victimized.

In general, the fear to become a victim is considered to be unrealistic. But, this is not true with regard to international crimes. Their unpredictability must necessarily lead to fear, especially since no individual alone can do anything in any part of the world to escape this danger.

Specific emphasis should also be given to the fact, that individual victims of crimes under international criminal law, *in general*, do not contribute in any measurable way to the commission of the crime. Thus, they cannot do much to prevent the crimes concerned, especially when direct confrontations are lacking, because weapons are far-reaching and the perpetrator cannot be seen. As far as armed conflicts are concerned, in addition, the uniform preserves the anonymity of the perpetrator. Uniforms, behind which persons can hide, not only reduce the natural reluctance, for instance to kill, but also hinder a "relationship" between perpetrator and victim. This may not only lead to the effect that perpetrators harm victims more easily and do not feel responsible for what they actually have done, because they may not even see "their" victims. It also makes it more difficult for the victims to participate in the process of international criminal justice. Quite often they can merely give rather vague hints concerning the identity of perpetrators. More concrete may be their testimony on situations like mass graves or destruction of property. But, in all cases, their fear for those who still may be in power at the local area, from where victims report atrocities, may be stronger than the desire to help to bring to justice those responsible.[47]

III. Task Assigned to the Permanent International Criminal Court

According to paragraph 5 of the Preamble of the Rome Statute, it is the aim of the community of nations "to put an end to impunity for the perpetrators

---

[46] See, for instance, O. Triffterer, *Viktimologische Besonderheiten im Umweltstrafrecht*, in: G. Kaiser/A. Eser (eds.) *Drittes deutsch-sowjetisches Kolloquium über Strafrecht und Kriminologie, Rechtfertigung und Entschuldigung - Umweltstrafrecht - Jugendkriminalität*, 1987, 141 et seq.

[47] See, for instance, D. Donat-Cattin in: O. Triffterer (ed.) *Commentary*, *supra* note 4, Article 68, especially margin Nos. 30 et seq.

of these crimes and *thus* to contribute to the prevention of such crimes".[48] More *explicit* statements on how to achieve prevention and to exercise the repressive function are contained in Article 28(a), for instance, by mentioning the failure "to exercise control properly", "to take all necessary and reasonable measures" available, and "to prevent or repress the commission or to submit the matter to the competent authorities for investigation and prosecution". In addition to these explicit references, all Articles of the Statute and the Court, exercising its jurisdiction on the basis of the Statute, serve the purpose "to prevent and repress" crimes under international law. Since this is the daily work of the Court, the Rules of Procedure and Evidence, still to be drafted by the Preparatory Commission and to be adopted by the Assembly of States Parties, should include details on means and measures contributing to the prevention of these crimes.

1. Basic Structures, Purpose and Tendencies

The Preamble further expresses that the victimization of "millions of children, women and men" by "unimaginable atrocities" not only "deeply shock the conscience of humanity", but also "threaten the peace, security and well-being of the world". Such aspects were the decisive factors for the agreement achieved, when 120 States adopted the Rome Statute to establish a permanent International Criminal Court.[49] "Affirming that ... (such crimes) must not go unpunished and that their effective prosecution must be ensured",[50] confirms the task assigned to the Court, to repress and thus to use the exercise of its jurisdiction (as one of several means available) to "contribute to the prevention of such crimes".[51] This clearly demonstrates the tendency to prevent such crimes with all means and measures. All organs of the Court, therefore, have to struggle with their whole energy, to fight such a criminality effectively, albeit with the help of the complementary national criminal jurisdiction, as long as this domestic level is not "unwilling or unable genuinely" to fulfil this function.

2. Contribution to the Prevention of Crimes by Exercising Jurisdiction

Besides those already mentioned, there are no explicit statements in the Statute on how to contribute to the prevention of crimes within the jurisdiction of the Court by exercising its judicial competence. We

---

[48] Emphasis added. See also above A II 3.

[49] Preamble paragraph 2 and 3 as well as O. Triffterer in: O. Triffterer (ed.), *Commentary*, *supra* note 4, Preamble margin Nos. 8 et seq.

[50] Brackets added.

[51] Preamble paragraph 6; brackets added.

therefore have to look, for instance, at the procedure provided to see, if and perhaps how the Court can or ought to manage this task.[52]

a) Initiation of proceedings, investigation and prosecution The initiation of criminal proceedings already raises the interest of the public, especially when crimes of violence or inhuman and degrading treatment are involved. While the mere demonstration of violence leading to personal benefits may stimulate criminality, the demonstration that justice is on the way to make the perpetrator "pay" for his or her illegal actions, at least make potential perpetrators aware of the risk they run when committing such crimes. This may not have a too great preventive effect, as long as the rate of perpetrators caught is rather low. But, the deterrent effect may increase, when it becomes clear that perpetrators, who could not be brought to trial because of their absence, finally may have other disadvantages, which may perhaps be even greater than those resulting from punishment: The loss of political influence and personal positions, official capacity and power by which other persons or institutions could be dominated, especially by abuse of such power.[53]

It has to be admitted that such side-effects of an initiation of proceeding could be dubious, because they may violate the presumption of innocence and even be abused for political purposes. But all these objections can be taken care of by corresponding measures, like thresholds as provided in Article 15 or a neutral, objective reporting system, clearly expressing the procedural situation, in which all allegations raised have not yet been confirmed in a public trial, dominated by the rule of law and the principle of a fair trial. When proceeded *proprio motu*, such side effects are to a certain extent unavoidable and thus legitimate, in the interest of finally to achieve justice, at the end of the procedure.

Keeping this in mind, it can be experienced by the praxis of the ICTY and the ICTR that already the initiation of proceedings cause the attention of a broad public, including those potential perpetrators, who have the power to commit or are already suspected of having committed such crimes. In addition, public reaction to the initiation of investigating procedures, when persons in positions of power have failed to obey law (or merely violated moral standards), supplies further evidence that already at such an early stage, at least the possibility exists to take influence on the prevention of future crimes by demonstrating what the judicial and, above

---

[52] For the difficulties and the need for empirical research see above A I and II 2. See also the UN discussion guide metioned in *supra* note 6. For the purpose of sentencing in international criminal law see J.Ch. Nemitz, *supra* note 15.

[53] For further details, see below b.

all, the political consequences may be, if the alleged responsibility can be proved.[54]

With all due respect to the presumption of innocence and the need for secret initiations of proceedings, in order not to endanger their success, it is the task of the Court and its organs, to balance between the necessity to sufficiently inform the public and the risk of, thus, endangering further investigations and rights of suspects, victims and witnesses. As far as admissible, press releases, therefore, might be - as for the ICTY and the ICTR - continuously issued on all activities, based on facts, concerning situations in which crimes under international law have been committed. It could be helpful to analyse - as far as possible and admissible - the alleged power structures and further details, about where the causes and responsibilities for such abuse of power lie and how they could - presumably - have been prevented. The more detailed such information is, the easier it can be associated with similar positions of power and persons acting in a comparable official capacity. Such an association makes the preventive effect more easy to develop, for instance, by a control exercised by democratic institutions or by the public, which by its voting power is the real sovereign.

Of course, as soon as a specific person is under the suspicion of having committed such a crime, the public reporting has to be more careful, avoiding names, but describing situations and organizational positions of power which may have caused or at least have made it possible to commit such crimes. In addition, only a well-founded and in an understandable language phrased report may make the public aware of the seriousness of the event and of the endeavours of the community of nations, to prevent such crimes by repressing those which have already been committed.

Precisely elaborated standards have to be applied, also during *all investigations and prosecutions*. It appears advisable, for instance, to choose a reporting system which clearly differentiates between alleged and already established facts, giving due respect to the presumption of innocence. The more transparent such reports are, including the context of alleged structures of power out of which the crime may have been committed, the more understandable appears the engagement of the

---

[54] The initiation of proceedings on the *national* level, for instance, against US President Bill Clinton in the case of Monica Lewinski 1999 - and now against the former German Chancellor Helmut Kohl, because of undeclared money for his party - concern quite different allegations compared to those falling within the jurisdiction of the Court. But, the *political* consequences, for instance, to be forced to resign of positions of power, may have the same preventive effect as punishment in cases where such "official capacity" is the condition for a repetition of the criticized behaviour, independent of whether this amounts to a crime or is below the level of the *ius puniendi*.

community of nations. Perpetrators have to be convinced that this community will use all its power to prevent and "to put an end to impunity for the perpetrators of these crimes".

The situation in Kosovo and the NATO bombing in early 1999 have drawn *additional* attention to the fact that there already exists an ad hoc international criminal jurisdiction and that this will be extended by the *permanent* International Criminal Court. It, therefore, can be expected that press releases of the Court will have even an increased impact on building awareness of what is right and wrong all over the world.[55]

b) Decisions supported, confirmed or taken by the Pre-Trial Chamber It follows by the very nature of criminal proceedings that, when a case is not acquitted, but investigation continues, the suspicion (slowly) may become more reasonable, intensive and well-founded. To be able to follow such a procedure of (slowly) establishing the proof for an international criminal responsibility may have, even if only an *intermediate* result without prejudice on the final decision of the Court, a preventive effect on potential perpetrators as well as on the public, if reported correspondingly. The possibility to achieve such results increases as soon as one of the *Chambers* of the Court gets involved in the investigation; because until now, prosecutors – regretfully – are deemed to be less objective than judges. The first possibility for such an involvement of judges exists according to Article 15 paragraph 3, "if the Prosecutor concludes that there is a reasonable basis to proceed with an investigation". Because, if the Pre-Trial Chamber, "upon examination of the request and the supporting material", confirms this evaluation for a crime within the jurisdiction of the Court, "it shall authorise the commencement of the investigation, without prejudice to subsequent determinations by the Court ...", paragraph 4.

Similar preventive and repressive effects may have "[p]reliminary rulings regarding admissibility" according to Article 18, because they are based on an intensified suspicion and, therefore, demonstrate that the probability of a trial *may* come closer. The same is true with regard to "[c]hallenges to the jurisdiction of the Court or the admissibility of a case", which have been *un*successful and thus resulting in the decision of the Court, "that it has jurisdiction ... and determine the admissibility of a case...", Article 19 paragraph 1.

Such decisions may effect situations and/or individual perpetrators. But there are others which concern primarily individual perpetrators and, therefore, are more suitable to have preventive and repressive effects on the

---

[55] For worldwide activities, creating already awareness by discussing the ratification and implementation of the Rome Statute, see O. Triffterer, *Implications*, *supra* note 10.

suspect and on potential other perpetrators as well as on the public. I may recall in this context especially Article 58 "[i]ssuance by the Pre-Trial Chamber of a warrant of arrest or a summons to appear" as well as Article 61, "[c]onfirmation of the charges before trial"; in the first two cases, mentioned in Article 58, a Pre-Trial Chamber has to be convinced, that "there are reasonable grounds to believe that the person has committed a crime within the jurisdiction of the Court", in Article 61, "*to confirm* the charges on which the Prosecutor intends to seek trial", after she or he has supported "each charge with sufficient evidence to establish substantial grounds to believe that the person committed the crime charged".[56] A case, thus "controlled" by a Pre-Trial Chamber composed of independent judges, is of more importance than decisions of the Prosecutor. Even though prosecutors and judges are equally independent and obliged to find the truth, which means investigating in favour and against the accused with equal care, public opinion assumes judges to be more neutral than Prosecutors, because the latter is seen, even in civil law countries, as one of the two adversary parties in criminal proceedings.

The thus confirmed indictments and international warrants of arrest of the ICTY against, for instance, Karadzic and Mladic, were, so far, not successful, as both persons could not be brought to trial, even though in other cases, the same procedure has been successful. But they resulted in a loss of political and military power, which were the basis for their alleged crimes. By thus abolishing a condition for committing the crimes mentioned in their indictments, these cases have a strong preventive effect on the two indicted persons and perhaps also on potential perpetrators in comparable official capacities. In addition, both suspects can no longer travel abroad without taking the risk of being arrested, which limits their personal freedom and broadly make them unsuitable to act in any important official capacity. Furthermore, the international reputation of their State would be endangered if they were entrusted with any official function.[57] With Milosevic the *legal* situation *before the Court* is the same. How much preliminary measures for the purpose of forfeiture may "incommodate" him and persons in comparable positions, is not known to the author.[58]

c) Public trial and sentencing It goes without saying that a verdict at the end of a public trial, finally establishing "the truth", is one of the most important contributions of criminal proceedings to the prevention of such crimes. It clearly demonstrates the situation, which has been carefully

---

[56] Emphasis added; Article 58 paragraph 1(a) and Article 61 paragraph 1, 2 and 5, respectively.

[57] See also O. Triffterer, *Strafgerichtshof*, *supra* note 33, 549 et seq.

[58] For the last aspect, see also below C IV.

investigated and the facts, which the judges are convinced of, as well as how the international community treats perpetrators found guilty. The penalties available according to Article 77, imprisonment up to 30 years or lifelong, and, only *in addition*, fines, mirror the gravity of the crimes falling within the jurisdiction of the Court.

Public trials followed by sentencing thus demonstrate that perpetrators will "not go unpunished"; the *repressive* function of international criminal jurisdiction, therefore, prevents at least this perpetrator from committing crimes during the time of imprisonment. In addition convicted and imprisoned persons lose all their positions of power and thereby their basis to commit crimes by abuse of power. The demonstration of the last consequence to the public and all potential perpetrators may even have a greater deterrent effect with regard to all crimes falling within the jurisdiction of the Court than the penalty imposed.

It can hardly be evaluated what expectation may result to a greater preventive effect, to be imprisoned or to lose all official capacity and thereby personal power. To believe in a preventive effect of criminal law and its enforcement is, as we all know, an optimistic view. But, even though such results are extremely difficult to be measured, it is generally agreed upon that the enforcement of criminal law is an indispensable condition without which preventive effects cannot be achieved.[59]

d) Enforcement of the sentences Not only the delivery of the "decision or a summary thereof ... in open Court", Article 74 paragraph 5, but, in addition, the enforcement of sentences, is an opportunity to contribute to the prevention of crimes within the jurisdiction of the Court. Part 10 of the Statute provides that an engagement of States for this enforcement is independent of whether that State has participated before in the case concerned.

States enforcing sentences of imprisonment will be, even if they have before not taken any action in the case concerned, more aware of and better informed about the underlying situation and the final decision of the Court than others, not involved at all. Not only the relevant State authorities, especially those concerned with the (funding of the) prison system, but also the public will take notice of what precisely has happened and thus can evaluate whether it was worthwhile to commit the crime. Both will accompany the case during the whole time of imprisonment, as provided in Article 103. In addition, since enforcement will be assigned according to the "principles of equitable distribution", as provided in

---

[59] Law enforcement in this sense is also restorative justice, the concept of which includes all aspects of diversion. See to this concept the UN discussion guide for the 10th Congress on Crime Prevention and Treatment of Offenders, April 2000, *supra* note 6.

paragraph 3 subparagraph (a), this possibility to contribute to the prevention of further crimes may even exist for people who are otherwise not at all familiar with or engaged in the field of *international* criminal justice.

The same is true with regard to the "Enforcement of fines and forfeiture measures", Article 109. Such measures may concern primarily the State, where the perpetrator has committed his or her act. But quite often, third States are used by persons abusing their power to harbour their wealth needed, for instance, in order to survive after they lost their position of power and to take care of other needs, for instance, for their health and the "well-being" of their family. The execution of such measures, therefore, may lead to a *preventive* effect by information even in those States, which otherwise may not have any experience with crimes under international law.

3. Preventive Effects Apart from Exercising Jurisdiction

The idea of a criminal responsibility directly under international law, executed by an *international* criminal jurisdiction, has received unexpected attention since the 1990s when, in the context of the belligerent struggles and crimes committed on the territory of former Yugoslavia and Rwanda, finally, the ICTY and the ICTR were established in 1993 and 1994 respectively. Even for those engaged for decades in this field, it was surprising that the UN shortly thereafter established an ad hoc Committee followed by a Preparatory Committee for the Establishment of a (permanent) International Criminal Court. The work carried out in these institutions was well enough prepared to be presented to a broad public and the mass media. Nevertheless, it was astonishing that both showed an unexpected strong interest, when finally the Rome Conference convened in June 1998 to fulfil its mandate, assigned to it by the General Assembly, to finalize and adopt a convention on the establishment of an international criminal court. It cannot be overlooked that the interest and engagement of more than 800 non-governmental organizations in this issue was also promoted by the fact that, meanwhile, the ICTY and the ICTR had started to operate and published their first decisions. It was the first time since Nuremberg that world public opinion saw, with regard to an ad hoc jurisdiction, the serious concern of the world community to "put an end to impunity and thus contribute to the prevention" of the classical Nuremberg crimes.

Since then, public and individual information and awareness of the importance of the issue has permanently increased. Even though the precise date of the entry into force of the Statute is not predictable, in most States proceedings for the signature, ratification and implementation of the Statute are initiated. Above all, a discussion started on the national, regional and broader international levels, which developed to be - on very different occasions - an *anticipated* contribution to the prevention of "the most serious crimes of concern to the international community as a whole", even before the Court starts operating.

This influence should not be underestimated. Already now, all States in all continents are confronted with the fact that with the deposit of the 60th ratification instrument "An International Criminal Court ('the Court') is hereby established", Article 126 in connection with Article 1 sentence 1 of the Statute. Therefore, there is almost nobody within the classical institutions of a State, the legislature, the executive and the judiciary, who does not know, at least, that "something" is coming, which they may have to deal with independently, whether the respective State becomes a State Party or not. Being aware of this fact is, in their own interest, because the Court, in a very limited way, has the task of controlling those in power and, if necessary, prosecute them for abuses amounting into one of the most serious crimes of concern to the community of nations. Thus, the legal and political debates on ratification and implementation create a far greater awareness as ever before of what is right or wrong according to the well established, but partly newly defined standards of international criminal law. This is true especially with regard to the possibility that individuals, independent of their official capacity, can soon be held responsible *directly* before an *international* criminal court. These discussions make people, on a broad scale, aquainted with the crimes listed in the Statute and their prosecution. In addition, they demonstrate to potential perpetrators, what they have to expect, if they abuse their power and thus violate values and interests of the international community as a whole, in a very severe way.

This can be proven, for instance, by the fact that the military authorities in many States are strongly engaged in this process. The mere fact that quite a number of them favour the implementation of at least all crimes listed and defined in the Statute into domestic codifications, show their deep concern for clarification, in order to be able to work better in a *preventive* way in their fields of responsibility. When military institutions support the idea to include such crimes into their military codes or into the general penal code, they do so because they have to inform all relevant personnel within their sphere of influence about the precise legal and factual situation, and what they may have to face when not obeying the legal order established by the Rome Statute.

Since the jurisdiction of the Court is complementary to national jurisdiction, every responsible State official must be interested to inform all potential perpetrators, and especially the military, of what will be established in the near future. This information is needed, because thereafter any shielding of perpetrators no longer remains without negative consequences for the respective State: In cases of unwillingness or unableness of States to investigate and prosecute genuinely, especially their own nationals, the jurisdiction of the Court may be activated, Article 17 or Article 20 paragraph 3. In addition, the preventive effect of creating consciousness may be considerably increased by the application of these laws. Even though the Court does not yet exercise its jurisdiction, the decisions of the ICTY and the ICTR clearly indicate that the law will be applied even to Heads of States and other persons in "official capacity", independent of the fact whether an arrest warrant can be executed now, later or perhaps never.

Therefore, it may be assumed that the preventive effect of the Statute is rather large even before it comes into operation. Those having to deal with these processes must consider all substantive and procedural aspects as well as the consequences of non-obedience in detail. This lies in the interest of all persons in power positions, which, if abused, could result in the commission of relevant crimes, and also concerns the international political reputation of their State. Both aspects may deter or are at least a strong argument for advocating with all means and measures, the prevention of such crimes on all State levels.[60]

In addition, the endeavours being made public by reporting part of the discussion within their countries, show that the persons in power accept their international responsibility for abuses of such power and, thereby, demonstrate their willingness to prevent such acts. This increases their *internal* and their *international* political reputation. Therefore, *politicians* should be included and individually addressed during the ratification and implementation procedures and informed comprehensively about the jurisprudence of the ICTY, the ICTR and the coming ICC: because it often is not the military, but the political level which decides about "programmes", for instance, for ethnical cleansing or other crimes against humanity and war crimes. Such information may be an especially helpful contribution to the prevention of crimes within the jurisdiction of the Court in cases where those persons may not be aware of the fact that not only those executing the crime or participating in its commission, but also those silently tolerating it, may be held responsible, especially for command responsibility, according to Article 28.

---

[60] See for details O. Triffterer, *Implications*, *supra* note 10.

C. RESULT AND CONCLUSIONS

I. A comparison between the task of the ICC and domestic criminal law leads to the result that, in principle, the preventive and repressive functions are the same: On both levels, criminal law is not dispensable and how to achieve the most effective prevention or deterrence is disputed.

The structure of "the most serious crimes of concern to the international community as a whole", falling within the jurisdiction of the Court, is typically shaped by an abuse of power of persons, holding official capacity in the sense of Article 27, even though their participation may not be stronger than by silent toleration. Article 28 makes this "non concern" expressly a basis for criminal responsibility.

II. Such an attitude or "non concern" of persons having political or military power, which may amount to be "part of a plan or policy", makes prevention more difficult than on the national level. States can confront perpetrators of crimes under national law, if necessary, with the full force of State power, executed by all its three branches: the legislature, the executive and the judiciary. They are even effective against organized international crimes, especially when States cooperate in this field of legal and factual assistance in criminal matters, as, for instance, with the help of EUROPOL.

The international community, on the contrary, has a rather complicated legislative procedure, no executing power and its judiciary is only beginning to operate on a world wide scale. The effectiveness of the ICC, therefore, depends on how much States "cooperate fully" with the Court in the sense of Article 86.

To be effective in preventing crimes is often, in addition, aggravated, because those persons in power and equipped with the possibility to stop all crimes in their sphere of influence, may be needed for the restoration of peace and are protected by State institutions, more or less dominated by their own or the power of their (political) friends. In order to prevent further large scale crimes, therefore, it may be recommendable or even unavoidable, not to bring them to trial by force of the international community. It may be even advisable, to start, instead, a procedure of reconciliation, as long as thereby a greater preventive effect can be achieved as by criminal procedures. However, such a substitution of criminal justice has to be handled with extreme care, in order not to raise the impression that criminal justice is negotiable.

III. With the establishment of the two ad hoc Tribunals, for former Yugoslavia and for Rwanda, and now the ICC, the international community has new organs to exercise its inherent *ius puniendi*. However, the member States are the executive force of this community. If the respective State is not willing or able to prosecute or surrender persons responsible for crimes within the jurisdiction of the Court, the international community has to use its power as far as possible.

Persons abusing their political or military positions of power lose the basis of their future criminality, when losing their power and influence. The strong mutual dependence of States enables the international community to take influence on the international political reputation of States and those leaders, supporting or committing crimes of concern to the international community as a whole. If the sanctions for such crimes include the loss of power, the preventive effect of the Court can be increased.

IV. The Court, as already the ICTY and the ICTR, is, as ultima ratio, organ of the international community, which is not only legally competent, but also capable to take such an influence. The danger that the Court may be used for political purposes, is excluded. The Statute provides sufficient guarantees against a political abuse of this new position of power of the international community, which the Court demonstrates, especially by the principle of complementarity and the trigger-mechanism established in Part 1.

When finally operating, the Court processes several possibilities to contribute to the prevention of such crimes. The initiation of proceedings before the Court is one of these opportunities. Its effectiveness has been confirmed in many cases on the national level. Just because this measure may be effective, its political abuse must be absolutely excluded, if the international community is not to lose its moral and legal legitimization to prevent and repress crimes under international law.

The possibility to contribute to the prevention of such crimes exists at all stages of criminal proceedings, gaining importance when Chambers of the Court get involved, for instance, by issuing "a warrant of arrest or a summons to appear", Article 58, or "confirmation of the charges before trial", Article 61. Such measures, at least, limit the possibility of the persons to leave their own country and, thus, exercise their official capacity in the interest of their State abroad. Trial, sentencing and enforcement of sentences are additional measures to build awareness by demonstrating that international criminal law will be enforced and that the international community will try, with all means and measures, "to put an end to impunity for the perpetrators of these crimes and thus to contribute to the prevention of such crimes". Examples by the ICTY and the ICTR have shown that States react very sensitively, when such decisions of the Tribunals are published worldwide.

V. How sensitive the international community, including potential perpetrators, has become, can be seen by the discussion about the signature, ratification and implementation proceedings which started shortly after the adoption of the Statute at the Rome Conference on 17 July 1998. All States become more and more aware that it is their responsibility, not only not to commit such crimes, but also to prevent their commission with all means available on the domestic level. The military branches especially appear to be aware of their command responsibility and, therefore, promote in many States an implementation of the Statute into the domestic legislation. Such a procedure by, for instance, literally integrating the definitions of crimes, provides the best guarantee for a broad knowledge of all issues concerned. It can best reach those who may be tempted to commit such crimes on all levels of hierarchic structures and, therefore, can contribute to prevent the commission of such crimes, often by just one single word. To ensure that States can take care of their role, to be primarily responsible for the prosecution of the crimes falling within the jurisdiction of the Court, they have, for instance, to investigate and prosecute such crimes according to the principle of universality.

VI. It is the aim of my presentation to inspire considerations on how to use all possibilities of the Rome Statute to prevent crimes falling within the jurisdiction of the Court and, perhaps, in addition, other crimes punishable directly under international criminal law. There is agreement that the best protection for the values inherent to the community of nations is to abolish the causes for such crimes and thus to prevent crimes before they occur. But, as long as this is not achieved, we have to use all our energy to find, develop and exhaust all legitimate means and measures to meet and fight these crimes. Whatever we will do, it has be adapted to the specific dynamic and pattern of these crimes.

This task raises the need for more detailed, empirical investigations on the availability, suitability and admissibility of preventive common actions, because peace and justice can only be restored in an imperfect way by criminal jurisdiction. I would be grateful if I have contributed some ideas to this common, future task.

19. The International Criminal Court and National Jurisdictions

FLAVIA LATTANZI*

1) Introduction

At first sight, when I was asked to intervene at this conference on the topic of the relationship between the International Criminal Court (ICC) and national jurisdictions, I was inclined to focus my attention on the co-operation between domestic legal systems and the Court in light of Part IX of the Rome Statute. However, I decided not to address this subject, on which much has been and more will be written by commentators of the Statute.[1]

I have therefore chosen to approach a thematic area with lesser technical profiles, but better placed in the framework of a conference on the ICC as "a challenge to impunity" and within a panel discussion on the prospects of international criminal justice after the Rome Conference. My presentation relates to the current status of the Statute, namely, when it is not yet entered into force, thus the Court is not operational, and there are not great expectations that it will be so soon.[2] Pessimism relating to the prompt entry into force of the Statute, upon deposit of 60 instruments of

* Professor of International Law, University of Teramo; Member of the Italian Delegation to the Rome Conference on the International Criminal Court.

[1] See the commentary of Part 9 of the Statute in *Commentary on the Rome Statute of the International Criminal Court, Observers' Notes, Article by Article*, Triffterer ed., Baden-Baden, 1999, p. 1045 ff., Rinoldi and Parisi, *International Co-operation and Judicial Assistance between States Parties and the International Criminal Court*, in Lattanzi and Schabas eds., *Essays on the Rome Statute of the International Criminal Court*, L'Aquila, 1999, p. 339 ff. and Palmisano, *The ICC and Third States*, *ibidem*, p. 391 ff.

[2] As of today - 1 September 2000, latest revision of this paper - 98 States have signed the Statute and 15 States have ratified it (Senegal, Trinidad and Tobago, San Marino, Italy, Ghana, Fiji, Norway, Belize, Tajikistan, Iceland, Venezuela, France, Belgium, Canada and Mali).

ratification, is often manifested: this attitude would lead to "temporarily nullify" the usefulness of the work completed in Rome on 17 July 1998.

Conversely, the aim of this paper is to demonstrate the impact of the ICC law-making process on national jurisdictions and – in general terms – on the normative content of domestic legal systems, before and independently from the entry into force of the Rome Statute. I wish to demonstrate that this law-making process has produced significant results ever since the Geneva sessions of the International Law Commission,[3] through the New York sessions of the Ad Hoc and Preparatory Committees,[4] and - above all - the Rome Conference of the Plenipotentiaries.[5]

I will, therefore, try to show that the impact of the Statute is, although randomly, already manifest in several distinct areas of law, without forgetting to consider the contradictions between the positions of States at the Rome Conference and their concrete practice in international relations. The task of national jurisdictions, as well as that of international criminal jurisdictions, will be to solve these contradictions, including conflicts of interpretations, in favour of the positions expressed in the letter and spirit of the Rome Statute.

I believe, indeed, that the very adoption by a wide majority of States of the ICC Statute – notwithstanding the contrary vote of important forces of the international community, like the United States of America – has already such a positive effect, which is due to increase, on national normative and jurisdictional systems that it has already influenced the development of norms and enforcement measures in the prevention and adjudication of acts of genocide, crimes against humanity and war crimes.

---

[3] The United Nations General Assembly (UNGA) mandated the International Law Commission (ILC) in 1989 [Cf. GA Res. 44/39(1989), in UN Doc. A/44/770 (1989)] to prepare a Draft Statute for an ICC in the framework of its works on the elaboration of a Draft Code of Crimes against the Peace and Security of Mankind. The ILC Draft Statute was approved and transmitted to the UNGA in 1994 [*Report of the International Law Commission, 46th session*, in UN Doc. A/49/10 (1994)].

[4] In 1994 and 1995, the UNGA created two Committees (entities composed by States), the ad hoc Committee on the Establishment of an ICC (1995) and the Preparatory Committee on the Establishment of an ICC (PrepCom) (1996-1998). The Draft Statute of the PrepCom has been the basis for the discussions and deliberations at the Rome Conference (*reproduced* as an appendix to Lattanzi (ed.), *The International Criminal Court: Comments on the Draft Statute*, Napoli, 1998).

[5] The ICC law-making process continues in New York in the framework of the Preparatory Commission for the ICC, tasked to prepare - *inter alia* - the draft Rules of Procedure and Evidence and the Elements of Crimes. The Commission has just concluded its works on the above-mentioned instruments, which were approved by *consensus*. The Rome Statute has mandated their adoption to the Assembly of the States Parties that will be operational upon the entry into force of the Statute.

In fact, it cannot be ignored that the United States, even if it voted against the adoption of the Statute on 17 July 1998, has always been active – sometimes too much active... – in the elaboration of its provisions.[6] Several fundamental principles have been incorporated in the ICC legal framework also and especially because they were supported by the American administration: this is why the US negative vote in Rome cannot diminish the legal and political value of the principles enshrined in the Statute. As made publicly known by the US delegation in several occasions, their vote was solely aimed at rejecting the statutory provisions on the pre-conditions to the exercise of the Court's jurisdiction (Article 12), and it does not prejudice the legal status of the statutory sections on general principles of international criminal law and "international criminal procedure", neither the principles relating to the role and rights of victims in the proceedings, nor, above all, the principle of individual criminal responsibility under international law for offences other than war crimes committed in international armed conflict (the most "consolidated" area of international criminalization):[7] namely for war crimes in internal armed conflicts, crimes against humanity and crimes of aggression (Article 5).

The achievements of the Rome Statute in the affirmation of general principles of international criminal law, which I will now briefly analyse,

---

[6] The United States has been very active also in the negotiation of the Elements of Crimes. The US delegation was particularly prepared and available to constructive dialogue with delegations that defended the contents of the Rome Statute, while other delegations pretended to modify the statutory definitions of crimes through an *ex novo* drafting process of the elements. However, the US activism has not always been directed to the advantage of the effective functioning of the Court-to-be: this especially happened in the preparation of the Draft Rules of Procedure and Evidence. The worst result of these negotiations has been "obtained" with the compromise text of *Rule 19.9* relating to Article 98, paragraph 2, of the Statute, now Rule 195 of the consolidated Draft Rules of Procedure and Evidence (see UN Doc. PCNICC/2000/INF/3/Add.1, at p. 89, available at http://www.un.org/law/icc/statute/rules/rulefra.htm), which has been surprisingly entitled "Provision of information". This Draft Rule attempts to modify Article 98(2) of the Statute by barring the possibility for the Court to even request a State Party to surrender an individual who would be "protected" by agreements – such as the NATO Status of Forces Agreement (S.O.F.A.) – that oblige the requested State (Party) to obtain the consent of the State of nationality of the suspect (requested by the Court) before authorizing his surrender to an international criminal jurisdiction, or his extradition to a third State or, even, his prosecution before the State of the territory in which a crime was allegedly committed. However, as it is stated in Article 51, paragraph 4 and 5, of the Rome Statute, and as re-affirmed on 30 June 2000 by the interpretative statements (in the conformity with the Statute) on Rule 19.19 of several delegations participating in the Preparatory Commission – Cf. "statements" of Angola, Ivory Coast, Cuba, New Zealand, Nigeria and Portugal on behalf of all member States of the European Union, contained in UN Doc. PCICC/2000/INF/4 dated 13 July 2000 (*distr.: Limited*) - the Rules of Procedure and Evidence [alike the Elements of Crimes] can not modify or amend the Statute: in case of conflict, the latter shall always prevail.

[7] Cf. Article 5, Rome Statute.

represent the essence of that "challenge to impunity" at the core of the theme proposed by the organizers of this Conference.

Of course, the effective functioning of the International Criminal Court, once operational, will naturally ensure a general and systematic "challenge to impunity". In light of the principle of complementarity with domestic jurisdictions, the Statute provisions will surely impact on all "States of good will", which will diligently prosecute and adjudicate the crimes under the Court jurisdiction: and this will be true also for those States that would have decided not to accept this jurisdiction. The future practice of the ICC will, indeed, bring about a definitive continued development of international criminal law, together with a uniform standard of application of principles and provisions that will penetrate national justice systems, and that will certainly operate as a deterrent to the prospective perpetration of *delicta iuris gentium*. On this specific aspect of "general prevention" I shall return in my concluding remarks.

2) Harmonizing Domestic Legal Systems to the Rome Statute in Light of the Principle of Complementarity

a) The Complementarity of the ICC Jurisdiction Also with Respect to the Jurisdictions of States non Parties to the Rome Statute

The founding principle that governs the exercise of the ICC jurisdiction is the principle of complementarity, operating even before the pre-conditions to ICC competence, namely its acceptance by the territorial or the national State.[8]

Just in virtue of this principle, the provisions of the ICC Statute have already had a breaking impact on States' justice orders.

In fact, the exercise of the Court's jurisdiction is triggered only by the unwillingness of States to prosecute or by the inability in case of a collapse of the judicial system or in case of lack of effective means at

[8] Cf. Article 12, Rome Statute, entitled *Preconditions to the exercise of jurisdiction*, which reads as follows:
"1. A State which becomes a Party to this Statute thereby accepts the jurisdiction of the Court with respect to the crimes referred to in Article 5.
2. In the case of Article 13, paragraph (a) or (c), the Court may exercise its jurisdiction if one or more of the following States are Parties to this Statute or have accepted the jurisdiction of the Court in accordance with paragraph 3. (a) The State on the territory of which the conduct in question occurred or, if the crime was committed on board a vessel or aircraft, the State of registration of that vessel or aircraft; (b) The State of which the person accused of the crime is a national."

national level.[9] The lack of implementation in domestic legal orders of applicable international standards, including the Statute itself[10] - as referred to in Article 21 -, could lead to the Court's decision of the admissibility of a case, as a consequence of the "incapability" of national jurisdictions to provide justice in the case. National jurisdictions will then be barred to re-try the individuals tried before the ICC by the principle of *ne bis in idem*, as stipulated in Article 20 of the Statute.[11]

All States in the world, including non Parties to the Statute, would therefore be involved in the process of its "implementation" *lato sensu*, if they will want to avoid that in particular crimes allegedly committed in their territory, or by their public officials or just by their nationals in the territories of third States - whether or not such States would have consented to the Court's jurisdictions[12] - would be subjected to Court's proceedings. In fact, the principle of complementarity plays in favour of national jurisdictions of States non Parties to the Statute also in case of initiation of the proceedings by a State referral or by the Prosecutor on her own motion and, therefore, in case of the ICC competence on the basis of its acceptance by the territorial or national State. In fact, according to Article 18, in application of the complementarity, "the Prosecutor shall notify all States Parties and *those States, which, taking into account the information available, would normally exercise jurisdiction over the crimes concerned...*".

Furthermore, one should be aware that the Court would be able to act also without the consent of the State of nationality or the territorial State if its jurisdiction will be "triggered" by the referral of a situation by the UN Security Council according to Chapter VII of the Charter.[13] Thus, the ICC will be "empowered" to complement and eventually replace domestic jurisdictions also of States which would not have ratified or acceded to the Statute or which would not have had accepted *ad hoc* the Court's jurisdiction under Article 12(3). This is an additional argument that should lead all member States of the United Nations to equip themselves with implementing legislation to fulfil the almost revolutionary regime of

---

[9] In this respect, see paragraph 3 of Article 17, Rome Statute.

[10] These legal standards pertain both to substantive prescriptions and procedural requirements.

[11] Paragraph 2 of Article 20, Rome Statute, make unequivocal that "no person shall be tried by another [domestic] court for a crime referred to in Article 5 for which that person has already been convicted or acquitted by the [International Criminal] Court".

[12] In fact, through a referral of a situation to the Court by the United Nations Security Council, the ICC jurisdiction could be extended to crimes allegedly committed outside the territories of States Parties and not involving nationals of States Parties. See Article 13(b), Rome Statute.

[13] *Ibid.*

complementarity with the Court. Such a regime could become relatively soon a reality with the entry into force of the Statute and the definitive coming into being of the permanent Court.

Needless to say, some national systems are clearly moving in this direction through different legislative avenues, the appropriateness of which may vary from case to case.[14]

Some States are incorporating the Rome Statute first of all with a constitutional norm of referral, postponing the process of further specific implementation of its prescriptions. Other States prefer to postpone the ratification of the Statute to the process of its implementation. The ones and the others decide, sometimes, to utilize the occasion of the ratification of the Statute to realize a general implementation of international criminal law and international humanitarian law.[15]

It is clear that, in virtue of the referral contained in the Statute to customary international law, as well as to the general principles of law as applied by the legal systems of the world, each State will assess the necessity to adequate their own jurisdictional system not only to the specific norms of the Statute, but also to the international law of armed conflicts, whether internal or international in character, and to the broader body of "humanitarian law" also applicable in time of peace, as well as the principles of international criminal law.

Considering the potential "boomerang" effect of the Court on national justice system, some systems have indeed commenced a process of general implementation of humanitarian standards. Such a tendency has prevailed in some legal orders already in the course of drafting and negotiation of the Rome Statute.

This is the case of the Italian government, which launched on 9 January 1998 a draft bill (*disegno di legge n. 2984/1998*) for the implementation of the 1949 Geneva Conventions and the 1977 Additional Protocols thereto in the military penal code ("*adeguamento del codice penale militare di guerra alle Convenzioni del 1949 e ai Protocolli del 1977*"). The Italian draft bill of 1998 has been since then submitted to revision, insofar as it was inappropriately not designed to implement the already existing body of general international law protecting victims of *delicta iuris gentium*. As correctly affirmed by the jurisprudence of the International Criminal Tribunal for the Former Yugoslavia (ICTY), this

---

[14] For a review on the major legislative approaches to the ICC by States, reference is made to the volume Kress/Lattanzi (eds), *The Rome Statute and Domestic Legal Orders*, vol. I *General Aspects and Constitutional Issues*, Nomos/Il Sirente, L'Aquila, 2000.

[15] See Italian project of Law No. 2984/1998. For a commentary of the implementation of the ICC in Italy, see Benvenuti, *Italy, Implementation of the ICC Statute in National Legislation. Constitutional Aspects*, *ibid*, p. 123 ff.

area of law - through the criminalization of acts of individuals, including agents of States - extends its protection to the victims of internal conflicts,[16] as well as to the victims of systematic violations of human rights perpetrated in time of peace (or, more precisely, of so-called peace).

In conclusion, also in Italy, a new wave of enthusiasm brought by the establishment of the first permanent mechanism of international penal justice is leading to the defeat of certain "reductive" legislative policies regarding - at least - the "core crimes" under international law and is opening the system to the broader international criminal law framework.

However, it must be noted that "enthusiasm" is not enough, if one considers that, as of today, the Inter-ministerial Commission mandated to prepare this new legislation seems to be very far from realizing the ambitious objectives of the mandated legislation (*legge delega*) as originally conceived by the Government for the implementation of the Statute. This mandated legislation, containing general principles of legislation that the Parliament was requested to refer back to the Executive for the elaboration of detailed legislation, has been separated by the relevant Committee of the Italian Senate from the Italian ratification bill adopted in June 1999, which also contains a norm giving force of law to the Statute - annexed to the Bill - in the Italian legal order once the Statute itself would be entered into force (*ordine di esecuzione*).[17]

In my view, this separation of the *remaining* implementing legislation from the ratification bill has been *wisely* decided with the aim of permitting a timely ratification by Italy, a country which is highly engaged in the prompt creation of the Court and, therefore, in the world-wide campaign for the ratification of the Statute.

But the time has come, now, for the Italian legislator to seriously address the problem of the specific and detailed incorporation of the Statute in the Italian legal system, realizing the normative integration and modifications to existing laws that are deemed as necessary for the full functioning of the ICC.[18]

b) The Non-Applicability of Statutory Limitations

A brief observation must be made also with respect to the principle of non-applicability of statutory limitations (*imprescrittibilità*), as starkly provided for the crimes within the Court's reach by Article 29 of the Rome Statute.

This norm is not considered by all commentators as part of the body of customary international law, at least for some of the categories of

---

[16] See, on this subject, the report of Condorelli.

[17] See P. Benvenuti, *cit.*

[18] For a comparative approach to the subject, see the essays contained in Kress/Lattanzi, *id.*

offences included in the Rome Statute (crimes against humanity). In order to assess the impact of Article 29 on the domestic level, it is not avoidable to discuss the very nature of the non-applicability of statutory limitations. Here, I wish only to underline that the non recognition of this principle on the national level should be read by the Court as a manifestation of the unwillingness or inability of a State to repress a crime under the ICC jurisdiction. And I wish to demonstrate that this statutory provision - even if conventional in nature - shall not find obstacles in its incorporation in domestic legal systems.

I stress this consideration in light of the fact that during the discussion in the Italian Parliament of the ratification bill some members mistakenly perceived the incorporation of Article 29 as a threat. Such a perception is probably due to the false idea that the recognition of this principle in the Italian legal order could somehow infringe upon the established *praxis* - rather than the *principle* - applied by the Italian legislator on the statutory limitations of some ordinary crimes.

The resistance from national policy-makers against introducing the non-applicability of statutory limitations to the "core crimes" enlisted in Article 5 of the Statute is not founded on substantive grounds. In fact, the traditional *praxis* of limitations reflects the decreased substantive interest of the State to prosecute offences which occurred too much time before their potential adjudication, which is considered unuseful, unless the gravity of the offence would justify a different regime. On the contrary, the interest to prosecute the *delicta iuris gentium* corresponds to a universal need not only *ratione personae* and *ratione loci*, but also *ratione temporis*, essentially because the protected interest to international individual accountability for the most serious crimes is deemed as "inderogable and inalienable".

It is true that peace agreements until the Versailles Treaty included nearly always an amnesty clause for war crimes. But, the application of statutory limitations, as well as amnesties or general "pardons" was acceptable in those past historical periods because the regulations on war crimes were aimed at protecting governmental interests rather than the humanitarian ones. They were simply designed to serve a military powers' interest, namely the interest to maintain a minimum of civilized behaviour during the hostilities in order to allow a restoration of peaceful and business-like relations between ex-belligerents after the end of a conflict. Moreover, the war was considered an available remedy to solve disputes in accordance with the international law of the time. Conversely, contemporary international humanitarian law (IHL), as well as the broadest regulatory framework provided by the expansion of international human rights law, protect the essential interests of the individual as such. The duty of States not to apply to the "core crimes" under international law the statutory limitations such as amnesty laws and "pardon's" decisions is a logical consequence of the international criminal responsibility for grave violations of rules protecting fundamental rights of individuals as such.

Therefore, the prohibition to impose national statutory limitations - and, in my view, to adopt amnesties - with respect to genocide, crimes against humanity and war crimes (all covered by Article 29 of the Statute) is indeed a necessary corollary of the inderogable and "non-negotiable" political decision, re-affirmed as such in the Preamble of the Statute: the determination "to put an end to the impunity of the perpetrators of these crimes" (cf. fifth *considerando*). In the pursuance of this political goal lies the *raison d'être* of the ICC.

From a purely pragmatic perspective, the non-applicability of statutory limitations is a necessary feature to ensure the effectiveness of the ICC in its framework of international cooperation and inter-States judicial assistance. The weak indirect enforcement mechanism of the Court's orders and decisions is based on the collaboration rendered by sovereign States, without which this institution would be meaningless. This reality could lead to a long time-span of ICC proceedings, which could even be initiated by the Prosecutor only several years after the commission of a given atrocity. And these proceedings could be initiated just because of application by national courts of statutory limitations provided by the national legislation for ordinary crimes.

3) The Implementation of the Rome Statute in Domestic Legal Orders in Light of the Principle of Legality

The provision of paragraph 3 of Article 22 of the Statute relating to the principle of legality has a crucial importance. Whereby paragraph 1 contains the general principle *nullum crimen sine lege*, paragraph 2 stipulates its corollaries, in particular the statutory characterization of the legal precision of incriminating norms (*tassatività*) and the prohibition of analogy in the interpretation of the "codified" crimes (without forgetting the other corollary of Article 24, the principle of non-retroactivity).

The true fact that the principle of legality has been inserted in the Statute demonstrates also that international law has upheld it and its affirmation is not limited to national regulatory frameworks. The language of Articles 6, 7 and 8 of the Statute, like the decision to subordinate the attribution of the ICC competence on the crime of aggression to its definition (Article 5), is there to prove that the drafters of this instrument had a strong sensitivity towards legal precision and predictability in defining the contours of criminal offences.

Such a reality should open the door of national systems - and hopefully the mind of some jurists, often too inclined to interpret the principle of legality in a manner which I would define "nationalistic" - to the international quest for the effective prosecution of *delicta iuris gentium*. It is worthy to note that, during the more and more frequent discussions on this subject matter, a prejudice against the incorporation in domestic orders of international standards often emerges in the position of magistrates, other practitioners and jurists with expertise in national legal disciplines. This trend is reflected in the unacceptable theory that does not deem as applicable in domestic law the legal qualifications of crimes of war, genocide and crimes against humanity, including torture, if their method of implementation is simply made through referral, whether it is made through general referral - such as the one of the Italian Constitution, Article 10, referring to the applicability in Italy of all norms of general international law - or through the *ad hoc* referral to the provisions of a given international convention (*ordine di esecuzione*).

The pretension of these interpreters of domestic law conflicts with the very structure of some provisions of certain international treaties, such as the Rome Statute, which embody rules aimed at describing with legal precision the facts constituting crimes under international law qualified as *delicta iuris gentium* (except, perhaps, certain crimes against humanity). Provisions of this nature are *self-executing*, even if they often need to be completed by accurate provisions on penalties for their application by national tribunals. In my view, the direct applicability of these norms is at least certain in legal orders based on the *rule of law*.

According to an interpretation of the principle of legality that we would call "nationalistic", it would be instead necessary to implement the international norm through its re-formulation in a domestic legal instrument more or less independent from the international instrument, and not through a referral *sic et simpliciter* to the relevant provision(s) of an international convention or a custom. In the absence of such a re-written norm, notwithstanding the binding nature of laws containing the incorporation of international incriminating norms through referral, national systems would be deemed as not containing the definition of the crimes as provided by international law. National courts would therefore be barred from hearing cases on these crimes before such detailed implementing legislation.

In the framework of a research project on the ICC coordinated by the University of Teramo and involving the *Università cattolica di Milano* and the Universities of Firenze, Siena and Trento, a debate on the principle of legality led *also* some Italian penalists to reflect on the need of a new opening of domestic criminal law to international incriminating norms, thus considering with great ponderation the courageous position of the "internationalists", often misjudged as excessive and unfounded. This has become possible thanks to the Rome Statute. I hope that the new attitude could have a positive impact in the continuation of the proceedings before Italian Tribunals on certain grave crimes against humanity perpetrated in Latin America by past dictatorial regimes under the name of "Operation Condor".[19]

The provision of paragraph 3 of Article 22 appears to clearly represent a firm point in solving the dispute on whether or not the principle of legality was violated in Nuremberg and Tokyo. In fact, it is now impossible to deny that - and not only with respect to the jurisdiction of the Court - the legal qualification of *delictum iuris gentium*, in particular relating to individual conduct enlisted as act of genocide, or crime against humanity or war crime, is not an exclusive monopoly of States and their written penal codes, but it is dealt with primarily by international law, which has a force of "primacy".[20] This is true beyond the law codified in the Rome Statute, because it stems from the law of other previous international conventions on the subject, as well as the unwritten principles and norms of international custom, in line with Article 21 of the Statute.

Therefore, the crimes of international concern are not only those expressly disciplined in national legal orders. It is not anymore acceptable to argue that, in the absence of the express criminalization of this conduct under domestic law, it is illegitimate to make findings as of their binding nature to a given case directly under international law.

Of course, the Rome Statute is designed to ensure the respect of the principle of legality primarily before the Court itself, and not expressly by States - as other international agreements containing the *nullum crimen sine lege*. And it could not have been differently.

In fact, past international law instruments dealt with the principle of legality in order to engage States to its application within their legal

---

[19] It is necessary that grave charges of crimes against some Argentinean and Chilean military officials who participated in "Operation Condor" would be brought under the categorization of crimes against humanity by Italian authorities and not just simply ordinary crimes under domestic law. This will allow the potential application of certain principles of international criminal law not applicable to ordinary offences under Italian law.

[20] I hereby utilize the term primacy in a particular context. I believe that there should be a full presumption of conformity of internal legal orders of the member States of the United Nations with the customary and conventional provisions (the latter only for States Parties of the relevant conventions) that qualify crimes of international concern. In fact, these legal orders of the UN member States must reflect the reality that States shall all be "peace-loving States which accept the obligations in the [...] Charter" as a condition to be satisfied under Article 4(1) of the Charter to be admitted in the Organization.

orders, under the law enforcement action of national tribunals, because "l'effetto fondamentale del principio di legalità, ciò che più di ogni altra cosa ne fa una conquista irrinunciabile di civiltà giuridica, è che esso riduce notevolmente il rischio di *arbitrio dei Magistrati*, e cioè di coloro i quali, in modo più diretto ed immediato, possono disporre della potestà punitiva".[21]

As the aforementioned author correctly observes, the principle of legality has indeed the effect of ensuring that certain policies of criminalization of acts are applied according to the "general interest" codified by the legislator and not the individual interest or preference of the particular law enforcement agent, thus revealing the democratic foundation of the principle of legality.[22]

The principle and its corollaries as stipulated in Article 22 of the Statute have therefore not the same direct effect of protection against abusive interpretations of incriminating norms as the principle of legality in national law. I share the opinion of the same Author[23] also on this point. The Statute does provide the judges with the legal obligation to prosecute and condemn individuals only for the offences defined in the Statute itself, but such an obligation can not be read as functional to a "democratic legitimization" of the Court's activities, because such a "legitimization" is not at all needed, as far as the Rome Conference has confined its law making process to the codification, in a single written text, of patterns of conduct which for a long time has deserved punishment by widespread recognition of the entire international community.[24] The Rome Statute added more certainty to this recognition, and even more certainty will be added by the future jurisprudence of the ICC.

[21] Cf. Catenacci, *Il principio di legalità nello Statuto della Corte penale internazionale*, (*ed. provv.*) Pescara, 1999, p. 41.

[22] Translation from Catenacci (*ibid.*, p. 45), whose original text states that the function of the legality principle is to "assicurare la rispondenza delle scelte di incriminazione (e più in generale della politica criminale) ad *interessi generali e non di parte*, che solo la legge, come espressione della volontà popolare può garantire (di qui il fondamento democratico del principio di legalità)".

[23] *Ibid.*, p. 86 et ff.

[24] *Ibid.*, p. 90. In particular, the Author writes that "l'obbligo, per i giudici dell'ICC, di perseguire e condannare solo le condotte descritte ... [nello Statuto], non può leggersi come funzionale ad un tentativo di "legittimazione democratica" dell'attività della Corte per il semplice motivo che di simile "legittimazione" non vi era alcun bisogno, visto che la ... [Conferenza di Roma] si è limitata a codificare, in un unico testo scritto, condotte la cui meritevolezza di pena era già ampiamente riconosciuta e condivisa nella comunità internazionale".

4) The Irrelevance of Official Capacity

Article 27 of the Statute establishes the irrelevance of the official capacity of the suspected person (paragraph 2), thus posing a norm, which remains a milestone in the affirmation of the principle of individual criminal responsibility at least for the "core crimes" amongst the *delicta iuris gentium.*

This norm is clearly not new in the history of international relations *vis-à-vis* certain crimes. It was formulated in the Geneva Conventions with respect to war crimes committed in an international armed conflict, in the Genocide Convention, in the Torture Convention, in the Draft Code of Crimes against the Peace and Security of Mankind, in the Statutes of the two ad hoc Tribunals for the former Yugoslavia and for Rwanda. Remarkably, these latter institutions - especially the ICTR - are providing an extensive practice of application of this principle. Although few cases have been brought to trial, the ICTR has held the prosecution of important governmental figures (the so called "big fishes") to whom the principle of irrelevance of official capacity have been essential in the determination of guilty. Numerous domestic courts adjudicating on war crimes committed in international conflicts have applied the same norm quite consistently.

Unfortunately, this principle appeared not to have had any practice before national tribunals neither in cases of war crimes perpetrated in the course of internal armed conflict nor in cases of crimes against humanity committed in time of "peace" (i.e., by a dictator). Except in the recent, isolated, case of Pinochet, the norm on the irrelevance of official capacity did not find recognition in the light of the 1984 Convention against torture, even if this Convention has been incorporated in many national legal systems.

For example, the prosecution in the United States of the former ruler of Panama, Mr. Noriega, was conducted on the basis of allegations of "international illegal trafficking in narcotic drugs" – not crimes against humanity - and, unfortunately, in virtue of his arrest following an armed intervention. But, the use of armed force against a State could not represent a positive and legal solution to the problem of the impunity of "big" perpetrators of crimes of international concern. The only correct solution is just the application by national and international jurisdictions of the principle codified in Article 27 of the Rome Statute.

In the "Pinochet case" there have been several voices alleging a presumption of invulnerability, that Mr. Pinochet would have forever enjoyed as a benefit of his Head of State immunity, which should have covered the facts upon which he received charges. These voices have been so superficial that they did not reflect the sad reality that certain atrocities can be committed only if the perpetrator is a Head of State or Government. Such crimes involve activities of planning, organization and orders through a precise chain of command, and the principle of international criminal responsibility of individuals would have been completely nullified by the exclusion of its application against those with command responsibilities in the highest levels of a State organization which would utilize widespread or systematic crimes as a method of maintenance of power or a system of conduct of hostilities at war.

Notwithstanding the British Immunity Act recognizes an absolute immunity to be granted to Heads of States and does not explicitly exclude this immunity for *delicta iuris gentium*, the two decisions of the House of Lords excluded the exemption from criminal jurisdiction for the crime of torture and re-affirmed the irrelevance of the official position of Pinochet directly under international law. These historical decisions have been possible, in my view, because of the Rome Statute! The same "legacy" has to be found in the previous arrest of Pinochet in England upon request of Spanish authorities and the subsequent decisions of Chilean Courts, including the Supreme Court, that excluded the immunity of Pinochet on the alleged crimes against humanity (or, at least, of international concern) as they have been tentatively qualified in the charges brought against him by the Chilean competent jurisdiction.[25]

[25] Besides, in my view, the lively discussions on the method of incorporation of Art. 27 in the face of constitutional immunities demonstrate that at the domestic level obstacles do not exist for implementing the exception to these immunities. If in some domestic systems it needs a modification of constitutional provisions, in others - like the Italian and the French, for example - the constitutional legitimacy to the exception is given by a general constitutional represented by a constitutional norm. So, it is known that in French the Constitution was modified in the aim to specifically incorporate the ICC Statute. In Italy, it is not possible to ignore the opening to international standards that the Italian Constitution provides for the national legal order. In particular, Article 11 of the Constitution authorizes restrictions of the Italian sovereignty to allow the cooperation of Italy with international institutions operating for an international regime of peace and justice among Nations. The derogation from other fundamental principles (whether or not of a constitutional nature, with the exception of those representing the "hard core" of constitutional principles) is therefore permitted by the "opening clause" of Article 11. In line with the above, I believe that Article 11 will allow the automatic incorporation in the Italian legal order of all the norms pertaining to general principles of law applicable to the Statutory crimes, thus solving all potential conflicts with Italian constitutional norms. Such adjustments will enter into force upon the entry into force of the Statute, exactly when the incorporation bill by referral (*ordine di esecuzione*) adopted with the ratification bill of June 1999 will also have binding effect. By virtue of this interpretation of Article 11, any conflict between the Constitutional provisions and the ICC Statute will be solved in favour of the latter without the need of a constitutional amendment process. The further specific implementation of the Statute in the Italian legal order would be nevertheless possible only through the adoption of additional detailed legislation that would give effect to all non self-executing provisions of the Rome Statute.

Also the recent position on the 1999 Kosovo crises of the High Commissioner for Human Rights, Ms. Mary Robinson, is largely based on the "legacy" of the 1998 Rome Statute, and of course on the normative and jurisdictional framework provided by the ICTY Statute annexed to Resolution 827/1993 of the UN Security Council. After the bombings over Serbia, the High Commissioner underlined that the ICTY would have had jurisdiction both on the mass atrocities allegedly committed by the military and political leaders of Yugoslavia and on the alleged war crimes attributed to the military forces of NATO, or - more precisely - to certain member States of NATO. This position, consistent with the international law principle codified in Article 28 (*Responsibility of commanders and other superiors*) of the Rome Statute, could have led to the top of the chain of command of the organs of Government of Yugoslavia as well as to the ones of the member States of NATO. The Tribunal's Prosecutor has reached different conclusions, but she never made reference to an hypothetical principle of immunity from prosecution of the individual-organs or of irresponsibility of superiors (cf. *infra*).

And the lively discussions on the method of incorporation of Article 27 in national systems in the face of constitutional immunities demonstrate that the domestic orders are in a position to implement the exception to immunities.

So, I doubt that it would still be possible to give legal foundation to a rule exempting from immunity to the benefit of Heads of States or Government, or other high governmental or military authorities, if these individuals at the highest level of a chain of command were suspected of having committed the most horrendous crimes. On the contrary, it would be only feasible to make recourse to political justifications to bar certain prosecutions, thus without interfering in any manner whatsoever with a valid legal process, which shall not be subject to abuse.

5. The *Mens Rea*

Article 25 of the Statute, concerning the individual criminal responsibility of the authors of the crimes comprised in the Court's jurisdiction, provides for the responsibility not only of those who commit the offence (sub-section a), but also of those who order, solicit or induce the commission (sub-section b), facilitate the commission of such a crime, aid, abet or otherwise assist in its commission or its attempted commission, including providing the means for its commission (sub-section c), or in any other way contribute to the commission or attempted commission of such a crime by a group of persons acting with a common purpose (sub-section d).

Although in the latter form of criminal participation there is an additional requirement of intent and knowledge of the intent of other persons (i.e. the common purpose), this limitation does not restrict the already very inclusive precedent provisions, and it does not alterate the basic requirements of the subsequent sub-section f, which criminalizes attempts to commit the crimes in the Court's jurisdiction. In addition, for the acts of genocide, also those who directly and publicly incite others to commit genocide (sub-section e) are punishable thereof.

It shall be however noted that, with respect to the *mens rea* (intent and knowledge) of the "common purpose", an important interpretative contribution has been made by the ICTY in the *Furundzija* Judgment of December 1998.[26] In this decision, the Trial Chamber has been confronted with the legal question of whether the "ancillary perpetrator" should share with the "principal perpetrator" the same positive intent to commit the crime. The conclusion of the ICTY in *Furundzija* is that "mere knowledge" of the intent of the other co-perpetrators shall be sufficient to establish the responsibility of "secondary perpetrators" as participants in the criminal transaction:

> "[...] it is not necessary for the accomplice to share the *mens rea* of the perpetrator, in the sense of positive intention to commit the crime. Instead, the clear requirement in the vast majority of the cases is for the accomplice to have knowledge that his actions will assist the perpetrator in the commission of the crime. This is particularly apparent from all the cases in which persons were convicted for having driven victims and perpetrators to the site of an execution. In those cases the prosecution did not prove that the driver drove for the purpose of assisting in the killing, that is, with an intention to kill. It was the knowledge of the *criminal purpose* of the executioners that rendered the driver liable as an aider and abettor. Consequently, if it were not proven that a driver would reasonably have known that the purpose of the trip was an unlawful execution, he would be acquitted. (Cf. *Furundzija* Judgment, paragraph 245: *emphasis added by the author*.)

Therefore, the response of the Chamber has been clear in not requiring that the same positive mental element be proved, on the basis of the doctrine of "common purpose" codified[27] by Article 30 of the Rome

[26] Cf. ICTY, *Furundzija* Judgment, 10 December 1998, Case No. IT-95-17/1, paragraph 245.

[27] Paragraphs 237 to 240 of the *Furundzija* Judgment (*ibid.*) cite the position of several accused persons in the following post World War II cases: the *Einsatzgruppen* case and the *Hechingen Deportation* case.

Statute.[28] This Article is that is indeed entirely reproduced in a footnote of the judgment, thus bringing about the recognition of its character of general norm.

This may be cited as another example of influence of the Statute, even if not yet entered into force and, therefore, not yet having the status of a legally binding treaty.

6) Responsibility of Commanders and Other Superiors

Also Article 28 re-states an essential principle that, although it was already part of the written provisions of the 1949 Geneva Conventions, has been often disputed before national jurisdictions (as it happened in Italy in the recent proceedings against members of the Italian contingent which operated in Somalia in 1993, suspected of grave crimes against Somali civilian population). Reference is made to the principle of the responsibility of the superior. According to the Rome Statute,

> "A military commander or person effectively acting as a military commander shall be criminally responsible for crimes ... committed by forces under his or her effective command and control, or effective authority and control as the case may be, as a result of his or her failure to exercise control properly over such forces, where:
>
> (i) That military commander or person either knew or, owing to the circumstances at the time, should have known that the forces were committing or about to commit such crimes; and
>
> (ii) That military commander or person failed to take all necessary and reasonable measures within his or her power to prevent or repress their commission or to submit the matter to the competent authorities for investigation and prosecution."

I believe that after the adoption of the Rome Statute, in particular the provision at paragraph 1 of Article 28, no military commander would be anymore in the position to say, as it indeed happened in the Italian-Somali case,[29] that he did not know what some subordinates - indeed, few subordinates involved in isolated criminal acts, nevertheless of extreme

---

[28] See footnote appended to paragraph 244, *Furundzija* Judgment (*ibid.*).

[29] The case was brought before the Rome Military Court after an Italian magazine ("Panorama") published photographs showing that, *inter alia*, members of the Italian troops were applying electrodes to the testicles of an immobilized Somali prisoner in order to obtain information on the movement of a certain "military" faction which allegedly threatened the Italian camp.

gravity - were doing in "having fun" of the Somali civilian population instead of providing humanitarian assistance to it. Under normal circumstances, commanders are expected to know about the conduct of their subordinates, simply because this type of knowledge is part of nature of the command- and control-function that they are exercising over their troops.

7) The Rights of Victims

Another area of impact of the Rome Statute on domestic legislation is certainly the one of victims' rights, starting with the participation of victims in penal proceedings (Article 68, paragraph 3) and the right to reparations (Article 75).

The current time frame does not allow me to examine the norms contained in these Articles. I shall solely note that the Statutory provisions on victims' rights are surely going to have (and are slowly having) a progressive impact on the administration of justice in national penal systems, including those systems in which the access of victims to criminal justice has been neglected in name of an assumed policy of a national (or international) reconciliation.

This impact may be noticed also with respect to certain common law jurisdictions, where criminal justice reform projects are entailing a profound review of the participation of victims in penal proceedings and are introducing the possibility for criminal courts to decide on means of reparations for the benefit of victims, without obliging them to make recourse to civil proceedings.[30]

8) The Uniform Interpretation of International Criminal Law and International Humanitarian Law

In conclusion, I must mention a principal function of the permanent Court, once it is operational: the development of a "uniform interpretation" of the international law that it will apply. The ad hoc International Criminal Tribunals created by the Security Council currently perform this function.

These Tribunals have the principal mandate to prosecute, adjudicate and eventually punish those responsible for war crimes, crimes against humanity or genocide and to (re)affirm the principle of individual

---

[30] This seem to be one of the latest orientations of the British Home Office experts involved with the preparation of "draft legislation" to reform the criminal justice system and procedure of England, Wales and Northern Ireland.

criminal responsibility under international law. It is true, however, that its repressive function is obviously very limited. But it is also true that, in performing this principal function, it is inevitable for these Tribunals to produce a jurisprudence (to be uniformed by an Appeals Chamber common to both the ICTY and the ICTR) in which a more or less consistent interpretation of customary and conventional international law is developed.

In fact, as of now, the two ad hoc Tribunals have been mainly effective in pursuing this "instrumental function", thus essentially operating as finding mechanisms of applicable rules and principles of international criminal law and international humanitarian law. The particular significance of this "law-finding" function is immediately understood, if one thinks that there has been no international jurisdiction called to apply these subject matters after the codification of a new international humanitarian law in Geneva in 1949 and the subsequent adoption and entry into force of several multilateral instruments on (certain) crimes against humanity.

Notwithstanding that, as of today, the ICTY has produced "only" 14 judgments on first instance and 4 on appeal, while the ICTR has just completed 8 proceedings before the Trial Chambers and 2 before the Appeals Chamber, the Tribunals' decisions - including a great number of preliminary rulings and procedural orders - form an excellent compendium on the application to concrete cases of international humanitarian law and international criminal law, especially in the area of the definition of the elements of the offences, which are also violations of fundamental human rights.

The Tribunals' ancillary legal instruments, starting with the Rules of Procedure and Evidence have made an additional contribution. A wide range of issues has been satisfactorily dealt with by the Tribunals' practice: from the rigorous notion of State under international law,[31] to the definition of armed conflict of an international or non-international character; from the scope of application of the principle of individual criminal responsibility, to the ambit of protected persons by IHL and the definition of the "elements" of war crimes and crimes against humanity; from the responsibility of the superior, to the application of defences or attenuating and aggravating circumstances on sentencing.

Needless to say, an International Criminal Court with permanent and non-limited jurisdiction could much more effectively perform this

[31] I hereby reproduce the definition of State as contained in rule 2 of the Rules of Procedure and Evidence of the ICTY (available at http://www.un.org/icty): "a State Member or non-Member of the United Nations or a self-proclaimed entity *de facto* exercising governmental functions, whether recognised as a State or not".

function of uniform interpretation of the so-called international criminal law. I believe that this will continue to be the most important and challenging aspect of the relationship between international criminal jurisdictions and national legal systems.

Through their jurisprudence, international criminal jurisdictions may seriously contribute to the prosecution of *delicta iuris gentium*, even if they would be capable of conducting a relatively small number of proceedings. The 'availability" of international trials will stimulate the "genuine" prosecution on the national plain and will provide useful guidelines for a uniform interpretation and application of international standards in the areas of IHL, international criminal law and procedure (the latter being strongly influenced by international human rights law).

In general terms, the existence of an international criminal and permanent court will produce a strong deterrent effect, at least *vis-à-vis* the mentality of those who still believe that "at war" all types of violent behaviours are justified, and that national or international peace process shall be built upon the denial or negation of justice:[32] and so it will exercise that preventive function which is and must be the ultimate principal goal of every criminal justice mechanism.

---

[32] As I previously stressed, it shall not be underestimated the impact of a guiding jurisprudence of the ICC in the delicate area of the responsibility of subordinates, where a correct assessment of a "superior order" as a mitigating factor with respect to the penalty rather than a defence excluding criminal responsibility may finally prevail.

20. Follow up to Rome: Preparing for Entry into Force of the Statute of the International Criminal Court

WILLIAM A. SCHABAS*

The Diplomatic Conference that adopted the Rome Statute of the International Criminal Court completed a drafting process than began in 1994, or 1989, or 1948, or 1937 and perhaps even before, depending on one's perspective. The treaty will enter into force when sixty accessions, approvals, acceptances or ratifications have been deposited.[1] While this stage is obviously indispensable and fundamental, there are other important tasks to be carried out before the Court can be created. In order for States to be in a position to comply with their commitments under the Statute, legislative and possible constitutional changes may be required. Furthermore, even if the Statute enters into force, the Court cannot be operational unless several additional instruments are drafted. Until the entry into force of the Statute, when the Assembly of States Parties can begin to assume its responsibilities, this work is to be carried out by a Preparatory Commission.

* M.A. (Toronto), LL.D. (Montreal), Professor, Département des sciences juridiques, Université du Québec à Montréal. During the academic year 1998-99, the author is a Jennings Randolph Senior Fellow at the United States Institute of Peace, Washington.

[1] "Rome Statute of the International Criminal Court", UN Doc. A/CONF.183/9, (1998) 37 I.L.M. 999, Article 126(1).

Signature, Ratification, Acceptance, Approval and Accession

The Rome Statute remains open for signature at the United Nations Headquarters until December 31, 2000.[2] Signatory States may ratify, accept or approve the Statute by depositing instruments to this effect with the Secretary-General of the United Nations. Alternatively, States may skip the signature stage altogether and deposit instruments of accession. The Statute will enter into force on the first day of the month after the sixtieth day following the date of the deposit of the sixtieth instrument of ratification, acceptance, approval or accession[3] with the Secretary-General of the United Nations. Subsequently, for States that become Parties to the Statute after it has entered into force, it will enter into force with respect to such States on the first day of the month after the 60th day following the deposit by such State of its instrument of ratification, acceptance, approval or accession.

Although signature of a treaty may also, under certain circumstances, constitute a mean of indicating its acceptance,[4] Article 125 of the Rome Statute indicates that this is to be only a preliminary step, necessarily followed by deposit of instruments of ratification, acceptance or approval. Signature indicates an intention to become a State Party. It constitutes, in the words of the International Court of Justice in its advisory opinion on reservations to the Genocide Convention, "a first step to participation" in the treaty.[5]

Signature of the Rome Statute is an important development and it is not without legal consequences. Pursuant to Article 18 of the Vienna Convention on the Law of Treaties, a signatory State is obliged not to defeat the object and purpose of a treaty prior to its entry into force. Above all, signature of the Statute manifests the State's intent to prepare for ratification, acceptance or approval, a step that will almost invariably require changes to its domestic legislation.

Article 2(1)(b) of the Vienna Convention on the Law of Treaties states that "'ratification', 'acceptance', 'approval' and 'accession' mean in each case the international act so named whereby a State establishes on the international plane its consent to be bound by a treaty". States undertake such steps in accordance with their own particular traditions, laws and constitutions.

---

[2] *Ibid.*, Article 125.

[3] *Ibid.*, Article 126.

[4] *Vienna Convention on the Law of Treaties*, (1979) 1155 U.N.T.S. 331, Articles 11-12.

[5] *Reservations to the Convention on the Prevention and Punishment of the Crime of Genocide (Advisory Opinion)*, [1951] I.C.J. Reports 16, p. 28.

Changes to National Legislation

States intending to sign, ratify, accept, approve or accede to the Rome Statute should undertake a thorough examination of their own domestic legislation. Two distinct issues must be addressed: first, the State's legislation must enable it to comply with the obligations in the Statute concerning cooperation and enforcement; second, and in keeping with the principle of complementarity (preamble: "Recalling that it is the duty of every State to exercise its criminal jurisdiction over those responsible for international crimes"), the State's legislation should enable it to exercise domestic jurisdiction over the crimes and the individuals within the jurisdiction of the Court.

Cooperation and Judicial Assistance

It ought hardly to be necessary - *pacta sunt servanda* - but Article 86 of the *Statute* affirms a general obligation to cooperate: "States Parties shall, in accordance with the provisions of this Statute, cooperate fully with the Court in its investigation and prosecution of crimes within the jurisdiction of the Court". For further clarity, Article 88 declares that "States Parties shall ensure that there are procedures available under their national law for all of the forms of cooperation" specified in Part VIII, which concerns international cooperation and judicial assistance.

Probably the most vital of these obligations concerns "arrest and surrender". States will require legislation enabling them to arrest and detain persons sought by the Court, and furthermore to facilitate their "surrender". Suspects will be entitled to exercise all legal remedies to contest their arrest and transfer, of course, and these may become quite protracted, raising the issue of provisional release. While not ruled out by the Statute, the spirit of international prosecution for such serious crimes argues in favour of a rather high threshold for any assessment of interim release. A State whose laws granted interim release too readily, thereby jeopardizing the ability of the Tribunal to ensure offenders would be brought before it, could be deemed in breach of its duty to cooperate.

The Statute does not use the term "extradition", consistent with an approach to this issue already adopted in the statutes of the ad hoc Tribunals, which speak of "surrender or transfer" ("le transfert ou la traduction").[6] The argument is a semantic one: extradition applies between

---

6 "Statute of the International Criminal Tribunal for the former Yugoslavia", UN Doc. S/RES/827 (1993), Art. 29(2)(e); "Statute of the International Criminal Tribunal for Rwanda", UN Doc., S/RES/955 (1994), Art. 28(2)(e). Also: "Rules of Procedure and Evidence", UN Doc. IT/32, Art. 58.

States, surrender or transfer applies between one State and an International Court. But the International Court is really only the sum of its parts, and "transfer" or "surrender" is in a sense the "extradition" to a collectivity of States, acting together. The reason for what at first blush seems obtuse terminology is to respond to objections from States that have legislation, and sometimes even constitutional provisions, prohibiting the *extradition* of their own nationals.

It is difficult to predict how national courts will take to these distinctions, and there are few precedents. Three rationales have been advanced by academic writers for such prohibitions on extradition of nationals: national judges are the natural judges of the offence; a State must protect its own nationals; a foreigner would be subject to prejudice.[7] None of these are applicable to the International Criminal Court, especially given that the Court grants States Parties the first bite at the apple, in accordance with the principle of complementarity. Yet many national judges remain hostile to international justice, as can be seen in the embarrassingly tardy efforts of the United States to secure the transfer of a Rwandan suspect to the Arusha Tribunal.[8] That a national judge would consider a distinction between "transfer or surrender" and "extradition" to be little more than legal sophistry cannot be ruled out.[9] As a result, States whose national laws protect their own citizens from extradition may be required to enact appropriate amendments.

Penalties may also pose problems for some States with regard to transfer and surrender. Indeed, the issue was raised at Rome during the debates on the death penalty and life imprisonment, with some delegations noting their constitutional prohibition on extradition in the case of such severe penalties. For example, the Colombian constitution forbids life imprisonment, and presumably an accused could argue that eligibility for parole, as set out in Article 77 of the Statute, does not exclude the possibility of such a sentence.[10] Colombian courts might hold, by analogy

---

[7] Geoff Gilbert, *Aspects of Extradition Law*, Boston/Dordrecht/London: Martinus Nijhoff, 1991, p. 96.

[8] Robert Kushen, Kenneth J. Harris, "Surrender of Fugitives by the United States to the War Crimes Tribunals for Yugoslavia and Rwanda", (1996) 90 *A.J.I.L.* 254.

[9] According to Cherif Bassiouni, "[I]n most States, surrender is equivalent to extradition": M. Cherif Bassiouni, Peter Manikas, *The Law of the International Criminal Tribunal for the Former Yugoslavia*, Irvington-on-Hudson, New York: Transnational Publishers, 1995, p. 787.

[10] Gisbert H. Flanz, "Colombia", translated by Peter B. Heller, Marcia W. Coward, in Gisbert H. Flanz, ed., *Constitutions of the Countries of the World*, Dobbs Ferry, New York: Oceana Publications Inc., 1995, Art. 34.

with a recent decision of the Italian constitutional court,[11] that they cannot speculate upon whether or not parole might be granted, and therefore deny transfer or surrender. Nor should the prospect be gainsaid that sometime in the future, regional or universal human rights bodies might determine that the sentences allowed by the Rome Statute, specifically the possibility of life imprisonment without possibility of parole before twenty-five years, are in breach of international human rights norms.[12] States preoccupied by their compliance with the Rome Statute might be led to contemplate reservations to human rights treaties on this basis, although the compatibility of such reservations with the object and purpose of human rights instruments would be debatable.

Other important obligations with respect to transfer or surrender which may need to be addressed by domestic lawmakers are the duty to allow and facilitate transit of prisoners on their way to the Court, waiver of the rule of speciality, and the application of specific rules concerning competing requests for extradition. The practical application of these norms must be thought through carefully in order to avoid situations like that confronting the International Criminal Tribunal for Rwanda earlier this year. When the Prosecutor decided to discontinue a case against an individual sought for murder of the Rwandan Prime Minister and several Belgian soldiers, the Trial Chamber concluded that the Statute and the Rules left it no alternative but to liberate the suspect. Belgium intervened unsuccessfully before the Court in order to obtain custody.[13]

Obligations in the area of judicial cooperation are set out in Article 93. States Parties are required to comply with requests for assistance by the Court in relation to investigations or prosecutions. The list includes identification and location of persons or items, the taking of evidence, questioning of suspects, service of documents, execution of search and seizure, provision of records and documents, protection of witnesses and preservation of evidence. Most of these points are already the subject of bilateral arrangements in the area of international judicial cooperation, and the domestic legal mechanisms involved in giving effect to them are well-known.

National laws may also need to be adapted in order to ensure the immunity of Court personnel.[14] Moreover, States Parties are required to

---

[11] *Venezia* v. *United States of America*, Decision no. 223, June 25, 1996 (Constitutional Court of Italy).

[12] See, for example: Dirk Van Zyl Smit, "Life Imprisonment as the Ultimate Penalty in International Law: a Human Rights Perspective", (1999) 9 *Criminal Law Forum* (forthcoming).

[13] *Prosecutor* v. *Ntuyahaga* (Case no. ICTR-90-.40-T), Decision on the Prosecutor's Motion to Withdraw the Indictment, March 18, 1999.

[14] "Rome Statute of the International Criminal Court", *supra* note 1, Articles 4(2), 48(1).

ensure that effect may be given to fines or forfeitures ordered by the Court as part of the penalty, in accordance with Article 77(2).[15]

Two important norms in the "General Principles" part of the Statute should be examined by States reviewing their own legislation. First, the issue of immunity must be addressed. Article 27 of the Statute reiterates a principle recognized since the Nuremberg Charter with respect to official capacity of a Head of State. Yet the uncertain reflection of this principle in domestic law became a central issue in the recent proceedings directed against Augusto Pinochet. The apparent ambiguities of English law were sufficiently convincing for seven judges (one in the High Court, three in the Appeal Court and three in the House of Lords) to rule that Pinochet enjoyed full immunity as a former Head of State.[16] While the matter has now been settled appropriately, it underscores the importance of detailed review of national legislation on this count.

Similarly, while the non-application of statutory limitations for crimes within the jurisdiction of the Court might seem obvious in the light of General Assembly resolutions and similar pronouncements, many national penal codes lag far behind. Article 29 of the Statute declares that the crimes within the Court's jurisdiction are not subject to a statute of limitations. But as there is no provision within the Statute of the Court to suggest the contrary, Article 29 would seem to be totally superfluous. It testifies to the complex relationship between domestic legal systems and the international justice system established by the Rome Statute. Indeed, Article 29 would seem to be directed not at the International Criminal Court but rather at domestic legal norms that allow for statutory limitation.

The issue was debated throughout the *travaux* as one in which national and international law might find themselves in conflict, with several States expressing the progressive position opposed to statutory limitation, and others noting that it remained part of their national law.[17] The *travaux* of the Statute seem to suggest an ongoing ambiguity among at

---

[15] *Ibid.*, Art. 109.

[16] *R.* v. *Bow Street Stipendiary Magistrate and others, ex parte Pinochet Ugarte*, [1998] 4 All E.R. 897 (H.L.); *R.* v. *Bartle and the Commissioner of Police for the Metropolis and others, ex parte Pinochet*, March 24, 1999, English House of Lords, http://.www.parliament.thestationeryoffice.co.uk/pa/ld199899/ldjudgmt/jd990324/pino1.htm

[17] "Report of the *Ad Hoc* Committee on the Establishment of an International Criminal Court", UN Doc. A/50/52, para. 127, p. 29; "Report of the Preparatory Committee on the Establishment of an International Criminal Court", GAOR, Fifty-first Session, Supplement No. 10 (UN Doc. A/51/10), Vol. I, paras. 195-196, p. 45, para. 324, p. 68; *ibid.*, Vol. II, pp. 88-89; "Decisions Taken by the Preparatory Committee at its Session Held from 11 to 21 February 1997", UN Doc. A/AC.249/1997/L.5, pp. 24-25; "Report of the Inter-Sessional Meeting From 19 to 30 January 1998 in Zutphen, The Netherlands", UN Doc. A/AC.249/1998/L.13, pp. 57-58; "Draft Statute for the International Criminal Court", UN Doc. A/CONF.183/2/Add. 2, pp. 62-63.

least some States as to the scope of the norm prohibiting statutory limitations on international crimes, including genocide. During the 1960s, as the application of statutory limitations in national penal codes to Nazi war criminals began to appear possible, there was a movement to amend rules by which such prosecutions could be time barred. Accordingly, there were changes to domestic legislation.[18] On an international level, these developments took the form of General Assembly resolutions,[19] and treaties within both the United Nations system[20] and that of the Council of Europe.[21] Both instruments refer specifically to the crime of genocide as an offence for which there shall be no statutory limitation. The treaties have not been a great success in terms of ratifications; the United Nations instrument has only forty-three States parties. The low rate of ratification of the United Nations Convention has led some academics to contest the suggestion that this is a customary norm.[22] The French Cour de Cassation determined, in the *Barbie* case, that the prohibition on statutory limitations for crimes against humanity is now part of customary law.[23]

---

[18] Dick de Mildt, *In the Name of the People: Perpetrators: Perpetrators of Genocide in the Reflection of their Post-War Prosecution in West Germany*, The Hague/London/Boston: Martinus Nijhoff Publishers, 1996, pp. 29-30; Ingo Müller, *Hitler's Justice, The Courts of the Third Reich*, Cambridge, Massachusetts: Harvard University Press, 1991, pp. 243-249; Robert A. Monson, "The West German Statute of Limitations on Murder: A Political, Legal and Historical Exposition", (1982) 30 *Am. J. Comp. L.* 605.

[19] G.A. Res. 3 (I); G.A. Res. 170 (II); G.A. Res. 2583 (XXIV); G.A. Res. 2712 (XXV); G.A. Res. 2840 (XXVI); G.A. Res. 3020 (XXVII); G.A. Res. 3074(XXVIII).

[20] *Convention on the Nonapplicability of Statutory Limitations to War Crimes and Crimes Against Humanity*, (1970) 754 U.N.T.S. 73. See: Robert H. Miller, "The Convention on the Non-applicability of Statutory Limitations to War Crimes and Crimes against Humanity", (1971) 65 *A.J.I.L.* 476.

[21] *European Convention on the Non Applicability of Statutory Limitation to Crimes Against Humanity and War Crimes of January 25, 1974*, E.T.S. 82.

[22] Steven R. Ratner, Jason S. Abrams, *Accountability for Human Rights Atrocities in International Law, Beyond the Nuremberg Legacy*, Oxford: Clarendon Press, 1997, p. 126.

[23] *Fédération nationale des déportés et internés résistants et patriotes et al. v. Barbie*, (1984) 78 I.L.R. 125, p. 135. Also: France, Assemblée nationale, *Rapport d'information déposé en application de l'Article 145 du Règlement par la Mission d'information de la Commission de la défense nationale et des forces armées et de la Commission des affairees étrangères, sur les opérations militaires menées par la France, d'autres pays et l'ONU au Rwanda entre 1990 et 1994*, Paris, 1999, p. 286.

Complementary and Domestic Prosecution

The principle of complementarity recognizes that States themselves have priority over the International Criminal Court in the prosecution of offenders. Only when they fail to do so is the Court entitled to exercise jurisdiction.[24] But the Statute does not require States to prosecute individuals suspected of committing crimes within the Court's jurisdiction, even if the preamble states this to be "a duty". Indeed, the Court was created precisely because States do not assume their responsibilities. While the main culprits have been the States with jurisdiction on a territorial or personal basis, it is clear that there is also a profound reluctance to exercise universal jurisdiction, even where laws permit. The United States government learned this bitter lesson in 1997 and again in 1998 when it sought the cooperation of a State whose laws recognized universal jurisdiction and was also willing to undertake the prosecution of Pol Pot. Israel, Spain and Canada all declined the invitation. Some States, such as Canada, after enacting legislation to permit universal jurisdiction have in practice renounced its application in favour of simpler solutions such as deportation or expulsion. Spain's enthusiasm for the prosecution of Augusto Pinochet is a welcome sign that this historic reluctance may be abating, but it is far too soon to tell whether judge Baltazar Garzon's initiatives reflect a more general trend among States.

Yet it is clear that the International Criminal Court will not have the resources to assume the burden of impunity throughout the world. One of the important messages of the Rome Statute is that States must show more diligence in prosecuting the crimes of genocide, crimes against humanity and war crimes. It is to be hoped that States will be embarrassed when the Court attempts to exercise jurisdiction under the principle of complementarity. Their failings, whether it be in the exercise of territorial or personal, or even universal, jurisdiction, will become an indelible stain on the historical record. Should States take this as the message of the International Criminal Court, then they will also want to turn their attention to the legislative reflection of the substantive provisions of the Rome Statute.

The first task is the implementation of the offences defined by the Statute within national laws. Article 6 repeats the definition found in the Convention on the Prevention and Punishment of the Crime of Genocide. A recent study reaches the perhaps unexpected conclusion that most States have in fact implemented the Convention within domestic legislation, at the very least by including the definition of the offence within their penal

---

24 "Rome Statute of the International Criminal Court", *supra* note 1, Art. 17.

codes.[25] But the situation cannot be the same with respect to crimes against humanity and war crimes because of the originality of Articles 7 and 8. States should therefore amend their penal legislation so as to incorporate the new definitions of these crimes.

Some States do not provide for these "international crimes" in their national laws because they consider that what are, in essentially all cases, serious crimes against the person are adequately covered by the more classic criminal law offences of murder, rape, assault and so on. Upon closer examination, however, there are some troubling gaps, particularly when it comes to inchoate offences such as incitement. To the extent that the definitions themselves come close to the terms of Articles 6 to 8 of the Statute, there may still be problems with respect to criminal participation and the availability of defences. Reference has already been made to the issue of Head of State immunity, invoked with at least temporary success by Augusto Pinochet before the English courts. The Rome Statute departs from the terms of the ad hoc Tribunals and earlier models by allowing the defence of superior orders, although subject to very rigorous conditions.[26] Yet some States give this plea a much broader scope in their national legislation. Discrepancies also exist between the forms of criminal participation punishable under the Rome Statute - conspiracy, complicity and attempt - and those that exist in domestic codes, although this is probably little more than a detail. Of greater significance is the absence of command responsibility provisions from the vast majority of national penal codes. Unlike most provisions concerning criminal participation, which migrated from "general principles" into the international penal environment, command responsibility comes from the other direction, a creation of international law that has yet to make its place within domestic codes.

To the extent that national lawmakers take up this task seriously, it should result in a greater consistency between national penal codes, even those derived from different legal cultures and systems. The result may be something that comparative criminal lawyers have long dreamed of, a cosmopolitan criminal law, but one delivered by the unexpected midwife of an International Criminal Court.

---

[25] William A. Schabas, *The Law of Genocide* (forthcoming).

[26] "Rome Statute of the International Criminal Court", *supra* note 1, Art. 33.

The Work of the Preparatory Commission

The Rome Statute says nothing about the Preparatory Commission, whose earnest work began in February 1999. The Preparatory Commission is created by the Final Act of the Rome Diplomatic Conference, adopted at the same time as the Statute, on July 17, 1998.[27] Its purpose is to give the Court a head start and to ensure that certain elements necessary for its operation are already in place by the time the Statute enters into force. The instruments drafted by the Preparatory Commission will still require approval by the Assembly of States Parties. The Commission's members consist of those States that have signed the Final Act of the Rome Conference as well as other States "which have been invited to participate", although the Final Act does not say by whom. As a result, even States that have declared their opposition to the Statute and their refusal to sign, such as the United States of America, may participate actively in this phase of the work. On a very practical level, the Commission looks very much like the continuation of the Rome Conference, and it relies on the efforts of many of the same individuals who guided the work in June and July 1998. It is chaired by Canadian diplomat Philippe Kirsch, who also presided over the Committee of the Whole at the Rome Conference.

Resolution F of the Final Act mandates the Preparatory Commission to draft eight specific texts: Rules of Procedure and Evidence; Elements of Crimes; a relationship agreement between the Court and the United Nations; basic principles governing a headquarters agreement to be negotiated between the Court and the host country; financial regulations and rules; an agreement on the privileges and immunities of the Court; a budget for the first financial year; the rules of procedure of the Assembly of States Parties. The Commission is also assigned to pursue work on the crime of aggression, included within the subject matter jurisdiction of the Court but left undefined in the Statute. It is to propose a definition of the crime and the conditions under which the Court may exercise jurisdiction, an oblique reference to the debate about whether Security Council determination is a *sine qua non* for the prosecution of aggression.

According to the Final Act, the Preparatory Commission is to remain in existence until the conclusion of the first meeting of the Assembly of States Parties. The Assembly of States Parties can only meet after the entry into force of the Statute. For the time being, the General Assembly of the United Nations has authorized three sessions of the Preparatory Commission.[28] Although its involvement is not formally

---

[27] UN Doc. A/CONF.183/10.

[28] G.A. Res. 53/105.

required by the Final Act, the Assembly is financing the meetings and its approval is therefore of considerable practical importance. The first meeting was held from February 16 to 26, 1999; the other two will be convened from July 26 to August 13 and November 29 to December 17, 1999. Presumably the General Assembly will authorize further meetings at its 1999 session.

Two instruments to be drafted by the Preparatory Commission are of particular importance. These are the Rules of Procedure and Evidence, and the Elements of Crimes, defined in the Rome Statute as being sources of applicable law to be applied by the Court in additional to the Statute itself, and to the extent that they are compatible with it.[29] The Final Act requires the Preparatory Commission to complete its drafts of these texts before June 30, 2000, although there would seem to be no consequence should it fail to do so. The February 1999 session of the Preparatory Commission agreed that it should focus on these two instruments and, on a practical level, it divided into two working groups, one for each of them. It also decided to begin its consideration of the issue of aggression.

Rules of Procedure

In the earlier international criminal tribunals, the statutes were rather laconic on matters of evidence and procedure. This was left to the judges, who drafted their own rules. The Rome Statute places rather less confidence in the judges, and charges the Assembly of States Parties with adopting the Rules of Procedure and Evidence. As for the judges, they are empowered to adopt "Regulations", but even these are subject to subsequent approval by States Parties.[30] Several provisions of the Rome Statute refer to the Rules of Procedure and Evidence. They Rules are to establish: conditions for intervention of victims in proceedings;[31] procedures for considering defences not expressly contemplated by the Statute;[32] jurisdiction of a single judge of the pre-trial chamber;[33] excusing of a judge by the President;[34] removal or discipline of a judge, the Prosecutor, a Deputy Prosecutor, the Registrar or the Deputy Registrar;[35] publication of decisions of the court and use of the official languages;[36]

[29] "Rome Statute of the International Criminal Court", *supra* note 1, arts. 9(3), 51(5).
[30] *Ibid.*, Art. 52.
[31] *Ibid.*, Art. 15(3), 68(3), 76(2), 82(4).
[32] *Ibid.*, Art. 31(3).
[33] *Ibid.*, Art. 39(b)(3), 57(2)(b).
[34] *Ibid.*, Art. 41(1).
[35] *Ibid.*, Art. 46(1)(a), 46(4), 47.
[36] *Ibid.*, Art. 51.

measures to protect property ordered by the Pre-Trial Chamber;[37] functions and powers of the Trial Chamber;[38] evidentiary matters including oaths, weight, privilege and disclosure of national security information;[39] offences against the administration of justice and misconduct before the court;[40] penalty issues including assessment of fines, applicable mitigating and aggravating factors and criteria for reduction of sentences;[41] appeal procedures;[42] compensation of accused who are acquitted or released;[43] formalities of requests for State cooperation with the Court;[44] and equitable division of State responsibilities in imprisoning offenders.[45] Although the Statute is silent on this point, there is nothing to suggest that these references are exhaustive, and that the Rules may not address a range of other issues. Indeed, there were recommendations sprinkled throughout the *travaux préparatoires* to other aspects of the Court's operations that might be addressed in the Rules.[46]

At the February session, a number of rather thorough proposals dealt with the Rules. Australia[47] and France,[48] in particular, had clearly prepared for the meeting. The two delegations subsequently attempted to devise some compromise proposals. The Preparatory Commission decided to address rules pertaining to investigation and prosecution (Part 5), trial procedure (Part 6) and appeal and revision (Part 7). In fact, in its nine meetings it was not able to get much beyond issues raised by Part 5. A working draft was prepared containing provisions covering commencement

---

37 *Ibid.*, Art. 57(3)(e).
38 *Ibid.*, Art. 64(1).
39 *Ibid.*, Art. 69, 72(5)(d), 93(8)(c).
40 *Ibid.*, Art. 70, 71.
41 *Ibid.*, Art. 77(2)(a), 78(1), 110(4)(c), 110(5).
42 *Ibid.*, Art. 81(1), 81(2)(a), 81(3)(c)(ii), 82(1), 82(3), 84(2) *in fine*.
43 Art. 85(3).
44 Art. 87(1)(a), 87(2), 92(3).
45 Art. 103(3)(a).
46 See: "References to Rules of Procedure and Evidence found in the Rome Statute of the International Criminal Court and in relevant documents of the United Nations Diplomatic Conference of Plenipotentiaries for the Establishment of an International Criminal Court", UN Doc. PCNICC/1999/L.2.
47 "Proposal submitted by Australia", UN Doc. PCNICC/1999/DP.1; "Proposal by Australia", UN Doc. PCNICC/1999/DP.3.
48 "Proposal by France", UN Doc. PCNICC/1999/DP.2; "Working paper submitted by France", UN Doc. PCNICC/1999/DP.3; "Proposal by France on Rules of Procedure and Evidence", UN Doc. PCNICC/1999/DP.6; "Proposal by France on Rules of Procedure and Evidence", UN Doc. PCNICC/1999/DP.7 and Add. 1, Add. 2; "Proposal by France concerning the Rules of Procedure and Evidence", UN Doc. PCNICC/1999/DP.8 and Add.1, Add.2; "Proposal submitted by France concerning the Rules of Procedure and Evidence", UN Doc. PCNICC/1999/DP.10 and Add. 1; "Working paper submitted by France, Comments on the proposal by Australia contained in document PCNICC/1999/DP.1".

of investigation and proceedings, including notification of the decisions of the Prosecutor, procedure to be followed in the event of an application for review of a decision not to proceed with an investigation or not to prosecute and supervision by the Pre-Trial Chamber of decisions of the Prosecutor taken in the interests of justice; conduct of investigation and proceedings, including measures to restrict or deprive a person of liberty; disclosure of evidence; and closure of the pre-trial phase, including proceedings on confirmation of charges in the presence of the person; consequences of the decisions taken by the Pre-Trial Chamber, final decisions on confirmation, amendment of the charges, transition from the pre-trial phase to the trial and confirmation proceedings in the absence of the person charged. The draft reveals that the Preparatory Commission is particularly concerned about the participation of victims in the proceedings, as well as ensuring adequate disclosure of evidence to the accused. However, the defence is also required to disclose evidence to support an alibi defence or some other special defence. The Coordinator of the Working Group noted that the "fundamental issue" of the extent of disclosure obligations by the defence needs further consideration as part of its discussion on evidentiary rules. Study of this working draft is expected to be continued at the July/August session.[49] A "comprehensive discussion of the participation by victims in proceedings before the Court" is also promised for the July/August session.

Elements of Crimes

According to Article 9(1) of the Rome Statute, the Elements of Crimes "shall assist the Court in the interpretation and application of Articles 6, 7 and 8". The concept of "elements" was proposed by the United States, and accepted at Rome mainly because there seemed no substantive reason to oppose them, and most delegations had enough difficulties with the United States that there was no point in adding another item to the list. The approach seems derived from United States federal criminal legislation, which is obsessively codified and contains detailed definitions of offences. The concept is quite strange for most delegations, whose legal systems have functioned well enough without such detailed "elements", trusting their judges to understand terms like "murder" and "robbery" without too much need of elaboration.

---

[49] UN Doc. PCNICC/1999/WGRPE/RT.1; UN Doc. PCNICC/1999/WGRPE/RT.2; UN Doc. PCNICC/1999/WGRPE/RT.3; UN Doc. PCNICC/1999/WGRPE/RT.4.

The fact that there were no other enthusiasts for the idea of Elements of Crimes probably explains why little attention was given to the matter by delegations between the close of the Diplomatic Conference in July 1998 and the first session of the Preparatory Commission the following February. As for the United States delegation, its stunning setback at Rome may well have quenched any enthusiasm for advancing the substantive work on the Elements. The United States had prepared a draft elements paper prior to the Rome Conference in order to show delegates what it had in mind.[50] For the February Preparatory Commission session, it presented an entirely new document that smacked of hasty preparation and sophomoric research. Much valuable time was wasted at the February meeting as a result.

The February session of the Preparatory Commission studied the crimes of genocide as well as a limited list of war crimes committed in international armed conflict corresponding in general to the concept of "grave breaches" of the 1949 Geneva conventions. On the subject of genocide, the United States arrived with a proposal that varied considerably from its document a year earlier. Moreover, it did not even reflect traditional American concerns with the definition of genocide in the 1948 Convention, which is repeated textually in Article 6 of the Statute. For example, the United States has always been worried about the scope of the terms "in whole or in part" out of fear that accusations of genocide might be levelled with respect to rather isolated hate crimes.[51] As a result, its own domestic legislation provides that "in whole or in part" means "in whole or in substantial part".[52] A reservation it formulated at the time of ratification of the Convention says essentially the same thing. A student of the Convention might well have expected that this might be the principal concern of the United States in preparation of the Elements. In fact, the point isn't even addressed.

An amusing example of the amateurishness of the American draft of the Elements can be seen in its treatment of the fifth enumerated act of genocide, "[f]orcibly transferring children of the group to another group". Perhaps because of its concern about the age of recruitment into the armed forces, the American delegation suggested that an age limit for such child victims of genocide should be established, and that it should be fifteen

---

[50] "Proposal submitted by the United States of America, Annex on Definitional Elements for Part Two Crimes", UN Doc. A/CONF.183/C.1/L.10.

[51] United States of America, *Hearing Before a Subcommittee of the Committee on Foreign Relations, United States Senate, Jan. 23, 1950*, Washington: U.S. Government Printing Office, 1950, p. 12.

[52] *Genocide Convention Implementation Act of 1987* (The Proxmire Act), S. 1851, sec. 1093(8).

years of age. This, of course, provoked many delegations to remind the United States that there was a generally accepted definition of the term "child "in Article 1 of the Convention on the Rights of the Child, and that it is eighteen years of age. Possibly they also took some glee in teasing the United States, which is one of two States in the world (Somalia is the other one) not to have ratified the Convention. The upper age limit for "children" as victims of genocide by being transferred was never considered during the drafting of the Genocide Convention and has only arisen in the context of domestic implementing legislation. Two States parties to the Convention have seen fit to establish an upper age limit, of 18. Those two are Israel[53] and the United States.[54] The American delegation to the Preparatory Commission in February 1999 had not even bothered to read its own law!

Delegations responded by attempting to recraft the American proposals. They would have been better to start afresh. In any case, few of them were any better prepared than the United States. The provisional draft that resulted after eight sessions of the Working Group on the Elements of Crimes is a mixture of the obvious - calling into question the utility of the procedure - and of blatant legal errors. The issue that most troubled the Preparatory Commission was whether or not genocide required a plan, and whether or not the individual offender needed to have knowledge of such a plan. It should seem obvious enough that genocide cannot, in practice, be committed without a plan. Moreover, as a form of crime against humanity, it ought to meet the basic criteria for that crime and be either widespread or systematic. The American drafters borrowed some language from the definition of crimes against humanity, describing the intent of the *genocidaire* as "conscious furtherance of a widespread or systematic policy or practice aimed at destroying such group".[55] This made everybody intensely suspicious.[56] The American delegation would have been far better to stick with the formulation proposed prior to the Diplomatic Conference, that only required that "there existed a plan to destroy such group in whole

---

[53] *The Crime of Genocide (Prevention and Punishment) Law*, Laws of the State of Israel, Vol. 4, 5710-1949/50 P101, s. 1(b).

[54] *Genocide Convention Implementation Act of 1987* (The Proxmire Act), S. 1851, sec. 1093(1).

[55] "Proposal submitted by the United States of America", U.N. Doc. PCNICC/1999/DP.4.

[56] See, for example: "Proposal submitted by Colombia, Comments on the proposal submitted by the United States of America on Article 6: the crime of genocide (PCNICC/1999/DP.4)", UN Doc. PCNICC/1999/WGEC/DP.2, p. 2." Proposal by Algeria, Bahrain, Comors, Djibouti, Egypt, Jordan, Iraq, Kuwait, Lebanon, Libyan Arab Jamahiriya, Morocco, Oman, Palestine, Qatar, Saudi Arabia, the Sudan, the Syrian Arab Republic, Tunisia, United Arab Emirates and Yemen, Comments on the proposal submitted by the United States of America concerning terminology and the crime of genocide", UN Doc. PCNICC/1999/WGEC/DP.4, p. 3.

or in part".[57] In any event, the Coordinator of the Working Group produced a discussion paper that seemed to satisfy the "interested delegations". It described the mental element of genocide as being that: "[t]he accused knew or should have known that the conduct would destroy, in whole or in part, such group or that the conduct was part of similar conduct directed against that group".[58] This blatantly contradicts the Statute itself, which declares that an individual can be convicted only if it is proven that "the material elements are committed with intent and knowledge", something which is inconceivable with a "should have known" standard.[59] In any case, it is a fundamental precept that genocide is a crime involving the highest level of specific intent. The term "should have known" is a catch phrase meaning "negligence" that most beginning law students learn before their first examinations. The shortcomings of the American draft can be excused because they are only a starting point for discussion. But that the Working Group, after days of discussion, commits such fundamental legal errors raises questions about the validity of the exercise as a whole.

The Working Group also studied the Elements of war crimes committed in international armed conflict, as set out in Article 8(2)(a) of the Statute.[60] Here its work was facilitated considerably by a detailed paper prepared by the International Committee of the Red Cross that analysed the relevant provisions in light of the case law, the *travaux préparatoires* of the Geneva conventions, and other relevant sources.[61] But even with such assistance, the work seemed to progress terribly slowly. There was much debate about the proposal, in the United States draft, that suggested the war crime of murder was not committed if there was a "lawful justification or excuse". The United States said as an example that "the killing of an escaping prisoner of war would not result in culpability for this offence".[62] Of course, war wouldn't be war if there was no killing, and therefore not every case of "murder" can be a war crime. The Swiss and Hungarians addressed the same issue, but used the word "unlawfully", which seemed

---

[57] *Ibid.*, p. 1.

[58] "Discussion paper proposed by the Coordinator, Article 6: The crime of genocide", UN Doc. PCNICC/1999/WGEC/RT.1.

[59] "Rome Statute of the International Criminal Court", *supra* note 1, Art. 30.

[60] There were two proposals, from the United States (UN Doc. PCNICC/1999/DP.4/Add. 2), and from Hungary and Switzerland (UN Doc. PCNICC/1999/DP.5). Subsequently, other delegations made proposals: "Proposal submitted by Spain: working paper on the Elements of Crimes", UN Doc. PCNICC/1999/ DP.9/Add.2; "Proposal submitted by Colombia", UN Doc. PCNICC/1999/WGEC/Dp.3; "Proposal submitted by Japan", UN Doc. PCNICC/1999/WGEC/DP.5.

[61] At the request of several delegations, the ICRC paper was released as an official document: UN Doc. PCNICC/1999/WBEC/INF.1

[62] UN Doc. PCNICC/1999/DP.4/Add. 2, p. 4.

less troublesome.[63] The United States delegates pointed out that it must mean the same thing. A second issue of debate was the characterization of the conflict. The United States' language was "in the course of international armed conflict", while the Swiss and Hungarian proposal suggested "in the context of an international conflict". The issue of how to designate protected persons also arose. The United States proposal spoke of "one or more civilians taking no active part in hostilities or one or more combatants placed *hors de combat*". The Swiss and Hungarian text was ostensibly broader, referring to "persons or property protected under the provisions of the relevant Geneva Convention", and it was argued that this would cover other non-combatants such as war correspondents. To this, the United States answered that "persons protected by the Geneva Conventions" was in fact more restrictive, because it would exclude categories of civilians. The Working Group also spent some time considering the scope of the war crime of torture.

At the close of the session, the Coordinator of the Working Group prepared a discussion paper as part of a process of consensus building.[64] His text referred to conduct that took place "in the context of and [...] associated with an international armed conflict". The Swiss and Hungarian terminology dealing with protected persons was adopted. A general introductory paragraph dealt with the possible defences: "the elements presume that the conduct is not otherwise legally justified under applicable law referred to in Article 21, paragraph 1(b) and (c) of the Statute... Absence of a lawful justification for a particular action need not be proved by the Prosecutor unless the issue is raised by the accused."

The United States had also submitted a document concerning Elements from the standpoint of norms of individual criminal responsibility, which are developed in Articles 25 and 28 of the Statute.[65] It too was poorly drafted, for example in changing the offence of incitement to genocide from an inchoate crime that does not require any concrete result, as intended by the drafters of the 1948 Convention, to an offence where the accused "had the direct effect of causing one or more persons to commit the crime of genocide in question".[66] The proposal was not discussed in any detail, but it is obvious that many delegations consider it to be beyond the scope of the Elements. Their views are supported by a textual argument, namely that the provision creating the Elements, Article 9, appears immediately after the definitions of the crimes in Articles 6 to 8, and refers to "interpretation and application of Articles 6, 7 and 8". On the

---

[63] "Proposal submitted by Hungary and Switzerland", UN Doc. PCNICC/1999/DP5.

[64] "Discussion paper proposed by the Coordinator", UN Doc. PCNICC/1999/WGEC/RT.2.

[65] "Proposal submitted by the United States", UN Doc. PCNICC/1999/DP.4/Add. 3.

[66] *Ibid.*, p. 3.

other hand, there is some merit to the American proposal, because the interpretation and application of Articles 6, 7 and 8 necessarily involves consideration of the other provisions. Defining forms of criminal participation seems to be intimately bound up with the interpretation of the crimes themselves.[67] Logically, if the judges need assistance with the substantive definitions, they should also get help on these related matters. However, the reluctance of delegates to expand the Elements is understandable. If things continue in the same way, they will be wasting enough time on the Elements of Articles 6 to 9 without compounding their problems.

The Elements were probably a bad idea and ought to have been resisted more vigorously at Rome. The relevant concepts are being elaborated in the complex jurisprudence of the ad hoc Tribunals, with impressive results. Is it really necessary to define "torture", as the February meeting endeavoured to do, when a perfectly workable definition has been adopted by the International Criminal Tribunal for the former Yugoslavia.[68] As an early student of humanitarian law noted, what is done cannot be undone,[69] and the Elements are with us. Nevertheless, an appropriate methodology to their preparation could save the Preparatory Commission an immense amount of time, and result in a genuinely useful instrument. The work on genocide and crimes against humanity might well be delegated to a group of experts who would be charged with preparing a draft, replete with the appropriate references to the case law,[70] *travaux* and legal scholarship. This would provide a genuine basis for debate. The Preparatory Commission would focus its discussions and take its decisions based on what the law really is and where the interpretative problems lie.

Aggression

The Preparatory Commission also undertook what was carefully described as "a preliminary consideration of the modalities of discussion" for a definition of the crime of genocide.[71] However, the summary of the proceedings provides no details about the scope of these discussions. The

---

67 See for example: "Proposal submitted by Spain; working paper on Elements of Crimes", UN Doc. PCNICC/12999/DP.9, p. 4.

68 Furundzija.

69 Theodor Meron, "Crimes and Accountability in Shakespeare", in *War Crimes Law Comes of Age*, Oxford: Clarendon Press, 1998, pp. 67-121.

70 A French document reviewing applicable authorities on genocide is a helpful beginning in this respect: UN Doc. PCNICC/1999/WGEC/DP.1.

71 "Proceedings of the Preparatory Commission at its first session (16-26 February 1999), Summary", UN Doc. PCNICC/1999/L.3/Rev.1, para. 11.

Chair asked Tuvaku Manongi of Tanzania to serve as Coordinator for the definition of the crime of aggression. Everyone is aware, of course, that while the Court cannot operate without Rules and Elements, its creation will hardly be imperilled if work on the "a-word" does not advance. Many may in fact hope for such a result.

* * * * *

Solutions will be found to these problems, as they were at Rome. With ten days to go before the close of the Rome Conference, many participants, including the Bureau, questioned whether the work could be completed.[72] The determination to create the Court triumphed, and there is no reason to believe it will not do so again in this subsequent, preparatory phase. Crises like those in Kosovo underscore the urgency of the work and the need for the prompt creation of the Court. The rate of signature of the *Statute* is very encouraging, and entry into force may come sooner than many anticipate.

---

[72] Philippe Kirsch, John T. Holmes, "The Rome Conference on an International Criminal Court: The Drafting Process" (1999) 93 *A.J.I.L.* 2.

21. Current Political Developments and their Impact on the Future of the International Criminal Court

PHANI DASCALOPOULOU-LIVADA*

We have heard very interesting and thought-provoking reports and interventions on the ICC. While listening to them, my mind wandered back at the time when this whole exercise - I mean its preparatory phase - started, in 1994. Certainly, five years is not a long period of time, especially when dealing with a process such as the creation of an international institution of such major and unique importance. An International Criminal Court, that is, which will project itself - that's how we aspire for it to be well into the depths of the twenty-first century and beyond.

Still, somehow it seems to me that, in every other sense apart from time, the early 1990s are, perhaps, further removed from 1999 than the 1940s and the Nuremberg and Tokyo trial where our inspiration for the establishment of a permanent criminal court mainly derives from. Why is that?

I would submit that this is due to the radical changes in the political realities, which occurred at the end of this last and very significant decade of the twentieth century. It is my view that these changes affect the future ICC and the future of the international criminal justice in general. Let me explain.

When the drafting of the Statute started within the Preparatory Committee, the creation of the ICC was viewed, I believe, primarily as a means of excluding national sovereignty, to the extent feasible, to the benefit of objective truth and justice. The idea was, in general terms, that

* Legal Adviser, Legal Department, Ministry of Foreign Affairs, Athens.

the ICC would be an institution which would have the possibility to disregard national frontiers in order to be able to bring those accused of grave crimes to justice, under its close scrutiny and control and by applying the highest standards of objectivity and fairness. Obviously there were great difficulties to be overcome. An extreme but nonetheless illustrative example of the considerations involved is provided by the case of universal jurisdiction. The notion of universal jurisdiction was highly controversial exactly because it challenged not only national jurisdiction but went even further, challenging the right of a state to be bound by a treaty or not. Ultimately, the notion of universal jurisdiction put in question the very relevance of national sovereignty. The solutions adopted, such as, primarily, the safe haven of "complementarity" and the wise or, in any case, very carefully thought out, selection of States which are required to be members of the Statute for the Court to acquire jurisdiction in a specific case, stand witness to the difficulties that a number of States, particularly major powers, had with universal jurisdiction for the reasons I mentioned.

Some months later from the Rome Conference, however, events seem to have bypassed us. It seems, indeed, that in this short period of time which has elapsed from those discussions, political realities have created a drastically different environment. According to the thoughts of the Western world, it seems that the doctrine which takes precedence now in international politics, certainly not in hard-core international law as yet, is that of the subordination of the notion of national sovereignty to that of the protection of human rights and the rights of minorities (still, of course very exceptionally applied by its proponents). We have thus witnessed national sovereignty being set aside without even a resolution of the Security Council to this effect, on the sole resolution of a number of States, over the commission of grave crimes which undoubtedly concern the international community. Which leads me to believe that, had the PrepCom and the Rome Conference taken place now, the arguments of those in favour of wider powers for the ICC would have been infinitely stronger.

Be that as it may, the result is that the ICC now looks even more like an imperative need of the times. If, indeed, we are close to accepting that national sovereignty is to be set aside in certain cases, if, indeed, national frontiers are going to be less relevant where human rights are at stake, then we are definitely in dire need of an institution which will have the ultimate power to decide whether these human rights have indeed been violated and whether grave crimes have indeed been committed and by whom, that is to say we need the ICC to be established as soon as possible so that it may be able to judge all sides of the spectrum and so that every shadow of a doubt as to the facts, the intentions and the truth may be removed.

And of course it should be considered imperative that those who are now sensitive enough to take the protection of human rights in their own hands should also be consistent enough to be the first to join in the Statute and promote its creation by all means. Otherwise their commitment to human rights and justice will be marred by doubt and suspicion.

22. The Obligation to Cooperate with the International Criminal Court and States not Party to the Statute

GIUSEPPE NESI*

This paper will focus on international cooperation and judicial assistance. Namely, I will deal with the issue of the lack of cooperation by States ruled by Articles 87, para. 5 and 87, para. 7 of the Rome Statute of the ICC.

Of course, different consequences derive from the fact that the State that does not cooperate is, or is not, a State Party to the Statute. With regard to States that are Parties to the Statute, many norms, and in particular Article 86, oblige those States to cooperate. Those provisions are re-statements of norms that are regularly included in international treaties devoted to cooperation and judicial assistance. As regards third States, the Statute provides for the conclusion of general agreements or ad hoc agreements dealing with cooperation between the State and the ICC.

What happens if cooperation is not given? What are the consequences deriving from this lack of cooperation?

1) If the State that does not co-operate is a State party, the Court can denounce such a behaviour to the Assembly of States Parties or, if the situation was referred to the Court by the Security Council on the basis of Chapter VII of the UN Charter, to the Security Council.
2) If the State that does not cooperate is a third State that concluded an agreement with the Court, the Court informs the Assembly of States Parties or, if the situation was referred to the Court by the Security Council, the Security Council.

* Professor of International Law, University of Trento.

What happens if no agreement was signed and thus the third State is not bound by any conventional link? At first glance, it could be stated that a lack of discipline in that respect is inherent to Article 87, para. 5. According to the general rules of the law of treaties, such as "*pacta tertiis nec nocent nec prosunt*", the third State would be "alien" to any obligation to cooperate.

Nonetheless, two elements suggest that, under specific conditions, also States not Parties to the Statute that did not stipulate any cooperation agreement are bound to cooperate. I refer namely, on the one hand, to the modalities of referral of the situation to the Court; on the other, to the nature of the crimes that fall within the jurisdiction of the ICC according to Article 5 of the Statute.

As regards the first point, if the Security Council referred the situation to the Court in conformity with Chapter VII of the UN Charter, i.e. in a situation that is qualified as being a menace to international peace and security (Article 13, b), it is crystal clear that all States that are members of the UN – and not only those that are parties to the Statute – have the obligation to cooperate. In such a case the Security Council resolution through which the situation was referred to the ICC is the source of the obligation to cooperate for the States members of the UN *Mutatis mutandis*, this is what happened when the Security Council adopted the resolutions that established the ad hoc International Criminal Tribunals for Former Yugoslavia and for Rwanda.[1] Thus, a first widening of the obligation to cooperate to States that are not Parties to the Statute can be shaped.

Secondly, as regards the nature of the crimes that fall within the jurisdiction of the ICC, Article 5 lists genocide, crimes against humanity, war crimes. With reference to war crimes, they are crimes on which the States Parties to the Geneva Conventions of 1949 agree to undertake the obligation "to respect and to ensure respect" - according to common Article 1 - for international humanitarian law. I would like to recall that the obligation to respect and to ensure respect for international humanitarian law is deemed by the International Court of Justice an obligation of general international law (*Case concerning Military and Paramilitary Activities In and Against Nicaragua*).

In order to respect and to ensure respect for international humanitarian law, all States Parties to the Geneva Conventions (that not necessarily will be parties to the Rome Statute) are ready to cooperate, in conformity with Article 88, par. 1, of the First Additional Protocol of 1977,

---

[1] As noted by G. Palmisano, *The International Criminal Court and Third States*, in *Essays on the Rome Statute of the International Criminal Court*, F. Lattanzi and W.A. Schabas (eds.), vol. I, L'Aquila, 1999, pp. 391-426.

according to which, "The High Contracting Parties shall afford one another the greatest measure of assistance in connection with criminal proceedings brought in respect of grave breaches of the Conventions or of this Protocol".

Thus, the nature of the crimes that shall be punished by the Court leads to believe that all States Parties to the 1949 Geneva Conventions and to the First Additional Protocol, although they are not parties to the Rome Statute, have the obligation to cooperate in the repression of those crimes. There is no doubt that, when the International Criminal Court becomes operational, the cooperation in the repression of the crimes provided for by the Rome Statute will surely be one of the means through which the States Parties to the 1949 Geneva Conventions and to the First Additional Protocol can "respect and ensure respect" for international humanitarian law.

In this context, the conduct of States that do not comply with the obligation to cooperate with the ICC can be sanctioned by both other States and the Security Council of the UN In fact, also the United Nations has, among its tasks, to respect and ensure respect for international humanitarian law. The existence of such an obligation implies that the States that are members of the UN, in cooperation with the UN, on the basis of Article 89 of the First Additional Protocol, could intervene in cases of non-compliance with the obligation to cooperate in the repression of the crimes listed in Article 5 of the Rome Statute.[2]

In conclusion, an obligation to cooperate even for States not Parties that do not sign any cooperation agreement with the Court could be deduced from instruments different from the Statute. In this manner a contribution to fill the gap regarding the Statute's norms on the obligation to cooperate could be filled.

[2] According to Article 89 of the First Additional Protocol, "In situations of serious violations of the Conventions or of this Protocol, the High Contracting Parties undertake to act, jointly or individually, in co-operation with the United Nations and in conformity with the United Nations Charter".

23. Observations on the Appeal before the International Criminal Court

PATRIZIA DE CESARI*

1) Preliminary Remarks

The Statute of the Court provides an elaborate discipline for the review of decisions in second instance, of which I shall only analyse certain aspects. With the introduction of the appeal,[1] an innovative and important step, the Statute of the Court follows the same solution adopted by the International Criminal Tribunals for the former Yugoslavia and for Rwanda.[2] It provides, however, a more detailed and elaborate system of challenges.

First of all, it should be reminded that the Statutes of the Nuremberg and Tokyo Tribunals did not provide the possibility for a re-examination of the decisions in second instance. Article 26 of the Statute of

* Professor of Private International Law, University of Trento. Researcher in International Law, University of Milan.

[1] See the Rome Statute, Articles 81-83. For a short analysis on the appeal provisions of the Statute see: C. Staker in O. Triffterer (ed.), *Commentary on the Rome Statute of the International Criminal Court - Observers' Notes, Article by Article* (Nomos, Baden-Baden, 1999), p. 1246. P. Sand, R. Mackenzie, Y. Shany, *Manual on International Courts and Tribunals*, London, Edinburgh, Dublin, 1999, pp 269-271; H. Brady and M. Yennings, *Appeal and Revision* in R.S. Lee (ed.), *The International Criminal Court, The Making of the Rome Statute*, The Hague, London, Boston, 1999, pp. 294-303. See also: M. Galasso, *Appeal and Revision in front of the International Criminal Court* in F. Lattanzi (ed), *The International Criminal Court, Comments on the Draft Statute*, Naples 1998.

[2] See at this regard Article 25 of the Statute of the International Criminal Tribunal for the Former Yugoslavia (hereinafter ICTY), UN Doc. S/25704 of 3 May 1993 and Article 26 of the Statute of the International Criminal Tribunal for Rwanda (hereinafter ICTR), UN Doc. S/RES/955(1994). For an analysis of appellate proceedings in the ICTY, see V. Morris and M.P. Scharf, *An Insider's Guide to the International Criminal Tribunal for the former Yugoslavia*, vol. I, at pp. 293-301. For a detailed analysis of ICTY jurisprudence, see S.D. Murphy, *Progress and jurisprudence of the International Criminal Tribunal for the Former Yugoslavia*, in AJIL, 1999, pp. 57-97.

the Nuremberg Tribunal very clearly established that the decisions were final and without possibility for an appeal.

After the establishment of the Nuremberg Tribunal, however, the right of the convicted person to a review of the declaration of guilt or of conviction by a higher level of jurisdiction has been recognized in different international instruments adopted in the field of human rights. Article 14(5) of the International Covenant of Civil and Political Rights, of 19 December 1966, adopted by the General Assembly of the United Nations,[3] states that "Everyone convicted of a crime has the right to his conviction and sentence being reviewed by a higher tribunal according to law". The same principle is stated in Article 2(1) of Protocol n. 7 annexed to the European Convention of Human Rights, adopted in Rome, 4 November 1950.[4] Finally, Protocol n. 11 annexed to the same Convention[5] introduces a new set of rules creating a system of substantial redress against the decisions of the European Court of Human Rights, when these, in accordance with Article 43, may be referred to the enlarged division of the Court (Grand Chamber).

These instruments, however, only provide a minimum level of guarantees, while the Statute of the International Criminal Court recognizes ample guarantees for a fair trial to every person who is subject to its jurisdiction. In fact, while the above-mentioned instruments only recognize a general right of appeal against the decisions of guilt or conviction, the Statute of the International Criminal Court goes beyond; among the grounds for appeal it not only provides error of fact, error of law, procedural errors and the disproportion between the crime and the sentence, but also any other ground that affects the fairness or the reliability of the proceedings or decision.

It must be added that while the Statute of the Court also provides the possibility of lodging an appeal against decisions made during the initial stage of the trial, the Covenant on Civil and Political Rights and

[3] Published in UNTS, vol. 999, p. 171 and vol. 1057, p. 407. The Covenant came into force on 23 March 1976. For a general analysis of the Covenant see: Capotorti F., *Introduzione ai patti internazionali sui diritti dell'uomo,* Padova, 1967.

[4] See the text of the Convention in UNTS, vol. 87, p. 103 and of Protocol n. 7 in ILM 1985, p. 435. It is only with Protocol n. 7 that the European Convention has adopted a provision on the right of the re-examination of the First Instance decision. For a comment on the Convention and Protocols see: L.E. Pettiti, E. Decaux, P.H. Imbert, *La convention européenne des droits de l'homme, Commentaire Article par Article,* 1995, Paris, p. 1087; see also: J. Harris, M. O'Boyle, C. Warbrick, *Law of the European Convention on Human Rights,* London, Dublin, Edinburgh, 1995.

[5] See Protocol n. 11 in *ILM,* 1994, p. 960. This Protocol came into force on 1 November 1998.

Protocol n. 7 provide the right of appeal only against the final decision on guilt or conviction.

Furthermore, while Protocol n. 7 and the New York Covenant - the latter with the possibility of making reservations to Article 14(5), which member States have often made - provide an exception to the right to have the conviction or the sentence reviewed in second instance when the convicted person has been judged in first instance by a court of the highest jurisdiction,[6] the Statute of the International Criminal Court guarantees instead the right of appeal to every person who is subject to its jurisdiction, independently of its official qualification.

A further guarantee of a fair trial is also given by the provision of the Statute, which provides that the judges assigned to the Appeals Division of the Court shall serve only in that division for their entire term of office.

2) The Organ of Appeal of the International Criminal Court

Article 34 of the Statute of the Court provides for the creation of an Appeals Division, added to a Trial Division and a Pre-Trial Division.[7] The Appeals Division is composed of the President and four other judges (Article 39(1)), who, like all the judges of the Court, are chosen from persons of high moral character, impartiality and integrity who have all the qualifications required in their respective States for the appointment to the higher judicial offices. The judges perform their functions with complete independence. The judge who presides over the Appeals Chamber is by law the President of the Court who is elected by an absolute majority of the judges. In the Appeals Division, the judicial functions of the Court are carried out by the Appeals Chamber, which is composed of all the judges of the Appeals Division (Article 39(2)(b)(i)). The judges assigned to the Appeals Division shall serve only in that division and for the entire term of

[6] See Article 2 of the Seventh Protocol. For a short comment see D.J. Harris, M. O'Boyle, C. Warbrick, *Law of the European Convention*, cit. pp. 566-567.

[7] The Trial Division and the Pre-Trial Division shall be composed of not less than six judges. Each division shall contain an appropriate combination of expertise in criminal law and procedure and in international law. The Pre-Trial and the Trial Division shall be composed predominantly of judges with criminal trial experience (Article 39). On the structure of the Court and on the composition of the Chambers see: G. Nesi, *The International Criminal Court: its Establishment and its Relationship with the United Nations System; its Composition, Administration and Financing* in F. Lattanzi (ed), *The International Criminal Court*, cit. pp. 171-192. See of the same author, *The Organs of the International Criminal Court and Their Functions in the Rome Statute. The Assembly of States Parties*, under print for the publication in F. Lattanzi and W.A. Schabas (eds), *Essays on the Rome Statute of the International Criminal Court*, vol. I, L'Aquila 2000, pp. 233 ff.

their office (Article 39(3) and (4)). The Rules of Procedure and Evidence shall ensure their independence and impartiality even with regard to the State of origin of the judges.

The organ entitled to the review of the decisions is thus an internal organ of the Court and in the performance of its functions it shall also ensure a uniform case law.

3) The Appeal against a Decision of Acquittal or Conviction or against a Sentence

An appeal against a decision of acquittal or conviction or against a sentence of the Trial Chamber can be brought by the Prosecutor or the convicted person (or the Prosecutor acting on the person's behalf).

The Statute, however, distinguishes different kinds of appeal according to the author of the appeal and to the type of acts under challenge.

In the case of an appeal brought by the Prosecutor the Statute provides that the revision is made on grounds of error of fact, error of law, procedural errors (Article 81(1a)) and in case of disproportion between the crime and the sentence (Article 81(2a)). Hence, the grounds on which the Prosecutor can bring an appeal are rigorously provided.

On the contrary, both the convicted person and the Prosecutor - on that person's behalf - may load an appeal not only on the error of fact, error of law, procedural errors but also on any other ground that affects the fairness or reliability of the proceedings or decision (Article 81(1b)). Thus, the grounds on the basis of which it is possible to load this type of appeal are wider than the Prosecutor's appeal.

At first sight this latter form of appeal could seem to be creating uncertainty and confusion since it could violate the principle of specificity, which has been conceived for the appeal, if not also appear discretionary in nature. Still, it must be kept in mind that the appeal is strictly linked to the principle of substantial justice, which is pivotal to the appeal itself. However, in no case, when the decision or sentence has been appealed only by the person convicted, or the Prosecutor on that person's behalf, it cannot be amended to his or her detriment (Article 83, para. 2(b)).

On appeal, the Appeals Chamber shall have all the powers of the Trial Chamber. If the Appeals Chamber finds that the proceedings appealed from were unfair in a way that affected the reliability of the decision or the sentence, or if it finds a factual, legal or procedural error, which materially affected the decision or the sentence, it may reverse or amend the decision or sentence or order a new trial before a different Trial Chamber. If necessary, the Appeals Chamber may permit the introduction of new evidence before it, or send the case on remand to the original Trial Chamber to determine factual issues and report back to the Appeals Chamber accordingly.[8]

According to Article 81(2)(b) the Appeals Chamber empowered to re-examine the decision may, if it considers that there are grounds on which the conviction might be set aside, wholly or in part, invite the Prosecutor and the convicted person to submit grounds under Article 81, para. 1(a) or (b), and may render a decision on conviction in accordance with Article 83. The provision in Article 81(2)(b) introduces, therefore, new grounds of appeal, which integrate the *thema decidendum* and supports new issues and pleadings for the appeal. Seemingly, it could represent a partial overcoming of the principle *tantum devolutum quantum appellatum.*[9] In the text prepared by the Preparatory Committee, Article 82 provided that the accused would only be able to raise defences in the appeal proceedings which had already been raised in the Trial Chamber or if resulting from the proceedings in that Chamber. This provision was deleted because many delegations asserted that such a provision would preclude fresh evidence which arises after the trial and would penalize an accused whose defence counsel had not raised certain pleadings and evidence at the trial.

The appeal has suspensive effect. Article 81(4) provides for the suspension of the enforcement of a decision or of a sentence, before the terms for loading the appeal expire and during the course of the proceedings of the appeal.

4) Appeal against Interlocutory Decisions

One of the features of the system of appeal provided in the Statute is, objectively speaking, the possibility to load an appeal against an ample series of decisions and sentences.

In fact not only the decisions of acquittal or conviction or the sentences listed in Article 81, but also a series of other decisions, which are listed in Article 82 and provided also in other provisions of the Statute, may be challenged before the Court. These kind of decisions in the Draft Statute for the International Criminal Court,[10] prepared for the Conference of Rome, were defined interlocutory decisions. This term no longer appears in the actual text of the Statute, which regulates in Article 82 the appeal of decisions, which are made during the course of the proceedings. In addition

---

[8] See Art. 83, para. 2.

[9] See in that sense M. Galasso, *Appeal and Revision*, cited at note 1, p. 303.

[10] UN Doc. A/CONF. 183/2 Add:1, 14 April 1998. See Art. 81.

to the convicted person, also the State concerned and the Prosecutor may load an appeal against decisions and orders as provided by Article 82. This type of appeal refers to preliminary decisions, which may cause direct damage to the rights of the person subject to the trial, in particular, rulings which decide on the lack of jurisdiction *ratione materiae* and *ratione temporis* and exceptions of admissibility.

The appeal against these decisions may be examined, discussed and decided by the Appeals Chamber before and separately from the discussion on the merit.

The decision of the Appeals Chamber, which rejects or admits these challenges, therefore, ends a procedural issue during the course of the trial on the merit. It represents thus an instrument for the expeditious definition of pleas. These pleas are in fact often presented by the convicted person with the aim of delaying the definition of the trial.

The Statute of the Court provides this kind of appeal also against other types of decisions. In particular, the possibility of loading an appeal against decisions given during the proceedings and which are referred immediately to the Court, is provided against orders, which grant or deny the release of persons who are being investigated or prosecuted.

The Prosecutor and the person subject to the trial may also make an appeal against decisions with which the Pre-Trial Chamber, acting on its own initiative and without the request of the Prosecutor, has issued orders and warrants for the purpose of an investigation. These types of decisions are adopted on an *expedited basis* in order to take testimony or a statement from a witness or to examine, collect or test evidence, which may not be available subsequently for the purpose of the trial.

The interlocutory appeal may also be made against a decision that involves an issue that would significantly affect the fair and expeditious conduct of the proceedings or the outcome of the trial, and for which, in the opinion of the Pre-Trial or Trial Chamber, an immediate resolution by the Appeals Chamber may materially advance the proceedings.

The State concerned or the Prosecutor may load an appeal on an *expedited basis* against a decision of the Pre-Trial Chamber made under Article 57(3d) when the latter has authorized the Prosecutor to take specific investigative steps within the territory of a State Party without having secured the cooperation of that State under Part 9 if, whenever possible having regard to the views of the State concerned, the Pre-Trial Chamber has determined in that case that the State is clearly unable to execute a request for cooperation due to the unavailability of any authority or any component of its judicial system competent to execute the request for co-operation under Part 9.

Furthermore, also the legal representative of the victims, the convicted person or a bona fide owner of property adversely affected by an order under Article 75 and regarding the request of reparations, including restitution, compensation and rehabilitation, may appeal against this order, as will be provided in the Rules of Procedure and Evidence.

It is important to emphasize the fact that the interlocutory appeal does not of itself have suspensive effect on the trial, unless the Appeals Chamber so orders, upon request, in accordance with the Rules of Procedure and Evidence.

The possibility to make an appeal against certain types of interlocutory decisions was already provided with regard to the decisions of the International Criminal Tribunal for former Yugoslavia and it had been introduced by modifying Article 72, para. B of the Rules of Procedure and Evidence, adopted by the Tribunal in February 1994.[11] This provision originally regulated the right to present preliminary pleas and it established that they were decided by the Chamber of first instance *in limine litis* and without the possibility of making an interlocutory appeal, with the exception of decisions on lack of jurisdiction. All the other decisions on preliminary issues could therefore be appealed together with the final decision of the Court of First Instance. With subsequent amendments to the Rules of Procedure, the possibility of loading an interlocutory appeal was extended to decisions concerning other preliminary motions on condition that the interlocutory appeal was admitted by at least three judges of the Appeals Chamber and provided that the appeal was made on the grounds of a "serious cause", which in the current text, adopted 12 November 1997, has been substitued with "good cause".

The decisions of the Appeals Chamber of the Tribunal for former Yugoslavia represent useful case law precedents for explaining the nature and scope of the interlocutory appeal. The Appeals Chamber had already made decisions on appeals of this type. In particular, in the *Tadic* case, in the decision of 2 October 1995,[12] the Appeals Chamber has examined the legitimacy and admissibility of the interlocutory appeal made by the convicted person and concerning an issue of jurisdiction, in accordance with Article 72, para. B of the Rules of Procedure and of Evidence.

---

[11] The last Amendments of the Rules have been adopted in November 1999. See the ICTY web site http://www.un.org/icty/basic/rpe/amendment.

[12] See ICTY Decision on the Defence Motion for Interlocutory Appeal on Jurisdiction - *Prosecutor* v. *Dusko Tadic*, Appeal Chamber, October 2, 1995-IT-94-1-T and in 35 *ILM*, 32, 1996 p. 35. Many of the decisions referred to in this discussion may be found in the ICTY web site: www.un.org/icty.

In the decision on interlocutory appeal of 14 October 1996, in the *Blaskic* case,[13] the Appeals Chamber has stated that the grounds for appeal were not based on a "serious cause". In determining whether there was a "serious cause", the Appeals Chamber has decided that the pleading must show that a "serious error was made that may cause substantial prejudice to the accused or is detrimental to the pursuit of justice, or which raises issues not only of general importance but also directly linked to the development of the trial itself, since the decision of the Appeals Chamber is due to have an effect on the proceedings before the Trial Chamber". However the new term "good cause", used in Article 72, seems to be indicating a lower level of evaluation of the grounds to appeal in order to allow a wider scope of action.

The Appeals Chamber with its case law has thus clearly defined the sphere of application of this type of appeal and it has clarified that it concerns exclusively preliminary issues.

In the *Celebici Camp* case, 22 November 1996,[14] the Court has stated that the interlocutory appeal cannot be lodged with regard to a request of temporary release and in the *Blaskic* case, 14 October 1996, it has excluded that it may be brought with regard to a request of protective measures for the witnesses.

If an issue is not a preliminary one, it may nevertheless be subject to the interlocutory appeal in the hypothesis in which the rejection of this form of appeal may prejudice the case in an irreparable way or the issue appears to be pivotal for the trial itself or under international law.

An interlocutory appeal, however, may be made against an issue, which does not concern the preliminary proceedings of the trial if the rejection of this form of appeal may prejudice the case in an irreparable way or the issue appears to be pivotal for the trial or under international law. An interlocutory appeal based on these grounds was lodged by the accused Delalic when the Chamber of First Instance asked the defence to indicate the identity of its own witnesses seven days before the revelation of the identity of the witnesses of the Prosecutor. In the *Celebici Camp* case the Appeals Chamber, 4 March 1998,[15] rejected the interlocutory appeal deeming that the decision of the Chamber of First Instance did not cause a

[13] See Blaskic Proceedings, IT-95-14 "Laska Valley", Appeal Chamber, 14 October 1996, Decision on Application for Leave to Appeal (Protection of Victims and Witnesses).

[14] Appeals Chamber, Delalic et al, IT-96-21 "Celebici", Decision on Application for Leave to Appeal (provisional release) by Hazim Delic.

[15] See Appeals Chamber, 4 March 1998, Decision on Application of Defendant Zejnil Delalic for Leave to Appeal against the Decision of the Trial Chamber of 19 January 1998 for the Admissibility of Evidence. Delalic et al., IT-96-21 "Celebici".

prejudice of such a nature to the defence as to have a significant impact on the development and on the result of the trial.

The case law of the organ of appeal is also interesting with regard to the rights of the accused during the trial once the interlocutory appeal has been admitted. As regards to this, the Appeals Chamber has not allowed the accused to bring new pleas, which had not been brought before the Chamber of First Instance.

Hence, in the *Celebici Camp* case, the Appeals Chamber (decision of 6 December 1996)[16] has rejected the interlocutory appeal based on grounds of "lack of jurisdiction" of the Court made by the accused Delic and on the effort to show that the indictment was incomplete and in violation of the principle *nullum crimen sine lege*.

The interlocutory appeal may also be made by subjects who are not Parties in the case, especially States, that are directly affected by a Trial Chamber's decision, to seek interlocutory review by the Appeals Chamber so long as the decision concerns "issues of general importance relating to the powers of the Tribunal". This possibility is provided by a new provision, Article 108 bis,[17] and it has been already used by Croatia in the *Blaskic* case by the interlocutory appeal against the Trial Chamber decision of 18 July 1997. On January 1997 with an oder (called *subpoena*) of a judge of the Tribunal, the Croatian Minister of Defence was forced to hand in some documents. In the case of not obeying to the order, the Minister would have had to present himself before the Court to give explanations. Croatia had refused to obey contesting the legitimacy of the order. The Chamber of First Instance stated that the Court had the power to address binding orders *subpoena* to States or organs of the State. Croatia challenged this decision and the Appeals Chamber pronounced on this interlocutory appeal (decision of 29 October 1997).[18] Preliminary the

[16] Appeals Chamber, 6 December 1996, Decision on the Application for Leave to Appeal by Hazim Delic (Defect in the form of the Indictment) Delalic et al., IT-96-21 "Celebici".

[17] Adopted by the Tribunal on 24 July 1997. The Rule 108 bis (Request for Review) provides:

"(A) A State directly affected by an interlocutory decision of a Trial Chamber may, within fifteen days from the date of the decision, file a request for review of the decision by the Appeals Chamber if that decision concerns issues of general importance relating to the powers of the Tribunal.

(B) The party upon whose motion the Trial Chamber issued the impugned decision shall be heard by the Appeals Chamber. The other party may be heard if the Appeals Chamber considers that the interests of justice so require.

(C) The Appeals Chamber may at any stage suspend the execution of the impugned decision.

(D) Rule 116 *bis* shall apply *mutatis mutandis*."

[18] Appeals Chamber, Decision on the Admissibility of the Request for Review by the Republic of Croatia of an Interlocutory Decision of a Trial Chamber (Issuance of *Subpoena*

Chamber noted that, since the term *subpoena* includes the notion of compulsory order, such an order can be directed only at individuals acting in their private capacity and not at the States. However the Chamber agreed that the ICTY may issue binding orders to States, since it must be able to take such steps to effectively investigate crimes, collect evidence, summon witnesses and have indicted, arrested and surrendered to The Hague. Furthermore, the application of this authority is not limited to the States of the former Yugoslavia but is extended to all the United Nations member States. The Appeals Chamber also found that the ICTY has no enforcement powers over the States and its only recourse is to report such noncompliance to the Security Council.

In conclusion, we can assert that in the context of ad hoc international criminal courts there has been a relevant strengthening of the instrument of interlocutory appeal, which is reflected in the adoption of this type of appeal, as provided in the Statute of the International Criminal Court, which has even given more importance to it elaborating a detailed and articulated discipline. We can state that the strengthening of this form of appeal responds to two fundamental principles: the economy of the trial and the full guarantee of a fair trial to the accused.

Duces Tecum) and Scheduling Order, *Blaskic* case, IT-95-14 "Lasva Valley". For a commentary of the decision see: Y. Nouvel, *Précisions sur le pouvoir du Tribunal pour l'ex-Yougoslavie d'ordonner la production des preuves et la comparution des témoins: l'arrêt de la chambre d'appel du 29 Octobre 1997 dans l'affaire Blaskic* in *R.G.D.I.P.*,1998, pp.157-164.

24. Some Remarks on the Settlement of Disputes in the Rome Statute of the International Criminal Court

FRANCESCA TROMBETTA-PANIGADI*

Article 119 of the Rome Statute of the International Criminal Court concerns the settlement of disputes which can arise among two or more States Parties with regard, on one hand, to judicial functions of the same Court and, on the other hand, to the interpretation or application of the Statute.

This provision specifies, in its first paragraph, that any dispute concerning the "judicial functions" of the Criminal Court shall be settled by the decision of the same Court. One may wonder which judicial functions of the Court can create disputes between member States. We have to exclude that disputes regarding the Court's competence to decide on jurisdiction in a concrete case can be included in the notion of "judicial functions". The *Kompetenz-Kompetenz* of the Court is in fact explicitely recognized in Article 19 of the Statute, which underlines that the Court satisfies itself that it has jurisdiction in any case brought before it and that it may, on its own motion, determine the admissibility of a case in accordance with Article 17. The power of international tribunals to determine their own jurisdiction is generally recognized in international practice. It is in fact a necessary component in the exercise of judicial function and does not need to be expressly provided for in the constitutive documents of those tribunals, although this is often done.[1]

* Researcher in International Law, University of Trento.

[1] See recently Appeal Chamber of the International Tribunal for the Prosecution of Persons Responsible for Serious Violations of International Humanitarian Law Committed in the Territory of Former Yugoslavia since 1991, 2nd October 1995, decision on the Defence

With regard to judicial functions of the Court in specific proceedings, it seems difficult to imagine that judicial functions can create disagreements among States, as the Criminal Court has jurisdiction on crimes committed by individuals and not on disputes among States. Therefore, it seems that questions - such as those relating to its jurisdiction *ratione temporis*, to preconditions to the exercise of jurisdiction, to issues of admissibility of a case, to the applicable law, to preventive and interim measures, to admissibility of evidence, to the testimony of witnesses, to their protection and the protection of victims, to the reparations to victims, to the imposition of penalties on convicted persons, to the admissibility and to the conditions of appeal - will be raised by individuals and by their lawyers. Therefore, at least directly, they cannot concern member States, nor create disagreements or disputes among them.

If this is correct, we should read Article 119 in a different way and consider its second paragraph as the provision having a general character and the first paragraph as a "final clause" or safeguard provision, aimed at avoiding the danger of external interferences. It will be the Court's task to single out and specify the border, which can be tenuous and not always easily identifiable, between disputes regarding judicial functions submitted to the jurisdiction of the Court and other disputes submitted to the regime set forth in the second paragraph.

The second paragraph is related to disputes between two or more States Parties dealing with issues on interpretation and application of the Statute. In this case, it seems easier to imagine which kind of disputes the provision refers to: obligation to cooperate fully with the Court in its investigation and prosecution of crimes within the jurisdiction of the Court (Article 86 and following), obligation to provide assistance in relation to investigations or prosecutions (Article 93), obligation of States Parties to finance (Article 113 and following).[2]

Any dispute relating to the interpretation or application of the Statute will be subject to a procedure different from that applicable to disputes concerning judicial functions. First of all, the dispute shall be settled through negotiations, which are to be concluded within three months of their commencement. In case negotiations do not have a positive conclusion and do not settle the dispute, the said provision specifies that the dispute shall be referred to the Assembly of States Parties, established under Article 112 of the Statute. The Assembly may itself seek to settle the

---

Motion for Interlocutory Appeal on Jurisdiction in *Prosecutor* v. *Tadic,* case No. IT-94-1-AR72 (reprinted in 35 ILM 32, 1996.).

[2] See some suggestions of disagreements which can be included in para. 2 in Clark, in O. Triffterer (ed.), *Commentary on the Rome Statute of the International Criminal Court - Observers' Notes, Article by Article* (Nomos, Baden-Baden, 1999), p. 1246.

dispute, and in this respect it has also explicit powers to establish subsidiary bodies as necessary (Article 112, para. 4), including committees or working groups for such purposes.

The Assembly may also make recommendations on further means of settlement of the dispute. Among these further means, Article 119 expressly mentions referral to the International Court of Justice in conformity with the Statute of that Court.

It is possible to make some further remarks on this provision. First of all, the Assembly of States Parties cannot go beyond recommending States among which the dispute arose to refer the dispute to the International Court of Justice, because the Assembly is neither an organ of the United Nations nor a specialized agency. Therefore the Assembly will not be entitled to request the Court an advisory opinion under Article 96 of the UN Charter.[3] Moreover, referral to the ICJ will be possible only when all States Parties to a dispute have recognized as compulsory the jurisdiction of the Court, under Article 36, para. 2 of the Statute of the ICJ. Even if it seems to me highly doubtful, one may wonder whether it could be in some way admissible to consider the second paragraph of Article 119 as a declaration of the recognition of compulsory jurisdiction of the Court, obviously limited to this matter.

Leaving the settlement of this kind of dispute to a reliable and experienced court such as the ICJ is probably a reasonable solution, being that the ICJ is a preconstituted tribunal, which works with pre-established rules. Nevertheless, in my opinion, referral to the ICJ should regard only the most delicate and important questions, which could probably concern the failure by a State to comply with a request to cooperate (Article 87) or perhaps disagreements regarding the finances of the ICC (Article 113 and following) or the management of the Trust Fund which is to be created for the benefit of victims (Article 79) or again claims to protection of national security information (Article 72). Other non judicial disputes relating to the interpretation and the application of the contents of the rules contained in

---

[3] In the same sense Clark, quoted supra, note 2, p. 1249, who points out that, however, "there is some, as yet inconclusive, practice to be placed against these considerations of principle". In 1957, the General Assembly authorized the International Atomic Energy Agency to request advisory opinions of the ICJ; the validity of this authorization has been debated and the Agency has never sought an advisory opinion. More recently, the 1993 Convention for the Prohibition of the Development, Production, Stockpiling and Use of Chemical Weapons and on Their Destruction contains a provision (Article 14, para. 5) which empowers the Conference and the Executive Council separately (two organs of the Organization for the Prohibition of Chemical Weapons set up under the Convention) to request the ICJ to give an advisory opinion on any legal question arising within the scope of the activities of the Organization. An agreement between the Organization and the United Nations shall be concluded for this purpose (32 ILM 800, 1993).

the Statute - such as decisions on removal from office of a judge, the Prosecutor or Deputy Prosecutor, the Registrar or Deputy Registrar (Article 46), disputes on whether a particular candidate for election as a judge has the necessary qualifications (Article 36), similar questions about potential prosecutors or registrars (Articles 42 and 43), some questions on privileges and immunities (Article 48) - should be better settled through ad hoc negotiations without any referral to the ICJ.

25. The Status of Third States before the International Criminal Court

GERHARD HAFNER*

A) Introduction

On the occasion of the ceremonial opening for signature of the Rome Statute of the International Criminal Court in Rome on 18 July 1998, the Secretary General of the United Nations called the establishment of the Court "a gift of hope to future generations, and a giant step forward in the march towards universal human rights and the rule of law".[1] Thus, it is to be expected that this statute will put into life an international judicial institution which is competent to try the most cruel crimes such as genocide, crimes against humanity, war crimes and, at a later stage, acts of aggression committed by individuals.

Despite the hopes carried with the signature of the Statute, some States still do object to the establishment of the International Criminal Court (ICC). The objection was already manifested by the seven negative votes at the last decision on the adoption of the Statute;[2] it can likewise be queried whether the abstention of twenty States was not also a reflection of such a position of these States with regard to the Statute. It is therefore to be assumed that at least these States will hesitate to adhere to the ICC in the foreseeable future so that their status as States not Parties to the Statute (further: "third States") will be of significance still for some years to come.

---

* Member of the International Law Commission.

[1] http://www.un.icc

[2] See Philippe Kirsch, John T. Holmes, *The Rome Conference on an International Criminal Court*, in: 93 AJIL (1999), vol. 1, 10; Roy S. Lee, *The Rome Conference and its Contribution to International Law*, in: Roy S. Lee, *The International Criminal Court - The Making of the Rome Statute*, The Hague-Boston-London 1999, 26.

It seems therefore worthwhile to scrutinize their status in relation to the ICC, in particular as far as their standing before the Court is concerned.[3]

B) The ICC and Third States

1. The Effect of the ICC on Third States

Beside the necessary restrictions of the sovereignty of States Parties through the establishment of the ICC,[4] one of the most widespread objections to the establishment of the ICC among the opponents relates to its effect on third States resulting from its jurisdiction.[5]

Contrary to the usual judicial institutions which decide disputes directly involving States and which therefore are immediately debarred from taking actions with effect on third States,[6] the jurisdiction of the ICC which, as opposed to the International Court of Justice (ICJ), addresses individuals is nevertheless, although only indirectly, linked with States. Hence, it is much more likely that the exercise of jurisdiction by the ICC could affect interests of third States if for instance nationals of a third State are tried by the ICC or this State has already undertaken investigations[7] and the State wishes to protect either its national or its jurisdiction against the ICC. This situation could most likely occur when the ICC exercises jurisdiction over an act which also falls under the jurisdiction of a third State.[8]

The question of the jurisdiction of the ICC was discussed during the elaboration of the Statute at length. The concept of universal

[3] This paper is not deemed to analyse the whole spectrum of the relation of third States to the ICC, but only the *ius standi*.

[4] According to China, for instance, the universal jurisdiction provided in the Statute "directly infringed on the judicial authority of States", quoted in Lee, op. cit. (fn. 2), 582.

[5] Cf. David J. Scheffer, *The United States and the International Criminal Court*, in: 93 AJIL 1999, vol 1, 18.

[6] See in particular the discussions regarding the competence of the ICJ in this regard in conjunction with the judgment of the ICJ in the Case concerning East Timor, ICJ Rep 1995, 90; B. Ajibola, *The International Court of Justice and Absent Third States*, in: 4 African YIL (1996), 85; Peter D. Coffman, *Obligations Erga Omnes and the Absent Third States*, in: 39 GYIL (1996), 285.

[7] These are the most probable cases in which States would like to exclude the competence of the ICC.

[8] This situation is not confined to cases where the national of a third State is tried by the ICC (because the incriminating act occurred in the territory of the third State), but could also exist when this State can exercise jurisdiction over non-nationals.

jurisdiction could not be included in the Statute as such,[9] it was done so only to a certain extent in Article 12 which entitles the Court to try cases involving suspects being nationals of third States, as long as the crime was committed on the territory of States Parties, or the suspects were nationals of States Parties, involving crimes committed on the territory of third States. But even this solution is being said to contradict the principle of *pacta tertiis nec nocent nec prosunt* as enshrined in Article 34 of the VCLT[10] and considered as forming a fundamental principle of treaty law.[11]

Whatever the value of this argument might be, the jurisdiction of the ICC and that of third States could become subject to a mutual concurrence in the same manner as that of States Parties, so that a decision of the preceding jurisdiction is required also with respect to third States. Although it is the Court which decides on this issue due to its general competence,[12] States enjoying such concurrent jurisdiction must have a right to challenge this decision, irrespective of whether or not they are Parties to the Statute. The question therefore arises in which manner even States not Parties to the Statute are granted the right to defend their interests before the ICC.

2. *Meaning of "Third States"*

Despite the obviously clear definition of third States in the Vienna Convention on the Law of Treaties (VCLT)[13] which reflects the undisputed common use in international law,[14] the full scope of the term of third States if applied to the Statute becomes a little less clear. It can be asked whether the usual definition still encompasses, for instance, States Parties which excluded the Court's jurisdiction with respect to certain crimes, respectively States not Parties which accepted the exercise of jurisdiction by the Court with respect to a crime, or States which concluded agreements on cooperation with the ICC according to Article 87(5). Three different

---

[9] The universal jurisdiction was reflected in a proposal by Germany, doc. A/AC.249/1998/DP.2; see E. Wilmshurst, *Jurisdiction of the Court*, in: Lee, *op. cit.* (fn. 2), 132; cf. also Zimmermann, *Die Schaffung eines ständigen Internationalen Strafgerichtshofes*, in: 58 ZaöRVR 1998, 84.

[10] "A treaty does not create either obligations or rights for a third State without its consent."

[11] Scheffer, *op. cit.* (fn. 5), 18.

[12] Cf. Article 19(1) "The Court shall satisfy itself that it has jurisdiction in any case brought before it. The Court may, on its own motion, determine the admissibility of a case in accordance with Article 17." (Article 17 is the basic Article on complementarity).

[13] Article 2(1) lit. h reads: "'Third State' means a State not a party to the treaty".

[14] Cf. Neuhold Hanspeter, *Völkerrechtlicher Vertrag und Drittstaaten* (Treaties and Third States), Berichte der Deutschen Gesellschaft für Völkerrecht, Heft 28, 54.

situations can therefore be distinguished: this term could address third States not only

(i) in relation to the administration of the Statute, but also
(ii) in relation to the jurisdiction[15] and
(iii) to the duty of cooperation.[16]

Hence, although the meaning of "third States" in relation to the Statute as the antithesis to States Parties corresponding to the meaning as used in the VCLT is very clear, the meaning of third States in relation to certain legal consequences under the Statute entails some different consequences and there exist a certain divergence of the scope of States which belong to the different groups of third States. Notwithstanding these divergences, one must proceed from the usual understanding of third States in the sense of the VCLT with regard of the Statute as such.

a) The consequences of these different meanings for the interpretation of Article 14 on the referral by a State Party Two conclusions regarding Article 14(1)[17] on the referral by a State Party can be drawn from this

---

[15] The category of third States in the usual sense does not coincide with the group of States which are not bound by the jurisdiction of the Court. As far as the jurisdiction of the Court according to Article 12 is concerned, it is the acceptance of the jurisdiction which serves as the decisive criterion for defining third States in relation to the jurisdiction, although the "automatic" jurisdiction necessarily includes States Parties within this category. This particular meaning of third States, albeit only in relation to the jurisdiction for war crimes, applies to those States Parties which excluded the jurisdiction of the ICC relating to war crimes for a transitional period according to Article 124. Similar is the position of States which do not accept an amendment to the Statute according to Article 121(5), adding a new crime to the existing ones under the jurisdiction, as far as this new crime is concerned. It seems justified to interpret the "acceptance of such amendments" in Article 121(5) as amounting to an "acceptance of jurisdiction" regarding the new crime in the sense of Article 12. In contrast, States not Parties, which nevertheless accepted the exercise of jurisdiction by the Court with respect to a crime pursuant to Article 12(3), remain third States in the usual sense although they cannot be regarded as third States in respect of this jurisdiction.

[16] Article 87(5) authorizes the Court to conclude cooperation agreements on assistance to the Court with third States. Despite their relation to the Court on the basis of such agreements and their status as States Parties to such agreements, such States undoubtedly remain third States in respect of the Statute so that they cannot participate in the administration of the latter. Likewise, they cannot be qualified as States which have accepted the jurisdiction of the Court, either generally or for certain crimes, so that they also remain third States in relation to the jurisdiction of the Court with all the consequences ensuing therefrom for the scope of jurisdiction. The conclusion of such agreements, therefore, does not extend the jurisdiction of the Court since Article 12 only relates to States which have accepted the jurisdiction either by becoming Party to the Statute or by an explicit acceptance of the jurisdiction. This requirement excludes any implicit acceptance of jurisdiction.

[17] "A State Party may refer to the Prosecutor a situation in which one or more crimes within the jurisdiction of the Court appear to have been committed requesting the Prosecutor to

construction: On the one hand, this provision which speaks of "States Parties", has to be understood as entitling even a State which excluded the jurisdiction for war crimes under Article 124 to refer a situation relating to such crimes to the ICC since these States nevertheless remain States Parties in the usual sense. The same conclusion can be applied to a State which has not accepted an amendment broadening the jurisdiction of the Court since it still maintains the status as State Party so that even with respect to these new crimes such States can refer a situation to the Court; there is no justification envisageable to distinguish between both categories of States.[18] Hence, the State Party which did not accept an amendment adding a new crime to the jurisdiction of the ICC, will nevertheless be entitled to refer a situation regarding such crimes to the ICC.

Although this conclusion can be deemed as void of any substantial political significance in view of the right of the prosecutor to act *proprio motu* on the basis of any information, it has nevertheless a certain bearing insofar as in such a case, contrary to the cases of referral by a State Party or the Security Council, the prosecutor is under the duty to submit his or her decision on the investigations to the Pre-Trial Chamber according to Article 15.

On the other hand, a further consequence of this interpretation of Article 14(1) is that, with regard to a situation which is referred to the ICC by States which did not become Parties to the Statute, but have accepted the jurisdiction of the ICC under Article 12(3) or concluded cooperation agreements, the Prosecutor is still bound to seek an explicit authorization by the Pre-Trial Chamber before investigations could be started.

b) The consequences of these different meanings for the duty of cooperation

In contrast, the duty to cooperate is imposed on any State Party pursuant to Article 86 in respect of those crimes which are under the jurisdiction of the Court.[19] This latter restriction could warrant an interpretation according to which a State which has excluded the jurisdiction of the Court under Article 124 or has not accepted the jurisdiction established by an amendment eschews the duty of cooperation with regard to the crimes

---

investigate the situation for the purpose of determining whether one or more specific persons should be charged with the commission of such crimes."

[18] It would also be difficult for such a State to anticipate for which crimes suspects will be tried by the ICC. It can also not be excluded that a person will be accused for crimes against humanity instead of war crimes since there exist a certain overlapping of the crimes. Cf. Wilmshurst, *op. cit.* (fn. 9), 139.

[19] Article 86 reads: "General obligation to cooperate.
States Parties shall, in accordance with the provisions of this Statute, cooperate fully with the Court in its investigation and prosecution of crimes within the jurisdiction of the Court."

under this part of the jurisdiction.[20] Since however, as to the duty of cooperation, Article 87 only proceeds from a dichotomy of States Parties and States not Parties,[21] the duty of cooperation under the Statute must encompass all State Parties in relation to all crimes falling under the jurisdiction of the Court, irrespective of whether or not they have excluded or not accepted the jurisdiction for some of the crimes. Any other interpretation would open a lacuna of cooperation in relation of such States, which is not envisaged by the Statute.

The duty of cooperation, however, reaches beyond the States Parties since it includes States not parties which otherwise have accepted the exercise of jurisdiction by the Court with respect to the crime in question; they are consequently not third States in relation to the duty of cooperation, limited, however, to these crimes.[22] Likewise they are subject to such duty third States which have concluded cooperation agreements according to Article 87(5), but only within the term of the relevant agreement.[23]

Hence the category of States being subject to the duty to cooperate goes beyond States Parties by including States which have accepted a certain scope of jurisdiction or have concluded a cooperation agreement.

C) Status of Third States in Proceedings before the ICC

In the following text, the term "third States" is used as relating to such States in the sense of the VCLT, irrespective of whether or not the relevant State is a third State in relation to the jurisdiction or duty of cooperation.

---

[20] Article 89(1) which determines: "States Parties shall, in accordance with the provisions of this Part and the procedure under their national law, comply with requests for arrest and surrender" would have to be interpreted accordingly.

[21] The States not Parties are addressed in Article 87(5) pursuant to which the Court can conclude cooperation agreements with such States. In this case, such States are then bound to cooperate according to the terms of this agreement.

[22] Article 12(3): "If the acceptance of a State which is not a Party to this Statute is required under paragraph 2, that State may, by declaration lodged with the Registrar, accept the exercise of jurisdiction by the Court with respect to the crime in question. The accepting State shall cooperate with the Court without any delay or exception in accordance with Part 9."

[23] Article 87(5): "The Court may invite any State not Party to this Statute to provide assistance under this Part on the basis of an ad hoc arrangement, an agreement with such State or any other appropriate basis.

Where a State not Party to this Statute, which has entered into an ad hoc arrangement or an agreement with the Court, fails to cooperate with requests pursuant to any such arrangement or agreement, the Court may so inform the Assembly of States Parties or, where the Security Council referred the matter to the Court, the Security Council."

In view of its particular structure and its focus on individual responsibility, the Statute takes into account the possibility of interests of third States being affected. Although the Court is obliged to satisfy itself that it has jurisdiction in any case brought before it and may, on its own motion, determine the admissibility of a case in accordance with Article 17,[24] the Statute nevertheless accords to third States a right to defend their interests before the Court, in particular the lack of jurisdiction of the Court or the admissibility of a case.[25] Consequently, the reference in the Statute to "States" as distinguished from "States Parties" encompasses all States,[26] thus reaching beyond the personal scope of the Statute so that also Article 19(2)(b)[27] which only speaks of "State" without any further specification has to be interpreted in this sense. This consideration is corroborated by the subsequent Article 19(2)(c) which refers to States (without qualifying them as parties) from which acceptance of jurisdiction is required. This situation can only occur with respect to non-Parties so that the term "States" as such necessarily includes third States.[28]

This right of standing extended to any State warrants the conclusion that "complementarity" is of universal nature comprising also third States,[29] the Court, in deciding its jurisdiction, has to take into account

[24] Article 19(1): "The Court shall satisfy itself that it has jurisdiction in any case brought before it. The Court may, on its own motion, determine the admissibility of a case in accordance with Article 17."

[25] This right was already provided in the draft of the ILC, according to which "interested States" were entitled to challenge jurisdiction and admissibility (cf. Draft Articles 34, 35 and 36; in: *Report of the International Law Commission on its Forty-Sixth Session, Draft Statute for an International Criminal Court*, 2 May-22 July, 1994, General Assembly, 49th Sess., Supp. No. 10, A/49/10, 1994). Hence, despite the need of explicit acceptance of the jurisdiction by State Parties it was felt necessary to establish such a right in the interest of any State.

[26] It may of course be asked whether it includes also international organizations. However, this question is still of less importance since they do not yet possess their own nationals, nor territory or a criminal jurisdiction which could be affected by a procedure before the ICC.

[27] Article 19(2) reads: "Challenges to the admissibility of a case on the grounds referred to in Article 17 or challenges to the jurisdiction of the Court may be made by:
(a) An accused or a person for whom a warrant of arrest or a summons to appear has been issued under Article 58;
(b) A State which has jurisdiction over a case, on the ground that it is investigating or prosecuting the case or has investigated or prosecuted; or
(c) A State from which acceptance of jurisdiction is required under Article 12."

[28] It would be unreasonable to interpret Article 87(2)(c) as addressing only State Parties which made a declaration under the transitional provision of Article 124, but, within the transitional period, accepted the jurisdiction of the Court for specific war crimes pursuant to Article 12(3) since it is doubtful whether the wording of the latter provision envisages such a possibility.

[29] Cf. Palmisano Giuseppe, *The International Criminal Court and Third States* (to be published), 4.

also the situation in third States or the judicial activities performed by them.

1. The Organs of the Court Involved in this Standing

Article 19(2)(b) is therefore the basic provision granting third States standing in procedures before the ICC, either before a Prosecutor, Pre-Trial, Trial or Appeal Chamber:

- In the case of a request for deferral according to Article 18, the State addresses its request to the Prosecutor which, however, can be overruled by the Pre-Trial Chamber. Since, however, the Statute is silent in this regard, it has still to be decided whether the requesting State will have a standing before the Pre-Trial in such a review procedure.
- The challenges to the jurisdiction or admissibility have to be presented to the Pre-Trial, after confirmation of the charges to the Trial Chamber.[30]
- The appeal to a decision in these cases has to be presented to the Appeal Chambers.[31]

2. The Substance of Presentations before the ICC by Third States

The general capability of third States to appear before the Court is not to be understood as authorizing any State to present any matter relating to a given case before the ICC. Like in the case of States Parties, two different conditions have to be met by the relevant third State, one *ratione personae*, the other *ratione materiae*.

a) The restrictions ratione personae As far as the *ratione personae* condition according to Article 19(2) litt. b and c is concerned, solely that State is entitled which either "has jurisdiction over a case", but only "on the ground that it is investigating or prosecuting the case or has investigated or prosecuted", or from which "acceptance of jurisdiction is required under Article 12". The latter category obviously reflects the broader interest the national State of the suspect or the State on whose territory the alleged crime was committed has in the proceedings since its standing is not contingent upon own investigations or prosecutions. In sum, it can be derived from these criteria that these provisions justify the standing under either by their own procedural activities of the relevant State or by the

[30] Article 19(6).
[31] See *infra*.

relation to the crime expressed by territoriality or by the nationality of the suspect.

A different matter is the case of Article 18 which provides a separate possibility to exclude activities by the prosecutor since any State "which is investigating or has investigated its nationals or others within its jurisdiction with respect to criminal acts which may constitute crimes referred to in Article 5" may request the deferral of investigations. The wording of Article 18 does not contain any reason to assume that only State Parties could be authorized to raise this ground so that third States too, enjoy a standing before the ICC for making such a request.

b) The restrictions ratione materiae Concerning the *ratione materiae* condition, this right of standing of third States depends on certain conditions the relevant third State has to meet - this right is granted only to those States which can establish a certain interest in the given case as defined in the Statute. The crucial issue which decides on the availability if the concrete right of standing is therefore the matter which the State is permitted to present to the Court.

The Statute distinguishes three different grounds in this respect: the challenge for grounds of inadmissibility as referred to in Article 17, for lack of jurisdiction and for reason of national procedures pursuant to Article 18.

As far as other devices included in the Statute are concerned, which aim at protecting third States, such as Article 90(4) and (6) dealing with competing requests from the Court and from third States or Article 98 on the immunity enjoyed by a third State, the third State is not granted standing before the ICC enabling it to invoke these rights.

(i) Grounds of inadmissibility referred to in Article 17

Article 17[32] which reflects the basic idea of complementarity limits the admissibility of a case before the ICC by four different criteria:

---

[32] Cf. Art. 17: "Issues of admissibility

1. Having regard to paragraph 10 of the Preamble and Article 1, the Court shall determine that a case is inadmissible where:

(a) The case is being investigated or prosecuted by a State which has jurisdiction over it, unless the State is unwilling or unable genuinely to carry out the investigation or prosecution;

(b) The case has been investigated by a State which has jurisdiction over it and the State has decided not to prosecute the person concerned, unless the decision resulted from the unwillingness or inability of the State genuinely to prosecute;

(c) The person concerned has already been tried for conduct which is the subject of the complaint, and a trial by the Court is not permitted under Article 20, paragraph 3;

(d) The case is not of sufficient gravity to justify further action by the Court.

- the unwillingness of a State genuinely to carry out the investigation or prosecution;
- the inability of a State genuinely to carry out the investigation or prosecution;
- double jeopardy;[33]
- lack of sufficient gravity.[34]

The joint reading of Articles 17 and 19 reveals that the first three grounds can be invoked by third States only if they have carried out investigations, but that the fourth can be presented also by third States without own investigations or proceedings being carried out if the suspect is their national or the crime was committed on their territory.

---

2. In order to determine unwillingness in a particular case, the Court shall consider, having regard to the principles of due process recognized by international law, whether one or more of the following exist, as applicable:
(a) The proceedings were or are being undertaken or the national decision was made for the purpose of shielding the person concerned from criminal responsibility for crimes within the jurisdiction of the Court referred to in Article 5;
(b) There has been an unjustified delay in the proceedings which in the circumstances is inconsistent with an intent to bring the person concerned to justice;
(c) The proceedings were not or are not being conducted independently or impartially, and they were or are being conducted in a manner which, in the circumstances, is inconsistent with an intent to bring the person concerned to justice.
3. In order to determine inability in a particular case, the Court shall consider whether, due to a total or substantial collapse or unavailability of its national judicial system, the State is unable to obtain the accused or the necessary evidence and testimony or otherwise unable to carry out its proceedings."

[33] Cf. Art. 20: "Ne bis in idem
1. Except as provided in this Statute, no person shall be tried before the Court with respect to conduct which formed the basis of crimes for which the person has been convicted or acquitted by the Court.
2. No person shall be tried before another court for a crime referred to in Article 5 for which that person has already been convicted or acquitted by the Court.
3. No person who has been tried by another court for conduct also proscribed under Articles 6, 7 or 8 shall be tried by the Court with respect to the same conduct unless the proceedings in the other court:
(a) Were for the purpose of shielding the person concerned from criminal responsibility for crimes within the jurisdiction of the Court; or
(b) Otherwise were not conducted independently or impartially in accordance with the norms of due process recognized by international law and were conducted in a manner which, in the circumstances, was inconsistent with an intent to bring the person concerned to justice."

[34] There is no need to scrutinize theses grounds in more details in this context since they are not reserved to third States, but apply also to State Parties. It should only be noted that according to Rule 5.1 of the Rules of Procedure and Evidence (Determination of reasonable basis to proceed with an investigation under Article 15; UN Doc. PNICC/1999/L.3 Rev.1) the requirement of "reasonable basis" to proceed with an investigation under Article 15(3) is interpreted in the sense of Article 53(1)(a)-(c).

The question may, however, be raised as to whether additional criteria determine the admissibility which could be invoked by a State. In this regard, it could be asked whether a State, for instance, could claim inadmissibility when the Security Council has taken a decision of deferral according to Article 16.

(ii) Lack of jurisdiction

The States referred to in Article 19(2) are also entitled to challenge the jurisdiction of the Court. The reference in this provision to the ground that the relevant State "is investigating or prosecuting the case or has investigated or prosecuted" seems to suggest that a State having jurisdiction may challenge only the admissibility of the case. The chapeau of paragraph 2 which refers to both grounds for a challenge, namely, admissibility and jurisdiction, however, leaves no doubt that such States are also entitled to challenge the jurisdiction of the ICC.

The jurisdiction is defined by limits in time, in persons[35] and in the matter respecting the crime. The time aspect of the jurisdiction is addressed by Article 11, the personal aspect by Article 12 and the substance aspect by the definitions of crimes (Articles 5-9).

(iii) Delay of investigations according to Article 18

According to a proposal put forward by the United States,[36] Article 18 gives a State the right to request a delay of the investigations for six months if the prosecutor wants to act either upon referral of a situation by a State Party or *proprio motu.*[37] This right also amounts to a limit to admissibility of a case before the ICC depending on an individual State's exercise of its own criminal jurisdiction. Again, not only States Parties are entitled to such a request, but all States so that even third States can resort to it.

3. Communications with Third States

The standing of third States in procedures before the ICC requires certain communications between these States and the ICC which only would enable them to benefit from this right. The Statute reflects this necessity

---

[35] This is to be understood as a reference to the element of jurisdiction which is defined by the States which must have accepted the jurisdiction.

[36] Arsanjani H. Mahnoush, *The Rome Statute of the International Criminal Court*, in: 93 AJIL (1999), vol. 1, 27.

[37] Therefore, this possibility does not apply to cases of a referral of a situation by the Security Council acting under Chapter VII of the Charter of the United Nations according to Article 13(b). This exception is based on the predominant position of this main organ of the United Nations and its competence to take decisions binding all member States of the United Nations.

insofar as it requires the Prosecutor to notify "all States Parties and those States which, taking into account the information available, would normally exercise jurisdiction over the crimes concerned"[38] the commencement of the investigations. Cases of a referral by the Security Council are exempted from this requirement so that only in such a case measures taken by the ICC could be kept under non-disclosure as is provided, for instance, in Rule 53 of the Rules and Procedures of the ICTY.[39]

But in all other cases, the wording of Article 18 definitely guarantees that third States are informed provided they "normally exercise jurisdiction over the relevant crimes". It will be only a matter for the Rules of Procedure and Evidence, if not of the future practice of the ICC, to define under which circumstances the "normal exercise of jurisdiction" can be assumed, whether the basic assumption should be based on the universal or only a territorial or personal jurisdiction exercised by States. Whatever the result of this practice will be, it can be expected that States addressed by Article 19(2)(c) undoubtedly will fall within this category whereas problems and lack of communication could arise if a jurisdiction exercised by States as referred to in 19(2)(b) is not considered as such a normal exercise of jurisdiction.

The communication between third States and the ICC is not restricted to such initial information, but continues even thereafter so that the Prosecutor and the Pre-Trial Chamber are permanently kept apprised of whether the relevant situation still exists. Contrary to Article 18(5) which takes into account the particular situation of third States since it obliges only States Parties to comply with the request of the Prosecutor for further information, the corresponding Article 19(11) does not make such a distinction. According to the fundamental principle of *pacta tertiis nec nocent nec prosunt*, one has nevertheless to proceed from the expectation that the Prosecutor cannot impose such a duty on a third State without the latter's explicit consent. It would certainly be difficult to identify the challenges to jurisdiction or admissibility presented by a third State as such a prior consent since the challenges are based on a right in favour of third States for which the consent can be presumed[40] whereas the duty necessarily requires an explicit consent in writing.[41]

---

[38] Article 18(1).

[39] http://www.un.org/icty/basic.htm

[40] Article 36(1) of the Vienna Convention on the Law of Treaties reads: "Treaties providing for rights for third States

1. A right arises for a third State from a provision of a treaty if the parties to the treaty intend the provision to accord that right either to the third State, or to a group of States to which it

4. *Appeals by Third States*

Despite the risk of a delay of the procedure,[42] but for the sake of fairness[43] and certainly also for that of the protection of sovereignty, States, States Parties as well as third States, are granted a right of appeal against decisions on claims presented by them. In this regard, Article 18(4) as well as Article 19(6) provide a right of appeal to the Appeal Chamber in accordance with Article 82 dealing with appeals against interlocutory decisions.[44] The latter provision, however, does not reflect this right explicitly since it refers only to "either party" which may appeal a decision with respect to jurisdiction or admissibility,[45] without clarifying the meaning of "party". Nevertheless this latter expression seems to encompass not only individuals such as the accused and the Prosecutor, but also States insofar as they are entitled to take part in proceedings. The Statute's text does not indicate a different interpretation since the only distinction between party to a proceeding and States allowed to intervene in a proceeding made in the Statute, namely in Article 50, ensues from Article 72(4) which explicitly grants such a right of intervention.

5. *The Right of Intervention*

The use of the expression "State" without any further qualifier in Article 72 on the protection of national security information induces the conclusion that this provision also refers to third States and grants them a right of intervention. Doubts can nevertheless be raised since the text stipulates duties which can be imposed only on States Parties; its paragraph 7, for instance, contains a cross reference to another provision of the Statute, namely Article 87(7), which undoubtedly only applies to States Parties.[46] It

---

belongs, or to all States, and the third State assents thereto. Its assent shall be presumed so long as the contrary is not indicated, unless the treaty otherwise provides."

[41] Article 35 of the Vienna Convention on the Law of Treaties reads: "Treaties providing for obligations for third States

An obligation arises for a third State from a provision of a treaty if the parties to the treaty intend the provision to be the means of establishing the obligation and the third State expressly accepts that obligation in writing."

[42] Helen Brady, Mark Jennings, *Appeal and Revision*, in: Lee, *op. cit.* (fn. 2), 300, speak of the risk paralysing the process.

[43] *Ibid.*

[44] Helen Brady, Mark Jennings, *Appeal and Revision*, in: Lee, op. cit. (fn. 2), 299.

[45] Article 82(1).

[46] As to the vagueness of the formulation of this Article and the discrepancies therein see Donald K. Piragoff, *Protection of National Security Information*, in: Lee, *op. cit.* (fn. 2), 294.

could also be argued that Article 72 in its entirety does not refer to third States in view of Article 73 which explicitly addresses third States. It must, however, at the same time be admitted that the substance of these two provisions differs insofar as Article 72 relates to national security information, Article 73 to any confidential information,[47] so that Article 72 forms a *lex specialis* in relation to Article 73. In sum, despite the difficulties this provision offers, one cannot but accept the interpretation that Article 72 applies also to third States insofar as the relevant information is a matter of national security.[48] Hence, any third State is entitled to intervene in the proceedings according to paragraph 4. Admittedly, the very vague wording of this provision does not permit a *prima facie* evident interpretation so that Piragoff is quite correct when he raises questions as to the applicability to third States without offering answers.[49]

One possible interpretation could be based on the addition "in order to obtain resolution of the issue in accordance with this Article" to the right of intervention. It makes this right of intervention purpose related and justifies a conclusion that this right includes also duties which are immediately related to the exercise of the right of intervention so that this right can be resorted to only if the relevant State is ready to accept the conditions under which this right can be enjoyed. Hence, if a State wishes to exercise this right of intervention, it must assume the corresponding duty referred to in Article 72(5), namely to search for a resolution in cooperation with the "Prosecutor, the Defence or the Pre-Trial Chamber or Trial Chamber, as the case may be". If the right of intervention is exercised by a third State, the duty of information on the inability to disclose the information spelled out in paragraph 6 as well as the remedial consequences for non-disclosure contained in paragraph 7 would likewise apply to such States.

However, if a third State chooses not to resort to this right of intervention, then Article 73 becomes relevant since its general formulation permits its application to information considered as affecting national security. According to the last sentence of this Article, if the third State does not consent to the disclosure of the document, the Court can only take note of this nature of the document without possessing any remedial means.

---

[47] *Ibid*, 292.

[48] *Ibid*, 292.

[49] *Ibid*, 292.

D) Conclusions

Establishing jurisdiction in relation of individuals confronts the ICC necessarily with the criminal jurisdiction of States and generates some overlapping jurisdiction. Since the possible conflict of jurisdictions does not exist in relation to State Parties only, but to any State, any such State must have the possibility to defend the exercise of its own jurisdiction. This survey establishes that the Statute provides ample opportunity even for third States to defend their criminal jurisdiction and the principle of complementarity.

The need to provide this right is prompted by the particular nature of the ICC addressing individuals, not States, and deciding on individual instead of State responsibility. It also reveals that the nature of the ICC is totally different from that of institutions competent to settle disputes between States since it reflects a vertical or public law approach contrary to the horizontal, civil or private law approach which underlies the latter. At the same time, the position of third States provided in the Statute, which is difficult to reconcile with classic doctrines, reveals that the Statute, indeed, is breaking new grounds in international law. It is one of the most striking recent examples which prove that modern international law can no longer be seen as regulating solely relations between States.

If the ICC has the last decision on whether a State, including a third State, exercises its jurisdiction in an appropriate manner and the jurisdiction of the ICC, consequently, is considered a possible breach of the principle *pacta tertiis nec nocent nec prosunt* and a threat to the sovereignty of third States,[50] the standing before the ICC as provided in the Statute gives third States sufficient possibility to defend their sovereignty. It will be a duty of the Preparatory Commission for the International Criminal Court[51] to elaborate appropriate regulations within the Rules of Procedure and Evidence which are able to ensure this right.

---

[50] Cf. Palmisano, *op. cit.* (fn. 29), 6.

[51] The Preparatory Commission for the International Criminal Court was established in accordance with resolution F adopted by the United Nations Diplomatic Conference of Plenipotentiaries on the Establishment of an International Criminal Court on 17 July 1998.

26. Criminally Protected Legal Interests at the International Level after the Rome Statute

LORENZO PICOTTI*

1) Introduction: New Prospects for International Criminal Law

Ratification of the Statute[1] of the International Criminal Court raises many questions and expectations among criminal law experts. Among these, the specific nature of the legal rights and interests protected under the court's jurisdiction are especially interesting and worth noting. The task of the Court is to exercise a supra-national *punitive power* directly over persons responsible for serious crimes which threaten the "peace, security and well-being of the world" (Preamble, para. 2) so that those persons should not go unpunished. The Court does not replace the jurisdiction of States nor their duty to exercise it, but acts as a complement to national jurisdictions.[2] What

---

* Professor of Criminal Law, University of Trento.

[1] Adopted in Rome July 17, 1998 (by a vote of 120 to seven, with twenty-one countries abstaining), was ratified with Italian Statute of July 12, 1999, N. 232, in *Gazz. Uff.* Suppl. ord. of July, 19, 1999, N. 167; with unofficial Italian Translation of the Statute in Annex. First Commentaries (with other unofficial Italian Translation) in Vassalli, G., *Statuto di Roma. Note sull'istituzione di una Corte penale internazionale*, in *Riv. Studi Poli. int.*, 1999, N. 261, p. 9 ff.; Reale, E.P. (ed.), *Lo Statuto della Corte penale internazionale*, Padova 1999; Tisci, G. (ed.), *La Corte penale internazionale*, Napoli 1999. In the international doctrine see the Commentary of Lee, R. (ed.), *The International Criminal Court. The Making of the Rome Statute*, The Hague, London, Boston, 1999; Triffterer, O. (ed.), *Commentary on the Rome Statute of the International Criminal Court*, Baden Baden, 1999; Bassiouni, M.C. (ed.), *International Criminal Law. III: Enforcement*, 2nd ed., 1999, Section IV, p. 595 ff.; Ambos, K., Guerrero, O.J., *El Estatuto de Roma de la Corte Penal International*, Bogotà, 1999.

[2] The principle, stated in the Preamble's penultimate paragraph ("The International Criminal Court...shall be complementary to national criminal jurisdictions"), given that as provided in para. 5 ("...it is the duty of every State to exercise its criminal jurisdiction over those responsible for international crimes") it is expressly included in Article 1 ("the power of

is of great importance in this connection is the statement, altogether original in international law, that the Court's power is autonomous and *permanently* attributed to it as a judicial authority independent of the States which have established it and of the Charter of the United Nations (Preamble, para. 9).

The rights protected under the Court's jurisdiction together with the *General Principles of Criminal Law* are an extremely important aspect of the Statute as regards criminal law, and not just for scholars. These two parts of the Statute help to define the Court's real international reach. Starting from these substantive elements of international criminal law we can formulate the *rights* and *interests* protected under this "new" system in conceptual terms.

The new system of international criminal law stems from a *juridical network* of various sources,[3] rather than from the Statute alone, since it explicitly refers to national criminal law systems, to international law in general, and to the "creative" function of the Court itself.[4] The heterogeneous nature of these sources allows ample room for a scholarly, theoretical reflection on new concepts and categories of criminal law, as a prelude to their systematic arrangement.

This is the task to which scholars of criminal law must offer their specific expertise and critical faculties, although legal scholarship is not

---

jurisdiction" of the Court over natural persons "is complementary to national criminal jurisdictions") and codified as the condition for bringing action in Articles 17 and ff. Underlines this Principle Jescheck, H.-H., *La Corte penale internazionale. Precedenti, lavori preparatori , statuto*, in *Indice penale*, 2000, p. 297 ff.

[3] Fronza, E., *I crimini di diritto internazionale nell'interpretazione della giurisprudenza internazionale: il caso Akayesu*, in Illuminati, G., Stortoni, L., Virgilio, M. (eds.), *Crimini internazionali e giustizia. Dai Tribunali Internazionali alle Commissioni Verità e Riconciliazione*, Torino 2000, p. 96 s. Speaks of a "hybrid", in conformity with the most currently and negative evaluation Virgilio, M., *Verso i principi generali del diritto criminale internazionale*, *ivi*, p. 41 s., especially 46 f.

[4] Illuminating in this connection is Article 21, placed at the end of the preceding and heterogeneous Part 3 and dedicated (also) to the "law applicable by the Court by virtue of which, alongside the Statute and the procedural rules and evidence (letter *a*), the Court must also consider "wherever necessary, the treaties applicable and the principles and rules of international law, including the *consolidated principles* of international law on armed conflicts" (letter *b*: my italics); and "if lacking, *general principles of law derived by the Court* on the basis of domestic law of the world's legal systems, including, where necessary, the domestic law of the States that would have had jurisdiction over the crime" (letter *c*: my italics), save of course the faculty of applying "the principles of law and juridical norms resulting from the interpretation of its own preceding decisions" (para. 2). It is thus recognized, albeit only in an integrating role and with precise limiting guarantees in para. 3, a plurality of "extra-legal" sources, including a partial jurisprudence "creation" of law, that goes beyond the mere interpretation of individual written laws that is more closely in accord with the tradition of *common law* systems than with systems of *civil law* (like Italy).

named among the sources of international criminal law (due to the principle of legality expressed in Article 22 of the Statute).

However, juridical decisions are used to round out the sources of international non-criminal law:[5] and can certainly contribute to a theoretical reflection on criminal law as well.

Indeed, scholars of criminal law, used to working within the formal constraints of a national system, may welcome the arrival of novel elements which can stimulate modification of their methods and viewpoints and can also offer them a chance to reconsider a *general* theory of crime.

2) Remarks on the "General Section" of the Substantive Criminal Law Codified by the Rome Statute

In addition to making provisions for the institution itself and the essential procedural rules and functioning of the Court, the Rome Statute *codifies* the substantive part of the new international criminal law set forth in a "general section" (the altogether new element in the history of international law[6]) and in a more consolidated and broader "special section" referring to crimes, which have largely been dealt with in prior conventional provisions or other international sources, and to judicial applicability, analysis and established principles.

These provisions necessarily operate in conjunction with the "general principles" of criminal law set out in part 3, Articles 22-33, which help to determine the actual extent and reach of international crimes, either by circumscribing or extending them (see the requisites of the psychological element for individual crimes in Article 30, or reasons for not prosecuting Articles 31-33; the provision for criminal responsibility and liability for participating in or attempting to perpetrate a crime Article 25, para. 3, a-f).

Then we need to consider that here however it is impossible to analyse them[7] (see para. 7).

---

[5] See Bassiouni, M.C., *Le fonti e il contenuto del diritto penale internazionale. Un quadro teorico*, Milano 1999, p. 21 f.

[6] Jescheck, H.-H., *La Corte*, cit., p. 305.

[7] A general Commentary Schabas, W.A., *Principios general del derecho penal*, in Ambos, K., Guerrero, O.J., *El Estatuto*, cit., p. 269 f.

3) The "Special Section" as the Result of Views Shared by the International Community

Before we analyse the crimes listed in the "special section" of this nascent international criminal law, we should remember not to consider them merely as a mandate to pass judgment, however much the title of part 2 might seem to suggest that function ("Jurisdiction, Admissibility and Applicable Law"). In addition we should not be discouraged from our task simply because Article 5 states that this section will define the *subject* (crime) over which the Court *has jurisdiction*.

Instead, the prosecution of specific crimes is the very reason why the Court was established, as the initial paragraphs of the "Preamble" state. Indeed, as *such grave crimes threaten the peace, security and wellbeing of the world* (Preamble, para. 3) and are *of concern to the international community as a whole* (Article 5, para. 1). Just because the rights to be protected are so important, they gave rise to such an ambitious project and help to identify *the most serious crimes* which the world community believes must be prosecuted and prevented (expressly noted in the Preamble, para. 5).

It is in this convergence of views that the *common bonds* uniting peoples and the *shared heritage* of their cultures (Preamble, para. 1) come to the fore and, despite their diversity, make impunity for the perpetrators of such crimes (para. 5) intolerable to all. Yet we should not overlook the paradox that although we all agree that certain essential *legal assets* must be protected, this does not guarantee that those who violate them will be prosecuted even within a single country (a *duty* as it is expressly put and reiterated in the Preamble's para. 6). This then is the reason why an International Criminal Court was founded to adjudicate such matters, *above and beyond* the single States (albeit only with "complementary" jurisdiction, para. 10), so as to assure the legal protection that some States do not guarantee.[8]

Unfortunately, the history of past centuries as well as today's events dramatically demonstrate just that States are often unable to use their own legal instruments to protect fundamental human rights[9] so solemnly proclaimed as pre-eminent and shared by the entire international community. This duty is even harder, not to say impossible, to fulfil wherever the crime against such *legal assets* is very serious, where

[8] On the nature of the compromise that this solution implies, see the analysis of Triffterer, O., *Die ständige Internationale Strafgerichtshof - Anspruch und Wirklichkeit. Anmerkung zum "Rome Statute of the international Criminal Court" vom 17. Juli 1998*, in *Gedächtnisschrift für Heinz Zipf*, Heidelberg 1999, p. 493 ff., and especially p. 522 ff.

[9] See in this connection Triffterer, O., *Die ständige*, cit., especially p. 503 ff.

"millions of children, women and men have been victims of unimaginable atrocities that deeply shock the conscience of humanity" (Preamble, para. 2). Indeed, the protection offered by a traditional criminal law of a single state has proved inadequate. Evidently, it is such a state's circumscribed territorial sovereignty that allows local political power to appropriate and make arbitrary use of the criminal legal system.

Nor can it be said, as has been suggested, that this need to overcome the structural limits of a given State's power to prosecute legitimizes a renewal of "natural law".[10] Rather, the need for an international court is the result of a broad, common, shared, supra-national basis of evaluations, principles, interests and rights of a "higher" nature. This common interest demands a consonant level of legal protection that is structurally guaranteed. Furthermore, international jurisdiction is required by the global aspects of development[11] underway not only in economic, production and trade relations but in social, cultural and human relations in general. Thus, integration and cooperation among peoples become necessary conditions to ensure the growing movement of the persons, goods, services, capital and information. Worldwide, sophisticated transportation systems and communications technologies accompany and strengthen this development. The conscious political choices of peoples to transform and respect these demands has to be grafted to the material conditions which make them possible.

4) Analysis of the Crimes Covered by the Statute

While this is a more concrete analysis, and certainly one more consonant with legal scholarship, note that it will be confined to categorizing the various crime, which actually constitute the real "special section" of the new international criminal law. A more detailed study of the individual crimes and their "constituent elements" (which will also be of use to the Court in interpreting and applying the individual provisions as set out in Article 9, para. 1) would in any case be premature, since the text the Preparatory Commission has made available still has to be approved by the

[10] See the basic reconstruction of Lattanzi, F., *Garanzie dei diritti dell'uomo nel diritto internazionale generale*, Milano 1983, p. 10 s. *passim*.

[11] For the manifold meanings intended with the use of this expression and its ramifications for law in general, see Ferrarese, M.R., *Le istituzioni della globalizzazione. Diritto e diritti nella società contemporanea*, Bologna 2000, with further references.

Assembly of States Parties (as provided by Resolution *F*, para. 5, *b*, appended to the Statute).[12]

As a working hypothesis, however, Articles 5, 6, 7 and 8 of the Statute can be studied to elicit the *traits common* to the crimes named there, a step that will also elucidate the distinguishing features of the different *legal assets* or rights to be protected under international criminal law.

1. The "Seriousness" of the Offence as Requisite

It would appear that in selecting the crimes to be covered in the Statute, the decisive factor was not so much a *property* or quality intrinsic to them as an extrinsic *quantitative fact* concerning the "seriousness" of said crimes, as expressed by the adjectives *grave*, *serious*, and the like, accompanying the indication of the crimes under the Court's jurisdiction in both the text proper (see Articles 1 and 5 in general and, in particular, Article 8 in its reference to war crimes) and the Preamble (paras. 3, 4 and 9). This concept is also recalled in their *objective* qualification as a "threat to the peace, security and wellbeing of the world" (Preamble, para. 3) alongside the *subjective* (or ideal) "(that) deeply shock" the international community and "conscience of humanity" (Preamble, para. 2).[13]

Thus, the four categories of international crimes listed in Article 5 (*a*: the crime of genocide; *b*: crimes against humanity; *c*: war crimes; *d*: the crime of aggression) refer not only to a large variety of *sources*, such as legal traditions, theories and principles of jurisprudence which provide a more precise delineation and discipline for them, but also to *types* of crimes and offences that are so heterogeneous that it seems questionable to reduce them to common *quality* traits.

Yet most of them are treated in provisions found in conventions, treaties and proceedings that have long been in force in international law,[14] as with the particular case of war crimes in their analytical list in Article 8.

---

[12] The final report of the Preparatory commission at 6 July 2000 PCNICC/2000/INF/3 and related appendices, including the text of the "elements of crimes", can be found at www.un.org/law/icc/statute/elements/english.htm. Amendments can be proposed by States Parties, the judges themselves and the Prosecutor (Article 9, para. 2), save the approval of the Assembly by a two-thirds majority. Both the "elements of crimes" and their amendments must in any case be "in conformity with" the Statute (Article 9, para. 3).

[13] For the requirement that such so-called *jus cogens* crimes of international criminal law meet the two requisites to "threaten the peace and security" and to "shock the conscience of humanity," see Bassiouni, M.C., *Le fonti*, cit., p. 71 ff. and footnote 177. As to the further requisite that the conduct is "the result of a State's action or of a policy in the State's favour" (*ibid*., p. 72), see para. 6 in the text *infra*.

[14] For a review, see Bassiouni, M.C., *Le fonti*, cit., p. 92 ff.; for an historical sketch, see Reale, E.P., *Lo Statuto di Roma della Corte penale internazionale*, in Id. (ed.), *Lo Statuto*, cit., especially p. 46 ff.

These crimes represent the most "stable" category, or "hard core" of international criminal law,[15] and are largely dealt with in national legal systems according to a tradition that is as long-standing as it is tragically ineffective in actually prosecuting or preventing them. The same would also hold, to a lesser extent, for the offences listed in Article 6 under the heading "crime of genocide", which is also dealt with in an international convention and has been incorporated into national legal systems, including Italy's,[16] and in significant judicial rulings of the ad hoc International Criminal Tribunals for Rwanda (ICTR) and the former Yugoslavia (ICTY).[17]

The remaining categories of crimes represent offences whose definition is less certain and still in the process of being consolidated. For example, *crimes against humanity* (Article 7)[18] risk overlapping in part *war crimes*, especially for those concerning violations during non-international armed conflicts (Article 8, *d* and *e*).[19] Yet their explicit provision has a marked significance in relation to decision-making in criminal policy by

---

[15] Amati, E., *La repressione dei crimini di guerra tra diritto internazionale e diritto interno*, in Illuminati, G., Stortoni, L., Virgilio, M. (eds.), *Crimini internazionali*, cit., p. 98 ff.

[16] The Convenzione for the Prevention and Prosecution of the Crime of Genocide was signed on 9 December 1948 and ratified by Italy as *legge 11 marzo 1952, n. 153*, although it was only by *legge 9 ottobre 1967, n. 962*, that provisions were made for the criminal offences. For the latter, see Grasso, G., *Genocidio*, in *Dig. Disc. Pen.*, vol. V, 1991, p. 399 ff., and the following footnote.

[17] For a thorough reconstruction of these crimes and a detailed analysis of the sentence handed down by the ICTR at Arusha in the Akayesu case (2 September 1998, Case 96-4-T, full text at the site: www/ictr/org) in which rape is held to be a stage in the destruction of the group in that it is designed to prevent births within it (especailly §732), see Fronza, E., *Gli atti di genocidio: percorsi di incriminazione*, PhD. thesis, Teramo, 1999, especially p. 187 ff.; and Id., *I crimini*, cit., p. 71 ff. See in the decisions of the ICTY (www.un.org/icty) the judgment concerning Kupreskic et al. of 14 January 2000, Case IT-95-16-T, which we will also return to *infra*. There have also been a number of indictments (and interim decisions) positing the crime of genocide: see the Prosecutor's *Indictments* against Radovan Karadzic and Ratko Mladic, 14 March 1995, and the more recent one against Momcilo Krajisnik, 21 March 2000, Case IT-00-39-1.

[18] For the origins of this category, see Fava, M.M., *Le origini della nozione di crimini contro l'umanità*, in *I diritti dell'uomo*, 1996, p. 31 ff., and in general Bassiouni, M.C., *Crimes against humanity in international criminal law*, Dordrech-Boston-London, 1992.

[19] The risk of "overlapping" has been rightly underscored by Vassalli, G., *Statuto*, cit., p. 16, according to which the problem of distinguishing crimes against humanity from war crimes, especially concerning acts committed in the course of armed conflicts *not* of an international character, can lead to controversy over the extent of and limits to the Court's jurisdiction, at least in the first seven years referred to in Article 124, by making it possible not to accept its jurisdiction for the war crimes as provided in Art. 8.

the international community, as is also corroborated by the broad-based application made of it by the ICTY.[20]

In the last case, *the crime of aggression*, the only example of the category "crimes against peace", its configuration has been left entirely to a future definition (Article 5, para. 2) as no agreement has been reached, except in the sense that it could be "consistent with the relative provisions of the Charter of the United Nations" and, hence, also with the wording of the UN's General Assembly Resolution approved in 1974:[21] this shows that it depends on conditions of a purely political nature as to how its content is to be defined and the relative jurisdiction is to be exercised.[22]

2. Comparison to Rights (Legal Assets) Protected against Common Crimes

The rather fragmentary picture of sources and offences takes on a greater unity if we goes beyond the provisions of the Statute and, in conformity with the system's transnational reach, compare the individual crimes listed in Articles 6, 7 and 8, to each other and to certain conventional crimes in national criminal codes of justice. Even a rather summary comparison shows that many of the provisions set forth indeed appear to be similar and overlap both one another and the *common crimes* at the core of every national criminal justice code, since they are offences against the essential *legal assets*, whether individual or collective. They seem to share less however with international statutes.

We can take any one of a number of examples: *life* for instance: violated by any of the numerous crimes implying the killing or in any event the death of human beings, as for example, those listed in Articles 6(a), 7(a) and 8(a)(i) and (c)(i); or a person's physical and psychic *integrity and health* violated by the various forms of bodily and metal harm, torture, suffering, mutilations inflicted on victims as exemplified in Articles 6(b), 7(f) and (k), 8(a)(iii) and (c)(i); or even one's personal and moral *freedom* deprived or compromised by kidnapping, illegal incarceration, deportation, hostage-taking, serious moral violence as exemplified in Articles 6(e), 7(e) and 8(a)(vii) and (c)(iii); or *sexual freedom* deprived by rape, sexually abusive treatment, enforced prostitution and forced pregnancy, and the like,

---

[20] Of the numerous rulings, see especially the judgment of 14 January 2000, Case Kupreskic et al., IT-95-16-T, which squarely faces the issue of *mens rea* and *actus reus* for the alleged crimes, and the alleged "concurrence" of international crimes and their interrelatedness (especially, §§677 s.).

[21] General Assembly Resolution 3314 (XXIX), 14 December 1974.

[22] On the issues debated in regard to its wording and protocols, see Zimmermann, A., *Article 5*, in Triffterer, O. (ed.), *Commentary*, cit., No.18 ff., p. 23 ff., which in any case underscores the will to let the Security Council retain a decisive role in whether to persecute this crime or not.

as provided in Articles 7(g) and 8(b)(xxii) and (e)(vi); or even the *freedom of speech* and *to exercise one's civil and political rights* violated by racial persecution, discrimination, abolition and suspension of rights as exemplified in Article 7(h), especially in the light of para. 2(g), which explicates the concept of "persecution," and 8(b)(xiv); or *heritage* subjected to destruction, appropriation, damage to assets, sacking, arbitrary criminal confiscation as exemplified in Articles 8(a)(iv), (xiii) and (xvi) as well as (e)(v) and (xii).

Taken individually, such crimes could be prosecuted as common offences like murder, inflicting bodily harm, kidnapping, assault and battery, rape, injury, damage to property, and the like (respectively exemplified by Articles 575, 582, 630, 615, 609 *bis*, 594, 635, etc. of the Italian criminal code). So it is clear that there must be *other* recognizable traits that distinguish the various crimes examined above from these (and other) *common crimes*. Indeed, even the group of international crimes are divided into distinct categories which evidently affect the severity of the offence and, hence, connote the rights or juridical assets considered worthy of protection under international criminal law.

5) The Peculiar Nature of Conflicting Interests as "Specific Trait" of the Crimes Provided for in the Statute

Indeed, analysing more carefully the *entire* normative context in which the individual crimes listed in the Statute's provisions are expressed, suggests that it is their introductory clauses that need to be reevaluated. Indeed, these sometimes even require that the individual agent, or the "group" to which he/she belongs, or on whose behalf he/she is operating, be pursuing a particular intentional subjective end, which does not coincide with the crime's usual "subjective element", as defined or required in general terms by Article 30 of Statute.

As an example of the first type, take the paragraph 1 of Article 7 concerning crimes against humanity. According to it, the crime must be "committed as part of a widespread or systematic attack directed against any civilian population, with knowledge of the attack"; an example of the second type is found in Article 6, on genocide, which requires the "intent to destroy, in whole or in part, a national, ethnical, racial or religious group".

If we apply the basic principles developed and argued elsewhere in the analysis of crimes with "further" or "specific" intent (called with *dolo specifico* in the traditional terminology of Italian legal doctrine and jurisprudence)[23] we will see that these elements, do not only list the requisites of subjective guilt, but also contribute to the objective definition of the crime's entire constituent "act" - an act that does not end in mere perpetration or basic fact as represented by the individual physical and material elements describing external behaviour and occurrences. Indeed, we should consider their teleological or instrumental *connection* to their broader underlying intent or purpose, and indeed all the elements constituting the criminal act, elements which include not only the material occurrence of the action itself, but also the subjective requisites or qualification role of the position and the traits of the active agent and passive subject.

From data like these, read according to the teleological canons of interpretation, we can elicit the peculiar features of the relationship between agent and victim (these latter would also include collective subjects like ethnic or racial "group" and a broader collectivity like "civilian population"), which is *part* of the specific *conflict of interests* that frames, in its *objective dimension*, the "typical fact" constituting the crime. By elucidating the characteristic "cause" of the criminal conduct, which is often reflected in the "specific intent" of the agent identified in the provision of law (and as such is to be kept distinct from the mere subjective motive),[24] we can recognize the overall *objectivity* of the typical crime and even the nature of the rights or *legal assets* specifically *offended*.

6) The Conflicting Kinds of Relationship Constituting the Crimes under Study

By re-examining the various categories of crimes considered above, we can see that in regard to *genocide* (Article 6) "...with intent to destroy, in whole or in part, a national, ethnical, racial or religious group, as such" the statute must be able to bring into *specific* relief the material acts it describes. Indeed, this ability is the mirror image of the objective requisite for the criminal act that is directed against the victims "members of the group" (as in *a*, *b*, *c*, *e*) or "against group" as such (*c* and *d*).

---

[23] See our *Il dolo specifico. Un'indagine sugli 'elementi finalistici' delle fattispecie penali*, Milano 1993, especially p. 533 ff.

[24] On the weight of subjective elements and, especially, "intent" in criminal acts (as those expressed by the traditional idea of *dolo specifico*, or intentional harm, in Italy) with respect to the harmfulness of a crime and, correlatively, to the *legal asset* protected, as well as on their distinction from the subjective motive, see our *Il dolo specifico*, cit., especially p. 547 ff.

It is thus clear that acts of genocide must always be characterized by an *objective* conflict between the specific interest ("causal") in the group's *destruction*, which must underpin and indeed determine the conduct of the agent or aggressors, and that of the individual victims, or even of the group as such, who have been *so* harmed.[25] By conceiving the very idea of *typical fact* in terms of conflict, the interest of the group (its freedom to exist and develop as such) is not placed alongside or added to the violated right of the individual victim, unlike what the pluri-offense concept of the crime would suggest and is usually posited in principle.[26] Rather, the violation of the latter appears as *instrumental* because it is specifically and typically "caused" by the *actual* pursuit of the interest to violate the freedom to exist and develop of the group, which is *thus* harmed. The "criminal fact" thereby acquires an overall dimension that is *objectively* broader and more significant than either the mere material act itself. In fact, the act is qualified, and also qualifies the legal asset harmed, by the specific "causal interest" pursued and carried out by the agent or the group to which the agent belongs.[27]

Even in the framework of *crimes against humanity* the "common" element that *specifies* the various acts of killing, extermination, enslavement, deportation, imprisonment, torture, rape, sexual abuse, forced prostitution, persecution, as well as any other act of similar nature, is their perpetration in "*as part of* a widespread or systematic attack directed against *any civilian population*" (Article 7, para. 1). The particular *type of relationship* constituting these crimes (in the light of the provision's further defining element "attack directed against any civilian population", para. 2, *a*) therefore connotes not so much the "multiplicity" of the acts themselves

---

[25] See the ICTY decision of 14 January 2000, Case Kupreskic et al. (IT-95-16-T), which in the destruction of the village of Ahmici in Bosnia Erzegovina and in the massacre of more than one hundred of its Muslim civilian inhabitants by Croatian militiamen ruled out genocide and held that it was a crime against humanity because the intention was not to destroy the ethnic Muslim group as such but to expel it from the village (see, especially, §751).

[26] Thus concludes the analysis of Fronza, E., *Gli atti di genocidio*, cit., p. 168, and 192, in reference to rape as an instrument of group destruction upheld by the ICTR in the *Akayesu* case. In contrast, by going beyond (in the text's viewpoint) the arbitrary reduction of the protected right to the static dimension of the individual as mere target of the act considered in isolation, it is possible to seek responses that are more satisfying than those of the compromise-based (only apparent) pluri-offence equivalent of the various protected *legal assets*. Generally about the offence of Genocide see Gil Gil, A., *Derecho penal International - Especial consideración del delito de genocidio*, Madrid 1999, especially p. 159 f.

[27] Significant here is the *purpose* or *intention* of the group as the participant must have *knowledge* of it to establish his or her personal criminal liability in contributing to the perpetration of the crime (Article 25, para. 3, *d*).

("a course of conduct involving the multiple commission of acts referred to") as the fact that these acts are committed "pursuant to or in furtherance of a State or *organizational policy* to commit such attack".

Thus the individual acts and crimes set forth take on an international nature in that they are *instruments* wielded with knowledge and the intent to pursue an aggressive *type of relationship* by *politically* organized agencies (even the State itself or other organizations) *against* an entire "civilian population" taken as a collectively passive subject that is the target of the "repeated" commission of said criminal acts. Even more evident is the importance of such a view when we consider the peculiar relation of war between two States (or between groups, organizations or organized State agencies). It connotes war crimes, not only in international armed conflicts (Article 8, para. 2, *a* and *b*), but also in the more controversial case of armed conflicts of a *non*-international nature (Article 8, para. 2, *c* and *e*).

Note that this is a specific *type of relation* which qualifies and indeed constitutes the essential constituent element *common* to the criminal acts perpetrated in multiple commission as listed in the above article,[28] even apart from *any* requisite ("*in particular* when committed as part of a plan or policy or as part of a large-scale commission of such crimes", Article 8, para. 1) with respect to which the same considerations as those set forth for crimes against humanity would hold. Here, actually, we have the characteristic dimension of the *relationship* "*of war*", which is absent instead in crimes against humanity. This dimension *sufficiently* specifies the objective type of all these criminal acts, though they overlap the others in their individual material nature. The validity of this point is confirmed by the provision of a normative limit to the framework of the crimes committed in "an armed conflict not of an international character", Article 8, *c* and *e*. In wording that is in part coincident with *d* and *f* of the same Article, the provisions covering these criminal acts do not apply to mere "situations of internal disturbances and tensions, such as riots, isolated or sporadic acts of violence or other acts of a similar nature".

---

[28] It is to be recalled (para. 3, *supra*) that only "serious" violations of the Geneva Conventions and of the laws and customs applicable in international armed conflicts are held to be "war crimes" as provided in Article 8, letters *a, b, c* and *e*. On this requisite, which surely introduces broadly flexible margins in criminal law, see the critique in Vassalli, G., *Lo Statuto*, cit., p. 15, where he speaks of the "price paid to the principles of legality and certainty", for the demand of a general nature not to involve the Court in deciding minor crimes, which is also reflected in the provision of Article 17, letter *d*; and for the more specific "removing" war crimes from the criminal acts of international character subject to the Geneva Conventions or customary law.

For the purposes of the Statute then, the definition of a war crime for violations committed in *non*-international armed conflicts does not refer to an individual act or conduct, which among other things can overlap a criminal act in international conflicts or even common crimes of another nature. Rather, the decisive factor is the particular *military* characteristic and the specific dimension and *political importance* of the *type of relation* made manifest in such acts (established between parties considered collectively and before an individual victim is concerned) - characteristics that are not found in mere situations of riots or internal disorder. The counter-limit is also significant in this connection. It is provided only in Article 8, *f*, sentence 2 (but not in *d*), by virtue of which the term "war crimes" is to be applied when the acts in question are committed in non-international armed conflicts "that take place in the territory of a State when there is *protracted* armed conflict between governmental authorities and *organized armed groups* or between such groups" (my italics).

The important politico-military dimension, which turns up in these cases of non-international armed conflict, again qualifies *identical* acts as "international" crimes. It is needless to add that the particular nature of the "relation of aggression" that is established between States, or with or between militarily organized political agencies, also represents the constituent element for the *crime of aggression* provided for in Article 5, *d*, the key issue in the legal definition of which surely depends on the political nature of this type of relation.

7) Concluding Remarks: Qualifying International Legal Interests and their Effects on Individual Guilt

We can assume correctly that the provisions of the Statute specifically qualify *common traits* of international criminal acts. More precisely, these characteristic traits appear to be represented by the particular *political and even a military* dimension of the differing *types of relation* which inform the various criminal acts.

The harm perpetrated against international legal rights or *juridical assets* occurs when the committing of such act is supported and characterized by the pursuit of the interests of organizations or organized political groups, or even of the State itself, i.e. when a *conflict* arises with collective or political interests, and not only with the rights and interests of individual victims, taken individually.

It is only in the former situations that a certain type of relation is established. This happens when a *de facto* army of a political or military power perpetrates the aforementioned abuses as instruments of a programme harmful to the international order, so that the criminal acts are raised to the status of "international crimes".

We need to consider one other question concerning the subjectivity of responsibility or liability. The new criminal law incorporated in the Statute regards the "criminal liability of natural persons" (Article 25, para. 1) in such a way as not to overlap or compromise the direct responsibility of States in international law (as expressly provided in Article 25, para. 4). The system thus permanently and directly calls upon the individual agent as such to respond to the entire international community for his or her position or action, thereby removing any immunity that may derive from or be guaranteed by the agent's political office, membership in a group or organization that exercises political or military power, even a State that is apparently or formally legitimate.

Offices like Head of State, member of government or parliament, or representative or agent thereof, a traditional source of immunity for individuals by virtue of reciprocal recognition among States, does not exempt anyone from personal criminal responsibility (as expressly provided in Article 27). Quite the contrary. The current position of the international community, as expressed in the Statute, considers the exercise of such power or military command, even if legitimate for an individual State, a source of the *special* extension of criminal responsibility. There are thus more severe disciplinary provisions for "military commanders" and other "hierarchy superiors" who are in a position to guarantee, control and even to punish subordinates who commit international crimes (Article 28).

On the other hand, even for the inferior ranks of a hierarchy or subordinates obedience to an (illegitimate) order retains only a very *limited* efficacy as an excuse (Article 33), given that the person must deal directly with an international *judicial* system whose principles and values are shared by the supra-national community and to which his own behaviour and judgment must conform.

This is a radical reversal of prospective with respect to the past, when the hierarchically organized structure of the State and armed forces lent itself to depersonalizing and to exonerating the individual from responsibility (not just criminal) for his or her decisions and actions. This new view is reflected today even in the judgment of guilt for criminal acts committed which arise from legal duties and constraints. The norms of the international legal system prevails, not only over those of all other groups, but also over those posited by the State itself, which may not comply with said principles and values in policy generally, especially when of a military nature. Indeed, no one will be able to invoke as an excuse a mistake of law "as to whether a particular kind of conduct is a crime", as expressly provided in Article 32, para. 2.

PROSPECTS FOR THE FUNCTIONING OF THE INTERNATIONAL CRIMINAL COURT

27. Some Practical Remarks on the Early Functioning of the International Criminal Court

TULLIO TREVES*

1. I will briefly consider some institutional and financial aspects of the International Criminal Court from which some difficulties might arise for its early functioning.[1] These difficulties are mostly of a practical nature. They stem nonetheless from a legal origin. This is the fact that the Court is the product of a treaty and that, consequently, its Statute is binding only for the States ratifying it or acceding to it. This fact is the most fundamental difference with the Tribunals for crimes committed in the former Yugoslavia and in Rwanda. They were created by resolutions of the Security Council under Chapter VII of the Charter. Their constitutive instruments are, consequently, binding on all members of the United Nations.

In my observations I will draw some lessons from the experience of the international tribunal to which I have the honour to belong, the International Tribunal for the Law of the Sea. This tribunal is also the

---

* Judge of the International Tribunal for the Law of the Sea, Hamburg; Professor of International Law, University of Milan, Faculty of Law.

[1] On the preparatory work for the provisions in the Rome Statute concerning institutional and financial aspects, see S. Rama Rao, "Financing of the Court, Assembly of the States Parties and the Preparatory Commission", in R. Lee (ed.), *The International Criminal Court, The Making of the Rome Statute*, The Hague, London, Boston, 1999, 399-420; see also G. Nesi, "The International Criminal Court: Its Establishment and its Relationship with the United Nations System; its Composition, Administration and Financing", in F. Lattanzi (ed.), *The International Criminal Court, Comments on the Draft Statute*, Naples, 1998, 187-191.

product of a treaty. It works within an institutional and financial framework comparable to that envisaged for the International Criminal Court.

2. The daunting tasks entrusted to the Preparatory Commission[2] indicate that the States which adopted the Rome Statute have concerns similar to those of the States signatories of the Law of the Sea Convention. The latter States worked for more than a decade in the Preparatory Commission of the International Seabed Authority and the International Tribunal for the Law of the Sea, not only to solve the problems of detail necessary to ensure the launching of the Authority and the Tribunal, but also in order to overcome some difficulties of principle concerning the Authority which made it impossible for an important group of States to ratify the Convention or to accede to it and for the Convention to become universal in scope. As is well known, these endeavours were not successful and the difficulties mentioned could be overcome only through an Agreement, introducing amendments to the Convention, adopted in 1994, few months before the Convention entered into force.[3]

In light of this precedent a certain measure of scepticism as regards the success of the Preparatory Commission in paving the way for widening the support for the Court seems reasonable. It is, however, a fact that the option of instituting the Court through a resolution of the Security Council, which would have ensured its universality, has not been chosen. Undoubtedly, there were strong political and legal reasons for not making such choice. Moreover, to amend the Statute with the purpose of increasing the number of States supporting it may also not be an advisable choice, at least for the time being. In light of the subject-matter of the jurisdiction of the Court, to pay too high prices for obtaining this result may not be acceptable. It seems imperative not to give further arguments to those that already now see the Statute as an instrument designed to placate the consciences of "virtuous" States and not really to prosecute and punish those who commit "the most serious crimes of international concern".[4]

Consequently, the difficulties depending on that the Statute is a treaty which binds only the States Parties to it have to be seen as an unavoidable aspect of the functioning of the Court.

---

[2] They are listed in the Annex to the Final Act of the Rome Conference (doc. A/CONF.183/C.1/L.83, 1988).

[3] Agreement relating to the Implementation of Part XI of the United Nations Convention on the Law of the Sea of 10 December 1982, adopted by the United Nations General Assembly with Res. 48/263 of 28 July 1994. On this agreement see T. Treves, "Entry into force of the United Nations Law of the Sea Convention: the Road towards Universality", Al-Nauimi and Meese (eds.), *International Legal Issues Arising Under the United Nations Decade of International Law*, The Hague etc., 1995, pp. 443-480.

[4] Article 5, para. 1, of the Rome Statute.

3. It is not, however, my intention to dwell on all the possible difficulties the Court may encounter because its Statute is not an universally ratified treaty. I shall only consider some practical difficulties of an institutional and financial nature. Comparative observations in light of the experience of International Tribunal for the Law of the Sea will be helpful.

A first comparative observation concerns the question whether it is wise to set up the Court as soon as the 60 ratifications needed for the entry into force of the Statute are reached. When the Law of the Sea Convention reached 60 ratifications and entered into force in 1994, the contracting parties felt that it was too soon for setting up the International Tribunal for the Law of the Sea. They felt that the Tribunal would have had a stronger basis, politically and financially, with a higher number of States Parties. They found legal devices for fixing the election at a date about one year later than that which was prescribed by the Convention.[5] This new time limit permitted the deposit of further instruments of ratification. The prospect of the election of judges stimulated States to become Parties. When the elections were held on 1 August 1996, the parties entitled to participate were a hundred, representing, in a rather balanced way, all continents and legal systems.[6]

Other relevant comparative observations concern the institutional framework. The International Criminal Court is based on an Assembly of the States Parties. This Assembly is similar to, but far from identical from, the Meeting of the States Parties of the Law of the Sea Convention upon which the Law of the Sea Tribunal is based. In both cases, the main tasks of these organs are the election of the judges (to which, in the case of the Assembly of the States Parties to the Rome Statute, must be added that of the Prosecutor) and the adoption of the budget of, respectively, the Court and the Tribunal.[7]

Before dealing with the differences between the two bodies, it seems necessary to underscore that the main problem facing them is, at least to a certain extent, the same. This is the problem of the relationship

---

[5] See the documents LOS/PCN/L.115, para. 37 (1994) and SPLOS/3, para 16 (1994) and Treves, "The Law of the Sea Tribunal: its Status and Scope of Jurisdiction after November 16, 1994" in *Zeischrift ausl. oeff. Recht u. Voelkerrecht*, vol. 55, 1995, 421, at 422-425. According to Article 4, para. 2, of the Statute of the Tribunal the first election of the judges should have been held in May 1995. Following the decisions of the Meeting of the States Parties it was held on 1 August 1996. The Rome Statute provides more flexibility, as it does not say when should the process of nominations of candidates be started and when should the Assembly for the election of judges be convened.

[6] SPLOS/14 paras 13-31 (1996).

[7] Rome Statute, Articles 36, 42 para. 4, and 112, para. 2*d*. Statute of the International Tribunal for the Law of the Sea, Articles 4 and 19 and rules 69 and 73 of the Rules of Procedure for the Meetings of States in doc. Parties SPLOS/2 rev.3 (1995).

between the Court and, respectively, the Tribunal, and the United Nations. Such relationship may be an uneasy one.

Especially in the early years after entry into force of the Statute, the Assembly will presumably be composed of a relatively small number of States. There will be many States belonging to the United Nations but not to the Assembly. And yet the Court, which is elected by the Assembly, has been conceived as a universal body claiming to work for mankind as a whole. Particularly if among the States not represented in the Assembly there will be States that oppose the Court, political and practical difficulties may arise. The situation of the Meeting of the States Parties to the Law of the Sea Convention is similar, as the Law of the Sea Convention has also been conceived as a universally applicable treaty. The Tribunal and, in particular, its Sea-bed Disputes Chamber, is the judicial custodian of the principle of the "common heritage of mankind". The uneasiness of the relationship with the United Nations, in the case of the Meeting of the States Parties, has, however, been removed to great extent by the high number of its component States (they are now 132) and by the decision, mentioned above, to elect the Tribunal only when such number had become much higher than the required 60.

A significant difference between the Assembly of the Parties to the Rome Statute and the Meeting of the States Parties to the Law of the Sea Convention is that the Statute provides for the establishment of a Bureau of the Assembly with the task to "assist the Assembly in the discharge of its responsibilities" (Article 112, para. 3c). It has 18 members elected for three years (Article 112, para. 3a). The Meeting of the States Parties to the Law of the Sea Convention also has a Bureau. Nothing is said in the relevant provision (Rule 24 of the Rules of procedure of the Meeting of States Parties) of its "representative character" and of the need to take into account "equitable geographical distribution and the adequate representation of the principal legal systems of the world" which are mentioned by the Rome Statute as regards the Bureau of the Assembly of the States Parties (Article 112, para. 3a). The provision is based on those usually found in Rules of procedure of international gatherings. The task of the four vice-presidents who compose the Bureau together with the president is simply to assist the latter "in the general conduct of work which falls within the competence of the President". Its members remain in function up to the meeting following the one that elected them (Rule 19), but no particular task is entrusted to them for the inter-sessional period.

The presence of such a representative Bureau should be a useful device to ensure the permanency and continuity of the institutional framework within which the Court functions. While more important than those of the Bureau of the Meeting of the States Parties to the Law of the

Sea Convention, the tasks of the Bureau, as set out in the Statute, are, however, rather limited. They consist in assisting the Assembly, but with no decision-making powers even in urgent situations. Potentially, the right granted to the Bureau to convene on its own initiative special sessions of the Assembly (Article 112, para. 6) might be the most powerful tool in its hands. The existence of the Bureau makes the institutional framework of the Court more elaborated and functional than that of the Tribunal. The Meeting of the States Parties of the Law of the Sea Convention holds only plenary sessions meeting normally once a year.

Another interesting difference is that in the Rome Statute there is a provision (Article 112, para. 8) which follows the well known Article 19 of the United Nations Charter in stating that: "A State Party which is in arrears in the payment of its financial contributions towards the cost of the Court shall have no vote in the Assembly and in the Bureau if the amount of its arrears equals or exceeds the amount of the contributions due from it for the preceding two full years. The Assembly may, nevertheless, permit such a State Party to vote in the Assembly and in the Bureau if it is satisfied that the failure to pay is due to conditions beyond the control of the State Party". This provision, which applies not only to the members of the Assembly but also those of the Bureau, aims at stimulating financial responsibility in the States Parties. Considering the financial difficulties met by other international institutions, including the International Tribunal for the Law of the Sea, because of late payment or of non-payment of contributions by member States, this seems an aspect where the Rome Statute improves on the Law of the Sea Convention's rules concerning the Tribunal.

There are further noteworthy differences between the Assembly of the State Parties of the Rome Statute and the Meeting of the State Parties of the Law of the Sea Convention. The first is that the Rome Statute provides for the setting up of subsidiary bodies of the Assembly, in particular in paragraph 4 of Article 112, which explicitly mentions "an independent oversight mechanism for inspection, evaluation and investigation of the Court, in order to enhance its efficiency and economy". I am not sure whether it is appropriate for an independent Court of law to be submitted to such a body. Certain precedents, in particular that of the Rwanda Tribunal, seem to indicate that means to ensure financial rigour may be necessary. Subsidiary bodies may be established according to the Rules of Procedure of the Meeting of States Parties of the Law of the Sea Convention (Rule 67). No indication as to the tasks to be performed by one or more of such bodies is provided. The idea to establish a Financial Committee (comparable to the ACEBQ of the General Assembly of the United

Nations) has been mentioned but met with some difficulties concerning its composition and functions.

The second difference is that the Rome Statute provides, in Article 119, for an albeit rudimentary system for the settlement of disputes, on which Francesca Trombetta Panigadi has developed some interesting thoughts in her contribution to the present volume. Nothing of this kind exists in the framework of the Meeting of the States Parties to the Law of the Sea Convention.

A third further difference lies in that the Meeting of the States Parties to the Law of the Sea Convention may be convened by the Secretary-General of the United Nations, while this is not allowed as regards the Assembly of the States Parties to the Rome Statute.

The comparative observations just made bring me to conclude that the Assembly of the States Parties to the Rome Statute is a reasonably self-contained organizational framework and that it is more independent from the United Nations than the already independent Meeting of the States Parties to the Law of the Sea Convention.[8]

4. I come now to the main point that prompted me to make these short remarks: the question of the financing of the Court and its connections with the Assembly of the States Parties. This aspect may prove decisive for the functioning or the non-functioning of the International Criminal Court.

Various proposals were discussed as regards the financing of the Court. They ranged from having the United Nations shoulder the financial costs of the Court, to having States Parties pay for these costs. The latter proposal was adopted. A compromise proposal which followed the model of the International Telecommunications Union, by dividing the membership into classes, each member of which would pay the same amount, thus lowering the burden of the highest contributors, was not accepted.

The system chosen is adapted from the scale of assessments of the United Nations. It is basically the same system adopted as regards the financing of the Law of the Sea Tribunal. According to this system, a few industrialized States face most of the financial burden. In the case of the Law of the Sea Tribunal, in light of the fact that the United States is not a Contracting Party, Japan, Germany, France, the United Kingdom and Italy alone pay more than 75 per cent of the bill.

The two systems are not, however, completely identical. Under Article 115 of the Rome Statute the expenses of the International Criminal

---

[8] See T. Treves, "The Law of the Sea 'System' of Institutions", in *Max-Planck Yearbook of United Nations Law*, vol. 2, 1998, 325, at 331-332, 335-337 and 340.

Court may also be provided by funds paid by the United Nations, subject to the approval of the General Assembly, "in particular as regards the expenses for cases referred to the Court by the Security Council". The logic is clear: whenever the Court has to perform tasks entrusted to it by the Security Council (which represents the United Nations as a whole) there is no reason why the United Nations should not pay. One may wonder, however, whether this is likely to happen in a situation (hopefully, but not necessarily, a transitional one) in which only some 60 or 70 members of the United Nations are Parties to the Statute and such memberships perhaps does not include one or more of the permanent members of the Security Council. In these circumstances political difficulties might arise which might block the use of resources for financing the activities of the Court out of the resources of the United Nations. The need for the approval of the General Assembly, set out in Article 115*b* of the Statute, in light the well known and rather complex procedure involving the Assembly's Committee on Administrative and Budgetary Questions (ACABQ), the Fifth Committee and the Plenary, is an indication that there will be no lack of fora in which these difficulties may emerge.

According to Article 115*b*, financing by funds of the United Nations is provided not exclusively but "in particular" in relation to expenses incurred due to referrals by the Security Council. It has been suggested that the expression "in particular" could be invoked by the Preparatory Commission set up by the Rome Conference in drafting the Financial Regulations mentioned in Article 113 of the Statute, in order to justify a provision according to which the United Nations would shoulder the start-up costs of the Court.[9] This is not, however, the only possibility. The Assembly of the Contracting Parties, once the Statute enters in force and before the establishment of the Court, could adopt an initial budget requiring the contracting parties to pay the necessary contributions. Both possibilities find a precedent concerning the institutions whose establishment is provided for by the Law of the Sea Convention. The financing of the International Seabed Authority was shouldered during the early years by the United Nations budget. Only one year after the definitive entry into force of the Agreement the autonomous financing system based on assessed contributions of member States started to apply.[10] To the contrary, the financing of the Law of the Sea Tribunal, with the exception of a very modest amount covering expenses prior to the establishment of the Tribunal, was covered from the beginning with the contributions of the States Parties to the separate budget of the Tribunal.

---

[9] A. Zimmermann, "The Creation of a Permanent International Criminal Court", in *Max-Planck Yearbook of United Nations Law*, vol. 2, 1998, 236 f.

[10] 1994 Agreement quoted *supra* at note 3, annex , sect. I, para 14.

A further difference, as far as funding is concerned, consists in that the Rome Statute mentions voluntary contributions from Governments, international organizations, individuals, corporations and other entities as possible sources of funds, although "in accordance with relevant criteria adopted by the Assembly of the States Parties" (Article 116). Nothing is provided in Statute of the Law of the Sea Tribunal. Voluntary contributions are not, however, excluded. They must be regulated by the financial regulations which the Meeting of the States should adopt, as they are in the United Nations Financial Regulations, which are applied on a provisional basis, *mutatis mutandis,* by the Tribunal.

The assessed contributions of the States Parties, together with the funds provided by the United Nations, are meant to cover not only the expenses of the Court but also those of the Assembly of the States Parties "including its Bureau and subsidiary bodies" (Article 115 of the Rome Statute). This enhances the autonomy of the Assembly from the United Nations in comparison with the Meetings of States Parties of the Law of the Sea Convention. The budget of the Law of the Sea Tribunal, financed by the assessed contributions of the States Parties, is only meant to cover the expenses of the Tribunal, while the expenses of the Meeting of the States Parties are shouldered by the United Nations Secretariat, in connection with the Secretary-General's task, as depositary, of convening the necessary meetings of the States Parties (Article 319, para. 1e, and see also Rules 25 and 26 of the Meeting of States Parties' Rules of Procedure).

As the precedent of the International Tribunal for the Law of the Sea shows, albeit within the framework of budgets which will unavoidably be more modest than those of the Court, the main concern for the proper functioning of the Court seems to arise from the possibility that adequate funding be available with continuity.

In both cases we have permanent judicial institutions whose expenses depend to a great extent on the amount of work to be undertaken within a given budget period. As regards the law of the Sea Tribunal, it is clear that each day in which the Tribunal is dealing with a case requires expenses, which would not be required otherwise, not only for interpreters, translators, precis-writers, reproduction of documents, but also for the very remuneration of judges, which depends in part on the number of days they exercise their functions (Statute of the Tribunal, Article 18, paragraph 1). In light of the text of the Rome Statute, it is not easy to say whether the same will be true in every detail as regards the Court. There is no doubt, however, that the expenses of the Court will depend to a great extent on the number and difficulty of the investigations and other activities of the Prosecutor and on the number and complexity of cases submitted to the Court.

In approving the budget for such judicial bodies, States may be tempted to provide funds only for a minimum of expenses - namely those necessary for the administrative functioning of the Court or Tribunal, possibly taking into account cases which at the time of approval of the budget are already on the list of cases. It seems rather unlikely that they will provide for cases which have not yet arisen, but which might very well arise during the period of time to which the budget applies. When such cases in fact arise, the expenses they entail are sources of difficulties which can only be met with funds destined to other uses (which is not always possible and legal) or with funds obtained after the fact, a procedure which is always costly and sometimes difficult.

To provide in the budget for the funds necessary to satisfy the needs of the Court of Tribunal that it is possible to foresee as likely makes easier to meet the expenses for some of the cases that may arise before such Court or Tribunal. This does not solve each and every difficulty. Forecasts about how many cases will arise in a given future period of time are far from easy to make. It may happen that funds prove insufficient to cover the expenses of all the cases that are submitted to the Court or Tribunal. It may also happen, however, that these funds remain wholly or in part unutilized. When the reluctance of States to provide funds whose need is not certain at the time of the adoption of the budget prevails, payments of supplementary funds becomes a necessity when the need arises because of submission of unbudgeted cases. Timely availability of such supplementary funds is, however, highly unlikely. Domestic decision-making processes, and in particular budget approval calendars, make late payment unavoidable for most States. Courts and Tribunals - which have the duty to attend to the cases submitted to them - are constrained to resort to sometimes unorthodox budget devices, including contracting loans.

The International Tribunal for the Law of the Sea was faced with the situation just described during its first year of life. The budget for 1996-97 provided for a certain amount to be spent on sessions of a non-judicial nature, needed especially in order for the Tribunal to adopt its Rules. It also provided for a modest amount for a possible first case which might have been submitted. In the middle of 1997, after having held a number of non-judicial meetings, the Tribunal considered that in order to conclude its work on the Rules, whose adoption was necessary for dealing efficiently with cases, one further meeting was necessary in the fall. No funds were available on the budget for this meeting. The Tribunal decided to utilize the amount set aside for the first case. This was approved by the Meeting of the States Parties held in May 1997 "as an exception" which should not constitute a precedent,[11] and the Tribunal was able to adopt its Rules at the end of October 1997. It so happened that a few weeks after the Rules were adopted the first case was submitted to the Tribunal, and that it was a "prompt release of vessels" case requiring immediate action according to Article 292 of the UN Law of the Sea Convention and the related provisions of the Rules of the Tribunal. The necessary expenses were met, in part, with money borrowed from the bank. To cover these expenses in 1998 the Meeting of the States Parties approved a supplementary budget for 1997. States Parties have paid - or are in the process of paying - their contribution to this supplementary budget together with their contribution to the 1999 budget. The amounts provided for in the supplementary budget are being credited to the Tribunal about two years after the expenses that have made them necessary were incurred.

Lack of funds for cases not foreseen in the budget is a problem arising unavoidably for international judicial bodies which, differently from the Tribunals for crimes in the former Yugoslavia and in Rwanda, are not part of a wider organization with a substantial budget and which, moreover, is permanently in session. For the reasons set out above, this problem does not seem to have a solution which is both simple and politically acceptable. In order to meet most, although not necessarily all, difficulties, it would seem advisable that States Parties provide in the budget for the Court of Tribunal amounts reasonable enough to cover cases not yet submitted when they adopt the budget, while establishing a contingency fund which would permit to use the amounts unspent during one year in the following year or years.

The existence of an institutional framework flexible enough to provide sufficient continuity is, nonetheless, a condition that must be satisfied in order to permit to the Contracting Parties to meet with the necessary timeliness the needs of the Court. Prompt payment of the contributions by all States Parties, and especially by those with the highest ones, is even more necessary as regards a judicial body, as the International Criminal Court, which functions within an autonomous institutional framework than it is as regards a Court or a Tribunal active within a broader institutional setting.

---

[11] Doc. SPLOS/24 para. 14 (1997) and doc. SPLOS/31, paras. 26-30 (1998).

28. Scenarios of Implementation of the Statute of the International Criminal Court

W. MICHAEL REISMAN*

With the adoption of the Statute of the International Criminal Court (ICC) by a diplomatic conference, there is now a significant possibility, though not a certainty, that the requisite number of ratifications will be achieved, the Statute will enter into force, and a permanent international criminal court will come into operation. Hence, the hitherto passionate discussions of whether the initiative to establish a permanent international criminal court is good or bad, wise or ill-conceived, timely or intemperate and whether, in the course of the long negotiations, this State behaved in good faith and that State not, will become increasingly historical or of purely academic interest. The practical question will become the effect the ICC, operating under its Statute, is likely to have on the international community's efforts to maintain minimum order and achieve a more optimum order and the strategic measures that may have to be taken in these regards. Answering that question requires us to discern the way the dynamics of world politics will operate with this new institution and the way the new institution, for its part, will operate and interact, synergize or collide, with a variety of other legal and political institutions, each of which is charged with responsibility for achieving its own objectives.

Until now, the Statute of the ICC has been appraised by many proponents and independent scholars in terms of some idealized model of law against which one can expose in the text of the Statute internal defects

* Myres S. McDougal Professor of Law, Yale Law School. I acknowledge the recommendations and critical comments of Mahnoush Arsanjani, Andrew Willard and Kate Hutchins.

or logical inconsistencies. This is an inappropriate and unrealistic standard: any multilateral instrument, at any level of social organization, must incorporate compromises - some of which may be internally inconsistent - in order to win the minimum support necessary for passage. The life of the law is not logic, Holmes said. The critical test of the utility of a legal instrument is less its internal consistency and more how it will operate in the contexts in which it is likely to be invoked.

In order to engage in such an intellectual exercise, scholars and policy scientists have long used the technique of inventing scenarios or constructs of the future as a means of testing the prospective operation of an instrument or a policy preference and to track the aggregate consequences of its application. I consider five factual scenarios or constructive futures in order to explore, under the different concatenations of factors in each, how the ICC Statute is likely to affect the achievement of the ultimate, ineluctable goals of international - indeed, all - politics: the maintenance or restoration of international and regional order, the restoration of order within States, and the achievement of justice.[1]

The Changing Role of the Military Instrument in World Politics

One new conditioning factor affects all the scenarios and merits some initial remarks. Though the idea of an international criminal tribunal has been discussed throughout the twentieth century, it was the apparently successful experience of the ad hoc Nuremberg and Far Eastern Military Tribunals[2] that forged popular conceptions about the possibilities and circumstances for using the technique of a permanent institution to dispense criminal justice in international politics. But proponents of the ICC frequently overlook the military-political paradigm that then obtained and was the precondition for the effective operation of Nuremberg and the Far Eastern Military Tribunals. At that time, the assumption was that war was to be waged in order to achieve victory; that the victorious army would seize the capital and control the government of the vanquished state; and that the victor could support or terminate the existing government as it wished. In brief, if one found oneself at war, one fought to win. Within this context, Nuremberg introduced the international trial as a technique of

---

[1] See, in this regard, W. Michael Reisman, *Institutions and Practices for Restoring and Maintaining Public Order*, 6 Duke J. Comp. & Int'l L. 175 (1995).

[2] This conclusion was not universally shared. See, e.g., Otto Kranzbuhler, *Nuremburg Eighteen Years Afterwards*, 14 DePaul L. Rev. 333 (1965); Onuma Yasuaki, *The Tokyo Trial: Between Law and Politics*, in *The Tokyo War Crimes Trial: an International Symposium* 45 (C. Hosoya et al. eds., 1986).

confirming the iniquity of the losers and their governmental practices and using the authoritative version of events duly proclaimed by the international tribunal as a strut in the reconstruction of the conquered State or, as the case was, of world order itself. But the point of emphasis was that the condition *sine qua non* for the trials was a total military victory.

Since 1945, international politics has seen what can be characterized as a paradigm shift with respect to the role of the military instrument in international politics. War is no longer conducted with a view to achieving a total victory, but rather with very limited objectives, such as winning some political advantage, securing the adjustment of a policy with an adversary, "degrading" the arsenal of an adversary, dumping obsolete ordnance, or maintaining one's credibility by confirming one's willingness and capacity to use military power. This change in strategic conception may be attributed to perceptions of greater interdependence and the consequent retro-costs of destroying an enemy; the destructiveness of modern weapons; and perhaps a heightened moral revulsion over the ever-widening collateral damage inflicted on non-combatants in modern warfare. There are also new internal political restraints operating on decisions to resort to intense coercion. The rank-and-file of democratic polities, which happen to command the most advanced military resources, have shown themselves disinclined, when they engage in elective conflicts, to pay the full price for achieving a comprehensive and enduring victory.

Because belligerents are unlikely to pursue or achieve complete victory, and tend rather to reach some accommodation with their adversaries, they are not likely to be able or to be inclined to place the leadership of an adversary in the dock of an ad hoc or permanent tribunal. Hence, the military and political preconditions of Nuremberg and Tokyo are unlikely to exist in many of the cases that may be brought to the ICC. Other than when the Security Council acts under Chapter VII of the UN Charter, the firm and imposed jurisdiction of Nuremberg and Tokyo is likely to be replaced by a consensual jurisdiction, in many instances requiring official collaboration from the State whose officials have been indicted. Presumably, unindicted officials from such a State would make the determination to submit to jurisdiction and either capture and surrender putative defendants themselves or to allow others to do so in their territory.

Five Scenarios

A) Conventional War

Traditionally, the law of armed conflict has assumed a war between two states, each with a hierarchically organized military force, confronting each other across a spatial domain and seeking to subdue the other by the delivery of kinetic weapons. While this is no longer the dominant form of contemporary warfare, it recurs and can still consume many lives. At present, Ethiopia and Eritrea are engaged in a major territorial war in this traditional format, one which has been extremely destructive of human life, but which has attracted relatively little attention from the international community.

If a war is pursued until victory, the political precondition of the Nuremburg paradigm will be fulfilled. But if the war is conducted according to contemporary practices and concludes in a negotiated settlement, with each government confirmed in place, then rendition of indicted persons to the ICC will depend on the consent and active participation of each of the governments concerned. In this scenario, that seems improbable, at least with respect to the leadership that has concluded the negotiated settlement: they are unlikely to agree to surrender themselves to an international criminal tribunal. If rendition of alleged war criminals occurs at all, it is likely to involve low-level token defendants. Should the prosecutor of the ICC undertake *proprio motu* prosecutions against the leadership of one or both sides, the action could conflict with the political settlement that had been achieved by the parties themselves or through the good offices of an international or regional organization. Thus, in the construct or scenario of large-scale conventional wars that may be fought in the coming decades (under the conditions we have projected), the ICC would appear to contribute little and could find itself in conflict with the Security Council or its regional proxy seeking to implement the UN Charter mandate to re-establish minimum world order and restore the peace.

B) Internal, Non-Ethnic and Non-Ideological War

Many states are still characterized by lack of internal elite consensus and the absence of effective procedures for the transfer of power. Such states are periodically disturbed by the purposive application of violence aimed at securing control of the apparatus of the State and, through it, access to the indulgences that are associated with it. Where these conflicts occur in acutely ideologized environments and each side feels that the entire future of the State and society is at stake, adversaries may concentrate on eliminating each other entirely. In non-ideological circumstances, however, these forms of internal violence are essentially "to-the-victors-go-the-spoils" struggles and are likely to be efficient and temporally short applications of violence, with destruction concentrated intensely on those who have or are seeking power; such conflicts are likely to inflict relatively little collateral damage.

It is difficult to see a role for the ICC in non-ideologized internal conflict. Rather, one would expect the ICC to be applied to conflict that involves ideological foes, with the large-scale bloodletting that usually attends it. That sort of conflict is likely to trigger Articles 6 to 8 of the Statute. The ICC's jurisdictional regime will be effective for this type of conflict only if the State concerned has become Party to the Statute. Even then, rendition of indicted parties is likely to be restricted to the losers, who may, as is often the case in these conflicts, have been the least ruthless and, as a result, least efficient of the contenders for power.

The operation of the ICC in these sorts of conflicts may collide with another international policy. A frequently used technique of the international community to resolve these types of internal wars is to "persuade" a leader who is believed to be the gravamen of the problem to depart voluntarily to a venue where he is assured immunity and can enjoy a "well-earned" retirement. The purpose of this sort of shabby swap is to allow a peaceful transition. Thus in the Philippines, Ferdinand Marcos was extricated from Manila, where he might otherwise have conducted a bloody last stand that might even have maintained his power, and was deposited in Hawaii where he could live his final days in tranquility. Idi Amin, the former dictator of Uganda, is now in Saudi Arabia. Mengistu Haile Mariam, the former dictator of Ethiopia, is in Zimbabwe (and latterly in South Africa in circumstances reminiscent of Augusto Pinochet's situation in the United Kingdom). In each case, the international community, in an efficient, if not very public fashion, was able to withdraw what seemed to be the political pathogen and then to allow a peaceful transition to ensue.

In all of these cases, a critical factor in securing the withdrawal of the dictator has been the assurance that he would be able to live in peace wherever he was dropped. This strategy is not a particularly proud one, but it is effective and relatively economical. With the ICC in operation, it will be more difficult to use. Consider: two and a half years ago, Hosni Mubarak, the President of Egypt, was reported to have proposed to Saddam Hussein asylum and protection in Egypt. Had Saddam accepted, it might have opened the way for internal political change and international reconciliation, a major prospective benefit for the Iraqi population. Similar suggestions have been made for a voluntary and judgment-proof exile of

Slobodan Milosevic to South Africa. Ironically, the international community has been more inclined to use this technique when the subject dictator is more, rather than less vicious. Yet these dictators are precisely the type of miscreant that the ICC Statute targets and with respect to whom States Parties will have committed themselves *aut dedere aut judicare*. Will this technique for resolving internal conflict be feasible when the ICC is operating?

In the past year, a number of commentators have observed that had the ICC been in operation, it would have been able to assume responsibility for the trial of General Pinochet. But this assumes, first, that General Pinochet would have permitted Chile to become or remain party to the Statute, and second, that General Pinochet, at the pinnacle of power, would have surrendered himself. Both assumptions are weak. Hence, the possibility that the ICC will respond constructively to crimes occurring in this species of internal conflict appears rather remote.

C) Internal Ethnic War

Internal ethnic conflicts have proved to be extremely destructive of human life and have been the scene of some of the most egregious atrocities. Indeed, much of the stimulus for the ICC has come from groups and individuals who have sought a means of deterring or at least arresting the impunity of perpetrators of atrocities in these types of conflicts. Where one ethnic group is primarily responsible for the atrocities and loses, the availability of an international criminal court to try those responsible for the atrocities seems particularly attractive, since it avoids the oxymoron of victors' justice by providing a judicial forum likely to be more neutral and more procedurally just then would be available within the disrupted State itself. Thus, the International Criminal Court might be preferable as the judicial forum for establishing accountability and punishing than would be an internal court, though serious scholars such as Professor Jose Alvarez have raised searching questions about this intuition.[3] Certainly, a system of internal trials after a particularly bloody ethnic war would probably be marked by vindictiveness and, if the court system had been disrupted in the conflict, it would be unlikely to achieve anything approximating an international standard. So, in this respect, the International Criminal Court could be beneficial. Yet it would also be asymmetrical in its application of justice, for it would be considerably more difficult to secure jurisdiction

---

[3] See Jose E. Alvarez, *Crimes of States/Crimes of Hate: Lessons from Rwanda*, 24 Yale J. Int'l L. 365 (1999).

over those who prevailed in the conflict - and their conduct might have been just as bad or worse than the conduct of those who lost.

Many of these conflicts have been resolved by compromise, with armistices and truth commissions or some similar internal arrangement that is far from the type of accountability that seems to be the fundamental impulse of the ICC. Where the conclusion of the conflict is a settlement, for example through a so-called "government of national unity" and is accompanied by some form of amnesty, independent action by the prosecutor of the ICC could actually undermine the settlement. The ICC Statute does not deal with amnesties; according to informed commentators, the issue was carefully avoided in the course of the negotiations. The government of France has indicated that it assumes that the ICC Prosecutor will exercise the discretion assigned to him or her in Article 56 of the Statute in these circumstances. Thus, the ICC could avoid a direct confrontation with the Security Council in circumstances in which the Council is interested in promoting a settlement as the means for terminating the internal violence. But this assumes that the Prosecutor will operate with the perspectives of members of the Security Council in mind, rather than the alternative perspective on which the ICC rests. Hence, one doubts whether this particular species of conflict is likely to be beneficially influenced by the ICC.

D) Internal Wars with External Intervention

The law of war has not had an effective external enforcing mechanism and it is not the type of law that has its own internal compliance incentives. Its effectiveness rests on the expectation of reciprocity for compliance and retaliation for non-compliance; where that expectation has not obtained, compliance has been low, because in the absence of an effective external enforcer that can impose costs for violations, there are significant incentives to ignore the restraints of the law of war. Expectations of reciprocity and retaliation depend upon a symmetry or power parity between belligerents. Ordering one's pilots to operate at 10,000 rather than 50,000 feet increases their vulnerability to ground fire but also increases the visibility of the target and reduces the amount of collateral damage. Flying at 50,000 feet reduces vulnerability and loss of planes and pilots, but increases the collateral damage caused to the adversary. If both belligerents have planes, both sides have an incentive to fly at the lower rather than the higher altitude insofar as it induces the other to do the same.

In UN interventions, there is likely to be an asymmetry, which may, indeed, encourage some states to participate in the UN force: UN forces will have most of the power and the target considerably less, while virtually all of the fighting will occur in the target's territory, with none in the territory of the States contributing to the UN force. Hence, there are few incentives for the UN force to increase its vulnerability (and the probability of casualties) in order to secure reciprocal behaviour from the target. Indeed, as this is elective conflict, the prospect of an increase in vulnerability and casualties may dissuade a government from committing its forces to the UN effort.

Imagine a scenario of a UN-authorized intervention into an internal conflict in order to secure a settlement and the establishment of what Judge Cassese has called "negative peace". Ironically, the International Criminal Court, with a standing jurisdiction over war crimes and greater capacity to secure custody of putative defendants from states inclined to participate in international actions, may limit the capacity of the UN to mobilize forces and use them effectively, since the ICC redresses the asymmetry or imbalance between the arsenals and capacities of the belligerents, which may be the very inducement for states to participate in UN actions.

E) Multilateral Interventions without UN Approval

Consider operations like those conducted recently in Kosovo and Serbia, which are arguably based on international support, but are conducted without formal international authorization. Here again, there is asymmetry between belligerents and, as a result of the nature of the internal policing dynamic or enforcing dynamic of the law of war - the implication of reciprocity or retaliation - there will be strong pressures on external participants to reduce their casualties by externalizing the risks of conflict onto the civilian population of the adversary, in ways likely to violate the laws of war. An international criminal court could act, to some extent, as a restraint on such actions by those stronger powers to the point where it may dissuade some of them *ab initio* from undertaking the risks of casualties in what is, for them, essentially an elective conflict. So, ironically, the operation of the ICC in this sort of scenario could deter the commission of war crimes, but it may also deter international action in response to grievous violations of internationally guaranteed human rights. Were this to happen, the existence of the ICC would actually increase impunity!

Conclusion

The artificial construction of alternative futures permits the scholar to assess the way an institution may work under different conditions and circumstances. I projected the existence and operation of the ICC in five scenarios of different types of armed conflict that are likely to trigger its jurisdiction and tried to assess the prospects of the achievement of its own special institutional goals as well as the impact its operation will have on goals such as the restoration and maintenance of internal and international order. With respect to its own goals, it appears that the ICC will have limited success in a number of probable scenarios. As for its impact on other minimum international goals, it appears that the ICC will contribute to the achievement of those goals in only one scenario, have indifferent effects in others, and probably obstruct the achievement of certain minimum goals in others.

29. Round Table: Prospects for the Functioning of the International Criminal Court*

ANTONIO CASSESE (CHAIRMAN)

The members of the panel are: Ambassador Philippe Kirsch, M.me Béatrice Le Fraper du Hellen, Professor Ted Meron, Professor Michael Reisman, Professor Tullio Treves and myself.

We have identified five main topics within the general issue of the future of the ICC.

First issue: possible scenarios of impact of the establishment of the ICC on world politics. It's a very general topic. Actually, we would like to ask ourselves to what extent will the ICC, once it is set up, impinge upon the role of the UN Security Council in the field of maintenance of peaceful relations. Will the ICC after its establishment have a bearing on international crises or, to borrow a concept from a famous political scientist Johann Galtung, will positive peace (i.e. realization of justice) replace negative peace (i.e. the absence of war)?

And on this particular topic, I will call upon Michael Reisman and Béatrice le Fraper du Hellen to make some brief comments.

The second topic we would like to discuss with you is less general. It relates to the problems that are still outstanding in the process of completion of the ICC legal framework. In particular, we would like to focus on some major elements of the rules of procedure, rules that are in the process of being drafted and, in other areas, the elements of crime. I would suggest that in particular, as far as the rules of procedure are

* This text is a transcription of the Round Table held in Trento on the 15th May 1999, and was not revised by the participants.

concerned, we should try to discuss whether or not there is a need to weld elèments of the inquisitorial model into the adversarial system. In other words, to take as much as possible some elements from the civil law systems and use them within the framework of the common law system, the adversarial system which is predominant in the Statute. In particular, we would like to focus on the role of victims and the accused in this area. As far as the elements of crime are concerned, one may wonder whether it is appropriate to set up a rigid list of elements of crime so as to leave very little leeway to judges. Judges, I think, will be faced with a sort of substantive criminal code, which will be difficult to apply and which will leave very little room for imagination and for innovative approach to criminal law. I hope that Ambassador Kirsch and Béatrice Le Fraper will make comments on this particular issue.

Third topic: how to speed up the process of ratification of the ICC Statute. Who should put pressure on Governments and Parliaments? This issue, we would like to set it aside and leave it to Ambassador Fulci, to discuss in his final statement. So, therefore, this will not be for the panel to discuss.

As for the fourth topic, we should discuss a major problem: the US position. Is it a major stumbling block to the establishment of the ICC or will what some labelled as "the US threat" prove in the end to be a sort of paper tiger? I will call upon Michael Reisman and Ted Meron to address this particular issue.

And finally, fifth topic, how to coordinate the future work of the ICC with that of the Tribunal for the former Yugoslavia and the Tribunal for Rwanda, and possibly also with the International Tribunal for Cambodia, if one day it is set up, according to the report prepared by a group of experts or with a national court to be set up by Cambodia. There may be problems of coordination.

However, before we start with item number one, I would like to ask Ambassador Kirsch to make a few introductory remarks. He was kind enough to accept a proposal that he should address the audience with a sort of overview of some outstanding problems.

PHILIPPE KIRSCH

There are really a few points I would like to make in introducing. They are not only based upon on what I've heard this morning and what has been said in the past couple of days, but also based on other seminars and conferences which I attended. I really have only three points.

The first point is that the ICC Statute that was adopted in Rome is the Statute we have and the only document we have. I'm not among those who say it is a perfect document. It is not a perfect document for many reasons: technical and political. Tullio Treves was saying earlier today that the ad hoc tribunals were established by the Security Council, and therefore are binding for every State, while the ICC, as a product of a treaty, does not: he is absolutely right. But this is also necessarily the political consequence of something else, which is one of the reasons why an ICC was established, was to move away, with apologies, the monopoly that the Security Council used to have. Once you want to move away the monopoly of the Security Council then you have to proceed by a treaty and that entails a number of concessions the Security Council never has to have. Having said that and knowing the imperfections of the Statute, technical and jurisdictional, you have to accept that the Statute is not going to be rewritten and you have to accept that we have to live with it. It has some constitutional consequences and some practical consequences. The constitutional consequence is that the Preparatory Commission which started sitting simply does not have the ability to change the Statute; that it can only be done by a review conference and a review conference can only take place a number of years from now, after entering into force of the Statute.

The practical consequence of the impossibility of changing the Statute is that even in technical work we have to be aware and conscious that a number of provisions in the Statute are the result of very, very difficult negotiations and reflect a balance of views.

Whether the balance is right or wrong in many cases can be argued, but that argument is to some extent irrelevant now; the balance is in the Statute.

So I think, generally speaking, what we should try to do is to make the Statute work and not get lost in too many theoretical discussions as to what the Statute should have been. I find that this kind of event, the Trento meeting, can be very useful in that kind of process because you all bring up some elements that other people have not thought of and which may eventually lead to a progress within the framework I indicated.

The second point I want to make is on the momentum that exists now behind the establishment of an ICC. As far as I am concerned, I see that the momentum continues to be sustained. It's true that you can look either way at the Pinochet case, the Kosovo case, or the Cambodian case; but the point is that ten years ago all of that would have been unthinkable, none of those issues would have arisen or would have appeared on the political screen.

My sense is that the document that was adopted, all the movement behind the creation of an ICC, is very different from any other treaty, in the sense that part of it does respond to States' interests, of course, but part of it's really based on much deeper concerns about the international society, and my impression is that this is not going to stop now. The ratification process, of course, is very slow because of the need for legislation and constitutional changes in some cases, but we have already eighty-two signatures, and all the signatures are not just pieces of paper. I think in those circumstances, where States have to change their legislation, signatures do reflect an intention to do that.

What is particularly interesting, I find, is that a number of States that abstained when the Statute was adopted, have now said very clearly that they do intend to become Parties to the Statute. Indeed, one of the three States that have ratified is a State that abstained under the adoption of the Statute and that, I think, is very significant. States that might have had concerns and questions about some aspects of the Statute, now those very same States are saying: well, the Statute is there, this is what we have and all things being considered, we are better off with an ICC - even if it is not perfect from our perspective - than without it.

My third and last point is that we are facing a long term and difficult work. We are in a situation where a culture of impunity still exists. It has behind it several decades of consistent impunity. And it's going to take a while for this to dissipate, to fade away. So there will be problems: ethical and serious political problems. My appeal is that we should not be discouraged in the short term by the problems that come up. We should try to resolve those problems in cooperation with those who do have a difficulty with the Statute, and not assume that, because there are difficulties, this is a lost cause. It's a very promising cause and we should keep our eyes on the ball, keeping in mind the final objective and continuing to work towards it despite the difficulties.

ANTONIO CASSESE

As for point one, may I comment? I understand your point as being a sort of appeal to outsiders, like Condorelli and myself, not to be too critical of the Statute. Don't shoot the pianist! We will not shoot the pianist.

Let us quickly move on to our panel discussion. We will start with item one: "Possible scenarios of impact of the establishment of the ICC on world politics".

MICHAEL REISMAN

Thank you very much. Before I begin I would like to thank the organizers, Professor Politi, Professor Nesi and the sponsor of this really remarkable conference. I have some comments, particularly on the first point that

Ambassador Kirsch made, which I think is a very telling and important point with respect to the constitutional structure of the world community. Since, Mr. Chairman, you are reserving a moment for discussing the relationship with the Security Council, I will defer that.

Much of the discussion in the last two days has either been an apology for the Statute, a defence of the myths of the Statute or an attack on the negotiating style of some of the participants. Let me say that this is only a legacy of the past. The Statute is there, we have it and it's a good probability, not a certainty, that there will be an International Criminal Court. I think, at this point, that the scholar has to look into the future, to try to understand the dynamics of world politics, and the way this new institution (the ICC) will operate and interact, synergize or conflict with a variety of other institutions and institutional objectives of international politics. What I propose to do is to consider a number of scenarios or constructive futures which are likely to engage the intention of the International Criminal Court when it's operating and to see how it works with respect to certain key goals: the maintenance or restoration of international order, the maintenance or restoration of order within States and the achievement of justice. In order to do that, I think we have to put into our picture the dynamics of the conduct of high level rulers, which are often a pre-condition for the types of crime that are spelt out in Articles 6 to 8 and which pose the problems that really are the predicate of the International Criminal Court. And we have to make a contrast between radical changes that have taken place in the conduct of armed conflicts and the object of armed conflicts since 1945. Up until 1945, military cadets understood that if you conduct a war, you conduct it to win, you conquer the army of the other side, you march victorious towards the capital, you do what you wish to the leadership of the other country. Since 1945, that has changed, there has been a substantial change. You no longer do final acts of conflict. You set up an International Criminal Court (Nuremberg), a military tribunal, and on the basis of that court you try the offenders who have been guilty of atrocities and you use that technique as a critical strike in the process of the reconstruction of the society that has been conquered. That is the new model. This is the paradigm that lies at the basis of the idea of an International Criminal Court.

But coinciding with the emergence of the Statute there have been fundamental changes in the way a war is now conducted; we no longer have this drive for victory, but in fact, we have a modern warfare and understanding that one will not push to the victory because it's too much destructive. It could, in fact, threaten oneself. Democratic policies engaged in elective conflicts are not going to pay the price of the final victory and so now warfare is conducted for political advantage, to secure adjustments within the policies of the target State, to degrade the arsenal - language that has been very common from the NATO spokesman during the Kosovo crisis - and to maintain the credibility of one's own entity as a political actor. In other words, one does not go to the point where one has complete victory over the adversary, and one is in a position then to place the leadership of the adversary in the dock for trial whether by an ad hoc tribunal or by a permanent tribunal. This is very important when you think about scenarios in which the International Criminal Court is going to operate, to think in terms of the conflicts that we are going to be engaged in the future, which I think are the sort of things in which the ICC will be engaged in.

The first is the conventional war, this is war in the nineteenth century model: armies of the two States run against each other across a fixed front and try to gain territory either for strategic or for some other purposes. This is a legacy of the past. Such a war is currently going on in the territory of Africa between Ethiopia and Eritrea. It has been extraordinarily destructive of human life. In one battle, 6 weeks ago, 30,000 people were killed. Causalities are at least over 100,000 in a war that looks to be a serial war. Now, the international community, under the new paradigm of conflict will not let one side or the other advance to total victory which would have been the predicate for the transfer of the losing side to an international tribunal. The international community will seek a ceasefire and then an accommodation, a settlement leaving the Governments of both sides intact. And in these circumstances, the possibility of trying the leadership of either States could in fact undermine the objective of what the Security Council would be trying to achieve. One would assume that neither State would be willing to initiate this if the Prosecutor were to initiate this *proprio motu*, under the authority that he or she will have under the Statute. There could be a potential conflict between the objective of the Security Council or of the international community to settle the conflict and the accountability objective sought by the Statute.

Second scenario is one of internal war that is ideological but not ethnic. This is a war that is fought between political parties, or political orders within a particular State. Struggles for power in Chile in early 1980s continued in the 1990s between relatively liberalizing and relatively conservatizing elements. Struggles for power within the Philippines. Struggles for power within Liberia... Here again, this is an internal war, this is not a war that immediately engages the attention of the international community.

Usually, the technique of the international community to resolve these wars, is to strongly seek to remove a particular leader who is believed to be a gravamen of the problem and to drop that person in some place which is safe, a place of asylum or a place of immunity, and to allow that person to enjoy the wealth that has been despoiled from the country concerned and at the same time to allow a peaceful transition. The model for this would be the Philippines where Ferdinand Marcos was removed and dropped in Hawaii, where he was allowed to live his final days. Idi Amin is now in Saudi Arabia, Mengistu, the dictator of Ethiopia, is now in Zimbabwe and so on. In each case, the international community, not in a very public fashion, but in a very efficient fashion, was able to withdraw what seemed to be the problematic element and allow peaceful transition. In all of these cases, a critical factor in securing the withdrawal of the dictator was the assurance that the dictator would be able to live in peace wherever he was dropped.

That is somehow doubtful now under the way the Statute will operate. This particular strategy - not a particular proud strategy but one that has been effective until now and relatively economical - probably it would be harder to conduct. I make you one example: two and a half years ago, the President of Egypt reportedly proposed to Saddam Hussein asylum and protection if he would have left Iraq and come to Egypt. I would think that that would have been a major benefit for the Iraqi population to internal changes that could hardly be worse and probably would be substantial and beneficial. It would be hard to conduct that kind of operation now, with the ICC, the way it is designed. And so there will be, maybe, a certain conflict between a set of practices that have been relatively covert but have been useful to stop internal conflicts of this type.

The next type of internal conflict that I would like to consider is a scenario where the internal conflict is marked by ethnic, deep ethnic strife. And this is something we find in the Balkans, we find it in Rwanda, we find it in the Sudan, and the question here is what will be the effect of the International Criminal Court beyond international efforts to resolve this type of conflict. For the most part, this conflict can be resolved either by one side prevailing, in which case the International Criminal Court would be preferable as a forum for trying and for accountability than would be an internal court, that probably would be marked by vindictiveness and certainly would be unlikely to achieve anything approximating an international standard. So, in this respect, the International Criminal Court, in the outcome of this type of unfortunately too familiar scenario, would probably be beneficial, although it would be asymmetrical, it will not be applied to those who won the conflict and they might be just as bad or worst than those who had lost. But the Court, in this scenario, provides a significant contribution.

I would like to talk about two other scenarios and obviously there could be many others and we could flash them out in great detail if we had enough time.

One is the scenario of the UN intervention authorized as a direct intervention into some sorts of internal conflicts as a way of securing a settlement and the establishment of "minimum order" or that what Professor Cassese calls "negative peace", citing Johann Galtung. Here I think that the International Criminal Court could probably play a very interesting role because the law of war traditionally depended upon a symmetry or parity of power between two States. The law of war does not, at least in its traditional form, have an external enforcing mechanism. The one side flies and plays at 1,000 feet rather than 30,000 feet because it increases the visibility of the target and reduces collateral damage with the expectation that the other side would do the same. So, if both sides have planes, both sides have a strong incentive to fly at 5,000 or 7,000 feet rather than 30,000 feet where the target is no longer visible and there is going to be much more collateral damage. In UN intervention, there would usually be a tremendous asymmetry that is the UN forces will have all the power, the target would relatively be little. In this respect, ironically, the International Criminal Court may act as a restraint on UN toward the third party on the outside since it introduces or redresses the asymmetry or unbalance that exists between the arsenals and capacities of the two powers.

And the same applies to a final scenario that I'll mention very briefly, and that is multilateral intervention without UN approval. For example, the operations that are being conducted just a few hundred miles from here with Italy as a major base: the operation in Kosovo against Serbia. And here again, you find an extraordinary asymmetry and as a result of the internal policing dynamic or enforcing dynamic, the implication of reciprocity or retaliation, that is fundamental to the law of war, is not operating. And so, in theory, an International Criminal Court could act, to some extent, as a restraint on the stronger powers. Ironically, since the stronger power will inevitably represent the powers of the international community, again, some iniquities or atrocities that stimulated the international intervention, the ICC will find itself in a curious way restraining or even abstracting some of these opportunities.

So, very briefly, using the technique of scenarios, or the artificial construction of futures, and trying to appreciate the dynamics that will operate in them, we can see that the ICC will in some circumstances be beneficial, in other circumstances may in fact be an obstruction to the achievement of minimum order, but of course, we all appreciate that justice has a price. We all understand that accountability cannot be achieved without the investment of a lot of treasure. And I presume that everyone who supports the Court is willing to make that investment.

BEATRICE LE FRAPER DU HELLEN

Although I don't want to dwell on history, if we want to speak about the prospects in the long term, in terms of what will happen in international politics with the intervention of the Court, we do have to know what expectations we had. This was already alluded to during our first session when we began the seminar, by Professor Mauro Politi and then by Ambassador Elaraby and others, when they spelt out what were the expectations of the Court. Politi spoke about the shadows and lights of the Statute and told us that the Statute was satisfactory, globally, in that it maintained enough independence and autonomy of the Court from the political area. Ambassador Elaraby stated that although his expectations had been the same, although he would have wanted that the Court should have such independence and autonomy in its functioning, he was not sure that such autonomy had been secured and said there was too much intervention by the Security Council.

The reason why I evoked those two interventions is that you have to understand that some delegations started the negotiations with entirely different perspectives. I must say for France that it was never an objective of France, when participating at the negotiations of the ICC, to achieve the creation of an independent judicial body. We wanted to ensure that the Court interact, synergize with other international bodies, especially in the field of maintenance of peace and security. I have sensed in this room the frustration of a lot of specialists in the field of international and criminal law. Each time we tried to go back to the law and study the Statute and the legal provisions of the Statute, we always had to go back at one point to international politics, finances, and we had to go away from the purity of law, if I may. But definitely the objective of France in the negotiations was not of a purely legalistic nature and our objectives were very closely linked to the need for the Court to contribute to the maintenance of peace and security. From our point of view, we think that we have inserted in the Statute a number of provisions which allow the Court, not the Court receiving instructions from the Security Council, but the Court itself, to be very much aware and to include in its activity those political concerns.

Let me point at some provisions in the Statute that we have introduced. One of them is certainly in Article 53 of the Statute on the beginning of investigation. Article 53 says that the Prosecutor, taking into account the gravity of the crime and the interest of victims, may consider that there are substantial reasons to believe that an investigation will not serve the interest of justice. The Prosecutor, taking into account the interest of justice, can decide not to open an investigation.

I thought it is a very important provision because it allows the Prosecutor to take into account the existence of a post-crisis situation; that is to say, like the South Africa situation today, the Guatemala, El Salvador situations a few years ago, when those countries, after a big crisis, dictatorships, atrocities, managed to find, sometimes with the help of the UN sometimes without, their own solutions to their problems. There were the Truth Commission in Guatemala, there is the Truth Commission in South Africa. And we have tried to give the Court the possibility to take into account the existence of such attempts at finding a solution. It will not always be linked to the intervention of the Security Council. That was not an objective *per se*. Our ambition, for the judges and prosecutors, is for themselves to try and reconcile the need for an independent judicial decision-making, and the need for the Court to contribute to international peace and security or rather, I should say, to reconciliation in those Countries where there had been big crises.

And for us, the prospects are quite good. I must say, I do not share the idea that there will always be contradiction between individual accountability and a peace settlement or a domestic political solution. Here, again, I'm not talking about a Kosovo-style situation. In the midst of a conflict, in the midst of terrible atrocities being committed, to my mind here, there is not much doubt about what kind of decision the Prosecutor will take, although I will not dwell further on the subject. But to us in Kosovo, individual accountability, the chain of command is quite clear; of course, judicial conclusions must be drawn from that. But there will be a time, where we will be in a post-crisis situation in the former Yugoslavia, where the Prosecutor and the judges will have to decide whether they want to continue investigating themselves, whether they want to continue prosecuting themselves, or whether it's time to let the Yugoslav people find their own solution. And we think that we have given the Court the right tools and the possibilities to take into account those evolutions.

I mentioned Article 53. Other important provisions are in the Articles on complementarity. When you read those Articles, they really leave the final choice to the Court to decide whether the Court should take jurisdiction or not. When you read the Statute, you might think that the Court will only base its decision on purely judicial analysis. Very frankly, I don't believe it. When you have to assess, and I draw your attention to those Articles (Articles 17, 18, 19), and when we ask the Court to assess whether a State is willing or unwilling to investigate or prosecute, whether a State is able or unable to prosecute or to investigate, this will be really in term of willingness to prosecute or to investigate.

I think there will also be, for the Court, a lot of political analysis to make. And here again, I want to stress that I'm not saying that the Court will receive instructions from the Security Council. We believe the Court will have in itself the possibility to respond to such situations.

I just want to remind you that Professor Fausto Pocar, yesterday, told us of the links between the Statute and human rights instruments. For us, it is obvious that the Court will not be impervious to what's happening in the human rights field and to all the thinking that is going on in the human rights field on things such as impunity. Authoritative scholars have written in the human rights field a lot of reports on impunity where they stressed the fact that there are a few criteria to be met for countries to find peace and reconciliation between themselves: rights of victims to know, rights of victims to reparation, rights of victims to justice. They stressed the fact that the recourse to an International Criminal Court is really the ultimate recourse. They stressed the fact that there are other solutions. And that is why the general reflection in this matter to us will have influence of the Court and we think the Court, the judges and the prosecutor, will be able on their own accord, as I said earlier, to conciliate the logics of justice and the logics of peace. It's rather an optimistic analysis that we will make on the future of the Court.

Before I conclude, I would just say a word on Article 60, on deferral, which has been considered as the proof that the Security Council would have too much influence on the International Criminal Court. I think the presentation made by Ms. Wilmshurst on the subject when she said: there are really a few cases when the Security Council will be able to reach a decision, to ask the Court to defer and in my opinion it will never need to do so. I don't think we will ever find ourselves in the situation where the Court will obstruct efforts to bring back peace, to stop the killings in a region. I cannot imagine such a situation where a prosecutor would willingly get involved into the situation while there are really positive efforts being made to stop a conflict. So, on these notes, I will stop. But there was a point I wanted to make here: there has been a lot of consent expressed during the negotiations by countries which had suffered delicate crisis internally and which had found their own solutions that the Court should be given the means to take into account the situation. I'm thinking again of South Africa, Salvador, Guatemala and others and I think we have found a quite balanced solution. It's all in the Statute. And I let you read it, study it, and speak international law about it in the future.

THEODOR MERON

Let me make it clear that I am speaking in my individual capacity. My association with the US Government is over.

The general question is the impact of the ICC on world politics. How much impact it will have on the real world. And I would like to relate it to a comment I heard yesterday from my friend, Richard Dicker, who said that the train has left the station and it's slowly proceeding to its destination. And I agree with him: the train has left the station, it is proceeding to a destination and it will get to a destination. What I do not know, is whether it will get to a Union Station, a Grand Central or a Gare de Lyon or to the sort of station that I know very well in the South of France, Brignon le Plagnole, about which nobody has heard and you have not missed much for not hearing about it.

The question is not whether the Court will survive and will be established. I'm sure it will. The question is how much relevance it will have to the real world, because comments by my colleague, Mike Reisman, today have demonstrated most of the myriads of conflict that we can expect in the future, are internal conflicts. Now, you know that the Statute, and this is a point on which I do not always agree with my colleague Mr. Kaul (but I do agree with him sometimes), when he spoke about the way the Statute, the jurisdiction is crafted, we have in fact created a Statute where to a large measure, we dispensed with State consent for operations by an army taking place outside of its territory, but we maintained the requirement for State consent for internal conflicts. Now, yes, we have a conflict like Yugoslavia, a conflict between Ethiopia and Eritrea but perhaps 90% or more of future conflicts, will be conflicts for whatever reasons, ideological or ethnic, conflicts which will take place within the country.

Now, there are two ways on which the Court could in fact be effective even for those conflicts:

If we have a large measure of cooperation between the P5 and the Security Council is willing to refer conflicts of this kind to the ICC, because then we, again, are not dependent on State consent. Now, leaving that aside, and leaving aside also the difficulty which at least for the moment would arise in the sense that the Court is not supported by the power of the principal superpowers, the Court could still be effective if the ratifications are adequate in number and particularly come from the right States. Now, the right States, I do not mean Germany or Austria, or Canada. I'm quite sure those Countries will never be involved in this sort of conflict, which can give rise to problems before the ICC, but the way I look now at the security situation, and there is a tremendously strong nexus between the security situation and the various countries of the world, and the process of ratification in the future, the picture that I see, it's not terribly encouraging. And this is the reason: a) in Africa I see collapse of security in very many countries. As a result of that, I agree there will be quite a few African ratifications, but not overwhelming, as I see the situation now. I expect very few, if any, ratification from Arab countries, perhaps Jordan, and I expect very few ratification in Asia and I'm much more optimistic, of course, about Latin America, but yet, I take into account some developments, say, in the Caribbeans, which are not terribly promising. For example, there is a strong move, as you know, among some Caribbean Countries, to severe jurisdictional links, the Privy Council, in London, in order not to be subjected to criticism or to appeals regarding capital punishment. It does not augur very well, the development in the UN Human Rights Commission, during the recent year, or 2 or 3, exemplifies a very strong emphasis on State sovereignty and protection of internal jurisdiction by very many of developing countries, but not only by them. I'm quite optimistic about the number of 60 but this is not as a person who has spent a lot of his years working on questions of humanitarian law. I regard the ICC as a very major historic establishment, first, because of the institution, second, because of the message of impunity, third, because of the advancement of human rights., I want the ICC to succeed. I see my friend Luigi Condorelli here. I don't want the ICC to become another Commission of fact finding under Article 90 of Additional Protocol I. It is in force. It has obtained enough countries. Now, how many of you know about the Commission, how many of you have heard about its relevance and impact on the real world, How do we go about it?

I don't see any easy answers to the problem raised by our brilliant leader Philippe Kirsch in the beginning. But I think that the Court, to be effective in the real world, and to have an impact, will need two things: that we will be forced to re-think how, in a reasonable manner, we can try to expand the jurisdiction to reach some internal conflicts. And I think that some developing countries or some countries that resent so much of the Security Council, should not be too negative about that, because in fact, expanding the jurisdiction, with regard to internal conflicts, not through the Security Council, will give them a certain satisfaction.

And the second point, and this is related to that, I personally believe for instance, that the US would be quite open and quite favourably disposed towards expansion of such jurisdiction. And the third thing, and I will stop and just mention the subject because I have been addressing this under the role of the US, the *quid pro quo* would be some kind of an accommodation enabling the US to become a supporter of the Statute. I don't think that we should discuss here the modalities or ways of this. The questions are technical. This should be an aim and we should not say: our work is done, we have a perfect product and we will not touch it, because very much is still at stake.

If the first and second and the third conflicts in which atrocities occur, after the entry into force of the Statute, are internal conflicts from countries that have not become parties and have not either accepted the jurisdiction, there might be a strong disillusionment. A human support and public support is a thicker thing, we cannot trust it. We have to work on that.

MICHAEL REISMAN

I would like to comment on Béatrice's very interesting observations. And in particular her notion that the Prosecutor will exercise the discretion available under the Statute, in ways that will make the ICC concordant with the Security Council.

With due respect, I think that that minimizes the revolution that was thought in Rome. Philip, in his opening remarks, was very explicit. I wrote down his words: "to get away from the monopoly and power of the Security Council". The Security Council operates according to a set of predicates which are mainly involved within the maintenance of minimum order in the world community. That is a Charter assignment and that trumps the notion of accountability. I think you minimize the fundamental conflict that was established here. Personally, one of my reservations about the Statute is precisely that it was an attempt to amend the Charter. The Charter is no more perfect than any other multilateral instruments that have been created trying to reach a compromise between the competing interests of many different parties. It does in my view recognize that the permanent members represent more than half the population of the world, most of its power, its indispensable military power for the projection of force beyond their territories and that any authorizing the international action has to incorporate them. Anyone who said through the debate on jurisdiction in the plenary that it will be presided over, could not but appreciate that this was an attempt to take this power away and to assign it to a different group to get away from the monopoly and power of the Security Council. We assume that having been accomplished, this institution will now move and operate like a mini Security Council in appropriate circumstances.

BEATRICE LE FRAPER DU HELLEN

I obviously assume the opposite and the reason why is as follows. I was just pointing out that in the Statute some provisions did not just happen to fall down from the sky. The complementarity provisions and the Article 53 provision are two provisions that France supported, that France wanted to insert in the Statute. It would be an exaggeration to say that we were ever planning to make the Court as a new form of political body, but we just wanted to give the Court the means to reconcile its independent decision-making with the objective of peace and reconciliation. As I said, we could have chosen an entirely different solution and refused the Prosecutor the possibility to have any discretion. There was a lot of discussion on Article 53, there was a lot of discussion not to have any mention of the possibility for the Prosecutor to have, as we say in France, *l'opportunité de poursuite*. Not everybody was in favour of this formula, giving the possibility for the Prosecutor not to open an investigation "in the interest of justice". You can see there was a lot of opposition to this provision because there are a lot of safeguards around this provision. It is written in the Statute that the Prosecutor's decisions under this Article, will be submitted to this provision of the pre-trial Chamber. So it is a very well-guarded discretion and, when I see such a very well-guarded discretion, the idea comes to my mind that maybe we think that the Prosecutor is going to use this discretion in some situation. As I said, it could be a situation where the Security Council is not really involved. It could be not a major crisis but a domestic conflict that has not yet emerged into a huge crisis. So, I want to be clear about that: we gave the Prosecutor and the judges the means to exercise this discretion if they want to use it, then you are right and there will be contradiction sometimes between political settlements and the action of the Court. I did not mention that but I do believe that sometimes we are still drawing too much on the experience of our own national Courts and when I hear the notion, this mention of individual accountability all the time like it was the only objective of the International Criminal Court, I must say, I do not share this view. We have created a *sui generis* institution. You are telling me we have created an entirely judicial body, I tell you to read the Statute. We have not created a purely judicial body.

PHILIPPE KIRSCH

I think we should distinguish the conditions that have surrounded the establishment of the Court, or the adoption of the Statute, and the way the Court is going to function. The Court was created in a political environment where there was a desire to create an institution that would be more independent. I don't think it is possible to argue with that because what the Security Council still does is to be selective, for good or bad reason, but it is very selective. Now, having said that, the Statute, even before moving to my next point, which is the function, the Statute is not a hardcore like-minded instrument. There are, as Béatrice said, a number of qualifications which were put into the Statute to allow eventually the functioning of the Statute in a way that would be reasonable. Now, one of those qualifications that have not been mentioned yet, is the process of selection of judges and the Prosecutor, who are supposed to meet certain high standards to be chosen. Now, I take very seriously what Ted was saying a few minutes ago about the right States being Parties to the Statute. I'm not sure I'm quite as pessimistic as Ted is, but it is sure that to be effective, the Court will have to have a very wide membership. When the Statute enters into force, the first members are probably going to be in fairly large numbers. Those States that are not directly involved in anything but are reasonable States: Germany, Austria, Canada. And my sense is that once the Statute functions and those judges are in place, they would normally know, that the best way of killing the Court would be to act in an unreasonable manner and to ignore, for example, the Security Council. My impression is that there will be a natural instinct to take account not only of purely legal considerations but also of policy and political factors. And it is so because, recognizing all that Michael was saying, I'm not sure I see the Court committing suicide by ignoring the political reality. I hope I am right. You may be right.

MICHAEL REISMAN

I have some experience on this personally. I was a member of the Inter-American Human Rights Commission and I was actually the author of the two Amnesty reports that condemned Uruguay and Argentina. You see the connection here already.

I studied it very carefully and I spent many sleepless nights. I appreciated, as well as anyone, how complex the situation was and all my colleagues of the Commission did as well. We were under tremendous pressure from the most important constituency in any human rights organizations which is the NGO community. The NGO community is just the electricity that drives human right. Make no mistake about it. It's no Government. I was very much aware of that. As a scholar, as a student of politics, it was perfectly clear to me that this was extraordinary complex issues, and in some circumstances, these amnesties were probably indispensable steps in the establishment of domestic peace and the achievement of the transition. But the more I thought about it, my colleagues thought about it, it was perfectly clear to us that there was no way that we could approve them. We had to say that there were violations of the human rights convention because if we didn't, you could take that human rights convention, and you could throw it in the garbage. You could just throw it in the trash.

There is a fundamentally different conception between the human rights movement, which is a radical movement in international politics, and the conceptions on which the Security Council rests.

Both of them are valid conceptions, both of them are coherent conceptions, and you're putting them to opposition. You say the judges are not going to commit suicide, they will basically stay out of these important cases. I think that the judges will assume that they're committing suicide if they don't do the courageous thing. In the Nicaragua case, a very doubtful case of jurisdiction, did the Court do the sensible thing? No.

I rest my case.

TULLIO TREVES

I will start from what Philip said at the beginning, the very words quoted by Michael: "The Court as a way to get out of the monopoly of the Security Council". There is one thing: the Security Council still retains an overwhelming power on these matters. My scenario is the following. Two or three years from now, the Statute enters into force, the Court is established. A problem arises, the Security Council has a choice whether to create a new ad hoc tribunal or use the Court.

Worse even: a problem that arises already is under the jurisdiction of an existing ad hoc tribunal. What happens? I think the ideal solution for everybody is that the new Court absorbs the ad hoc tribunals; they are not needed anymore. But this might happen only when the Statute has 150 or so parties including all the permanent members and so on. But if this has not happened when my scenario arises, we risk competing jurisdiction, prosecutors on both sides starting investigations. This is not a tolerable situation. And I think in this moment the ball comes back in the court of the Security Council and maybe (contrary to what Béatrice said) Article 16 might become very useful. The Security Council might defer the investigations of the new Court and leave room for the existing Court, like the Tribunal for Yugoslavia. Of course this is a transitory situation that might disappear in a few years but at the beginning the monopoly is still there.

ANTONIO CASSESE

If I may add just one footnote: I don't see any conflicts between the Rwanda and Yugoslavia tribunals because *ratione temporis* and *ratione loci* and *personae*, the new Court will not have any jurisdiction over facts happened before its establishment. So therefore, as I say, the Security Council will have to allow the Rwanda and Yugoslavia Tribunals to go on until the end of their mandates.

TULLIO TREVES

Sorry. We all hope that you are right but you might not be right on the Yugoslavia situation, because this is still ongoing and something can happen later on.

ANTONIO CASSESE

Yes, you are right. Everything can happen in Yugoslavia after the establishment of the ICC. Let us hope this will not happen.

As a chairman, I am in a very difficult position. I do not have enough time. I have to drop too technical topics. It would be better to concentrate on the one political issue which I think is of great interest for the audience, namely "The US position: a major stumbling block to the establishment of the ICC". So, let us concentrate on this topic. Ted Meron could probably make a few comments on this topic. He published an important article in the Washington Post, just a few weeks after the end of the Rome Conference.

THEODOR MERON

I am convinced that the present US Administration has a strong and indeed compelling interest in the establishment of an International Criminal Court that it could support. There is a very strong support for the idea of the US lending its power to the transformation of the vague or general idea of putting an end to impunity, to enter into an international institution. At the same time, it seems to me quite clear that without some kind of accommodation of US concerns, whether justified or not, with regard to Article 12 on jurisdiction, the hope expressed by many people, including our own NGO community, that the US will move towards supporting the Treaty, is an illusion.

This will simply not happen, and I believe that despite the enormous progress made in Rome towards accommodating many of the American concerns, checks and balances on the power of the Prosecutor, complementarity and other, there are problems in Washington which are not only of substance, there are also problems of psychology and mutual trust. And the effect is again, it's a purely empirical statement that there are no situations in the US history, at least not a recent history, when American

Presidents were ready to support and promote actively through the Senate law of war treaties, and I would categorize this for the ICC Statute, without the Department of Defense having a reasonable level of comfort.

And anybody who has any doubt about it, let that person think of Treaties such as the Ottawa Treaty but perhaps more pertinently about the experience that we have gained with regard to Additional Protocol I. I, myself, chaired the study group of the Council on Foreign Relations on Protocol I and we recommended the ratification and I followed that up with a strong editorial in the American Journal. We can shout twenty times a day or a hundred times a day, as long as the people in the Department of Defense do not feel comfortable with such thing, we will not have any result.

And there is one real problem. It's not just a problem of psychology and mutual confidence.

I already referred to the way in which the jurisdiction of the Statute has been crafted.

And there is a lack of symmetry between foreign operations and domestic operations. Now it is entirely possible in the thinking of many of the colleagues I know in the Department of Defense that in case of a future humanitarian intervention, even if it is authorized by the Security Council under Chapter VII, the country where atrocities are committed will - and we can learn from the experience of Yugoslavia accepting Article 36.2 so rapidly - for a specific case, the very Country where those multilateral or unilateral humanitarian actions will take place, will accept jurisdiction either to embarrass or more the Country which is carrying out that humanitarian intervention.

Now imagine for example the case of Yugoslavia but let's futurize it. Let's imagine that we are discussing the case of Yugoslavia after the entry into force of the Statute and let's imagine for a moment that an American pilot is shot down and promptly delivered up under accusations of war crimes or whatever it is to the Prosecutor. This would create for the US and for any other country intervening in such a situation, an extremely embarrassing situation which might eventually be resolved if we have good judges and good prosecutors and they are quite confident.

So, my conclusion is that we must think on some ways, some reasonable minimalist ways to create that level of comfort which would enable the US to move forward.

MICHAEL REISMAN

I don't follow the intricate details of the US position. The use of ad hoc international criminal courts seems to me to have been extraordinarily successful and one thing that concerns me is the credibility and plausibility of ad hoc tribunals after this exercise, since this exercise seems to raise doubts about the ultimate quality of them.

My own feeling is that the best way to have an ICC, would have been without Article 12 and with Article 13. And I'm directing maximum pressure, the extraordinary pressure that was able to focalize at Rome on the Security Council in the appropriate time.

My own sense is more pessimistic than Ted. I think, short of that, the US Senate will find it very difficult to participate.

THEODOR MERON

I would like to distinguish between two situations: American ratification of the Statute in the sense of obtaining Senate approval and American support of the Statute. As a matter of real life, even with a very high measure of support for something, experience shows that we need in the US, I don't know perhaps 15 or more years to ratify something which for some people is going to remain controversial.

So, as a practical person, many of you know that since Rome, I've been trying in various ways to produce a situation in which the US may be more supportive of the Treaty.

But leaving aside the possibility of Senate ratification, I think that we would really obtain something absolutely tremendous if we would have the Administration supporting the Treaty. There is so much that the US Government could do in political support, in financial support, when the first case comes up to the Security Council, a difficult US might be afraid of creating the precedent or even referring cases to the Court about which it feels uncomfortable.

So, my own personal goal it's not the Senate, because I think it's so far in the future. I would be very happy if we can arrive at the solution where the American administration can support the Treaty and this is my aim.

ANTONIO CASSESE

May I just make a comment on what Ted said about problems facing those poor people in the Pentagon when they say: to take up his example, if one of our pilots (a US pilot in Yugoslavia assuming that the ICC has jurisdiction over the war going on in Yugoslavia), assuming one of our pilots is shot down and apprehended by the enemy and surrendered to the ICC for a trial because he's accused of war crimes.

I fail to understand why this is so abhorrent to the Americans. If the prosecutor may produce evidence against this man because he is accused of war crimes and indeed he committed war crimes, let him be tried and sentenced. If he is actually accused for political reasons, and only because he is American, and the Yugoslavs claim he committed war crimes, but actually he did not commit any war crime, so he will be acquitted by the Prosecutor. He will not be even tried by the Court. The Prosecutor will dismiss the case saying he has not committed any war crime. If we were to apply another reasoning to the Americans, then we should apply the same reasoning to any pilot in the world, not only to American pilots but also to Germans, Italians, Yugoslavs, Rwandans, and so on. I don't see why we should follow this double standard. All those who belong to the American army, or to the American airforces, should be protected because they might be brought to trial under the pretext that they have committed war crimes. But the Court will be a very serious Court, the Prosecutor will be somebody highly professional. I fully agree with Philip, the selection of judges and prosecutors will be careful and you can trust that judges and prosecutors will be absolutely impartial, professionals of high calibre, and they will say: we would dismiss any charge which is based on political pretext and which is used only for political reasons.

I think we should convince the people from the Pentagon that they are totally wrong and that it's only because of their being shortsighted that they don't allow the State Department and the President to ratify or even support the ICC Statute. I am sorry, but I become a bit emotional when we discuss these matters.

BEATRICE LE FRAPER DU HELLEN

I am glad that the auditorium applaude you. Because I feel sorry sometime when we do not talk about politics. Now we do not talk about technical issues. Sometime we talk about psychology and mutual trust.

That was a very interesting point by Ted Meron, which was not only a legal problem but also a problem of psychology and mutual trust. We do have the same problem in France, I have to acknowledge that, and I want also to respond to Antonio Cassese about that. There is in the French military this fear that there might be a double standard at the very beginning of a case, because it's always more interesting to bring a complaint against an American, a military officer or a military from a Country which is a permanent member of the Security Council. It's always more interesting somehow to bring a complaint against those kind of personnel than against personnel from other countries. So, I think at the beginning, it's a fear in my military that there might be at the very beginning of a case a psychological double standard.

So, we have chosen a less radical solution than not signing and not ratifying the Convention. We are going to make a declaration under Article 124 and decline the jurisdiction of the Court for seven years in the field of war crimes and those seven years are really for us a way to build the confidence of our military towards the Court. We acknowledge that entirely. What we do not accept, in the American position and although we would very much like to have them on board, if only for the financial reasons explained this morning by Tullio Treves, that the absence of the Americans are going to cost us a lot of money, from France perspective, when we will be State Parties, although we would very much like to have them on board, there is no way we can support the idea that Article 12 of the Statute goes further and is in contradiction with a trend in international law.

There have been a lot of international conventions, where the jurisdiction criteria is much wider. Here we have an alternative jurisdiction criteria, either the state of nationality or the State where the crime was committed. The Torture Convention goes further as some of you probably know, for France, it would have been absolutely acceptable given the traditional jurisdiction criteria we have in France in relation to the nationality of the victim, nationality of the accused, territory where the fact was committed. We have those three. We could have even accepted another jurisdictional criteria which would have been the nationality of the victims. So, the idea that Article 12 has to be changed, goes really beyond what we can further in the future. I'll be writing on Article 12 to get the Americans on board, is something that we can't imagine.

On the other hand, we were very much ready to help as much as we could with the elements of crimes and the rules of proofs and procedure which are being discussed at the moment. We thought there was a good occasion to establish this trust in the Court by helping out, as much as we can, the American delegation. I should mention that France participated actively to the discussion on elements of crime when those elements are absolutely foreign to our legal tradition and to our understanding. And that was in order really to re-establish the confidence of the American delegation towards the Court, especially the military (because they are really attached to the elements of crime). So, again, I want to stress that there are some countries which do share the concerns of the Americans for the possible people's complaints that could be brought against our military involved in operations abroad. But we have found another solution and definitely the idea of amending Article 12 is very difficult for us, and we would highly recommend, if not for the US to reconsider, reread Articles 1 and 124, at least to participate very actively in the discussion on the rules of proofs and procedures and the elements of crime to see if we could not go forward.

PHILIPPE KIRSCH

First of all, most reasonable people and most reasonable States would very much like to have the US in a position of support to the Court. I won't comment on the US substantive position, first of all, because I can't in my position, and secondly, because that has already been done.

But I don't think that the problem for the US is a question of symmetry. It is not because the internal conflicts are not covered that they have problems with international conflicts because the symmetry was there, in our grasp, if the Korean proposal would have been adopted, where all conflicts had been adopted on the same way. I don't think the problem is a problem of symmetry. But I do believe that the US concerns about internal conflicts are genuine. I think it is possible that there will be double standards in the way the Court is approached. I think it is true that the US is a tempting target for some State and here is where we differ: my impression is that the Court will then being seized of a politically motivated action will be high reasonably; Michael thinks that maybe the Court will be unreasonably. There is no answer to that right now. That's the situation.

Now, getting back to the first point I made which is that we would very much like to see the US on board then the question is: how? And here is my question: we run into two simultaneous problems, and they are not consecutive, they are simultaneous. One is that the Statute cannot be changed, that is not my position. It is constitutional and I think that at the political level, virtually all States would very strongly resist an amendment to the Statute. Amendment or protocol or something that is in effect an amendment to the Statute.

I'm told that in the discussion on elements of crime, on the first day, every State said that elements of crimes had to be consistent with the Statute. Well, there is a message: so, one, the Statute cannot be changed.

The second is: let's assume complete good faith on the part of the US, no suspicion at all, but, how do you protect the US without protecting at the same time the Milosevic and Saddam Hussein, and all these people?

I just don't get it. I don't understand how it can be done. I link the two things because if the Statute could be changed, my view is doing it, and if it can't be changed, how do you do that? That is my question, it's a simple one.

THEODOR MERON

Let me first refer and point to the statement made by our moderator, Nino Cassese, and let me say that I'm not a representative from the US Government. I felt that in an academic setting, it's very important that some views should be presented candidly and openly even if they may be unpopular or this will not be a good academic discussion. So, there is no need to get excited about that. This is part of the picture that we would have to take into account.

The second point is, our chairman suggests, there will be one formula for the US, and one formula for others. I don't think that this is something that I spoke about. To the extent that there would be any adjustment of anything, they would apply across the board. Now, why, is the view of the Pentagon on those problems of humanitarian intervention exaggerated? It may well be. But the fact is that unless we are ready to address also psychology of institutions, then, we will not, because this is part of the political problem. Our chairman said: why is this problem different for Italy, Germany or Canada, and the US. Let us be realistic. If there are going to be humanitarian interventions, with all due respect to our Italian friends and allies, I don't think that much would happen unless American pilots are involved. Now, this may be a good thing, a bad thing, but it explains perhaps the sensitivity of those people who are afraid that in fact, there might be, at least initially, a political staging of things. Remember how Yugoslavia handled during the first few days the American soldiers who were captured. There were their strong elements of propaganda and they were mistreated, etc.

If you think that there can be a solution without taking into account those psychological things, then this is a mistake. Now, it may very well be, that in American history we have cyclical developments. It may very well be that we will move before long to a cycle of retrenchment in which all of us here will be coming to the Department of Defense and Department of State and begging them in fact to intervene in some kind of forcible role to save people from atrocities. What scares me, Nino, is that we, who in some situations will want that, we will not be able to obtain that even with Security Council's authorization because they will say: this does not resolve the problem of the initial embarrassment that would happen.

As regards the questions of our chairman, you have asked a question which is extremely compelling and the answer to this is so compelling in the sense that there should be no rules which would benefit only the US, they should benefit everybody. And because we don't want to create law cases for the future Pinochet and Pol Pot and Milosevic, then, we should try to device ways of doing things in a responsible way, which will not be able to be abused by internal dictators and potentates or tyrants who kill their own population.

ELIZABETH WILMSHURST

Ted has just mentioned the US pilot who is involved. UK pilots are frequently involved too. The answer we give to our Defence people is the word complementarity, which has not been mentioned yet.

In the example given by Ted, where the pilots are handed over to the ICC, we would expect the case to be declared inadmissible, because investigations would be undertaken certainly in the UK, or in the US as well.

That's the answer we give. I know it's not satisfactory to the US but it's enough for us.

PAOLO BENVENUTI

My question is the same: there is the complementarity principle, and it's clear that states like USA will use it. But, thereafter, it will be necessary, for them, to exercise their jurisdiction: and maybe in some cases (like in the Cermis one) their jurisdictional system could have some difficulties, and therefore the International Court could still play a role.

ANNALISA CIAMPI

I have a different question, that relates to implementing legislation and so may be connected to our next topic: the last one, "the process of ratification".

As far as I remember, the obligation to cooperate which is provided for in the Statute of the International Criminal Tribunal for former Yugoslavia, was interpreted by the Tribunal as establishing an obligation of conduct, not of result. And that implies that States will have to adopt (had to), and implement legislation upon the entry into force of the Statute. Now we have Article 88 in the Statute, which expressly provides for an obligation to adopt national procedures. So, now I come to my question, if this provision too is going to be read as establishing an obligation of conduct, my question is, first: how do we reconcile this with the hope that was expressed by some of our speakers that we shouldn't really be worried if implementing legislation will come later on and we should keep going on with ratification?

So, I understand that it will be politically significant but I think that implementing legislation should go on at the same time as ratification.

And my other question is: our task as scholars should be to clarify to States what obligations do arise for them from the Statute, and we haven't been able to do it so far, or, at least, I haven't been able to follow it at all, I mean, after two and a half days of listening to many problems, still it's not clear whether, just giving a few examples, substantive criminal provisions, we said, they do only concern jurisdiction of the Court, but at the same time, they will have an impact on national procedures. What does this mean? That States will have to take into account the definition of the crimes in the Statute or not? Again, the principle of individual criminal responsibility, in the respect of official capacity, do States will have to take this into account? And again, Article 99, execution of request, shall we give States some guidelines and so is it something that maybe could be done as a parallel process while the Committee is drafting the rules of procedures? So Parliaments will be able to do if we cannot do it as scholars. How will Governments and Parliaments be able to do it?

ANTONIO CASSESE

This topic will be addressed by Ambassador Fulci, in his final statement. I propose that we now stop. I will turn over the chair to Professor Politi so that Ambassador Fulci will be able to make a final address.

MAURO POLITI

I would like to call attention to the last part of our meeting. I just want to say that it is a great honour for me and pleasure to give the floor to Ambassador Paolo Fulci, permanent representative of Italy to the UN. Ambassador Fulci needs no presentation, he's well known for his strenuous and successful activity, as Italian Ambassador to the UN, for being in the frontline of numerous political battles at the UN, and for the tremendous support given to the project of an ICC. He's also currently President of ECOSOC.

I've had the privilege to work with him at the Italian Mission for more than 6 years and to share with him the joy of many successes, in particular, electoral successes.

And it is, as I said, a reason of great satisfaction for me to see him in this Law Faculty where I teach.

I welcome him in Trento very warmly and I give him the floor.

30. Conclusions

FRANCESCO PAOLO FULCI*

First of all let me reassure you. I'm one of those who believe that "speeches, to be good, are like a mini-skirt on a beautiful girl: short enough to attract attention, long enough to cover the essential".

I see around here faces of so many friends. First of all, Ambassador Elaraby, who has been a permanent representative of Egypt until a few weeks ago in New York. And he has already become a legend there. You have read in the Italian newspapers that Italy won a battle for the procedural rules for the reform of the Security Council: but the man behind it, the truly, inspiring force for that battle, the one who never for a moment had any doubt that there could be one, was Ambassador Elaraby. You know I'm referring to that resolution finally approved by acclamation which practically brought back legality to the process of the reform of the Council. It stated that no change, no amendment, no resolution which has to do with the reform of the Security Council, can be approved unless it has the vote of two-thirds of the member States of the United Nations, not that of those present and voting. I'm delighted that Ambassador Elaraby could give such an important contribution to your meeting. I heard that his speech was so very much appreciated.

And I'm also very glad to see, although he was many times on the other side of the fence, in this battle for the reform of the Security Council, Hans Peter Kaul, together with Elisabeth Wilmshurst.

And of course, I was very glad to see Professor Meron. Professor Cassese, I think when you say that he's really a champion of human rights, you really interpret the feeling that is widespread, but not only in this room, but everywhere.

---

* Ambassador, Permanent Representative of Italy to the UN. This text is a transcription of the speech held in Trento on 15 May 1999, and was not revised by the Author.

And many others I should mention. I must be frank. I don't think we would be here discussing, I don't think there would have been any Statute in Rome, if it had not been for Ambassador Kirsch.

We spent a lot of time together with them and Ambassador Elaraby in the Security Council, as elected members - and I underline, I never say non-permanent members, I say, elected members, truly representative of the international community and not imposed by the force of weapons and victory.

Let me come to the chief of my presentation. What is really important and urgent, is ratification. If we don't achieve ratification of sixty Countries, all this work has been totally in vain. And I think we must absolutely use the momentum. Because, if the momentum is not used, the risk is that, because there are many internal difficulties involved, the whole process comes to a stop, and this, we must absolutely avoid.

I have one suggestion. I know that what is absolutely necessary is a new lobbying effort, but a really strong determined one. In New York, the Italian Mission to the UN, has a long experience in lobbying. Our French friends used to say that we have "*la machine électorale italienne*". I must say that perhaps they realize how serious that *machine* is. So, what I suggest is that we must do something as we are doing in New York with "*la machine électorale italienne*".

How does this work? Well, I suggest that today we establish what I would call the "T82". "T" stands for Treaty, "T" stands for Trento, "82" stands for the 82 Countries who have signed but 79 of whom have not yet ratified. I think that we need the help of the distinguished representatives of serious societies, and I have in mind especially Richard Dicker, to whom I spoke a few minutes ago, and Bill Page. I take great pride in saying that I was the first President of the Security Council ever to allow a representative of an NGO into the room of the Security Council. And through the two of them, we must find in each of the 82 Parliaments a parliamentarian who is really dedicated, who is really enthusiast, and who would spend hours and hours following the process and reporting to a cell in New York that can be established in the office of the coordinator for the NGO'S Coalition for the ICC which has been so effective until now. And what would be the aim of this? The aim would be to create this sort of emulation among Parliaments that have not yet ratified. We do have enormous problems to face, I have always been convinced that the last thing that a country wants to give away is its jurisdiction, its penal jurisdiction, together with its secret services. You know I was once at the head of the Italian secret service, so I know what this exactly means. And I'm convinced that there are great difficulties. But having served myself as a liaison officer between the Parliament and the Italian Foreign Ministry, I have also learned that if you have a goodwill man inside the Parliament, who pushes for you, who goes and does even the minor jobs...I remember spending so much time to have the ratification that interested my Ministry printed. Most of the time, the ratification of Treaties are staying there because the printing office of the Chamber waits months and months. I remember that what usually took three or four months was done in half an hour, because I would not move from there until they printed it. And this is the way to do it if we want to get somewhere. And what can be done every two months is a focal point in New York, to let know to the other 82 what is happening in each capital. So that they know, they realize all at the same time and I think that this can be done and must be done if we want to get there. Believe me, 60 is not an impossible number, what is needed is that we are determined to get this ratification and only in these ways, only with this systematic and capillary action, it will be possible to make the Court become reality and to move from the culture of impunity to the culture of accountability.

This morning a television man was asking me: "don't you think these people here are visionary people, look at what they say: a challenge to impunity, do you think it will ever happen?" And I told him: "They are not visionary people, they are men and women with a great vision who believe in these things and will work for this to happen."

If you look at what happened in Kosovo, those who commit horrible crimes such as ethnic cleansing should know that they will not get away with it any longer. It will not be possible for them to say, we have acted under orders, under instructions, so we are not guilty. No, they know that they are guilty, so, already, the fact that the Tribunal, of which Prof. Cassese was President until recently, to which he's still a distinguished member, it works at least in the sense of a deterrent. It is a deterrent. Otherwise, if there was not the tribunal, if there was not this idea that there is no longer an impunity, believe me, there would be many more crimes than there are today.

Erratum

The first sentence of the text on the back of the book should read: This book focuses on the Statute of the International Criminal Court, gathering contributions by scholars and diplomats attending the 1999 Trento Conference in Italy.

FSC
www.fsc.org
MIX
Papier | Fördert gute Waldnutzung
FSC® C083411

Kolibri 360 GmbH
Ferdinand-Jühlke-Straße 7
99095 Erfurt, Deutschland
produktsicherheit@kolibri360.de